Wanderings of a Pilgrim
in Search of the Picturesque

MANCHESTER
UNIVERSITY PRESS

Exploring Travel

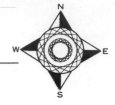

Series editors   Sara Mills and Jill LeBihan

Exploring Travel is a publishing initiative which makes accessible travel writing which may be out of print or difficult to obtain. Travel literature currently has enormous popular appeal, and there is widespread academic interest from a number of fields, including anthropology, colonial and post-colonial discourse theory, literary theory, history, geography and women's studies.

The series has two main aims. The first is to make available a number of key, edited texts, which will be invaluable to both the academic and general reader. The texts will be edited by scholars from a range of disciplines, and a full introduction to each edition will aim to set it within its socio-cultural context, and explain its literary and historical importance. The second aim of the series is to make available monographs and collections of critical essays on the analysis of travel writing. In this way, the *Exploring Travel* series aims to broaden perspectives on travel writing and the theoretical models used for its analysis.

Already published:

Tracey Jean Boisseau   *Sultan to sultan: adventures among the Masai and other tribes of East Africa, by M. French-Sheldon, 'Bébé Bwana'*
Simon Gikandi   *Uganda's Katikiro in England by Ham Mukasa*
Amanda Gilroy   *Romantic geographies: discourses of travel 1775–1844*
Neil L. Whitehead   *The discoverie of the large, rich and bewtiful empyre of Guiana, by Sir Walter Ralegh*

Forthcoming titles:

Sara Mills and Shirley Foster   *Women's travel writing: an anthology*

Wanderings of a Pilgrim in Search of the Picturesque

by Fanny Parkes

edited with notes and an introduction by

Indira Ghose and Sara Mills

Manchester University Press

Manchester and New York

distributed exclusively in the USA by Palgrave

Introduction and editorial matter copyright © Indira Ghose and Sara Mills 2001

The right of Indira Ghose and Sara Mills to be identified as the editors of this work has been asserted by them in accordance with the Copyright, Designs and Patents Act 1988.

Published by Manchester University Press
Oxford Road, Manchester M13 9NR, UK
and Room 400, 175 Fifth Avenue, New York, NY 10010, USA
http://www.manchesteruniversitypress.co.uk

Distributed exclusively in the USA by
Palgrave, 175 Fifth Avenue, New York, NY 10010, USA

Distributed exclusively in Canada by
UBC Press, University of British Columbia, 2029 West Mall, Vancouver, BC, Canada V6T 1Z2

British Library Cataloguing-in-Publication Data
A catalogue record for this book is available from the British Library

Library of Congress Cataloging-in-Publication Data applied for

ISBN 0 7190 5350 1 *hardback*

First published 2001

08 07 06 05 04 03 02 01   10 9 8 7 6 5 4 3 2 1

Typeset in Adobe Garamond 10 on 12pt
by Best-set Typesetter Ltd., Hong Kong
Printed in Great Britain
by Bookcraft (Bath) Ltd, Midsomer Norton

To our mothers

Contents

Contents

Contents

Illustrations

Preface

Fanny Parkes' *Wanderings of a Pilgrim in Search of the Picturesque* was originally published in 1850 in two volumes, amounting to over nine hundred
pages with numerous illustrations. We would like to have produced an exact
copy of that first edition, in order for the reader to get a sense of the scale
of the book and the amount and range of information which was included.
There are also good theoretical reasons why texts should be reproduced in
their entirety, rather than in a form and size which fits in with current concerns about readability and repetition. However, because of publishing constraints, we have had to edit the text to its current form, which we have
tried to do in as sympathetic and careful way as possible. We have omitted
sections of the text where the information which is provided is replicated
elsewhere in the book, and we have, on the whole, omitted material which
was reported at second-hand by Parkes. However, we have retained the
reports she gave from others of the harem, as this contrasts with her own
account, and we have also retained the accounts that she reports of thuggee,
since it is unusual for such violent acts to be described in women-authored
accounts of India at the time. We have tried to make it as clear as possible
where we have omitted material, and have made bridging statements where
necessary for the sake of continuity. The inconsistencies in spelling in
Parkes' text have been retained throughout.

Acknowledgements

We would like to thank the editors at Manchester University Press, Matthew Frost, Rachel Armstrong and Lauren McAllister, for their help in producing this edition; we are also very grateful to the anonymous reader of the manuscript who gave us insightful comments on the introduction. Thanks are also due to the thief who stole Indira's case in Germany containing her final copy of the manuscript, the slides of illustrations, and her original copy of *Wanderings of a Pilgrim*, for returning the case to the place where it had been stolen, thus saving us a great deal of work. Further, we wish to thank Carl Plasa at Cardiff University for all his generous help during the time the manuscript was stolen.

We would like to acknowledge our indebtedness for the footnotes provided in the edition edited by Esther Chawner, and published in Pakistan in 1975, which we have drawn upon in putting together the footnotes.

Part 1
Introduction

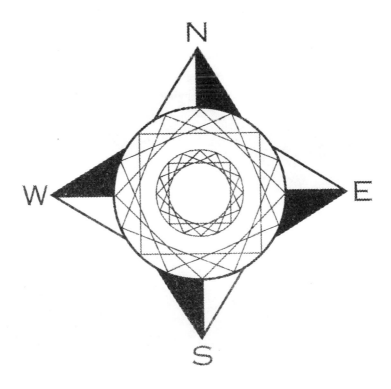

Introduction

Fanny Parkes lived in India as a memsahib for twenty-four years between 1822 and 1845.[1] She was the wife of a member of the Bengal Civil Service, Charles Crawford Parkes, who worked as a Collector of Customs at Calcutta and overseer of the ice-pits at Allahabad. Her position as an "incorporated wife", that is a woman who draws her status and rank from the position of her husband within an institution, is complex. (Callan and Ardener 1984; Gartrell, 1984). The stereotypical view of memsahibs and British women in India in general is fairly negative, and literary representations of them have focused on their small-mindedness, intolerance, vindictiveness, their dislike of Indians and their prudery (for example, E. M. Forster's representation of Mrs Turton in *A Passage to India*). Paradoxically, together with their supposed prudery, they also had a reputation for marital infidelity.[2] Even their lack of paid work is often held against them by critics; consider this representation of the memsahib by Stanford: "Women had always a great deal of time on their hands in which to brood about the heat and the futility of their lives, the lurking dangers, the snakes, and the diseases, their children at home and above all their hatred of letting any child grow up in India, with a *chi-chi* accent and all sorts of undesirable precocious ways which it had picked up from ayahs and bearers" (Stanford, 1962: 127).

Many historians have asserted that relations with Indians deteriorated markedly when British women started to settle in India (Hyam, 1990). However, this is a vast oversimplification of the situation, and constitutes a casting of blame on British women for the structural changes then going on in the colonial system. In her analysis of the figuring of the rape of white women within the colonised countries, Jenny Sharpe argues that, in some sense, British women in India were represented as at risk and rapable by dangerous "natives" to condone the violent acts which were meted out, in supposed retribution, against the growing nationalist movement by the

3

colonial powers (Sharpe, 1993). The stereotype of the fragile, distant, sexually endangered British woman was thus "produced" by the colonial powers in their efforts to deal with the difficulties of managing the violence and exploitation of the colonial relationship. In a similar way, it could be argued that the stereotype of the memsahib could also be seen to be "produced" by the colonial powers in their efforts to justify to themselves the fact that a changing colonial situation (greater numbers of English people in India, greater numbers of Indians working within the colonial system, a more formal colonial relation between India and England, a growing nationalist movement) had meant that there was, at one and the same time, a greater distance between Indians and themselves and also a greater difficulty in implementing colonial goals. Increased settlement brought about many changes and memsahibs became almost a symbol of these changes in the relation between British men and the Indian population as a whole. In fact, their presence was indispensable for colonial corporate identity and the policing of racial boundaries (Stoler, 1989: 640).

The British women in India cannot be seen as a homogeneous group, as they have often been portrayed. Fanny Parkes' writing is significantly different from that of her contemporaries such as Emily Eden and Emma Roberts. Indeed, Eden's sister Fanny comments rather scathingly on Parkes when she visits their camp: "We are rather oppressed just now by a lady, Mrs Parkes, who insists on belonging to our camp . . . She has a husband who always goes mad in the cold season, so she says it is her duty to herself to leave him and travel about. She has been a beauty and has remains of it, and is abundantly fat and lively. At Benares, where we fell in with her she informed us she was an independent woman" (Eden, cited in Robinson, 1990: 219).

By the time Parkes arrived in India, British women had been accompanying their husbands on visits, living in India and bringing up their children there since the end of the eighteenth century. Thus, she arrived in an India where there were fairly well-established communities of British men and women in Indian cities, and groups of British people who lived in the countryside, usually in houses grouped around administrative buildings. As Anthony King and others have shown, these communities did not live in close contact with the Indian population, since they were located at some distance from the Indian centres of habitation (King, 1976; 1984). This was because of British beliefs about hygiene and miasmic contagion which were current at the time. British middle-class women living in these communities generally came into contact with Indian servants and merchants on a day-to-day basis, and from time to time met aristocratic and upper middle-class, often Western educated Indians. However, unlike their male counterparts, they did not come into contact with the middle-class Indians who worked within the British administration from the beginning of the nineteenth century, or with the middle-class Indians with whom British men dealt in business or within the legal system. Thus, British women's contact with Indians was fairly limited and their primary contact was a rather close relationship with their many servants. This may have led to a rather stereotypical view of Indians on the part of British women and may have contributed to their behaviour towards Indians as a whole. The forms of behaviour which many of them adopted towards Indian people may have been as much to do with their assessment of appropriate behaviour towards servants which were formulated through English notions of class distinction, as they were to do with straightforward racism.[3] This can quite clearly be seen in accounts of women's travel writing to India and Africa in the nineteenth century, as Susan Blake has shown, where middle-class white women negotiated the complex terrain of relating to indigenous peoples who were less privileged than themselves and to whom they felt they had to appear authoritative (Blake, 1992).[4]

However, as can be seen from Parkes' writing, not all British women conformed to this stereotypical memsahib figure. Whilst Parkes does not by any means escape racism (she is necessarily implicated in colonial "othering" simply by the nature of her position within the colonial hierarchy), her writing differs quite substantially from the writings of many other British memsahibs. She writes that she loved exploring the country—while her husband was stationed in Allahabad, she describes spending most of her time travelling alone through the country, making trips up the Ganges, visiting the Taj Mahal at Agra, exploring Delhi and Lucknow, and making an expedition to the Himalayas. She displays an insatiable curiosity about Indian life and customs, learns to speak Urdu (she signs the fly-leaf of the book in the Persian script) and to play the sitar. Her journal, addressed to her mother in England, is crammed with background information on Indian mythology and details of famous sights gleaned from scholarly works. In fact, her journal resembles nothing so much as an exhaustive *omnium gatherum* of information on India, which ranges over a compilation of Oriental proverbs to recipes for producing perfumed tobacco cakes. Her voracious appetite for all things Indian is not limited to fact-gathering, however. She boasts a collection of Hindu idols "far superior to any in the (British) Museum" and much of her energy is devoted to finding new statues for her collection. Apart from idols, she collects butterflies, fossil bones and even possesses a zoological collection which she preserves in spirits. The description of collecting is, indeed, a key activity for Fanny Parkes.

Knowledge

This type of collecting, which seems so alien to current readers of Parkes' text, seems very much part of a Victorian episteme (a global system of structures for organising knowledge which seem self-evident within a particular culture), which makes this approach to the material world seem, for nineteenth-century writers, a relatively transparent way of organising material (Foucault, 1972; Mills, 1997; Young, 1993). The type and scale of her collecting strike the current reader, as much of this type of Victorian ordering does, as verging on the psychotic, with its linking together of dissimilar elements, use of endless lists and presentation of useful information to the reader. This constitutes a way of representing the world which developed particularly within the period of high British colonialism, where knowledge was amassed about the colonised countries as a form of asserting power over them (Richards, 1993).[5]

For British women of the mid-to-late nineteenth century, there were difficult choices to be made about presenting oneself as knowledgeable; as Sara Suleri has argued, Parkes has to justify publishing her account, whereas male travellers did not: "Parkes is from the outset troubled by the potential narcissism of which she may be accused, and tellingly anticipates such charges in her inscription of dedication: 'To the memory of My Beloved Mother, at whose request it was written, This Narrative is Dedicated: and if any of the friends, whose kind partiality has induced them to urge its publication, should think I have dwelt too much on myself, on my own thoughts, feelings and adventures, let them remember that this journal was written for the affectionate eye of HER to whom nothing could be so gratifying as the slightest incident connected with her beloved and absent child'" (Suleri, 1992: 83).

In describing plants in India, as Parkes frequently does, she would have had to decide whether to describe plants using the Latin names, the familiar British names, or to include the indigenous names. Each of these choices entailed certain ways of presenting oneself, since the Latin name would obviously have been read as a claim to scientificity, which the use of the common British name or a simple description in general terms would have avoided. In fact, Parkes chose to include all three names, sometimes spending far longer on details of the indigenous uses for the plant than she did for other information. Thus, rather than situating herself within the globalising Eurocentric discourses of categorisation for flora and fauna in other countries, and claiming an authoritative status, she instead aligns herself with indigenous knowledge, by cataloguing the plants' symbolic and religious function within the indigenous community. This is not an unproblematic move, since this too could be interpreted as a co-opting and powerful strategy, but it is an unusual feature, not often seen in travel writing in general and certainly not in women's travel writing of the period in India. Indeed, Robinson suggests that her passion for collecting and amassing knowledge might have led to the antipathetic relations between Parkes and other British women: "Much to the amusement of the other British wives, Fanny became an avid and knowledgeable student of Hindu life and history, and her book is heavy with old Indian proverbs and mythology. She speaks of 'us' Indians' and counts 'the native ladies of rank' amongst her dearest friends" (Robinson, 1990: 219). By positioning herself in relation to scientific knowledge, she can thus be seen as positioning herself in relation to the indigenous culture and in relation to the British community in India.

The Picturesque

The main discursive strategy that shapes Parkes' text is that of the Picturesque. Originally an aesthetic mode in landscape art that originated in the mid-eighteenth century, the Picturesque soon outgrew its beginnings in visual art. It percolated into travel writing as a rhetorical strategy that served specific functions for the traveller. In landscape art the concept of the Picturesque had been inspired by Edmund Burke's famous treatise on the notions of the beautiful and the sublime. Here, classical ideas about the aesthetic ideal of the beautiful were called into question. Similarly, the Picturesque was an aesthetics in revolt against Classical norms. Irregularity was now valorised as the most sought-after aesthetic element. Rugged, not smooth outlines were called for in landscape depiction. Further elements deemed as Picturesque were ruins, old cottages, rural inhabitants with their carts and horses, and especially exemplars of the rural poor like gypsies. Interestingly enough, as Elizabeth Bohls has argued, the high water-mark of the Picturesque coincided with a revolution in rural management: the large-scale enclosure of the English countryside, a movement that accelerated with the advent of the industrial revolution in the mid-eighteenth century. (Bohls, 1995) In fact, the quest for the Picturesque might well be seen as an attempt to elide or erase social reality in an idealisation of an old world order (Bermingham, 1986). People cultivating the land and shaping the land to their own needs do not feature in the Picturesque. Thus, land is represented as a material entity, a composition of light, shade and colour, by a disinterested spectator who sets him/herself apart from the landscape. The Picturesque is thus predicated on a power distance between the observer and the observed: those who represent and those who labour. This power difference is heightened when the Picturesque is employed within the context of colonialism. As Bohls argues: "Aesthetic discourse disclosed a heightened potential for contributing to the colonial project . . . as travellers began to inscribe the concept of disinterested contemplations on the landscape through scenic tourism". (Bohls, 1995: 48) This distance from the landscape, necessitated by the employment of the language of aesthetics, creates disjunctures within Parkes' text, since in addition to displaying her knowledge of aesthetic vocabulary, she is at pains to assert the intimacy of her relation to the landscape, especially in her descriptions of her sketches of landscapes and people.

In travel writing which addresses the notion of the Picturesque within the colonial context, idealisation is central. Here it is, above all, an Arcadian, classical past that is idealised. Edward Said has analysed the idealisation of the Oriental past as one of the corner-stones of what he terms Orientalism, a Western strategy of perceiving the Orient that often served the purpose of reasserting Western norms as superior (Said, 1978). By harking back to the golden age of the Orient, Western travellers were implicitly serving to define the contemporary Orient as decaying and culturally exhausted. In Parkes' case, as Suleri argues, "the shrines that Parkes seeks out are already relics, experiences to be represented with an elegiac acknowledgement of their vacated power" (Suleri, 1992: 83). The future, it was implied, lay in Western hands.

Fanny Parkes defines herself explicitly as a pilgrim in pursuit of the Picturesque. India, she considers, is an inexhaustible source of the Picturesque: "No country can furnish more or so many picturesque scenes as India" (p. 147). Her image of India is that of a land frozen in an aesthetic tableau. Accordingly, the India she depicts is dehistoricised and colonial rule is naturalised as an eternal state of affairs. Recent critics have scrutinised the implications of the Picturesque and have come to the conclusion that the Picturesque had acquisitive connotations that are not immediately apparent—"the discourse of the Picturesque intersects with and is shaped by the discourses of colonialism at various points". (Copley and Garside, 1994: 6). In addition to obscuring material relations of power, the Picturesque served to appropriate the country for aesthetic consumption. Thus Parkes' compulsive collecting of souvenirs is very much a part of the project of the Picturesque. The Orient is fetishised into curios that are available for commodity consumption at home. Parkes does not merely collect Oriental objects with passion, however. As Suleri has observed, her entire text is organised in the form of a haphazard collection of aesthetic experiences: "her two volumes map out an omnivorous and often maniacal consumption of the picturesque in all of its manifestations" (Suleri, 1992: 88). Her view of India is an obsessive accumulation of disparate elements—a stance that is reflected directly in the structure of her text with its remorseless compendium of information and breathless narrative pace.

Even the seeming sympathy which the text demonstrates to all things Indian must be scrutinised carefully. Although it has often been asserted that women travellers in colonised countries were more able to position themselves alongside the colonised in a critique of colonialism, and empathise with their plight because of their own oppression, such a position cannot be taken at face value (Youngs, 1997). The sympathy which many women travellers exhibit in their texts should instead be seen as a strategy perhaps as invidious as male colonisers' more open power strategies. In the case of Parkes, her seeming sympathy and love of the country must be examined since very often her enthusiasm for Indian religion ends with an erasure of differences between Islam, Hinduism and Christianity, in a move which ends with a containing of difference. She casts herself as a "pilgrim", a very resonant term within a country where pilgrimage served a significant purpose within many peoples' lives. Her shrine, however, is India itself. This should signal to the reader her sympathy for India and her alignment with Islam and Hinduism. However, her stance towards these religions often conflicts with this seeming empathetic move. She describes collecting religious icons and characterises a statue of the Hindu elephant god Ganesh as the god of writing; however, in this moving of Ganesh out of the sacred environment in which it functions, by acquiring the statue and treating it as an aesthetic object, and further, by including elements from Islam in her description of the statue, she effectively makes these religious objects into simple material objects, devoid of their meaning within a symbolic system. No matter how much she describes their use in devotional rituals, in effect she has destroyed their sacred function. As Suleri comments: "Much as Parkes' picturesque dehistoricises the subcontinent into an amorphous aesthetic space, it further desacralizes each icon that Parkes represents into an allegory of colonial ownership: at the end of the pilgrim's wanderings, Ganesh sits in Great Britain with a zoological composure, god no longer of writing but of the literal appropriation that Parkes' narrative delineates" (Suleri, 1992: 85).

There is, however, a further element that comes into play in the case of the Picturesque. Apart from the political implications underpinning the rhetorical strategy of the Picturesque, it served a further function for the traveller on a personal level. The Picturesque worked to impose a filter on the scene of the strange land; it literally served to insert an aesthetic frame between the traveller and the country he or she was visiting. The anxiety of travel, the fear and unease caused by the unfamiliar are effectively deflected and the traveller is insulated from their effects. By subsuming the Other to a picture the traveller is able to reassert control in what might well be a situation of cultural misunderstanding and tension.

In addition to serving as a way of aestheticising another country, the Picturesque also serves the purpose of allowing the narrator to present a great deal of seemingly random information. By categorising herself as a "picturesque traveller" as she does in the title of her book, Parkes signals also a certain stance towards the information she provides. This choice would be read as marking her text as that of an amateur, which has implications for how the information was judged. In this way, Parkes is able to present information to the reader without compromising her feminine status. However, Suleri suggests that there are a number of questions which impose themselves when we are considering the use of the picturesque by British women writers, which go beyond this consideration of femininity: "given the censored status of their discourse, what literary modalities allow even nonfictional texts by women writers to embody the veiled realities of colonial panic? How, furthermore, does the act of autobiography dilute or reify male historiography, as it inscribes a female and foreign body onto an Indian landscape? Despite the ostensible privacy of the picturesque—its impulse to be anecdotal rather than historical—could such a genre signify an Anglo-Indian breakdown of the boundaries between official and intimate languages? If so, the figure of woman writer as amateur could emblematize an unofficial fear of cultural ignorance shared equally by male and female imperialists, converting amateurism into an elaborate allegory through which Anglo-India examines in hiding colonialism's epistemological limits" (Suleri, 1992: 82). Whilst this critique is useful as a way of troubling the supposed transparency of Parkes' casting of herself as an amateur, it nevertheless masks some of the difficulties which we have already discussed concerning the way British women could situate themselves in relation to these discursive frameworks of scientific knowledge, aesthetics and colonialism.

In the case of women travellers in India, there were few alternatives other than the Picturesque to which they had access in handling their encounter with the country. The British women who were in India at the time of Fanny Parkes were not accorded a share in the administration of the country. Neither were they accorded the status of Oriental scholars, irrespective of the quality of the field work they might undertake uncovering inscriptions and exploring tombs. Even big game hunting was a field in which they were not permitted to disport themselves—though this was taken up with great enthusiasm by later generations of women travellers.

While Parkes quotes copiously from other experts on India—such as Colonel James Tod's authoritative *Annals and Antiquities of Rajasthan* (1829–32)—she remains painfully aware of the fact that she cannot quite measure up to their mark. "I have no tigers to kill", she remarks wistfully (p. 191). She has no tiger-hunts, eyewitness accounts of sati or real-life encounters with thugs to report, relying instead largely on second-hand reports. Her main claim to fame remains the aesthetic presentation of the country: "could my pencil do justice to the scenery, how valuable would be my sketch-book!", she remarks.

The zenana

There is one field in which women travellers alone were qualified to contribute to the production of knowledge about the Orient, and that was in their accounts of the harem or zenana. From the accounts of Lady Mary Wortley Montague (1763) onwards, British women published accounts of life in the secluded women's quarters in the houses of well-to-do Indian and Turkish men; very often these conflicted with travel writing by male writers who tended to focus on the harem as a sexualised zone, full of languid women, lying semi-naked waiting for the man to take his pleasure. As Rana Kabbani has shown these fantasies of the harem generally involved representations of Caucasian women in baths and seemed to be a vehicle whereby Western men could represent naked "white" women (Kabbani, 1986). Since the secluded women's quarters were generally not sexualised areas at all, but simply areas where women could safely congregate without fear of being disturbed by unknown males, many of the travel accounts of the harem by women express disappointment that what they see does not approximate to the literary or artistic representations of the harem (Ahmed, 1982; Jeffery, 1979; Lewis, 1996). Parkes is no exception, since although she describes some of the women of the zenana using the same eroticised discursive frameworks as male travellers before her, she is also at pains to describe the ways in which what she observed does not conform. She describes her distaste when some of the women take opium, and much of her description is taken up with distancing herself from these women. But perhaps most important is her involvement in those imperialist discourses whose aim is to uncover the harem, to make it available for Western males; the exotic, as Grewal argues, "so European in its opacity, allure and evil, was the aesthetic of a civilising endeavour that saw itself as the remover of darkness and mystery" (Grewal, 1996: 49). Nevertheless, in the case of eyewitness accounts of the harem by Western women a number of related topics, such as the issue of female spectatorship and questions of female desire are brought into focus (Ghose, 1998a). Debates on the female gaze, in particular in film studies (Mulvey, 1975; 1981; Stacey, 1994), have offered illuminating insights on the issue of what it means to look at "the other woman" from a woman's point of view. In her analysis of the position of female viewers of Hollywood films, Mulvey posits the female spectator as continually oscillating between a vicarious identification with a male perspective or a narcissistic identification with the female character as object of the male gaze. Other feminist critics have probed these ideas in a variety of areas. Thus, Reina Lewis (1996) has examined women Orientalist painters' representations of the harem and has described the differences between their representations and male art. In paintings by women artists, the harem is depicted as a social rather than an eroticised space. Billie Melman (1992), too, detects a domesticisation of the harem in the writings of women travellers.

To be sure, it remains indisputable that women travellers' descriptions of the harem cater to voyeuristic male fantasies and contribute towards the production of knowledge about the Other. Nevertheless, there is a palpable sense of excitement in Parkes' text that urges us to take Parkes' own pleasure and fantasy into account. There is an ambivalent interplay between desire and identification in the text that is, above all, attributable to the erotics of difference. For what the eyewitness accounts reveal are Western fantasies—both male and female—about the harem, not the material realities of the harem (or zenana) itself.

A further distinctive element in Parkes' description is the fact that in the zenana that she visits, rather than the one of which she includes second-hand descriptions, she meets a woman whose father is English and whose mother is Indian, and most of her difficulty with the women in the zenana seem to stem from her distaste with what she sees as a mixture of the Indian and the English (see Young, 1993). However, this seeming distaste at hybridity is tempered by the fact that she also represents herself as extremely proud to attend the wedding of Colonel Gardner's grand-daughter to an Indian prince. Parkes here seems to be operating on a complex mixture of class and racial lines, displaying her own snobbery, as well as her more stereotypical ideas about racial "mixing".

Whilst some of Parkes' depictions of Oriental women are imbricated with the project of Orientalism, the redeeming grace lies in her account of one particular relationship with an Indian woman—her friendship with the Baiza Bai. The Baiza Bai was a Maratha queen who had been deposed as queen of Gwalior by her adopted son. In this dynastic intrigue the British favoured a policy of non-intervention, even though the queen had hoped for support from the paramount power in regaining her throne. She was virtually doomed to a life in exile. Parkes encounters the queen during her stay at Fatighar where she was visiting a relative. Anxious to add a closer acquaintance with Hindu women to her collection of Oriental encounters, she strikes up an acquaintance with the queen's camp and spends much of her time among them. Despite her predilection for languid Oriental beauties, Parkes finds the energetic queen very much to her taste. Both share a passion for horses—the queen is known to have ridden into battle against the British under Governor-General Wellesley in her youth. There is a wonderful scene where Fanny Parkes tackles riding horses the Maratha style and in return teaches the court ladies how to ride side-saddle in the English manner. The contest is won by the Marathas in Fanny's eyes: "I thought of Queen Elizabeth, and her stupidity in changing the style of riding for women", she reflects. (p. 309). Unlike other women travellers in the nineteenth century, Parkes shows herself to be increasingly impatient with Western notions of feminine decorum.

Fanny Parkes represents herself as spending hours discoursing with the queen and her followers, and it is in these dialogues that the aspirations close to Fanny's heart become apparent. "We spoke of the severity of the laws of England with respect to married women, how completely by law they are the slaves of their husband, and how little hope there is of redress" (p. 311), she records. In deploring the oppression of women, both women seem to find mutual ground. Her outspoken feminism here contrasts markedly with that of other women travellers of the period. It is when Parkes permits the facade of the Picturesque imposed on her narrative to slip and her real concerns and anger to be glimpsed, that her account becomes most readable. Of course, a gloss must be applied to her relationship with the Baiza Bai. It might well be that the queen overestimates her political influence as an Englishwoman and is guided by expediency in her friendly relations with Parkes. Fanny Parkes, on the other hand, seems clearly thrilled to be able to add the acquaintance with a real queen to her list of acquisitions. There is no indication that Parkes attempts to intercede with the government on the Baiza Bai's behalf. Nonetheless, Parkes seems to identify herself with her concerns and remarks cryptically, "Were I an Asiatic, I would be a Mahratta." It is clear that Parkes is keen to present herself as someone on intimate terms with Indian aristocracy and indeed as a traveller who is effortlessly able to traverse the barriers between cultures. This perhaps serves to validate her narrative in much the same way as the endless listing of Indian devotional objects. Nevertheless, despite these caveats about her motivations, this representation of an egalitarian friendship with a high-ranking Indian woman suggests the possibilities of different kinds of relationships between memsahibs and Indian women, than those frequently encountered within literature and travel writing.

One of the most moving scenes in the latter part of her narrative is her description of a mound covered by memorials to women who have committed sati. Parkes is inspired by the scene to rage against the injustice meted out against women in both East and West. She does not merely deplore the fate of the victimised Indian woman, a refrain regularly churned out by generations of women travellers after her, which often serves to deflect critique from the state of Western women in society and to construct the Western woman as socially far more advanced than her Asian counterpart. Instead, she draws a provocative analogy between the fate of Indian and English women. The latter, while not subjected to widow-burning, were themselves victims of oppression. In effect, the lives were "one perpetual sati"—a life-long burden of sorrow (p. 382). This move to the assertion of sisterhood with Indian women is one which is fraught with difficulty, much as the move to assert a commonality of religious belief in her description of the statue of Ganesh. As many critics have shown (Burton, 1994; Jayawardena, 1995), British women often used appeals to the colonial authorities on behalf of Indian women as vehicles for the articulation of their own political agendas. "English feminists use the image of what they saw as victimized 'sisters' in India . . . in order to position themselves as English citizens when the notion of 'citizen' was itself gendered" (Grewal, 1996: 11). Thus, women travel writers' empathy with Indian women has to be treated with caution, without dispensing with it entirely; it is clear that they acted in a way which they felt was to the benefit of other women, but it clear that their motivations and the effects of their actions were more complex than they themselves realised. However, it could be argued that Parkes' position is slightly different from the stance of some feminists which is predicated on a construction of the Englishwoman as superior to and more advanced than the Indian woman. Parkes, in her analysis of sati and its relation to English women's position, declares English women to be every bit as oppressed as Indian women forced to commit sati.

Historical context

The use of the Picturesque denies Parkes the possibility of describing the actual state of relations within the British empire at the time. The India she inhabits is one where British rule has by and large been consolidated. With the defeat of the warrior clans of the Marathas in 1818 the last great opponent of the British on the Indian subcontinent was overcome. Since the death of Tipu Sultan, the powerful ruler of the state of Mysore in South India, who had formed an alliance with the French but had been defeated by the British in 1799, the French influence had long been reduced to a few coastal pockets, and the Mughal emperor Bahadur Shah was a virtual puppet of the British. The Mughal emperors had been pensioners of the British since 1803. An air of peace reigned, and energetic Governor-Generals like William Bentinck instigated a series of reforms: sati was outlawed in 1829, and thuggeeism eradicated.[6] At the same time the style of British rule changed perceptibly—the nabobs of the eighteenth century, who had ruled in opulent Oriental splendour, were replaced by serious-minded administrators, on whom the wave of evangelical feeling at home had left its mark. A feeling of contempt for Indians crept into the cross-cultural relations between the British and Indians—epitomised by the growing popularity of the term "nigger" (see Hutchins, 1967). In a sense Fanny Parkes' account, with her eagerness for contact with Indians, is touched by a sense of anachronism. During the end of her stay rumbles of discontent among the Indian population are discernible—a growing resentment that would explode a decade after her departure in the form of the revolt termed by the British the "Indian Mutiny" (now more usually viewed as the first event in the Indian war of independence).[7] Parkes' text refers to historical events such as the colonial wars and she discusses company policy, particularly when it impacts on British communities in India. But her primary focus is not on the larger political events. Instead, she gives valuable information about the conditions of life of the British in India, the number of servants they had, the events which shaped their everyday lives.

What makes Parkes' account so interesting is its significance for a study of the role of travel writing in producing and circulating images of the Other—and thus fashioning a definition of the self. As Edward Said has pointed out in his now classic study of representations of the Orient, Western travellers, scholars and artists used the Orient as a foil on which they could project their own cultural desires and anxieties. (Said, 1978) In the case of women travellers, the issue is further complicated by the undoubtedly emancipatory effect that travel brought with it. Travel enabled women to rebel against the constraints of the gender norms that relegated them to the sphere of domesticity. Furthermore, by writing accounts of their travels and thus producing a public self, women gained further access to the public sphere (Ghose, 1998a). This empowerment and rebellion against gender norms also functioned vicariously as a spur to fantasies of freedom for women readers of these accounts.[8]

Nonetheless, it is indisputable that women contributed to the discourses of empire through their travel writings and that their production of knowledge was deeply implicated in the relations of power (Mills, 1994). It is interesting to reflect that while Parkes was compiling her compendium of the Picturesque, colonial officials were consolidating colonial rule through the production of a vast amount of scientific knowledge of the country (Edney, 1997). The hysteria that Suleri has revealed as an undertow in the text is attributable to the anxiety haunting both these projects—the fear that the general project of "knowing" the Other was ultimately doomed to founder on the epistemic limits of colonial knowledge.

In the final analysis, Fanny Parkes' text offers a paradigm of British women's position in empire. In particular, the rhetoric of the Picturesque it employs, with its acquisitive connotations, and simultaneously its detachment from colonial reality, epitomises Western women's role as a spectator of empire. The Picturesque is predicated on an elision of social reality. Similarly, Western women often sought a transcendent observer stance that seemed to deny all implication in the ugly realities of colonialism. However, the very rootedness of her narrative in the mundanities of everyday life counteract that seeming distanced stance, as does her positioning of herself in relation to Indian people and culture; this complexity thus makes for a text which serves as a fascinating challenge to the stereotypes we have of British women in India.

Notes

1 Colonial officials had to stay for at least twenty-two years in order to qualify for a pension (Robinson, 1990: 219). There is considerable debate about the spelling of Parkes' name. Most critics list her as Parks (Suleri, 1992), but the Dictionary of Indian Biography (1906) lists her as Parkes. For the sake of consistency, we have chosen to refer to her as Parkes throughout.

2 We should not be surprised that the stereotypical views of memsahibs consist of contradictory elements, since their function is purely ideological. There are many accounts of the types of sexual liaisons which white women had either with white men or with indigenous men in India and Africa. For an account of sexual liaisons in Africa, see Fox, 1982, and for an account of male sexual exploits in India, see Hyam, 1990. One can tell that there were difficulties around women's sexual behaviour within the colonies because of the amount of intervention by the colonial authorities to police supposedly improper behaviour (see Ballhatchet, 1980).

3 There is a difficulty with using the term "racism" within this context because scientific racism did not become a formal, institutionalised system until the end of the nineteenth century; however it is clear that many Westerners operated within a

system of thinking whereby racial arrogance was ratified by being taken as a common-sense form of behaviour and thinking associated with their position of power within the colonial regime.

4 This is not an attempt to excuse or explain British women's racism towards Indians, but simply to try to understand the discursive parameters within which they formulated their own sense of what was appropriate behaviour towards others.

5 But as Bhabha (1994) has argued, this form of asserting control is never as simple as it appears. Rather than constituting a power relation, where the Other is controlled by being known, the Other in fact often inserts itself within the realm of the coloniser, and becomes part of the coloniser's way of thinking and understanding. See also Pratt (1992) and Whitehead (1997) for interesting discussions of the complex relationship between knowledge and colonial power.

6 The British found it important to eradicate certain cultural traditions which they considered barbaric, and this was one of the testing points of the British "civilising mission" in relation to its colonies. British women were instrumental in campaigning to end what they saw as oppressive practices in relation to Indian women. However as many feminists (such as Antoinette Burton, 1994) have argued, this seeming philanthropic concern of British women for their Indian "sisters" had complex and troubling implications. It was always predicated on an image of Indian women as inferior, and above all served to consolidate the Western woman's self-image as more liberated and civilised (see also Mohanty, 1988).

7 For a view of these discontents as a more openly politicised struggle against British colonial rule by subalterns, see Guha, 1983.

8 Given the nature of Parkes' text, it is therefore surprising that there has been so little critical work on it, apart from Sara Suleri's 1992 analysis.

Part 2

Wanderings of a Pilgrim in Search of the Picturesque

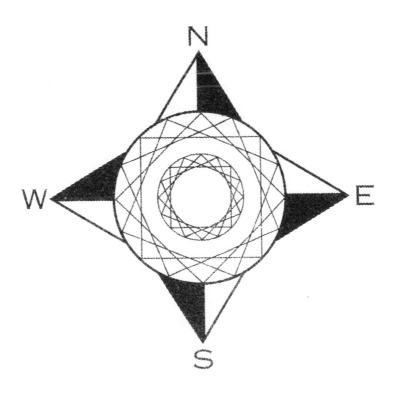

WANDERINGS OF A PILGRIM

IN SEARCH OF

The Picturesque,

DURING FOUR-AND-TWENTY YEARS IN THE EAST;

WITH

REVELATIONS OF LIFE

IN

THE ZENĀNA.

BY

فاني پاركس

ILLUSTRATED WITH SKETCHES FROM NATURE.

"Let the result be what it may, I have launched my boat."

IN TWO VOLUMES.

LONDON:

PELHAM RICHARDSON, 23, CORNHILL.

1850.

To the Memory

OF

MY BELOVED MOTHER,

AT WHOSE REQUEST IT WAS WRITTEN,

THIS NARRATIVE IS DEDICATED:

AND IF ANY OF THE FRIENDS,

WHOSE KIND PARTIALITY HAS INDUCED THEM TO URGE

ITS PUBLICATION,

SHOULD THINK I HAVE DWELT TOO MUCH

ON MYSELF, ON MY OWN THOUGHTS, FEELINGS, AND ADVENTURES,

LET THEM REMEMBER THAT

THIS JOURNAL WAS WRITTEN FOR THE AFFECTIONATE EYE

Of Her

TO WHOM NOTHING COULD BE SO GRATIFYING

AS THE SLIGHTEST INCIDENT CONNECTED WITH HER

BELOVED AND ABSENT CHILD,

فاني پاركس

INVOCATION.

Work-perfecting Gŭnéshŭ!　Salamut.
Gănésh!—Gănésh!
Two-mothered!　One-toothed!
Portly-paunched!　Elephant-faced Gŭnéshŭ!
Salām!!
Moon-crowned!　Triple-eyed!
Thou who in all affairs claimest precedence in adoration!
Calamity-averting Gănésh!
Salām!!
Thou who art invoked on the commencement of a journey,
the writing of a book,
Salām!!
Oh! Gănésh, "put not thine ears to sleep!"[1]
"Encourage me, and then behold my bravery;
Call me your own fox, then will you see me perform
the exploits of a lion!"[2]
"What fear need he have of the waves of the sea,
who has Noah for a pilot?"[3]
First-born of Mahādēo and Parvutī!
God of Prudence and Policy!
Patron of Literature!
Salām!!
May it be said,
"Ah! she writes like Gănésh!"

[1] Oriental Proverbs and Sayings.　　[2] Ibid.　　[3] Ibid.

Figure 1   Gănésh

A BENGALEE. WOMAN

Figure 2   Bengalī woman

Introduction

Gănésh, the Patron of Literature

"WHATEVER THE WANDERING TRAVELLER SAYS, HE DOES
SO FROM HAVING SEEN THAT OF WHICH HE SPEAKS."[1]

So many admirable works have appeared of late, illustrating scenes in India, both with pen and pencil, that I offer these sketches in all humility, pleading the force of example.

"THE CAMELS WERE BEING BRANDED WITH HOT IRONS FOR THE
PUBLIC SERVICE, AND THE SPIDER CAME TO BE MARKED ALSO."[2]

For four-and-twenty years have I roamed the world,—

"I NEITHER WENT TO MEKKA NOR MUDĪNA,
BUT WAS A PILGRIM NEVERTHELESS."[3]

The Frontispiece represents the idol Gănésh, the deified infant whom I have invoked.

The sign *Sri*, at the top of the page, implores his triple eyes to look with favour on the undertaking,—in the same manner that this sign, 4, the old heathen invocation to Jupiter, sought his blessing; and is equivalent to the usual invocation of the poets to the Muses,—the Muhammadan authors to the Prophet,—or the "Laus Deo," with which merchants' clerks formerly began their books,—a practice not yet quite extinct.

"Sri" is written at the top of all Hindī writings; the meaning of the word is "prosperity;" it is put as a title of respect before proper names; frequently they write the same word twice over ("Sri, Sri,")—or they write "Sri Gănésh." The Muhammadans, in a similar manner, dedicate their writings

---

[1] Oriental Proverbs.   [2] Ibid.   [3] Ibid.

to God by a character on the first page, which, as in short-hand writing, implies a whole sentence.

The history of Gănésh is as follows:

"I SPEAK TO THOSE WHO HAVE DAUGHTERS,
AND LET THOSE WHO HAVE SONS LISTEN!"[1]

Parvutī, the mountain-born, the daughter of the Himalaya, the mountain goddess, the mother of Gănésh the wisest of deities, on the birth of her son, charmed with his beauty, and proud of the infant, in the presence of the gods assembled in council, requested their congratulations on the happy event.

Shivŭ the destroyer, although he paid the compliments necessary on the occasion, ever avoided looking upon the child. The mother naturally reproved him; Shivŭ, annoyed at the rebuke, gazed upon the infant, whose beautiful head instantly withered away beneath a glance which none can endure and live.

Indra, the abode of the gods, resounded with the lamentations of Parvutī, who, struck with dismay, was inconsolable.

Brahma, having pity on her distress, bade her be comforted, and commanded Shivŭ to bring the head of the first animal that he should find lying with its head to the north.

This sleeping with the head to the north is unlucky, and ever to be avoided, it being forbidden by the Shăstr, and the penalty thereof death.

Shivŭ went forth: the first animal he encountered in the above-mentioned unlucky position being an elephant, he cut off its head, and, returning to the assembly of the gods, fixed it upon the body of Gănésh. Seeing this, the mother became frantic, nor could she be consoled until Brahma thus addressed her: "Lament not the fate of your child;—with the head of an elephant he shall possess all sagacity. In *pūja* Gănésh shall be invoked ere any other god be worshipped, hence shall he be greater than all the gods. Ere a pious Hindū commence any sort of writing, the sign of Gănésh shall he make at the top of the page, otherwise his words shall be folly, and his traffic a matter of loss. He shall be the patron of learning, his writing shall be beautiful.

"'Behold! he writes like Gănésh!' who shall say more?—with the simplicity of the child shall be united the wisdom of the elephant, his

[1] Oriental Proverbs.

power shall be all-seeing—The patron of literature and work-perfecting."

The daughter of the Himalaya listened to the words of Brahma, and the heart of the mother found consolation in the honours bestowed upon her child.

He is called two-mothered, uniting the elephant's head to his natural body, therefore having a second mother in the elephant.

In the wars of heaven he lost one tusk, hence his appellation one-toothed.

His quadruple hands and arms denote power. In one of his hands is the *ānkus*, the instrument with which the elephant is guided; in another a battle-axe. Being a child, and therefore fond of sweetmeats, a third hand bears a small cup filled with *pera*, a sweetmeat common in all bazārs; in the fourth he carries a short rosary, wherewith he counts his beads. Around his neck is twined the *Cobra-di-capello*, the holy serpent, whose hood is outspread upon his breast. This image is dignified by a frontal eye, signifying the sun, encircled by a crescent, a sol lunar emblem and mystical mark, hence "moon-crowned," "triple-eyed." His attendant, a rat, holding a *pera*, sweetmeat, is placed at his side: on his head is a crown, and around his limbs a yellow *dhotī*, a cloth of Benares tissue edged with gold. His body is covered with ornaments of rich jewellery, such as are worn by men in the East,—his single tusk is bound with gold,—his hands and feet are dyed with *menhdī*, hinnā. On each of his four arms are two *bāzūbands*, or armlets; and *chūrīs*, or bracelets, of massive gold, adorn his wrists. A golden plate on the back of the hand is fastened round the wrist by chains of gold, and from the upper part similar but finer chains pass over the back of the hand, and unite with rings on all the fingers and the thumb. This ornament is very peculiar; both hands are thus adorned. The *chaunrīs* above his head, emblems of royalty, are used by the attendant Brahmāns to keep off the flies; they wave them over the head of the idol during *pūja*.

Gănésh is seated on an altar, such as is used in the *mut'hs*, Hindū temples, surrounded by divers idols, sacred shells, and instruments of worship; small brass cups filled with oil, called *chirāghs*, are burned as lamps before the shrine. The worshippers pour oil and the holy water of the Ganges over the head of the god, which is thus bathed daily, and offerings of boiled rice and flowers are made at the time of prayer. The conch shell, which lies before him, is blown by the Brahmāns during the hours of *pūja* at different times—it is considered very holy—the priest holds it clasped in both hands, and blows into it from the top. The sound can be heard afar off, especially when on the river at the time of evening worship; it resounds from every side of the water, mingled with the ringing of the priest's bells and the sound of a sort of brass castanet, which they strike whilst chanting forth their prayers.

The opening of these shells is on the left side; but they say a shell is sometimes found with the opening on the right side, and its spiral involutions reversed; it is then called *Dūkshina Vúrtú*, and is valued at from three to five hundred rupees. Vishnŭ is said to hold a shell of this sort in his hand. Shells are placed with flowers around the idol, the bull-mouthed is considered sacred, and often adorns the shrine.

Small brass bells are used in worship; some are decorated with the image of Hunoomān, some with the sacred cow. They are rung during *pūja*, not only, it is said, to amuse the god, but to keep off evil spirits.

The shape of the spoon with which the rice or oil is put upon the head of the image is remarkably beautiful and antique. The top of the spoon bears the image of Gănésh, crowned by the *Nāgā*, or holy serpent, with a hundred heads, which are outspread, to screen him from the sun.

This idol is made of solid white marble, and weighs three hundred weight and a quarter. It is painted and gilt, as in the Frontispiece. It was brought down from Jeypūr to the sacred junction of the triple rivers at Prāg, at which place it came into my possession.

Although a *pukka Hindū*, Gănésh has crossed the *Kālā Pānī*, or Black Waters, as they call the ocean, and has accompanied me to England.

There he sits before me in all his Hindū state and peculiar style of beauty—my inspiration—my penates.

O Gănésh, thou art a mighty lord! thy single tusk is beautiful, and demands the tribute of praise from the Hājī of the East. Thou art the chief of the human race; the destroyer of unclean spirits; the remover of fevers, whether daily or tertian! The pilgrim sounds thy praise; let her work be accomplished!

SALĀM! SALĀM!

Chapter 1

Life in India

"I HAVE SEEN BENGAL: THERE THE TEETH ARE RED AND THE MOUTH IS BLACK."[1]

Calcutta has been styled the City of Palaces, and it well deserves the name. The Government House stands on the Maidān, near the river; the city, and St. Andrew's Church, lie behind it; to the left is that part called Chowringhee, filled with beautiful detached houses, surrounded by gardens; the verandahs, which generally rise from the basement to the highest story, give, with their pillars, an air of lightness and beauty to the buildings, and protecting the dwellings from the sun, render them agreeable for exercise in the rainy season.

The houses are all stuccoed on the outside, and seem as if built of stone. The rent of unfurnished houses in Chowringhee is very high; we gave 325 rupees a month for ours, the larger ones are from 4 to 500 per month.

The style of an Indian house differs altogether from that of one in England.

The floors are entirely covered with Indian matting, than which nothing can be cooler or more agreeable. For a few weeks, in the cold season, fine Persian carpets, or carpets from Mirzapore are used. The windows and doors are many; the windows are to the ground, like the French; and, on the outside, they are also protected by Venetian windows of the same description. The rooms are large and lofty, and to every sleeping-apartment a bathing-room is attached. All the rooms open into one another, with folding-doors, and pankhās are used during the hot weather. The most beautiful French furniture was to be bought in Calcutta of M. de Bast, at whose shop marble tables, fine mirrors, and luxurious couches were in abundance. Very excellent furniture was also to be had at the Europe shops, made by native workmen under the superintendence of European cabinet and furniture makers; and furniture of an inferior description in the native bazaars.

On arriving in Calcutta, I was charmed with the climate; the weather was delicious; and nothing could exceed the kindness we experienced from our friends. I thought India a most delightful country, and could I have

[1] Oriental Proverbs.

gathered around me the dear ones I had left in England, my happiness would have been complete. The number of servants necessary to an establishment in India, is most surprising to a person fresh from Europe: it appeared the commencement of ruin. Their wages are not high, and they find themselves in food; nevertheless, from their number, the expense is very great.

The Sircar

A very useful but expensive person in an establishment is a sircar; the man attends every morning early to receive orders, he then proceeds to the bazaars, or to the Europe shops, and brings back for inspection and approval, furniture, books, dresses, or whatever may have been ordered: his profit is a heavy per centage on all he purchases for the family.

One morning our sircar, in answer to my having observed that the articles purchased were highly priced, said, "You are my father and my mother, and I am your poor little child: I have only taken two annas in the rupee, dustoorie."

This man's language was a strong specimen of Eastern hyperbole: one day he said to me, "You are my mother, and my father, and *my God!*" With great disgust, I reproved him severely for using such terms, when he explained, "you are my protector and my support, therefore you are to me as my God." The offence was never repeated.

[. . .]

Dustoorie is an absolute tax. The durwān will turn from the gate the boxwallas, people who bring articles for sale in boxes, unless he gets dustoorie for admittance. If the sāhib buy any article, his sirdar-bearer will demand dustoorie. If the mem sāhiba purchase finery, the ayha must have her dustoorie—which, of course, is added by the boxwalla to the price the gentleman is compelled to pay.

Dustoorie is from two to four pice in the rupee; one anna, or one sixteenth of the rupee is, I imagine, generally taken. But all these contending interests are abolished, if the sircar purchase the article: he takes the lion's share. The servants hold him in great respect, as he is generally the person who answers for their characters, and places them in service.

It appeared curious to be surrounded by servants who, with the exception of the tailor, could not speak one word of English; and I was forced to learn to speak Hindostanee.

To a griffin, as a new comer is called for the first year, India is a most interesting country; every thing appears on so vast a scale, and the novelty is so great.

In *December*, the climate was so delightful, it rendered the country preferable to any place under the sun; could it always have continued the same, I should have advised all people to flee unto the East.

My husband gave me a beautiful Arab, Azor by name, but as the Sā'īs always persisted in calling him Aurora, or a Roarer, we were obliged to change his name to Rajah. I felt very happy cantering my beautiful high-caste Arab on the racecourse at 6 A.M., or, in the evening, on the well-watered drive in front of the Government House. Large birds, called adjutants, stalk about the Maidān in numbers; and on the heads of the lions that crown the entrance arches to the Government House, you are sure to see this bird (the hargilla or gigantic crane) in the most picturesque attitudes, looking as if a part of the building itself.

The arrival of the 16th Lancers, and the approaching departure of the Governor-general, rendered Calcutta extremely gay. Dinner parties and fancy balls were numerous; at the latter, the costumes were excellent and superb.

Dec. 16th.—The Marquis of Hastings gave a ball at the Government-house, to the gentlemen of the Civil and Military Services, and the inhabitants of Calcutta; the variety of costume displayed by Nawābs, Rajahs, Mahrattas, Greeks, Turks, Armenians, Mussulmans, and Hindoos, and the gay attire of the military, rendered it a very interesting spectacle. Going to the ball was a service of danger, on account of the thickness of one of those remarkable fogs so common an annoyance during the cold season at the Presidency. It was impossible to see the road, although the carriage had lights, and two mashalchees, with torches in their hands, preceded the horses; but the glare of the mashals, and the shouts of the men, prevented our meeting with any accident in the dense cloud by which we were surrounded.

Palanquins were novel objects; the bearers go at a good rate; the pace is neither walking nor running, it is the amble of the biped, in the style of the amble taught the native horses, accompanied by a grunting noise that enables them to keep time. Well-trained bearers do not shake the pālkee. Bilees, hackeries, and khraunchies, came in also for their share of wonder.

So few of the gentry in England can afford to keep riding-horses for their wives and daughters, that I was surprised, on my arrival in Calcutta, to see almost every lady on horseback; and that not on hired hacks, but on their own good steeds. My astonishment was great one morning, on beholding a lady galloping away, on a fiery horse, only three weeks after her confinement. What nerves the woman must have had!

Dec. 16th.—The Civil Service, the military, and the inhabitants of Calcutta, gave a farewell ball to the Marquis and Marchioness of Hastings, after which the Governor-general quitted India.

On Christmas-day the servants adorned the gate-ways with hārs, i.e. chaplets, and garlands of fresh flowers. The bearers and dhobees brought in trays of fruit, cakes, and sweetmeats, with garlands of flowers upon them, and requested bakhshish, probably the origin of our Christmas-boxes. We accepted the sweetmeats, and gave some rupees in return.

They say that, next to the Chinese, the people of India are the most dexterous thieves in the world; we kept a durwān, or porter at the gate, two chaukidārs (watchmen), and the compound (ground surrounding the house) was encompassd by a high wall.

1823. *Jan.* 12*th.*—There was much talking below amongst the bearers; during the night the shout of the chaukidārs was frequent, to show they were on the alert; nevertheless, the next morning a friend, who was staying with us, found that his desk with gold mohurs and valuables in it, had been carried off from his room, together with some clothes and his military cloak. We could not prove the theft, but had reason to believe it was perpetrated by a khansāmān (head table servant) whom we had discharged, connived at by the durwān and chaukidārs.

March 20*th.*—I have now been four months in India, and my idea of the climate has altered considerably; the hot winds are blowing; it is very oppressive; if you go out during the day, I can compare it to nothing but the hot blast you would receive in your face, were you suddenly to open the door of an oven.

The evenings are cool and refreshing; we drive out late; and the moon-light evenings at present are beautiful; when darkness comes on, the fire-flies illuminate the trees, which appear full of flitting sparks of fire; these little insects are in swarms; they are very small and ugly, with a light like the glowworm's in the tail, which, as they fly, appears and suddenly disappears: how beautifully the trees in the adjoining grounds are illuminated at night, by these little dazzling sparks of fire!

The first sight of a pankhā is a novelty to a griffin. It is a monstrous fan, a wooden frame covered with cloth, some ten, twenty, thirty, or more feet long, suspended from the ceiling of a room, and moved to and fro by a man outside by means of a rope and pullies, and a hole in the wall through which the rope passes; the invention is a native one; they are the greatest luxuries, and are also handsome, some being painted and gilt, the ropes covered with silk, and so shaped or scooped, as to admit their vibratory motion without touching the chandeliers, suspended in the same line with the pankhā, and when at rest, occupying the space scooped out. In the up country, the pankhā is always pulled during the night over the chārpāī or bed.

The weather is very uncertain; sometimes *very* hot, then suddenly comes a north-wester, blowing open every door in the house, attended with a deluge of heavy rain, falling straight down in immense drops: the other evening it was dark as night, the lightning blazed for a second or two, with the blue sulphureous light you see represented on the stage; the effect was beautiful; the forked lightning was remarkably strong; I did not envy the ships in the bay.

The foliage of the trees, so luxuriously beautiful and so novel, is to me a source of constant admiration. When we girls used to laugh at the odd trees on the screens, we wronged the Chinese in imagining they were the productions of fancy; the whole nation was never before accused of having had a fanciful idea, and those trees were copied from nature, as I have found from seeing the same in my drives and rides around Calcutta. The country is quite flat, but the foliage very fine and rich. The idleness of the natives is excessive; for instance, my ayha will dress me, after which she will go to her house, eat her dinner, and then returning, will sleep in one corner of my room on the floor for the whole day. The bearers also do nothing but eat and sleep, when they are not pulling the pankhās.

Some of the natives are remarkably handsome, but appear far from being strong men. It is *impossible* to do with a few servants, you *must* have many; their customs and prejudices are inviolable; a servant will do such and such things, and nothing more. They are great plagues; much more troublesome than English servants. I knew not before the oppressive power of the hot winds, and find myself as listless as any Indian lady is universally considered to be; I can now excuse, what I before condemned as indolence and want of energy—so much for experience. The greatest annoyance are the musquito bites; it is almost impossible not to scratch them, which causes them to inflame, and they are then often very difficult to cure: they are to me much worse than the heat itself; my irritable constitution cannot endure them.

The elephantiasis is very common amongst the natives, it causes one or both legs to swell to an enormous size, making the leg at the ankle as large as it is above the knee; there are some deplorable objects of this sort, with legs like those of the elephant—whence the name. Leprosy is very common; we see lepers continually. The insects are of monstrous growth, such spiders! and the small-lizards are numerous on the walls of the rooms, darting out from behind pictures, &c. Curtains are not used in Calcutta, they would harbour musquitoes, scorpions, and lizards.

The Chŭrŭk Pooja

The other day, hearing it was a Burra Din, (day of festival in honour of the goddess Kālee, whose temple is about a mile and a half from Calcutta,) I drove down in the evening to Kālee Ghaut, where, had not the novelty of the scene excited my curiosity, disgust would have made me sick. Thousands of people were on the road, dressed in all their gayest attire, to do honour to the festival of the Chŭrŭk Pooja, the swinging by hooks. Amongst the crowd, the most remarkable objects were several Voiragee mendicants; their bodies were covered with ashes, their hair clotted with mud and twisted round their heads; they were naked all but a shred of cloth. One man had held up both arms over his head until they had withered and were immoveable, the nails of the clenched fists had penetrated through the back of the hands, and came out on the other side like the claws of a bird. To fulfil some vow to Vishnoo this agony is endured, not as a penance for sin, but as an act of extraordinary merit. At first the pain must be great, but it ceases as the arms become benumbed. A man of this description is reckoned remarkably holy, having perfect dependence upon God for support, being unable, his arms having become immoveable, to carry food to his mouth or assist himself. Two or three other mendicants who were present had only one withered arm raised above their heads. Some Hindoos of low caste, either for their sins or for money, had cut three or four gashes in the muscular part of the arm, and through these gashes they kept running a sword, dancing violently all the time to hideous music; others ran bamboos as thick as three fingers through the holes in the arm, dancing in the same manner. One man passed a spit up and down through the holes, another a dagger, and a third had a skewer through his tongue.

A little further on were three swinging posts erected in this fashion; a post some thirty feet in height was crossed at the top by a horizontal bamboo, from one end of which a man was swinging, suspended by a rope, from the other end another rope was fastened to a horizontal pole below, which was turned by men running round like horses in a mill. The man swung in a circle of perhaps thirty feet diameter, supported by four iron hooks, two through the flesh of his back, and two in that of his chest, by which, and a small bit of cloth across the breast, he was entirely supported: he carried a bag in one hand, from which he threw sweetmeats and flowers to the populace below. Some men swing with four hooks in the back and four on the chest without any cloth, eight hooks being considered sufficient to support the body. The man I saw swinging looked very wild, from the quantity of opium and bengh he had taken to deaden the sense of pain. Bengh is an intoxicating liquor, which is prepared with the leaves of the Gánja plant (Canabis Indica).

Hindoos of the lower castes are very fond of this amusement, accidental deaths occasioned by it are reckoned about three per cent. Sometimes four men swing together for half an hour; some in penance for their own sins;

some for those of others, richer men, who reward their deputies and thus do penance by proxy.

Khraunchies full of nāch girls were there in all their gaily-coloured dresses and ornaments, as well as a number of respectable men of good caste.

I was much disgusted, but greatly interested.

Sentries from the Calcutta militia were stationed round the swings to keep off the crowd.

The men on the mound at the foot of the second swing run round with the bamboo frame which is connected with the pole, at the summit of which are the cross bamboos. As they proceed, the four men above swing merrily on their hooks, scattering flowers and sweetmeats on the people, and repeating verses and portions of the shāstrs.

Chapter 2

Residence in Calcutta

"DEBT IS A MAN'S HUSBAND."[1]

"i.e. A man in debt is always at the mercy of his creditors,
as a woman at her husband's."

1823, *May.*—The other evening we went to a party given by Ramohun Roy, a rich Bengallee baboo; the grounds, which are extensive, were well illuminated, and excellent fireworks displayed.[1]

[1] Oriental Proverbs.

[1] Raja Ram Mohun Roy, the Hindu religious reformer, campaigned against suttee and the control of the press.

In various rooms of the house nāch girls were dancing and singing. They wear a petticoat measuring, on dit, one hundred yards in width, of fine white or coloured muslin, trimmed with deep borders of gold and silver; full satin trousers cover the feet; the doputta, or large veil, highly embroidered, is worn over the head, and various ornaments of native jewellery adorn the person.

They dance, or rather move in a circle, attitudinizing and making the small brass bells fastened to their ankles sound in unison with their movements. Several men attended the women, playing on divers curiously-shaped native instruments.

The style of singing was curious; at times the tones proceeded finely from their noses; some of the airs were very pretty; one of the women was Nickee, the Catalani of the East.[2] Indian jugglers were introduced after supper, who played various tricks, swallowed swords, and breathed out fire and smoke. One man stood on his right foot, and putting his left leg behind his back, hooked his left foot on the top of his right shoulder; just try the attitude *pour passer le temps*. The house was very handsomely furnished, everything in European style, with the exception of the owner.

The children of Europeans in India have a pale sickly hue, even when they are in the best of health; very different from the chubby brats of England.

All the Indian fruits appear very large, and a new comer thinks them inferior in point of flavour to the European; as for the far-famed mangoes, I was disgusted with them, all those to be had at that time in Calcutta being stringy, with a strong taste of turpentine.

The fort is spacious and handsome, but very hot from the ramparts that surround it. The 44th Queen's have lost three officers by death, nine more have returned to England on sick certificate, and three hundred of the privates are in hospital; this in six months! The mortality amongst the privates has been dreadful, owing, I believe, to the cheapness of spirituous liquors, and exposure to the sun.

Port or sherry is seldom seen on table, during the hot weather; Madeira is not much used; Burgundy, Claret, and light French wines are very rationally preferred.[3]

Where the climate is so oppressive, what are luxuries indeed at home, are here necessary to health and existence; to walk is impossible, even the

[2] Nickee was heard by other Western women, Lady Nugent in 1812, Mrs Heber at Babu Rup Lal Mullick's and Emma Roberts in *Scenes and Characteristics of Hindustan*, 1835 stated that she was paid 1000 rupees per night.

[3] Wine displaced arrack punch in the eighteenth century as the most popular drink for the English in India. In the nineteenth century, beer generally replaced wine.

most petty Europe shop-keeper in Calcutta has his buggy, to enable him to drive out in the cool of the evening.

June 1st.—This is the first day of the month; the morning has been *very* hot, but at this moment the rain is descending, as if the windows of heaven were again opened to deluge the earth; the thunder rolls awfully, and the forked lightning is very vivid. I never heard such peals of thunder in Europe. No one here appears to think about it; all the houses have conductors, and as the storm cools the air, it is always welcomed with pleasure by those on shore.

Our friends who are going to Lucnow have hired their boats, an absolute fleet! I must describe the vessels.

1st. A very fine sixteen-oared pinnace, containing two excellent cabins, fitted up with glazed and Venetian windows, pankhās, and two shower-baths. In this vessel our friend, his lady, and their infant, will be accommodated.

2dly. A dinghee for the cook, and provisions.

3rdly. An immense baggage boat, containing all their furniture.

4thly. A vessel for the washerman, his wife, and the dogs.

5thly. A large boat with horses. 6thly. A ditto. What a number of boats for one family! The hire of the pinnace is twenty rupees a-day, about 2 *l.*; the other boats are also very expensive. They will be three or four months before they arrive at Lucnow; they quitted us the 12th of June.

I have now become acquainted with the three seasons in India; the cold weather, the hot winds, and the rains. The last have set in; it is quite warm; nevertheless, the rains descend in torrents for some hours daily: pankhās are still necessary.

The natives are curious people; my ayha was very ill yesterday, and in great pain, she would take no medicine unless from a doctor of her own caste; brandy was prescribed; she would not take it, said it was very wicked to drink it, that she would sooner die; therefore I was obliged to leave her to her fate, and sent her home to her friends; she is a good and honest servant.

In July, my husband was seized with one of those terrific Indian fevers, which confined him to his bed about fourteen days; he got up looking very transparent and ghostlike, and in a state of great debility, from which he was some time in recovering. Happily, he was saved from a premature epitaph.

I had great trouble with the servants, with the exception of five of them; a speech made by the ayha is worthy of record:—"It would be a great pity if the sāhib should die, for then—we should all lose our places!"—symptoms of fine feelings!

Lord Amherst arrived, and we attended a party given to those over whom he had come to reign.

There is much talk here of a passage to India by steam. [. . .] Heaven forefend that I should find myself in a steam-boat, in a fine rolling sea and a brisk gale, off the Cape. I should not hesitate to give the preference to the twelve hundred ton ship. Some of the old rich Indians, as they are called at home, will have full opportunity to try its safety before my time is come.[4] We have, however, established a steam-boat upon the Hoogly, which goes about four knots against tide; something prodigious in a river where the tide runs like lightning, and with tremendous force.

At this time we became anxious for an appointment up the country, at a cooler and healthier station than Calcutta, far removed from the damp, low, swampy country of Bengal Proper.

August 29th.—The Governor-general and Lady Amherst are great favourites in Calcutta; the latter renders herself particularly agreeable to her guests at the Government-house. The new Governor-general is so economical he has discharged a number of servants, quenched a number of lamps; on dit, he intends to plant potatoes in the park at Barrackpore; people are so unaccustomed to anything of the sort in India, that all this European economy produces considerable surprise.

It happens that in India, as in other places, they have an absurd custom of demanding a certain portion of the precious metals in exchange for the necessaries and luxuries of life, to procure which, if you have them not, you are forced to borrow from agents, the richest dogs in Calcutta: and why? Because, forsooth, they merely require *now* eight per cent, (formerly ten) added to which, after your debt reaches a certain amount, they oblige you to ensure your life, and in this ticklish country the rate of insurance is very high.

In the third place, which to us is the *argumentum ad hominem*, many and many are the lives that have been sacrificed, because poor miserable invalids have been unable from their debts to leave India. Interest—horrible interest—soon doubles the original sum, and a man is thus obliged to pay the debt three or four times over, and *after that he may* put by a fortune to support him in his native land.

Do not suppose I am *painting*; this is the plain fact, of which almost every month furnishes an example.

A man on first arrival (a griffin) cannot or will not comprehend that "one and one make eleven."[1]

---

[1] Oriental Proverbs.

[4] Here Parkes means to refer to the English living in India.

Sept. 7th.—Since our arrival we have been annoyed with constant robbery in the house. Seventy rupees were stolen one day, and now they have carried off about eighteen silver covers that are used to put over tumblers and wine-glasses to keep out the flies; in consequence we have discharged our Ooriah bearers, who we suspect are the thieves, and have taken a set of up country men.

Oct. 1st.—We have had a singular visitor, Shahzadah Zahangeer Zaman Jamh o Deen Mahomud, Prince of Mysore, the son of Tippoo Sāhib, and one of the two hostages.[5]

He resides in a house near us, and sent us word he would honour us with a visit. The next morning he called, and sat two hours. He had studied English for twelve months. Seeing a bird in a cage, he said, "Pretty bird that, little yellow bird, what you call?"—"A canary bird." "Yes, canary bird, pretty bird, make fine noise, they not *grow here*." In this style we conversed, and I thought my visitor would never depart. I was ignorant of the oriental saying, "Coming is voluntary, but departing depends upon permission;"[1] his *politesse* made him remain awaiting my permission for his departure, whilst I was doubting if the visit would ever terminate. At last he arose, saying, "I take leave now, come *gen* soon." The next day he sent three decanters full of sweetmeats, very like the hats and caps that used to be given me in my childish days, mixed with caraway comfits, and accompanied by this note:—

"Some sweetmeats for Missess—with respectful thanks of P. Jamh o Deen." I suppose my visitor Prince Jamh o Deen did not understand the difference between compliments and thanks. I did not comprehend why the sweetmeats had been sent, until I was informed it was the custom of the natives to send some little valueless offering after paying a visit, and that it would be considered an insult to refuse it.

[. . .]

Dec. 2nd.—Would you believe that we sit at this time of the year without pankhās, with closed windows, and our floors carpeted! In some houses, fires are adopted. We have not yet come to this, though I occasionally have found it cold enough to desire one. The mornings are delightful, and the nights so cold, I sleep under a silk counterpane quilted with cotton, called a Rezai.

---

[1] Oriental Proverbs.

[5] Prince Jama-uddin Sultan was the ninth son of Tippu Sultan. When Seringapatam, the capital of Tippu's kingdom of Mysore, was besieged in 1782, two of his sons were taken hostage by the Company but returned to him when he had discharged his obligations. On his death in 1799 all his sons were taken prisoner and sent to Calcutta.

The natives form images in clay; the countenances are excellent; the eyes, eyelids, and lips move remarkably well; they are very brittle; they represent servants, fakīrs, and natives of all castes: the best, perhaps, are to be procured in or near Calcutta; they are attired according to the fashion of the country, and cost from eight annas to one rupee each.

We are in the midst of our gaieties, balls, plays, and parties, agreeably varied. Our first meeting (the races) is held during this month; for we have our Derby, and Oaks, and Riddlesworth. The Riddlesworth is with us a very interesting race, all the riders being gentlemen, and sometimes ten or twelve horses starting. From the stand, of a clear morning, there is a good view of the horses during the whole of their course.

We have just received from China two magnificent screens, of eight panels each; they are exceedingly handsome, and keep out the glare by day and the air by night: I think I may say they are magnificent.

Amongst the ornaments of the household, let Crab the terrier be also mentioned; he is much like unto a tinker's dog, but is humorous and good-tempered, plays about, chases cats, and kills rats, not only in the stable, but house, and serves us in the place of a parvulus Æneas.

Chapter 3

Residence in Calcutta

January, 1824.—The advantages of a residence in Calcutta are these: you are under the eye of the Government, not likely to be overlooked, and are ready for any appointment falling vacant; you get the latest news from England, and have the best medical attendance. On the other hand, you have to pay high house-rent; the necessary expenses are great; and the temptations to squander away money in gratifying your fancies more numerous than in the Mofussil.

A friend, now high in the Civil Service, contracted, on his arrival here about eighteen years ago, a debt of 15,000 rupees, about 1500 *l.* or 1800 *l.* Interest was then at twelve per cent. To give security, he insured his life, which, with his agent's commission of one per cent, made the sum total of interest sixteen per cent. After paying the original debt five times, he hoped his agents upon the last payment would not suffer the interest to continue accumulating. He received for answer, "that interest never slept, it was awake night and day;" and he is now employed in saving enough to settle the balance.

I wish much that those who exclaim against our extravagances here, knew how essential to a man's comfort, to his quiet, and to his health it is, to have every thing good about him—a good house, good furniture, good carriages, good horses, good wine for his friends, good humour; good servants and a good quantity of them, good credit, and a good appointment: they would then be less virulent in their philippics against oriental extravagance.

15*th.*—The Governor-general has a country residence, with a fine park, at Barrackpore; during the races the Calcutta world assemble there: we went over for a week; it was delightful to be again in the country. Lady Amherst rendered the Government-house gay with quadrilles and displays of fireworks; but I most enjoyed a party we made to see the ruins of an ancient fort, near Cairipoor, belonging to the Rajah of Burdwan, about five miles from Barrackpore, and thought them beautiful.

The road was very bad, therefore I quitted the buggy and mounted an elephant for the first time, feeling half-frightened but very much pleased. I ascended by a ladder placed against the side of the kneeling elephant; when he rose up, it was like a house making unto itself legs and walking therewith.

We went straight across the country, over hedges and ditches, and through the cultivated fields, the elephant with his great feet crushing down the corn, which certainly did not "rise elastic from his airy tread." The fields are divided by ridges of earth like those in salterns at home; these ridges are narrow, and in general, to prevent injury to the crops, the mahout guides the elephant along the ridge: it is curious to observe how firmly he treads on the narrow raised path.

By the side of the road was a remarkable object:—

"The appearance of a fakir is his petition in itself."[1] In a small hole in the earth lay a fakir, or religious mendicant; the fragment of a straw mat

[1] Oriental Proverbs.

was over him, and a bit of cloth covered his loins. He was very ill and quite helpless, the most worn emaciated being I ever beheld; he had lain in that hole day and night for five years, and refused to live in a village; his only comfort, a small fire of charcoal, was kindled near his head during the night. Having been forcibly deprived of the property he possessed in the upper provinces, he came to Calcutta to seek redress, but being unsuccessful, he had, in despair, betaken himself to that hole in the earth. An old woman was kindling the fire; it is a marvel the jackals do not put an end to his misery. The natives say, "It is his pleasure to be there, what can *we* do?" and they pass on with their usual indifference: the hole was just big enough for his body, in a cold swampy soil.

There is a menagerie in the park at Barrackpore, in which are some remarkably fine tigers and cheetahs. My ayha requested to be allowed to go with me, particularly wishing to see an hyena. While she was looking at the beast, I said, "Why did you wish to see an hyena?" Laughing and crying hysterically, she answered, "My husband and I were asleep, our child was between us, an hyena stole the child, and ran off with it to the jungle; we roused the villagers, who pursued the beast; when they returned, they brought me half the mangled body of my infant daughter,—that is why I wished to see an hyena."

Before we quitted Calcutta, we placed the plate in a large iron treasure chest. A friend, during his absence from home, having left his plate in a large oaken chest, clamped with iron, found on his return, that the bearers had set fire to the chest to get at the plate, being unable to open it, and had melted the greater part of the silver!

It appears as if the plan of communicating with India by steam-boats will not end in smoke: a very large bonus has been voted to the first *regular company* who bring it about, and the sum is so considerable, that I have no doubt some will be bold enough to attempt it.

In Calcutta, as in every place, it is difficult to suit yourself with a residence. Our first house was very ill defended from the hot winds; the situation of the second we thought low and swampy, and the cause of fever in our household. My husband having quitted college, was gazetted to an appointment in Calcutta, and we again changed our residence for one in Chowringhee road.

Prince Jamh o Deen, hearing me express a wish to see what was considered a good nāch, invited me to one. I could not, however, admire the dancing; some of the airs the women sang were very pretty.

Calcutta was gay in those days, parties numerous at the Government-house, and dinners and fancy balls amongst the inhabitants.

A friend sent me a mouse deer, which I keep in a cage in the verandah;

it is a curious and most delicate little animal, but not so pretty as the young pet fawns running about the compound (grounds) with the spotted deer. The cows' milk generally sold in Calcutta is poor, that of goats is principally used: a good Bengallee goat, when in full milk, will give a quart every morning; they are small-sized, short-legged, and well-bred. The servants milk the goats near the window of the morning room, and bring the bowl full and foaming to the breakfast-table.

Feb. 27th.—My husband put into one of the smaller lotteries in Calcutta, and won thirteen and a half tickets, each worth 100 rupees: he sent them to his agents, with the exception of one, which he presented to me. My ticket came up a prize of 5000 rupees. The next day we bought a fine high caste grey Arab, whom we called Orelio, and a pair of grey Persian horses.[1]

Feb 28th.—TRIAL BY RICE.—The other day some friends dined with us: my husband left his watch on the drawing-room table when we went to dinner: the watch was stolen, the theft was immediately discovered, and we sent to the police. The moonshee assembled all who were present, took down their names, and appointed that day seven days for a trial by rice, unless, during the time, the watch should be restored, stolen property being often replaced from the dread the natives entertain of the ordeal by rice. On the appointed day the police moonshee returned, and the servants, whom he had ordered to appear fasting, were summoned before him, and by his desire were seated on the ground in a row.

The natives have great faith in the square akbarābādee rupee, which they prefer to, and use on such occasions in lieu of, the circular rupee.

[. . .]

The moonshee, having soaked 2 lbs. weight of rice in cold water, carefully dried it in the sun: he then weighed rice equal to the weight of the square rupee in a pair of scales, and, calling one of the servants to him, made him take a solemn oath that he had not taken the watch, did not know who had taken it, where it was, or any thing about it or the person who stole it. When the oath had been taken, the moonshee put the weighed rice into the man's hand to hold during the time every servant in the room was served in like manner. There were thirty-five present. When each had taken the oath, and received the rice in his hand, they all sat down on the

---

[1] Lotteries were a popular way of raising money for such causes as public buildings (e.g. churches, schools and town halls). So popular did they become that instead of being organised by groups of independent gentlemen they came under the control of commissioners appointed by the Government.

ground, and a bit of plantain leaf was placed before each person. The moon-shee then said,—

"Some person or persons amongst you have taken a false oath; God is in the midst of us; let every man put his portion of rice into his mouth, and having chewed it, let him spit it out upon the plantain leaf before him; he who is the thief, or knows aught concerning the theft, from his mouth it shall come forth as dry as it was put in; from the mouths of those who are innocent, it will come forth wet and well chewed."

Every man chewed his rice, and spat it out like so much milk and water, with the exception of three persons, from whose mouths it came forth as *dry* and as fine as powder. Of these men, one had secreted two-thirds of the rice, hoping to chew the smaller quantity, but all to no purpose; it came *perfectly dry* from his mouth, from the effect of fear, although it was ground to dust. The moonshee said, "Those are the guilty men, one of them will probably inform against the others;" and he carried them off to the police. It is a fact, that a person under great alarm will find it utterly impossible to chew and put forth rice in a moistened state, whilst one who fears not will find it as impossible to chew and to spit it out perfectly dry and ground to dust. An harkāra, in the service of one of our guests, was one of the men whom the moonshee pronounced guilty; about a fortnight before, a silver saucepan had been stolen from his master's house, by one of his own servants. Against another, one of our own men, we have gained some very suspicious intelligence, and although we never expect the watch to be restored, we shall get rid of the thieves. So much for the ordeal by rice, in which I have firm faith.

May 4th.—The weather is tremendously hot. A gentleman came in yes-terday, and said, "this room is delightful, it is cold as a well;" we have dis-covered, however, that it is infested below with rats and musk-rats, three or four of which my little Scotch terrier kills daily; the latter make him foam at the mouth with disgust. My little dog Crab, you are the most delightful Scotch terrier that ever came to seek his fortune in the East!

Some friends have sent to us for garden-seeds. But, oh! observe how nature is degenerated in this country—they have sent alone for vegetable-seeds—the feast of roses being here thought inferior to the feast of mar-rowfat peas!

The Toolsee

An European in Calcutta sees very little of the religious ceremonies of the Hindoos. Among the most remarkable is the worship of the toolsee, in honour of a religious female, who requested Vishnoo to allow her to become his wife. Lukshmee, the goddess of beauty, and wife of Vishnoo, cursed the woman on account of the pious request she had preferred to her lord, and changed her into a toolsee plant. Vishnoo, influenced by his own feelings, and in consideration of the religious austerities long practised by the enamoured devotee, made her a promise that he would assume the form of the shalgramŭ, and always continue with her. The Hindoos, therefore, keep one leaf of the toolsee under and another upon the shalgramŭ.—

"The sweet basil is known by its two leaves."[1] Throughout a certain month they suspend a lota (earthen vessel) over the toolsee filled with water, and let the water drop upon it through a small hole. The Hindoo, in the sketch "Pooja of the Toolsee," is engaged in this worship, perhaps reading the Purana, in which a fable relates the metamorphosis of the nymph Toolsee into the shrub which has since borne her name. The whole plant has a purplish hue approaching to *black*, and thence, perhaps, like the large *black bee* of this country, it is held sacred to Krishna, in whose person Vishnoo himself appeared on earth.

The Hindoos venerate three kinds of toolsee—the kala (*ocimum sanctum*), purple-stalked basil; the small-leaved toolsee; and the suffaid toolsee, white basil or Indian tea. The leaves of the latter are used by those in India who cannot afford the tea of China; they are highly aromatic. The Hindoos have faith in their power to cure diseases, and use them with incantations to dispel the poison of serpents.

This plant is held in estimation by the Mussulmāns as well as the Hindoos. It is recorded of the prophet that he said: "Hásan and Húsain are the best young princes of paradise. Verily, Hásan and Húsain are my two sweet basils in the world."

At Benares I saw, on the side of the Ganges, a number of pillars hollowed at the top, in which the Hindoos had deposited earth and had planted the toolsee; some devotees were walking round these pillars, pouring water on the sacred plant and making sālām. My bearers at Prag had a toolsee in front of their house, under a peepul tree; I have seen them continually make the altar of earth on which it was placed perfectly clean around it with water and cow-dung; and of an evening they lighted a little chirāgh (small lamp) before it. If one of these sacred plants die, it is committed in due form to Gunga-jee: and when a person is brought to die by the side of the sacred river, a branch of the toolsee, the shrub goddess, is planted near the dying man's head.

The shalgramŭ is black, hollow, and nearly round; it is found in the Gunduk river, and is considered a representation of Vishnoo; each should

[1] Oriental Proverbs.

have twenty-one marks upon it, similar to those on his body. The shalgramŭ is the only stone which is naturally divine; all the other stones worshipped are rendered sacred by incantations.

A pan of water is suspended over this stone during the hottest month in the year, exactly in the same manner as over the toolsee in the sketch; and during the same month another pan is placed under the stone, in which the water is caught, and drunk in the evening as sanctified.

Ward mentions that some persons, when ill, employ a Brahmin to present single leaves of the toolsee sprinkled with red powder to the shalgramŭ, repeating incantations.[2] A hundred thousand leaves are sometimes presented. It is said that the sick gradually recover as each additional leaf is offered. When a Hindoo is at the point of death, a Brahmin shows him the marks of the shalgramŭ, of which the sight is supposed to insure the soul a safe passage to the heaven of Vishnoo. When an Hindoo takes an oath, he places a sprig of toolsee on a brass lota, filled with the sacred water of the Ganges, and swears by Gunga-jee. If a small part of the pebble god be broken, it is committed to the river. I bought several of these stones from a Brahmin at the great Mela at Prag. I gave two old Delhi gold mohurs to a native jeweller, to make into an ornament for the forehead after a native pattern. My jemmadār took the mohurs, and, rubbing them on a shalgramŭ, gave it to me to keep, in order to compare the purity of the gold on its return when fashioned, with that of the red gold I had given the man to melt. In making fine jewellery the natives put one-fourth alloy; they cannot work gold so impure as that used by English jewellers, and contemptuously compare it to copper.

[. . .]

July 17th.— On this day, having discovered a young friend ill in the Writer's Buildings, we brought him to our house. Two days afterwards I was seized with the fever, from which I did not recover for thirteen days. My husband nursed me with great care, until he fell ill himself, and eleven of our servants were laid up with the same disorder.

The people in Calcutta have all had it; I suppose, out of the whole population, European and native, not two hundred persons have escaped; and what is singular, it has not occasioned one death amongst the adult. I was so well and strong—over night we were talking of the best means of escaping the epidemic—in the morning it came and remained thirty-six hours, then quitted me; a strong eruption came out, like the measles, and left me weak and thin. My husband's fever left him in thirty-six hours, but

[2] William Ward: *View of the History, Literature and Mythology of the Hindoos*, Mission Press, Serampore, 1816.

he was unable to quit the house for nine days: the rash was the same. Some faces were covered with spots like those on a leopard's skin. It was so prevalent, that the Courts of Justice, the Custom House, the Lottery Office, and almost every public department in Calcutta, were closed in consequence of the sickness. In the course of three days, three different physicians attended me, one after the other having fallen ill. It is wonderful, that a fever producing so much pain in the head and limbs, leaving the patient weak, reduced, and covered with a violent eruption, should have been so harmless; after three weeks, nobody appeared to have suffered, with the exception of two or three children, whom it attacked more violently than it did grown-up people, and carried them off.

The politicians at home have anticipated us in reckoning upon the probability of a Burmese war. We have hitherto been altogether successful. I saw yesterday a gold and a silver sword, and a very murderous looking weapon resembling a butcher's knife, but on a larger scale. A necklace (so called from its circling the neck, for it was composed of plates of gold hammered on a silken string), and some little squab images, gods, perhaps, taken from a chief, whom Major Sale of H. M. 13th, dispatched in an attack upon a stockade, leaving the chief in exchange part of the blade of his own sword, which was broken in his skull by the force of the blow that felled him.

It is an unlucky business: the Company certainly do not require at present more territory on that side India, and the expense to which Government is put by this elegant little mill, as Pierce Egan might call it, is more than the worthies in Leadenhall-street suppose.[3]

I see Lord Hastings is made Civil Governor of Malta! "To what base uses we may return!" I observe the motion to prevent the necessity of parents sending their sons to Haileybury has been lost. The grand object of the students should be the acquisition of the oriental languages; here nothing else tells.[4]

[. . .]

Sept. 1st.—The fever has quitted Calcutta, and travelled up the country state by stage. It was amusing to see, upon your return to the Course, the whole of the company stamped, like yourself, with the marks of the leech upon the temples. Its origin has been attributed to many causes, and it has been called by many names. The gentlemen of the lancet are greatly divided

[3] Leadenhall Street in London was where many of the major banks and financial offices were situated.

[4] In 1800 Lord Wellesley started Fort William College in Calcutta giving English boys a three year course in Indian languages, law and history, and later specialising only in languages. In 1806 the East India College was set up in Hertford giving two years' training; it moved in 1809 to Haileybury.

in their opinions; some attribute it to the want of rain, others to the scarcity of thunder and lightning this season. There was an instance of the same general fever prevailing in the time of Warren Hastings. Not a single instance has been heard of its having proved mortal to adults.

Extract from a homeward-bound epistle

"The cold season is fast approaching, when every one becomes, *per force*, most amiable. Indeed we are all creatures of a different order during this delightful time. You in England cannot fancy the sensible feeling of actual enjoyment our bodies and minds experience from this exhilarating change. We live upon the thought of it for months; it must beat the snake casting his skin. I feel quite invigorated even at *describing* its effects.

"We both continue excellently well, and persist in defying the foul cholera and all other tropical maladies. The hot season has passed, and the rains are setting in, rendering the air more temperate. We now occasionally enjoy a cool fresh breeze. A few days since I felt gay enough to fetch a walk in the evening, and got well ducked for my reward; also an appetite for dinner. *Apropos*, I rejoice to see that feeding is assuming the high place among the sciences which was always its legitimate right.

"Oh Dick! you may talk of your writing and reading,
Your logic and Greek, but there's nothing like feeding."

Dr. Kitchener has borrowed the most erudite and savoury parts of his two books from the 'Almanach des Gourmands,' a work well worthy of being placed in the hands of the rising generation as a standard book; I am sure it would be a perfect Kurān for an English lady. But, alas! in this savage place, *dindon aux truffes, omelette soufflée, vol au vent à la financière, coquille de volaille, paté de Strasbourg*, exist but in name. The thousand temptations which fascinate the eye and distract the choice in a French *carte à dîner*, rarely, very rarely appear. The beef of to-day succeeds to the mutton of yesterday; none of those "coruscations of genius, breaking like lightning from a cloud," which must now so frequently illumine the horizon of the London mahogany. But all is tame and unvaried, and man remains here comparatively dead to one of the noblest ends of his creation. I endeavour to struggle against this lifeless life by anticipating the time when I shall return to Europe, at the proper gourmand age of forty-five, with a taste corrected by experience, and a mouth open as day to melting delicacies.

"*Oct.*—We have heard with sorrow of the death of Lord Byron; the other evening, as we were driving past a Greek chapel on the banks of the Hoogly, prayers were being offered for the repose of the soul of the departed. We cannot join with the yelpers who cry him down on the score of his immorality; the seed he sowed must have fallen upon a soil villainously bad to have brought forth nothing but an unprofitable harvest. Mr. Hunt is publishing a translation of a work capable of producing more evil than any of his lordship's—Voltaire's 'Dictionnaire Philosophique' to wit. What is the correct story about the Memoirs? Are we to believe the papers?

"The cold weather has now begun. We have weddings and rumours of weddings. The precipitate manner in which young people woo and wed is almost ridiculous; the whole affair, in many cases, taking less than a month. Many young gentlemen become papas before they have *lawfully* passed their years of infancy. Marrying and giving in marriage is, in this country, sharp, short, and decisive; and where our habits are necessarily so domestic, it is wonderful how happily the people live together afterwards.

"*Dec.*—The races are beginning, the theatre in high force, fancy-dress balls and dinner-parties on the tapis, water-parties to the botanical gardens, and I know not what. My beautiful Arab carries me delightfully; dove-like, but full of fire.

"We shake off dull sloth, rise early, and defy the foul fiend. Many a nail is extracted, by this delightful weather, from our coffins. Calcutta opens her palaces, and displays hospitality, after a fashion which far outdoes that of you cold calculating islanders. And there is such a variety in our pastimes, and the season is so short,—about four months,—that we have no time to 'fall asleep in the sameness of splendour.'

"We were glad to hear our friend would not come out to India. It is a pity that men like him should be sacrificed—and for what? To procure a bare subsistence; for the knack of fortune-getting has been long since lost. Show me the man in these latter days who has made one,—always provided he be no auctioneer, agent, or other species of leech,—and we will sit down and soberly endeavour to make one for ourselves.

"A merry Christmas to you, dear friends; may you find it as great a restorer as we favourites of the sun and minions of the tropics!"

Chapter 4

Residence in Calcutta

January, 1825.—The cold weather is delightful, and a Persian carpet pleasant over the Indian matting, but a fire is not required—indeed, few houses in Calcutta have a fire-place. Ice is sent from Hoogly, and is procurable in the bazaar during the cold weather; it is preserved in pits for the hot season.

March 23rd.—I will describe a day at this time of the year. At 6 A.M. it is so cold that a good gallop in a cloth habit will just keep you warm. At 9 A.M.—a fine breeze—very pleasant—windows open—no pankhā.

3 P.M.—Blue linen blinds lowered to keep off the glare of the sunshine, which is distressing to the eyes; every Venetian shut, the pankhā in full swing, the very musquitoes asleep on the walls, yourself asleep on a sofa, not a breath of air—a dead silence around you.

4 P.M.—A heavy thunder-storm, with the rain descending in torrents; you stop the pankhā, rejoice in the *fraicheur*, and are only prevented from taking a walk in the grounds by the falling rain.

5 P.M.—You mount your Arab, and enjoy the coolness for the remainder of the day;—such is to-day.

April 11th.—The hot winds are blowing for the first time this year.

We understand that after twenty-five years' service, and *twenty-two* of actual residence in India, we of the Civil Service are to retire upon an annuity of 1000*l*. a year, for which we are to pay 50,000 rupees, or about 5000*l*. This, on first appearance, looks well for us and generous in the Company; but I should like first to know, how many will be able to serve their full time of bondage? secondly, what the life of a man, an annuitant, is then worth, who has lingered two and twenty years in a tropical climate?

May 9th.—The heat is intense—very oppressive. I dare not go to church for fear of its bringing on fits, which might disturb the congregation; you have little idea of the heat of a collection of many assembled in such a climate—even at home, with all appliances and means to boot for reducing the temperature, the heat is sickening. You in England imagine a lady in India has nothing to do. For myself, I superintend the household, and find it difficult at times to write even letters, there is so much to which it is necessary to attend. At this moment I would willingly be quiet, but am continually interrupted. The coachman, making his salām, "Mem sāhiba, Atlas is very ill, I cannot wait for the sāhib's return; I have brought the horse to the door, will you give your orders?" The durwān (gate-keeper), "Mem sāhiba, the deer have jumped over the wall, and have run away." The sirdar-bearer, "Mem sāhiba, will you advance me some rupees to make a great feast? My wife is dead." The mate-bearer then presented his petition, "Will the mem sāhiba give me a plaister? the rats have gnawed my fingers and toes." It is a fact that the lower part of the house is overrun with enormous rats, they bite the fingers and feet of the men when they are asleep on the ground.

The other evening I was with my beautiful and charming friend, Mrs. F——, she had put her infant on a mat, where it was quietly sleeping in the room where we were sitting. The evening darkened, a sharp cry from the child startled us—a bandicote rat had bitten one of its little feet!

It is reported the Burmese war is nearly finished. I hope it may be true; it is a horrible sacrifice of human life, a war in such a climate! I hear much of all the hardships of fighting against the climate endured by the military, from friends who return to Calcutta on sick leave.

When we arrived in Calcutta the only drive was on the Course, which was well-watered; a fine broad road has since been made along the side of the river, about two miles in length; it is a delightful drive in the evening, close to the ships.

The Course is deserted for the Strand.

June 25th.—The Furlough and Pension Fund for the Civil Service has been established; we subscribe four per cent. from our salary, for which we are allowed by Government six per cent. interest, towards the purchase of an annuity of 1000*l.* after twenty-five years service. A very strong induce-ment this to economy—yet human nature is very contrary . . . Never-theless, we will return home as soon as we can.

Our friend Mr. C——is going down to Bulloah, a savage spot, where he is to make salt; he takes down three couple of hounds to assist him in his labours.

Provided there is a good bulky dividend at the end of the year upon India Stock, the holders think the country flourishing in the greatest security. Every governor who is sent out is told that the principal thing to be con-sidered is economy. Lord Moira, who had a becoming horror of such *petitesses*, and who saw the political danger of carrying the cutting system into practice, in several instances refused to adopt the measures he was intrusted to execute. Yet India was never in a more flourishing state; divi-dends on India Stock never *looked up* more cheerfully. Lord Amherst has applied the paring-knife, and much good it has done;—the military ran

53

riot, the civilians were inclined to grow rusty, and India Bonds were very dismal and *looking down*.[1]

[. . .]

August 6th.—The natives, especially the Hindūs, are dying by hundreds daily in the damp and marshy part of Calcutta; 410 died in one night of cholera and fever, both of which are raging fearfully. They sleep in such swampy places, in the open air, it is only surprising they are not all carried off. Last month a fever amongst the Europeans was universal, many died of it; it has disappeared, and Calcutta is tolerably healthy; the cholera has not attacked the Europeans.

September 18th.—

[. . .]

The Burmese seem to have adopted the plan of the Russians, and left their infernal climate to fight their battles; it has done it most wofully—fever has killed more men than the sword. Our troops are now waiting for the breaking up of the rains, to recommence operations. It is supposed that they will meet with little difficulty in making their way to Amrapūrā, the capital; but if they do, it seems that the king and his court will not wait for their arrival, but start with their valuables to the mountains. There has been a sad waste of life and money. Commissioners have now been appointed. Report says that Sir Archibald Campbell's spirit is too bellicose; and the deputation (civil) to Rangoon is to check his warlike excesses. The company profess that they do not wish for an extent of territory; so that the present war has been entered into solely for the purpose of avenging the insults that have been offered to their arms. I wish most sincerely that they had been contented with holding what they had, instead of proclaiming war; and probably they may be of the same opinion. The papers say that a truce has been entered into with the Burmese, for the purposes of negotiation. Within these few days we have heard that it has been prolonged, in order that our terms might be submitted to the Golden Feet. It is to be hoped that they will not trample upon them, and that this most detestable war, which has cost so many lives and so much money, may be honourably concluded.

Lord Combermere has determined to proceed immediately to the Upper Provinces, and to have a fling at Bhurtpore.[2] There is no doubt as to the event being successful, but the natives have a great conceit about it; it is

[1] The Barrackpore Mutiny 1824.
[2] In 1805 the Rajah of Bharatpur renounced his allegiance to the Company and joined Holkar in attacking Delhi. Lord Lake besieged the fortress for several months but eventually had to make peace. In 1824 a usurper seized the throne and in 1826 Lord Combermore, the Commander in Chief, took the fort.

another Pucelle, as it has never yet been taken.[3] In Lord Lake's time, our troops were three times repulsed; but that is a tale of the times of old, when these matters were conducted on too small a scale. Now there is to be a fine park of artillery, fully capable of making an impression on the heart of this obdurate maiden. It will do much service in taking the conceit out of these people. They have songs, and even caricatures, in which Europeans are drawn as craving for mercy under their victorious swords, to the number of three or four to one Mahratta horseman. It is an old grudge, and our *sipahis* fancy the affair hugely. We took Bhurtpore last night over the whist-table, by a *coup de main*; I trust we shall be able to play our cards as well when before it. This will be of a different nature altogether from the vile Burmese war. Those who fall will die nobly in battle, not by the host of diseases by which our poor fellows have been sacrificed at Rangoon and Arracan.

The early marriages which take place in India were brought under my eye this morning. My ayha being ill, sent another to act for her during her absence; she is a pretty little woman, aged twenty-five, and has been married fourteen years!

The sickness in Arracan is dreadful; ship-loads of officers and men are arriving daily, with shaved heads and white faces, bearing testimony of the marsh fever, considering themselves most fortunate in having quitted the country alive.

Imagine living in a straw-shed, exposed to the burning sun and the torrents of rain that fall in this country; the nights cold, raw, and wet; the fog arising from the marshes spreading fever in every direction. Where the sword kills one, the climate carries off an hundred.

Oct.—Lord Combermere intends to render the cold weather gay with balls and dinner parties. His staff are quite a relief to the eye, looking so well dressed, so fresh and European. They express themselves horrified at beholding the fishy hue of the faces on the Course; wonder how they are ever to stay at home during the heat of the day, and sigh for gaiety and variety. Speaking of the ladies in the East, one of them said, "Amongst the womankind, there are some few worth the trouble of running away with; but then the exertion would be too much for the hot season; and in the cold, we shall have something else to think about!"

Dec. 1*st.*—We changed our residence for one in Middletonrow, Chowringhee, having taken a dislike to the house in which we were residing, from its vicinity to tanks and native huts.

---

[3] La Pucelle is the term generally used by the French to refer to Joan of Arc.

The house has a good ground floor and two stories above, with verandahs to each; the rent 325 rupees per month; the third story consists of bed-rooms. The deep fogs in Calcutta rise thick and heavy as high as the first floor; from the verandah of the second you may look down on the white fog below your feet, whilst the stars are bright above, and the atmosphere clear around you. The spotted deer play about the compound, and the mouse deer runs about my dressing-room, doing infinite mischief.

The Barā bazār, the great mart where shawls are bought, is worth visiting. It is also interesting to watch the dexterity with which seed pearls are bored by the natives. This operation being one of difficulty, they tell me seed pearls are sent from England to be pierced in Calcutta.

Chapter 5

Departure from the Presidency

1826.—LADY AMHERST is on horseback at gun-fire; few young women could endure the exercise she takes. She is an admirable equestrian, and possesses all the fondness of an Archer for horses. Her ladyship has won my heart by expressing her admiration of my beautiful Arab. His name originally was Orelio; but having become such a frisky fool, he has been rechristened 'Scamp.'

On the death of Lord Archer, in 1778, she "who knew and loved his virtues," inscribed the following sentence on his tomb: "He was the last male descendant of an ancient and honourable family that came over with William the Conqueror, and settled in the county of Warwick in the reign of King Henry the Second, from whom his ancestors obtained the grants of land in the said county."

When it was recorded on his monument at Tanworth that Lord Archer was the last of the male branch of the Archers who came over with the Conqueror, little did Lady Amherst (then the Hon. Miss Archer) imagine that, in her future Indian career, she would cross the path of the poor Pilgrim, the child of one of the noblest and best of men, who through Humphrey Archer, deceased 1562, is a direct descendant, in the male line, from our common ancestor, Fulbertus Sagittarius.[1]

March.—Lord Amherst has been recalled, a circumstance we regret. He has had great difficulties to contend with since his arrival; and now, just at the moment his troubles are nearly ended, he has been recalled. I believe his lordship signified to the Home Government his wish to resign.

In a climate so oppressive as this, billiards are a great resource in a private house; the table keeps one from going to sleep during the heat of the day, or from visiting Europe shops.

April 17th.—The perusal of Lady Mary Wortley Montague's work has rendered me very anxious to visit a *zenāna*, and to become acquainted with the ladies of the East. I have now been nearly four years in India, and have never beheld any women but those in attendance as servants in European families, the low caste wives of petty shopkeepers, and *nāch* women.

I was invited to a *nāch* at the house of an opulent Hindū in Calcutta, and was much amused with an excellent set of jugglers; their feats with swords were curious: at the conclusion, the baboo asked me if I should like to visit his wives and female relatives. He led me before a large curtain, which having passed I found myself in almost utter darkness: two females took hold of my hands and led me up a long flight of stairs to a well-lighted room, where I was received by the wives and relatives. Two of the ladies were pretty; on beholding their attire I was no longer surprised that no other men than their husbands were permitted to enter the zenāna. The dress consisted of one long strip of Benares gauze of thin texture, with a gold border, passing twice round the limbs, with the end thrown over the shoulder. The dress was rather transparent, almost useless as a veil: their necks and arms were covered with jewels. The complexion of some of the ladies was of a pale mahogany, and some of the female attendants were of a very dark colour, almost black. Passing from the lighted room, we entered a dark balcony, in front of which were fine bamboo screens, impervious to the eye from without, but from the interior we could look down upon the guests in the hall below, and distinguish perfectly all that passed. The ladies of the zenāna appeared to know all the gentlemen by sight, and told me their names. They were very inquisitive; requested me to point out my husband,

[1] See Appendix.

inquired how many children I had, and asked a thousand questions. I was glad to have seen a zenāna, but much disappointed: the women were not ladylike; but, be it remembered, it was only at the house of a rich Calcutta native gentleman. I soon quitted the apartments and the nāch.

[. . .]

April.—We heard, with sorrow, the death of Bishop Heber, from my sister at Cuddalore, whose house he had just quitted for Trichinopoly; after preaching twice in one day, he went into a bath, and was there found dead. It was supposed, that bathing, after the fatigue he had undergone, sent the blood to the head and occasioned apoplexy.[1]

[. . .]

May 18*th*.—Killed a scorpion in my bathing-room, a good fat old fellow; prepared him with arsenical soap, and added him to the collection of curiosities in my museum.

My Italian master praises me for application: he says, the heat is killing him, and complains greatly of the want of rain. When I told him we had had a little during the last two days, he replied, "You are the favoured of God in Chowringhee, we have had none in Calcutta." The natives suffer dreadfully. Cholera and the heat are carrying off three and sometimes five hundred a day.

An eclipse has produced a change in the weather, and the sickness has ceased in the bazārs.

August.—A gloom has been thrown over Calcutta; and Lord Amherst's family are in the deepest affliction, caused by the death of Captain Amherst, which took place a short time ago. His lordship, his son, and his nephew were seized with fever at the same time; Captain Amherst's became typhus, and carried him off. The family have proceeded up the country. All those who have the pleasure of their acquaintance, sympathize most deeply in their affliction; they are much respected.

Oct. 18*th*.—My husband having received an acting appointment at Allahabad, we prepared to quit Calcutta. The distance by the river being eight hundred miles, and by land five hundred, we determined to march up stage by stage, sending the heavy baggage by water.

On quitting the Presidency, a great part of our furniture, horses, &c. were sold. I had refused 2000 rupees for my beautiful Arab; but determined, as economy was the order of the day, to fix his price at 2500. The pair of greys, Atlas and Mercury, carriage-horses, sold for 2200 rupees, 300 less than they

---

[1] Reginald Heber was the second Bishop of Calcutta. He wrote *Narrative of a Journey thorough the Upper Provinces of India 1824–26*, John Murray, 1828.

cost; they, as well as Scamp, were too valuable to march up the country. This will give you some idea of the price of good horses in Calcutta. One morning a note was sent, which I opened (having received instructions to that effect), requesting to know if the grey Arab was for sale. I answered it, and mentioned the price. The gentleman enclosed the amount, 2500 rupees, about 250 *l.*, in a note to me, requesting me to keep and ride the horse during the remainder of my stay in Calcutta, and on my departure to send him to his stables. For this charming proof of Indian *politesse*, I returned thanks, but declined the offer. I felt so sorry to part with my beautiful horse, I could not bear the sight of him when he was no longer my own: it was my own act; my husband blamed me for having sold a creature in which I took so much delight, and was not satisfied until he had replaced him by a milk-white Arab, with a silken mane and long tail. Mootee, the name of my new acquisition, was very gay at first, not comprehending the petticoat, but on becoming used to it, carried me most agreeably. A fine Scotch terrier was given me to bear me company on the journey, but he was stolen from us ere we quitted Calcutta.

The people in Calcutta abused the Upper Provinces so much, we felt little inclination to quit the city, although we had applied for an appointment in the Mufassil.[2] Imagining the march would be very fatiguing, I went on board several pinnaces; they did not please me; then I crossed the river to see the first dāk bungalow, and brought back a good account.

Nov. 22nd. —We quitted Calcutta, crossed the river to the bungalow, on the New Road, stayed there one day to muster our forces, and commenced our journey the next.[3]

Our marching establishment consisted of two good mares for the Stanhope, two fine saddle Arabs for ourselves, two ponies, and nine hackeries, which contained supplies and clothes, also a number of goats, and two Arabs, which we had taken charge of for a friend. We travelled by the Grand Military road, riding the first part of the stage, and finishing it in the buggy.

30th.—I now write from Bancoorah, some hundred miles from the Presidency. Thus far we have proceeded into the bowels of the Mufassil very much to our satisfaction. The change of air, and change of scene, have wrought wonders in us both. My husband has never felt so well in health or so *désennuyé* since he left England. I am as strong as a Diana Vernon,

---

[2] Mufassil: outside the settled communities. The Upper Provinces were the Gangetic Plain between Benares and Delhi excluding Oudh.

[3] The New Road from Calcutta to Benares crossed the hilly countryside of Bihar, whereas the Old Road went through the towns on the Ganges.

and ride my eight or ten miles before breakfast without fatigue. We have still some four hundred miles to march; but the country is to improve daily, and when we arrive at the hills, I hear we are to be carried back, in imagination, to the highlands of Scotland. I have never been there; *n'importe*, I can fancy as well as others. We rejoiced in having passed Bengal Proper, the first one hundred miles; the country was extremely flat, and, for the greater part, under water, said water being stagnant: the road was raised of mud, high enough to keep it above the swamp; a disagreeable road on a fly-away horse like my new purchase; low, marshy fields of paddy (rice) were on either side: sometimes we came to a bridge, surrounded by water, so that instead of being able to cross it, you had to ford the nullah (stream) lower down. No marvel, Calcutta is unhealthy, and that fevers prevail there; the wind flowing over these marshes must be charged with malaria.

Bancoorah has a bad name. It is remarkable that almost all the horses that are any time at the station, go weak in the loins.

Dec. 2nd.—We reached Rogonautpoor, a very pretty spot, where there are some peculiar hills.

[. . .]

The country from this place, through Ranachitty to Dunghye, is most beautiful; fine hills, from the tops of which you have a noble and extensive view. Sometimes I was reminded of my own dear forest, which in parts it much resembles. The weak Calcutta bullocks finding it hard work, we were obliged to hire six more hackeries. We rode the whole of this stage. The road was too bad, and the hills too steep, for the buggy; but as it was nearly shaded the whole distance by high trees, the heat of the sun did not affect us. Tigers are found in this pass; and when Mootee my Arab snorted, and drew back apparently alarmed, I expected a *sortie* from the jungle. At this stage a horse ran away in a buggy, alarmed by a bear sleeping in the road. [. . .]

En route were several parties of fakirs, who said they were going to Jugunnath.[4] These rascals had some capital tattoos with them. Several of these men had one withered arm raised straight, with the long nails growing through the back of the hand. These people are said to be great thieves; and when any of them were encamped near us on the march, we directed the chaukidārs (watchmen) to keep a good look out, on our horses as well as our chattels. The adage says of the fakir, "Externally he is a saint, but internally a devil."[1]

---

[1] Oriental Proverbs.

[4] This temple of Jugannath is situated five miles from Ranchi, built on the same plan as the temple of Jugganath at Puri.

[. . .]

At Baroon we bought some uncut Soane pebbles, which turned out remarkably good when cut and polished. We rode across the Soane river, which was three miles in breadth, and had two large sand-banks in the middle of the stream. Wading through the water was most troublesome work on horseback. Twice we were obliged to put the horses into boats, they struggled, and kicked, and gave so much trouble. The Arab 'Rajah' jumped fairly out of the boat into the stream. The mares worked hard getting the buggy across the deep sand; they went into and came out of the boats very steadily.

On our arrival at Sahseram, a native gentleman, Shah Kubbeer-oo-deen Ahmud, called upon us. At tiffin-time he sent us some *ready-dressed* native dishes; I was much surprised at it, but the natives told me it was his usual custom. In the evening, some fireworks, sent by the same gentleman, were displayed, particularly for my amusement. The town is very ancient, and there are numerous remains of former magnificence rapidly falling into decay. The tombs are well worth a visit.

Dec. 23rd.—We arrived at Nobutpoor, a very pretty place. The bungalow is on a high bank, just above the Curamnassa river. To the right you have a view of a suspension-bridge, built of bamboo and rope; on the left is a suttee-ground, to me a most interesting sight. I had heard a great deal regarding suttees in Calcutta, but had never seen one; here was a spot to which it was customary to bring the widows to be burned alive, on the banks of the Curamnassa, a river considered holy by the Hindoos.

In the sketch I took of the place are seven suttee mounds, raised of earth, one of which is kept in good repair, and there are several more in the mango tope to the left. The people said, no suttee had taken place there for twenty years, but that the family who owned the large mound kept it in repair, and were very proud of the glory reflected on their house by one of the females having become suttee. A fine stone bridge had been begun some years before by a Mahratta lady, but was never finished; the remains are in the river. The touch of its waters is a dire misfortune to an Hindoo; they carefully cross the suspension-bridge.

The next stage took us to the Mogul Serai; and, some rain having fallen, we felt the difference between the cold of the upcountry and the fogs of Calcutta.

Dec. 25th.—Arrived at Benares; and here, again, crossing the Ganges was a great difficulty. The Arab 'Rajah' was so extremely violent in the boat, that we were obliged to swim him over. At length we reached the house of a friend in the civil service, and were well pleased to rest from our labours.

Rising and being on horseback by four A.M. daily, is hard work when continued for a month.

My husband, finding it necessary to reach Allahabad by the 30th, left me at Benares, to discharge the Calcutta hackeries, to get others, and to continue my journey. During my stay, our friend took me into the holy city, and showed me a great deal of what was most remarkable. Long as I had lived in Calcutta, I had seen very little of native life or the forms of pooja. The most holy city of Benares is the high place of superstition. I went into a Hindoo temple in which pooja was being performed, and thought the organ of gullibility must be very strongly developed in the Hindoos.

It was the early morning, and before the people went to their daily avocations, they came to perform worship before the idols. Each man brought a little vessel of brass, containing oil, another containing boiled rice, another Ganges' water and freshly-gathered flowers. Each worshipper, on coming into the temple, poured his offering on the head of the idol, and laid the flowers before it; prayed with his face to the earth, then struck a small bell three times, and departed. The Hindoo women follow the same custom.

There were numerous uncouth idols in the temple. A black bull and a white bull, both carved in stone, attracted many worshippers; whilst two *living* bulls stood by the side, who were regarded as most holy, and fed with flowers.

If an Hindoo wishes to perform an act of devotion, he purchases a young bull without blemish, and presents him to the Brāhmans, who stamp a particular mark upon him; he is then turned loose, as a Brāhmani bull, and allowed to roam at pleasure. To kill this animal would be sacrilege. When they get savage they become very dangerous. The Brāhmani bulls roam at pleasure through the bazaars, taking a feed whenever they encounter a grain shop.

We ascended the minarets, and looked down upon the city and the Ganges. Young men prefer ascending them at early dawn, having then a chance of seeing the females of some zenana, who often sleep on the flat roof of the house, which is surrounded by a high wall. From the height of the minarets you overlook the walls. I thought of Hadji Baba and the unfortunate Zeenab, whom he first saw spreading tobacco on the roof to dry. The shops of the kimkhwāb and turban manufacturers, as also of those who prepare the silver and gold wire used in the fabric of the brocade worked in gold and silver flowers, are well worth visiting.

Beetle wings are procurable at Benares, and are used there for ornamenting kimkhwāb and native dresses. In Calcutta and Madras, they embroider gowns for European ladies with these wings, edged with gold; the effect is beautiful. The wings are cheap at Benares, expensive at other places.

I was carried in a tanjan through Benares. In many parts, in the narrow streets, I could touch the houses on both sides of the street with my hands. The houses are from six to seven stories high.

In one of these narrow passages it is not agreeable to meet a Brāhmani bull. Four armed men, barkandāzes, ran on before the tanjan to clear the road. I procured a number of the brazen vessels that are used in pooja. On my return we will have it in grand style; the baby shall represent the idol, and we will pour oil and flowers over his curly head.

The cattle live on the ground-floor; and to enter a gay Hindoo house, you must first pass through a place filled with cows and calves; then you encounter a heavy door, the entrance to a narrow, dark passage; and after ascending a flight of steps, you arrive at the inhabited part of the house, which is painted with all sorts of curious devices. I visited one of these houses; it was furnished, but uninhabited.

The contents of the thirteen small hackeries were stowed away upon four of the large hackeries of Benares, which started on their march with the buggy and horses. For myself, a dāk was hired.[5] Our friend drove me the first stage, and then put me into my palanquin. I overtook the hackeries, and could not resist getting out and looking into the horses' tents. There they were, warm and comfortable, well littered down, with their sā'īses asleep at their sides; much more comfortable than myself during the coldness of the night, in the pālkee. The bearers broke open one of my bahangīs, and stole some articles.

I reached Raj Ghāt early, and crossed the river. The fort, with its long line of ramparts, washed by the river, and the beauty of a Dhrumsālā, or Hindoo alms-house, on the opposite bank, under one of the arches of which was an enormous image of Ganěsh, greatly attracted my attention. I watched the worshippers for some time, and promised myself to return and sketch it.

The carriage of a friend was in waiting at this spot, and took me to

---

[5] To travel dak means to travel by palanquin carried by relays of bearers. One travels at night and rests during the day. Eight bearers were needed: four to carry and four to run alongside. They travelled between stages set at 10–14 miles apart. The palanquin was like an oblong chest with sliding doors and with a mattress and pillow inside. Very little luggage could be carried in a palanquin apart from refreshment for the traveller; light luggage would be carried in baskets, called bahangis, suspended on poles which were carried by the bearers.

Papamhow, where I rejoined my husband. Notwithstanding the difficulties, which according to report we expected, we made good progress, and arrived at Allahabad on the 1st of January, after a very pleasant trip.[6] Indeed, this short time we agreed was the most approaching to delightful that we had passed in India; the constant change of scenery, and the country very beautiful in some parts, with the daily exercise, kept us all, horses included, in high health and spirits. We travelled at the rate of about fifteen miles a day, making use of the staging bungalows that have been erected for the accommodation of travellers, as far as Benares; thence we travelled by dāk to Prāg, the distance being only ninety miles. So much for our journey, which, considering our inexperience, I think we performed with much credit to ourselves.

A friend received us at Papamhow with the utmost kindness, housed and fed us, and assisted us in arranging our new residence, which, by the bye, has one great beauty, that of being rent free: no small consideration where the expense of an unfurnished house is equal to that of a small income in England.[7] Said house is very prettily situated on the banks of the Jumna, a little beyond the Fort. We like our new situation, and do not regret the gaiety of the City of Palaces; indeed, it now appears to me most wonderful how we could have remained there so long: in climate there is no comparison, and as to expense, if we can but commence the good work of economy, we may return on furlough ere long.

The peaceful termination of the war with Ava was one of the happy events of this year.

---

[6] Allahabad was called Prayag in ancient times, meaning a confluence since it was situated at the junction of the Ganges and the Jumna.

[7] No trace of the house remains now but its location is easily found. The Parkes paid no rent since Charles was Collector of Customs. Because of the position of Allahabad there was a great deal of traded material such as cotton, salt, grain and sugar to tax.

Chapter 6

Life in the Mufassil

"PLANT A TREE, DIG A WELL, WRITE A BOOK, AND GO TO HEAVEN."[1]

January 1827.—It is usual in India for those newly arrived to call upon the resident families of the station; the gentleman makes his call, which is returned by the resident and his family; after which, the lady returns the visit with her husband. An invitation is then received to a dinner-party given in honour of the strangers, the lady being always handed to dinner by the host, and made the queen of the day, whether or not entitled to it by rank.

Our *debût* in the Mufassil was at the house of the judge, where we met almost all the station, and were much pleased that destiny had brought us to Prāg. Prāg was named Allahabad when the old Hindoo city was conquered by the Mahomedans. We were very fortunate in bringing up our horses and baggage uninjured, and in not having been robbed *en route*. Lord Amherst has lost two horses, and his aide-decamp three: guards are stationed around the Governor-general's horse-tents and baggage night and day, nevertheless native robbers have carried off those five animals. His lordship is at present at Lucnow.

We have spent the last three weeks most delightfully at Papamhow. Every sort of scientific amusement was going forward. Painting in oil and water colours, sketching from nature, turning, making curious articles in silver and brass, constructing Æolian harps, amusing ourselves with archery, trying the rockets on the sands of an evening, chemical experiments, botany, gardening; in fact, the day was never half long enough for our employment in the workshop and the grounds.

Papamhow is five miles from our own house, standing on higher ground and in a better situation, on the Ganges; when we can make holiday, we go up and stay at *our country house*, as our neighbours call it.

The old moonshee is cutting out my name in the Persian character, on the bottom of a Burmese idol, to answer as a seal. What an excellent picture the old man, with his long grey beard, would make! I have caught

[1] Guzrattee Proverb.

65

two beautiful little squirrels, with bushy tails and three white stripes on their backs; they run about the table, come to my shoulder, and feed from my hand.

May.—Our friend at Papamhow is gunpowder agent to the Government, and manager of the rocket manufactory; his services are likely to be fully exerted, as it is reported that Runjeet Singh is not expected to live four months, being in the last stage of a liver complaint, and that his son, it is thought, will hoist the standard of rebellion.[1] What gives foundation for this, is, that Lord Combermere is about to make the tour of the Upper Provinces, and that a concentration of forces is to take place on the frontier, under the pretext of a grand military inspection and review. There is no doubt as to who will go to the wall.

We have just received news of the death of Lord Hastings, and learn from the same papers, that Lord Amherst has been created an earl, and Lord Combermere a viscount.

We have been occupied in planting a small avenue of neem-trees in front of the house; unlike the air around the tamarind, that near a neem-tree is reckoned wholesome:—according to the Guzrattee Proverb, we had made no advance on our heavenward road until the avenue was planted, which carried us on one-third of the journey. No sooner were the trees in the ground, than the servants requested to be allowed to marry a neem to a young peepul-tree (ficus religiosa), which marriage was accordingly celebrated by planting a peepul and neem together, and entwining their branches. Some pooja was performed at the same time, which, with the ceremony of the marriage, was sure to bring good fortune to the newly-planted avenue.

The neem is a large and beautiful tree, common in most parts of India (melia azadirachta), or margosa-tree; its flowers are fragrant—a strong decoction of the leaves is used as a cure for strains.

Oil is prepared from the berry of the neem, (neem cowrie, as they call it,) which is esteemed excellent, and used as a liniment in violent headaches brought on by exposure to the sun, and in rheumatic and spasmodic affections. The flowers are fragrant: any thing remarkably bitter is compared to the neem-tree; "yeh duwa kŭrwee hy jyse neem:" this medicine is bitter as neem.

The bacäin, or māhā nimba, (melia sempervivens,) a variety of the neem-tree, is remarkably beautiful. "The neem-tree will not become sweet though watered with syrup and clarified butter."

My pearl of the desert, my milk-white Arab, Mootee, is useless; laid up

---

[1] Ranjit Singh unified the Punjab 1799–1839.

with an inflammation and swelling in his forelegs; he looks like a creature afflicted with elephantiasis—they tell us to keep him cool—we cannot reduce the heat of the stable below 120°!

I feel the want of daily exercise: here it is very difficult to procure a good Arab; the native horses are vicious, and utterly unfit for a lady; and I am too much the spoiled child of my mother to mount an indifferent horse. [. . .]

Oct. 27th.—The weather is now very pleasant, cold mornings and evenings; the end of next month we hope to begin collecting the ice, which is quite a business in this country. The next four months will be delightful; March will bring in the hot weather, and in April we shall be roasted alive.

Dec. 31st.—For the last three weeks I have been gadding about the country, the gayest of the gay. A friend at Lucnow invited me to pay her a visit, at the time Lord Combermere was to stay at the residency. Having a great desire to see a native court, and elephant and tiger fights, I accepted the invitation with pleasure.

Accompanied by an aide-de-camp who was going to see the tamāshā, I reached Lucnow after a run of three nights. Mr. Mordaunt Ricketts received me with great kindness; I spent a few days at the residency, and the rest with my friend.

On the arrival at Lucnow of his excellency the commander-in-chief, the king of Oude, Nusseer-ood Deen Hyder, as a compliment to that nobleman, sent his son, prince Kywan Jah, with the deputation appointed to receive his lordship, by whom the prince was treated as the walī-uhd, or heir-apparent.

The first day, Lord Combermere and the resident breakfasted with the king of Oude; the party was very numerous. We retired afterwards to another room, where trays of presents were arranged upon the floor, ticketed with the names of the persons for whom they were intended, and differing in their number and value according to the rank of the guests. Two trays were presented to me, the first containing several pairs of Cashmere shawls, and a pile of India muslin and kimkhwāb, or cloth of gold. The other tray contained strings of pearl, precious stones, bracelets, and other beautiful native jewellery. I was desired to make my salām in honor of the bounty of his majesty. As soon as the ceremony had finished, the trays were carried off and placed in the Company's treasury, an order having arrived, directing that all presents made to the servants of the Company should be accepted,—but for the benefit of the state.

That night his majesty dined at the residency, and took his departure at ten P.M., when quadrilles immediately commenced. The ladies were not allowed to dance while his majesty was present, as, on one occasion, he said, "That will do, let them leave off," thinking the ladies were quadrilling for his amusement, like nāch women. The second day, the king breakfasted with Lord Combermere, and we dined at the palace.

During dinner a favourite nāch woman attitudinized a little behind and to the right of his majesty's chair; at times he cast an approving glance at her performance. Sometimes she sang and moved about, and sometimes she bent her body *backwards*, until her head touched the ground; a marvellously supple, but not a graceful action.

The mornings were devoted to sports, and quadrilles passed away the evenings. I saw some very good elephant fights, some indifferent tiger fights, a rhinoceros against three wild buffaloes, in short, battles of every sort; some were very cruel, and the poor animals had not fair play.

The best fight was seen after breakfast at the palace. Two battaire (quails) were placed on the table; a hen bird was put near them; they set to instantly, and fought valiantly. One of the quails was driven back by his adversary, until the little bird, who fought every inch of his forced retreat, fell off the table into my lap. I picked him up and placed him upon the table again; he flew at his adversary instantly. They fight, unless separated, until they die. His majesty was delighted with the amusement.

[. . .]

On quitting the presence of his majesty, a harrh, a necklace of silver and gold tissue, very beautifully made, was placed around the neck of each of the guests, and atr of roses put on their hands.

The resident having sent me a fine English horse, I used to take my morning canter, return to cantonments, dress, and drive to the presidency to breakfast by eight A.M. The horse, a magnificent fellow, had but one fault,—a trick of walking almost upright on his hind legs. It was a contest between us; he liked to have his own way, and I was determined to have mine.

The dinners, balls, and breakfasts were frequent. Lord Combermere was in high good humour. His visit lasted about eight days, during which time he was entertained by the resident in Oriental style.

My journey having been delayed for want of bearers for my palanquin from Cawnpore, I arrived at Lucnow too late to see the ladies of the royal zenāna. The lady of the resident had been invited to visit their apartments the day before my arrival. She told me they were very fine, at least the dopatta (veil) was gay in gold and silver, but the rest of the attire very dirty. They appeared to have been taken by surprise, as they were not so highly ornamented as they usually are on a day of parade. I felt disappointed in being unable to see the begams; they would have interested me more than the elephant fights, which, of all the sights I beheld at Lucnow, pleased me the most.

I returned home at the end of December. The resident had the kindness to give me an escort of Skinner's horse, to protect my palanquin, and see me safely out of the kingdom of Oude, as far as Cawnpore, which, being in the Company's territories, was considered out of danger; and during the rest of the journey I was accompanied by two gentlemen.

[. . .]

In my vanity I had flattered myself dulness would have reigned triumphant at Prāg; nevertheless, I found my husband had killed the fatted calf, and "lighted the lamp of ghee;"[1] *i.e.* made merry.

I sent a little seal, on which this motto was engraved, "*Toom ghee ka dhye jalāo*," to a lady in England, telling her ghee is clarified butter. When a native gives a feast, he lights a number of small lamps with ghee. If he say to a friend, "Will you come to my feast?" the answer may be, "Light thou the lamp of ghee;" which means, "Be you merry, I will be there." Therefore, if you accept an invitation, you may use this seal with propriety.

Chapter 7

Residence at Allahabad

Jan., 1828, *Leap Year.*—I BEFORE mentioned we had accomplished one-third of our way to heaven, by planting an avenue; we now performed another portion of the journey, by sinking a well. As soon as the work was completed, the servants lighted it up with numerous little lamps, and

[1] Oriental Sayings.

strewed flowers upon its margin, to bring a blessing upon the newly-raised water. From Hissar we received six cows and a bull, very handsome animals, with remarkably fine humps, such as are sold in England under the denomination of buffalo humps, which are, in reality, the humps of Indian cows and oxen.

[. . .]

Jan.—Our garden was now in good order; we had vegetables in abundance, marrowfat peas as fine as in England, and the water-cresses, planted close to the new well, were pearls beyond price. Allahabad is famous for the growth of the finest carrots in India. At this time of the year we gave our horses twelve seer each daily; it kept them in high health, and *French-polished* their coats. The geraniums grew luxuriantly during this delightful time; and I could be out in the garden all day, when protected by an enormous chatr, carried by a bearer. The up-country chatr is a very large umbrella, in shape like a large flat mushroom, covered with doubled cloth, with a deep circle of fringe. Great people have them made of silk, and highly ornamented. The pole is very long, and it is full employment for one man to carry the chatr properly.

The oleander (kanér), the beautiful sweet-scented oleander, was in profusion,—deep red, pure white, pink, and variegated, with single and double blossoms. I rooted up many clusters of this beautiful shrub in the grounds, fearing the horses and cows might eat the leaves, which are poisonous. Hindoo women, when tormented by jealousy, have recourse to this poison for self-destruction.

The Ice-pits

Jan. 22nd.—My husband has the management of the ice concern this year. It is now in full work, the weather bitterly cold, and we are making ice by evaporation almost every night. I may here remark, the work continued until the 19th of February, when the pit was closed with 3000 mann,—a mann is about 80 lbs. weight. There are two ice-pits; over each a house is erected; the walls, built of mud, are low, thick, and circular; the roof is thickly thatched; there is only one entrance, by a small door, which, when closed, is defended from the sun and air by a jhamp, or frame-work of bamboo covered with straw.

The diameter of the pit, in the centre of the house, is large, but the depth not great, on account of the dampness of the ground. At the bottom is a small well, the top of which is covered over with bamboo; a channel unites it with a dry well on the outside, still deeper than itself, so constructed, that all the water collected in the pit may immediately run off through this duct,

Figure 3   The ice pits

and be drawn up from the external well. This keeps the pit perfectly dry—
a material point. The interior is lined, from top to bottom, with chatā'īs
(mats), three or four deep, which are neatly fastened by pegs round the
inside; mats are also kept ready for covering in the top of the pit. Some
ābdārs recommend a further lining of sulum (cotton-cloth), but it is
unnecessary.

The ground belonging to the ice concern is divided into keeārees, or
shallow beds, very like saltern-pans in England, about six feet square and a
cubit in depth; between them are raised paths.

When the weather in December is cold enough to induce us to suppose
water will freeze at night with artificial aid, the business of ice-making com-
mences. At the bottom of the keeārees, the shallow square beds, a black-
looking straw is spread about a foot in depth, called "pooāl," which is
reckoned better for the purpose than wheat-straw. Some ābdārs think sugar-
cane leaves the best thing to put under the pans in the ice-beds; next
in estimation is the straw or grass of kodo (the *paspalum frumentaceum*);
and then rice-straw, which is called "puwāl," or "pooāl," though the term
"pooāl" is not applied exclusively to the straw of rice. The highest temperature at which ice was made in 1846, at Cawnpore, was 43° of Fahrenheit,

or 11° above freezing point. At each of the four corners, on the pathway, is placed a thiliyā (an earthen jar), which is filled by a bihishtī with water. The pooāl straw in the shallow beds must be kept perfectly dry, to produce evaporation and the freezing of the water in the little pans placed upon it; should rain fall, the straw must be taken up and thoroughly dried before it can again be used.

It is amusing to see the old ābdār who has charge of the ice concern, walking up and down of an evening, watching the weather, and calculating if there be a chance of making ice. This is a grand point to decide, as the expense of filling the pans is great, and not to be incurred without a fair prospect of a crop of barf (ice) the next morning. He looks in the wind's eye, and if the breeze be fresh, and likely to increase, the old man draws his warm garment around him, and returning to his own habitation,—a hut close to the pits,—resigns himself to fate and his hubble-bubble. But should there be a crisp frosty feeling in the air, he prepares for action about 6 or 7 P.M., by beating a tom-tom (a native hand-drum), a signal well known to the coolies in the bazaar, who hasten to the pits. By the aid of the little cup fastened to the long sticks, as shown in the sketch, they fill all the rukābees with the water from the jars in the pathway. Many hundred coolies, men, women, and children, are thus employed until every little pan is filled.

If the night be frosty, without wind, the ice will form perhaps an inch and a half in thickness in the pans. If a breeze should blow, it will often prevent the freezing of the water, except in those parts of the grounds that are sheltered from the wind.

About 3 A.M. the ābdār, carefully muffled in some yards of English red or yellow broad cloth, would be seen emerging from his hut; and if the formation of ice was sufficiently thick, his tom-tom was heard, and the shivering coolies would collect, wrapped up in black bazār blankets, and shaking with cold. Sometimes it was extremely difficult to rouse them to their work, and the increased noise of the tom-toms—discordant native instruments— disturbed us and our neighbours with the pleasing notice of more ice for the pits. Each cooly, armed with a spud, knocked the ice out of the little pans into a basket, which having filled, he placed it on his head, ran with it to the ice-house, and threw it down the great pit.

When all the pans had been emptied, the people assembled around the old ābdār, who kept an account of the number at work on a roll of paper or a book. From a great bag full of pice (copper coins) and cowrie-shells, he paid each man his hire. About ten men were retained, on extra pay, to finish the work. Each man having been supplied with a blanket, shoes, and a heavy wooden mallet, four at a time descended into the pit by a ladder, and beat down the ice collected there into a hard flat mass; these men were constantly relieved by a fresh set, the cold being too great for them to remain long at the bottom of the pit.

When the ice was all firmly beaten down, it was covered in with mats, over which a quantity of straw was piled, and the door of the ice-house locked. The pits are usually opened on the 1st of May, but it is better to open them on the 1st of April. We had ice this year until the 20th of August. Each subscriber's allowance is twelve ser (24 lbs.) every other day. A bearer, or a cooly is sent with an ice-basket, a large bazār blanket, a cotton cloth, and a wooden mallet, at 4 A.M., to bring the ice from the pit. The ābdār, having weighed the ice, puts it into the cloth, and ties it up tightly with a string; the cooly then beats it all round into the smallest compass possible, ties it afresh, and, having placed it in the blanket within the ice-basket, he returns home. The gentleman's ābdār, on his arrival at his master's house, re-weighs the ice, as the coolies often stop in the bazaars, and sell a quantity of it to natives, who are particularly fond of it, the man pretending it has melted away *en route*.

The natives make ice for themselves, and sell it at two annas a seer; they do not preserve it for the hot winds, but give a good price for the ice stolen from the sāhib loge.[1]

For the art of freezing cream ices to perfection, and the method of making them in India, I refer you to the Appendix.

As the ābdārs generally dislike rising early to weigh the ice, the cooly may generally steal it with impunity. The ice-baskets are made of strips of bamboo covered inside and out with numdā, a thick coarse woollen wadding. The interior is lined with dosootee (white cotton cloth), and the exterior covered with ghuwā kopra, a coarse red cloth that rots less than any other from moisture.

The basket should be placed on a wooden stool, with a pan below to catch the dripping water.

Calcutta was supplied, in 1883, with fine clear ice from America, sent in enormous blocks, which sold at two annas a seer, about twopence per pound: this ice is greatly superior to that made in India, which is beaten up when collected into a mass, and dissolves more rapidly than the block ice. It is not as an article of luxury only that ice is delightful in this climate, medicinally it is of great use: there is much virtue in an iced night-cap to a feverish head. The American ice has not yet penetrated to the Up Country; we shall have ice from Calcutta when the railroads are established. No climate under the sun can be more delightful than this during the cold

---

[1] European gentleman.

weather, at which time we enjoy fires very much, and burn excellent coal, which is brought by water from Calcutta. The coal mines are at Burdwan, 100 miles from the presidency. In Calcutta it costs eight annas a mann; here, if procurable, it is one rupee: this year we had fires until the 29th of February.

After a good gallop round the Mahratta Bund, on Master George, a remarkably fine Arab, with what zest we and our friends partook of Hunter's beef and brawn!—as good as that of Oxford; the table drawn close to the fire, and the bright blaze not exceeding in cheerfulness the gaiety of the party!

March 31st.—How fearful are fevers in India! On this day my husband was attacked; a medical man was instantly called in, medicine was of no avail, the illness increased hourly. On the 9th of April, the aid of the super-intending surgeon was requested; a long consultation took place, and a debate as to which was to be employed, the lancet, or a bottle of claret; it terminated in favour of the latter, and claret to the extent of a bottle a day was given him: his head was enveloped in three bladders of ice, and iced towels were around his neck. On the 17th day, for the first time since the commencement of the attack, he tasted food; that is, he ate half a small bun; before that, he had been supported solely on claret and fresh straw-berries, being unable to take broth or arrow-root.

Not daring to leave him a moment night or day, I got two European artillerymen from the fort, to assist me in nursing him. On the 23rd, the anxiety I had suffered, and overexertion, brought on fever, which confined me to my chārpāī for seven days; all this time my husband was too ill to quit his bed; so we lay on two chārpāīs, under the same pankhā, two artillerymen for our nurses, applying iced towels to our heads, while my two women, with true native apathy, lay on the ground by the side of my bed, seldom attending to me, and only thinking how soon they could get away to eat and smoke. The attention and kindness of the medical men, and of our friends at the station, were beyond praise. Thanks to good doc-toring, good nursing, and good claret, at the end of the month we began to recover health and strength.

May 18th.—The ice-pits were opened, and every subscriber received twenty-four pounds weight of ice every other day—perfectly invaluable with a thermometer at 93°! Our friends had kindly allowed them to be opened before, during our fevers. It is impossible to describe the comfort of ice to the head, or of iced-soda water to a parched and tasteless palate, and an exhausted frame.

April.—Lord Amherst was requested by the directors to remain here until the arrival of Lord William Bentinck; and such was his intention, I believe, had he not been prevented by the dangerous illness of lady Sarah; and by this time, it is possible the family are on their way home. Mr. Bayley is Viceroy, and will reign longer than he expected, as Lord William Bentinck does not sail before January.

Our politicians are all on the *qui vive* at the *mêlée* between the Russians and Persians, and the old story of an invasion of India is again agitated:— we are not alarmed.

June 7th.—The weather is more oppressive than we have *ever* found it; the heat intolerable; the thermometer, in my room, 93°, in spite of tattees and pankhās. Allahabad may boast of being the oven of India; and the flat stone roof of our house renders it much hotter than if it were thatched.

We were most fortunate in quitting Calcutta; this past year the cholera has raged there most severely; the Europeans have suffered much; many from perfect health have been carried to their graves in a few hours.

A novel and a sofa is all one is equal to during such intense heat, which renders life scarcely endurable.

[. . .]

12th.—We have had a most miserable time of it for the last two months; this has been one of the hottest seasons in recollection, and Allahabad has well sustained its *sobriquét* of Chōtā Jahannum! which, being interpreted, is Hell the Little. Within these two days the state of affairs has been changed; we are now enjoying the freshness of the rains, whose very fall is music to our ears: another such season would tempt us to quit this station, in spite of its other recommendations.

Lord William Bentinck arrived July 3rd. The new Bishop of Calcutta is gone home, obliged to fly the country for his life; indeed, he was so ill, that a report of his death having come up here, some of his friends are in mourning for him; but I trust, poor man, he is going on well at sea at this minute.

Sept. 8th.—My verandah presents an interesting scene: at present, at one end, two carpenters are making a wardrobe; near them is a man polishing steel. Two silversmiths are busy making me some ornaments after the Hindostani patterns; the tailors are finishing a gown, and the ayha is polishing silk stockings with a large cowrie shell. The horses are standing near, in a row, eating lucerne grass, and the jumadār is making a report on their health, which is the custom at twelve at noon, when they come round for their tiffin.

Yesterday a mad pariah dog ran into the drawing-room; I closed the doors instantly, and the servants shot the animal: dogs are numerous and dangerous at some seasons.

[. . .]

Aug. 21st.—It is thought the gentleman, for whom my husband now officiates, will not rejoin this appointment; should he be disappointed of his hope of reigning in his stead, he will apply for something else rather than return to Calcutta, which we do not wish to see till the year of furlough, 1833–4. Meantime we must make it out as well as we can, and live upon hope, with the assurance that *if* we live, we shall *not* die fasting.

I wish the intermediate years would pass by as quickly as the river Jumna before our house, which is in such a furious hurry, that it is quite awful to see the velocity with which the boats fly along. Both the Ganges and the Jumna have this year been unusually high, and much mischief to the villages on the banks has been the consequence. There was a report the day before yesterday, that the Ganges, about a mile from this, had burst its banks. Luckily it was false; but it was a very near thing. Since then the river has sunk nearly twenty feet, so that we have no fear at present. The Jumna was within six feet of our garden bank.

Of the climate we cannot form a fair opinion, but it is certainly very superior to any they have in Bengal. This year has been most unnatural; no regular hot winds, unexpected storms, and the rains delayed beyond their proper season. Allahabad is called the oven of India, therefore I expect to become a *jolie brune*, and the sāhib well-baked.

We have just received telegraphic intelligence of the bishop's death at the Sandheads, where he was sent on account of severe illness, which terminated fatally on the 13th instant. It is said, that *three* bishops are to be imported, the late consumption having been so great. They ought to make bishops of the clergy who have passed their lives in India, and not send out old men who cannot stand the climate.

We have the use of a native steam-bath, which is most refreshing when the skin feels dry and uncomfortable. There are three rooms—the temperature of the first is moderate; that of the second, warmer; and the third, which contains the steam, is heated to about 100°. There you sit, until the perspiration starts in great drops from every pore; the women are then admitted, who rub you with besun[1] and native hand-rubbers,[2] and pour hot water over you until the surface peels off; and you come out a new creature, like the snake that has cast its skin. One feels fresh and elastic, and the joints supple: the steam-bath is a fine invention.

Oct. 1st.—The first steamer arrived at Allahabad in twenty-six days from Calcutta; the natives came down in crowds to view it from the banks of the Jumna; it was to them a cause of great astonishment.

---

[1] The flour or meal of pulse, particularly of chanā (cicer arietinum).
[2] Khīsās.

Chapter 8

Life in the Zenāna

"SHE WHO IS BELOVED, IS THE WIFE'."

Oct. 1828.—A letter just received from a lady, a friend of mine, at Lucnow, is so amusing and so novel, I must make an extract:—

"The other day, (Oct. 18th,) was the anniversary of the King of Oude's coronation; and I went to see the ceremony, one I had never witnessed before, and with which I was much gratified. But the greatest treat was a visit to the begam's afterwards, when the whole of the wives, aunts, cousins, &c., were assembled in state to receive us.

"The old begam (the king's mother), was the *great lady,* of course, and in her palace were we received; the others being considered her guests, as well as ourselves.[1] It was a most amusing sight, as I had never witnessed the interior of a zenāna before, and so many women assembled at once I had never beheld. I suppose from first to last we saw some thousands. *Women-bearers* carried our tanjans; a regiment of female gold and silver-sticks, dressed in male costume, were drawn up before the entrance; and those men, chiefly *Africans,* who were employed inside the zenāna (and there were abundance of these frightful creatures), were all of the same class as the celebrated Velluti. The old begam was without jewels or ornaments, likewise a very pretty and favourite wife of the late king, their state of widowhood precluding their wearing them. But the present king's wives were most superbly dressed, and looked like creatures of the Arabian tales. Indeed, one was so beautiful, that I could think of nothing but Lalla Rookh in her bridal attire.[2]

"I never saw any one so lovely, either black or white. Her features were perfect; and such eyes and eyelashes I never beheld before. She is the favourite queen at present, and has only been married a month or two: her

---

[1] The Padshah Begum, widow of Ghazi-uddin Hyder, was not the king's mother, who was a slave.

[2] Lalla Rookh, in Thomas Moore's poem of that name (1817), the supposed daughter of Aurungzeb, Emperor of Delhi. On her journey from Delhi to Kashmir, she is entertained by the young Persian poet Fer'amorz, who relates the four tales of the romance, and with whom she falls in love.

age about fourteen; and such a little creature, with the smallest hands and feet, and the most *timid, modest* look imaginable. You would have been charmed with her, she was so graceful and fawn-like. Her dress was of gold and scarlet brocade, and her hair was literally strewed with pearls, which hung down upon her neck in long single strings, terminating in large pearls, which mixed with and hung *as low* as her hair, which was curled on each side her head in long ringlets, like Charles the Second's beauties.

"On her forehead she wore a small gold circlet, from which depended (and hung half-way down her forehead) large pear-shaped pearls, interspersed with emeralds. The pearls were of this size and form, and had a very becoming effect, close upon the forehead, between the eyes. Above this was a paradise plume, from which strings of pearls were carried over the head, as we turn *our hair.*

"I fear you will not understand me. Her ear-rings were immense gold-rings, with pearls and emeralds suspended all round in long strings, the pearls increasing in size. She had a nose-ring also, with large round pearls and emeralds; and her necklaces, &c., were too numerous to be described. She wore long sleeves, open at the elbow; and her dress was a full petticoat, some dozen yards wide, with a tight body attached, and only open at the throat. She had several persons to bear her train when she walked; and her women stood behind her couch to arrange her head-dress, when in moving her pearls got entangled in the immense dopatta of scarlet and gold she had thrown around her. How I wished for you when we were seated! you would have been delighted with the whole scene. This beautiful creature is the envy of all the other wives, and the favourite, at present, of the king and his mother, both of whom have given her titles—the king's is after the favourite wife of one of the celebrated kings of Delhi, 'Tajmahŭl,' and Nourmahŭl herself could not have been more lovely.

"The other newly-made queen is nearly *European*, but not a whit fairer than Tajmahŭl.[3] She is, in my opinion, plain, but is considered by the native ladies very handsome; and she was the king's favourite until he saw Tajmahŭl.

"She was more splendidly dressed than even Tajmahŭl; her head-dress was a coronet of diamonds, with a fine crescent and plume of the same. She is the daughter of an European merchant, and is accomplished for an inhabitant of a zenāna, as she writes and speaks Persian fluently, as well as Hindostani, and it is said she is teaching the king *English*; though, when we spoke to her in English, she said she had forgotten it, and could not reply. She was, I fancy, afraid of the old begam, as she evidently understood

[3] She was a Miss Walters.

us; and when asked if she liked being in the zenāna, she shook her head and looked quite melancholy. Jealousy of the new favourite, however, appeared the cause of her discontent, as, though they sat on the same couch, they never addressed each other. And now you must be as tired of the begams, as I am of writing about them.

"The mother of the king's children, Mulka Zumanee, did not visit us at the old queen's, but we went to see her at her own palace: she is, *after all*, the person of the most political consequence, being the mother of the heir-apparent; and she has great power over her royal husband, whose ears she boxes occasionally.

"The Delhi princess, to whom the king was betrothed and married by his father, we did not see; she is in disgrace, and confined to her own palace. The old begam talked away to us, but appeared surprised I should admire Tajmahŭl more than the English begam, as she is called,—*my country-woman* as they styled her!

"Poor thing, I felt ashamed of the circumstance, when I saw her chewing pān with all the gusto of a regular Hindostanee."

The above letter contains so charming an account of Lucnow, that I cannot refrain from adding an extract from another of the same lady.

"At the residency, on such a day as this, the thermometer is seldom short of 100ⁿ!

"Did you ever hear of Colonel Gardner? he is married to a native princess. The other day he paid Lucnow a visit. His son's wife is sister to the *legal* queen of our present worthy sovereign of Oude. Colonel Gardner came on a visit to the begam's father, Mirza Sulimān Sheko, a prince of the house of Delhi, blessed with fifty-two children, twelve sons and forty daughters. Did you ever hear of such enormity? the poor papa is without a rupee, his pension from government of 5000 rupees a month is mortgaged to his numerous creditors. He has quarrelled with his illustrious son-in-law, the king of Oude; and Colonel Gardner has come over with the laudable purpose of removing his family from Oude to Delhi, where they will have a better chance of being provided for.

"Indeed, the other day, seventeen of the daughters were betrothed to seventeen princes of Delhi: this is disposing of one's daughters by wholesale! is it not? Colonel Gardner, who is a very gentlemanlike person, I hear, of the old school, was educated in France some fifty years ago. He gave a description of his sojourn amongst this *small family* in the city, in these words,—'I slept every night with the thermometer at 100°, and surrounded by 500 females!'

"What a situation! I do not know which would be the most overpowering, the extreme heat, or the incessant clack of the forty princesses and their attendants. It reminds me of the old fairy tale of the 'Ogre's forty daughters with golden crowns on their heads.'"

On dit, the English begam was the daughter of a half caste and an English officer; her mother afterwards married a native buniyā (shop-keeper). She had a sister; both the girls lived with the mother, and employed themselves in embroidering saddle-cloths for the horses of the rich natives. They were both very plain; nevertheless, one of them sent her picture to his majesty, who, charmed with the portrait, married the lady. She had money in profusion at her command: she made her father-in-law her treasurer, and pensioned her mother and sister.

The Suttee

A rich buniyā, a corn chandler, whose house was near the gate of our grounds, departed this life; he was an Hindoo. On the 7th of November, the natives in the bazār were making a great noise with their tom-toms, drums, and other discordant musical instruments, rejoicing that his widow had determined to perform suttee, *i.e.* to burn on his funeral-pile.

The magistrate sent for the woman, used every argument to dissuade her, and offered her money. Her only answer was, dashing her head on the floor, and saying, "If you will not let me burn with my husband, I will hang myself in your court of justice." The shāstrs say, "The prayers and imprecations of a suttee are never uttered in vain; the great gods themselves cannot listen to them unmoved."

If a widow touch either food or water from the time her husband expires until she ascend the pile, she cannot, by Hindoo law, be burned with the body; therefore the magistrate kept the corpse *forty-eight* hours, in the hope that hunger would compel the woman to eat. Guards were set over her, but she never touched any thing. My husband accompanied the magistrate to see the suttee: about 5000 people were collected together on the banks of the Ganges: the pile was then built, and the putrid body placed upon it; the magistrate stationed guards to prevent the people from approaching it. After having bathed in the river, the widow lighted a brand, walked round the pile, set in on fire, and then mounted cheerfully: the flame caught and blazed up instantly; she sat down, placing the head of the corpse on her lap, and repeated several times the usual form, "Ram, Ram, suttee; Ram, Ram, suttee;" *i.e.* "God, God, I am chaste."

As the wind drove the fierce fire upon her, she shook her arms and limbs as if in agony; at length she started up and approached the side to escape. An Hindoo, one of the police who had been placed near the pile to see she had fair play, and should not be burned by force, raised his sword to strike her, and the poor wretch shrank back into the flames. The magistrate seized and committed him to prison. The woman again approached the side of the blazing pile, sprang fairly out, and ran into the Ganges, which was within a few yards. When the crowd and the brothers of the dead man saw this, they called out, "Cut her down, knock her on the head with a bamboo; tie her hands and feet, and throw her in again;" and rushed down to execute their murderous intentions, when the gentlemen and the police drove them back.

The woman drank some water, and having extinguished the fire on her red garment, said she would mount the pile again and be burned.

The magistrate placed his hand on her shoulder (which rendered her impure), and said, "By your own law, having once quitted the pile you cannot ascend again; I forbid it. You are now an outcast from the Hindoos, but I will take charge of you, the Company will protect you, and you shall never want food or clothing."[4]

He then sent her, in a palanquin, under a guard, to the hospital. The crowd made way, shrinking from her with signs of horror, but returned peaceably to their homes; the Hindoos annoyed at her escape, and the Mussulmans saying, "It was better that she should escape, but it was a pity we should have lost the *tamāshā* (amusement) of seeing her burnt to death."

Had not the magistrate and the English gentlemen been present, the Hindoos would have cut her down when she attempted to quit the fire; or had she leapt out, would have thrown her in again, and have said, "She performed suttee of *her own accord*, how could *we* make her? it was the will of God." As a specimen of their religion the woman said, "I have transmigrated six times, and have been burned six times with six different husbands; if I do not burn the seventh time, it will prove unlucky for me!" "What good will burning do you?" asked a bystander. She replied, "The women of my husband's family have all been suttees, why should I bring disgrace upon them? I shall go to heaven, and afterwards re-appear on earth, and be married to a very rich man." She was about twenty or twenty-five years of age, and possessed of some property, for the sake of which her relatives wished to put her out of the world.

If every suttee were conducted in this way, very few would take place in India. The woman was not much burned, with the exception of some parts on her arms and legs. Had she performed suttee, they would have raised a

[4] The Company's policy was not to interfere with indigenous customs, so they took no action against suttee until 1813, when it was ordered that a magistrate had to be present. This implied that the practice was sanctioned and so the number of suttee increased. From 1818 a group of Hindu reformers, led by Ram Mohun Roy, organised campaigns against suttee, and in 1828 the Government consulted officials as to the feasibility of outlawing it. Bentinck declared it illegal in 1829 in Bengal and in 1830 in Madras and Bombay.

little cenotaph, or a mound of earth by the side of the river, and every Hindoo who passed the place returning from bathing would have made sālām to it; a high honour to the family. While we were in Calcutta, many suttees took place; but as they were generally on the other side of the river, we only heard of them after they had occurred. Here the people passed in procession, flags flying, and drums beating, close by our door. I saw them from the verandah; the widow, dressed in a red garment, was walking in the midst. My servants all ran to me, begging to be allowed to go and see the tamāshā (fun, sport), and having obtained permission, they all started off, except one man, who was pulling the pankhā, and he looked greatly vexed at being obliged to remain. The sāhib said, the woman appeared so perfectly determined, he did not think she would have quitted the fire. Having performed suttee according to her own account six times before, one would have thought from her miraculous incombustibility, she had become asbestos, only purified and not consumed by fire. I was glad the poor creature was not murdered; but she will be an outcast; no Hindoo will eat with her, enter her house, or give her assistance; and when she appears they will point at her and give her abuse. Her own and her husband's family would lose caste if they were to speak to her: but, as an example, it will prevent a number of women from becoming suttees, and do infinite good: fortunately, she has no children. And these are the people called in Europe the "mild inoffensive Hindoos!"

The woman was mistress of a good house and about 800 rupees; the brothers of her deceased husband would, after her destruction, have inherited the property.

The burning of the widow is not commanded by the shāstrs: to perform suttee is a proof of devotion to the husband. The mountain Himalaya, being personified, is represented as a powerful monarch: his wife, Mena; their daughter is called Parvuti, or mountain-born, and Doorga, or difficult of access. She is said to have been married to Shivŭ in a *pre-existing* state when she was called Sŭtēē. After the marriage, Shivŭ on a certain occasion offended his father-in-law, King Dŭkshŭ, by refusing to make sālām to him as he entered the circle in which the king was sitting.

To be revenged, the monarch refused to invite Shivŭ to a sacrifice which he was about to perform. Sŭtēē, the king's daughter, however, was resolved to go, though uninvited and forbidden by her husband. On her arrival, Dŭkshŭ poured a torrent of abuse on Shivŭ, which affected Sŭtēē so much that she died.

In memory of this proof of great affection, a Hindoo widow burning with her husband on the funeral-pile, is called a Sŭtēē.

The following passages are from the Hindoo Shāstrs:—

"There are 35,000,000 hairs on the human body. The woman who ascends the pile with her husband, will remain so many years in heaven."

"As the snake draws the serpent from its hole, so she, rescuing her husband (from hell), rejoices with him."

"The woman who expires on the funeral-pile of her husband, purifies the family of her mother, her father, and her husband."

"So long as a woman, in her successive transmigrations, shall decline burning herself, like a faithful wife, on the same fire with her deceased lord, so long shall she not be exempted from springing again to life in the body of some female animal."

"There is no virtue greater than a chaste woman burning herself with her husband:" the term Sŭtēē, here rendered "chaste" is thus explained; "commiserating with her husband in trouble, rejoicing in his joys, neglecting herself when he is gone from home, and dying at his death."

"By the favour of a chaste woman the universe is preserved, on which account she is to be regarded by kings and people as a goddess."

"If the husband be out of the country when he dies, let the virtuous wife take his slippers (or any thing else which belongs to his dress) and binding them, or it, on her breast, after purification, enter a separate fire."

Mothers collect the cowries strewn by a sutēēn as she walks round the pile, ere she fires it, and hand them round the necks of their sick children as a cure for disease.

[. . .]

The suttee took place on the banks of the Ganges, under the Bund between the Fort and Raj Ghat, a spot reckoned very holy and fortunate for the performance of the rite.

Several of our friends requested me, in case another suttee occurred, to send them timely notice. Five days afterwards, I was informed that a rānee[1] was to be burned. Accordingly I sent word to all my friends. Eight thousand people were assembled on the suttee-ground, who waited from midday to sun-set: then a cry arose—"The mem sāhiba sent us here! the mem sāhiba said it was to take place to-day! see, the sun has set, there can now be no suttee!" The people dispersed. My informant told me what he himself believed, and I mystified some 8000 people most unintentionally.

Temple of Bhawānī and suttees, Alopee Bagh

In Alopee Bagh, in the centre of a large plantation of mango-trees, is a small temple dedicated to Bhawānī; there is no image in it, merely a raised altar,

[1] A Hindoo queen or princess.

on which victims were, I suppose, formerly sacrificed. Each of the small buildings on the right contains the ashes of a suttee; there are seven suttee-graves of masonry on this, and six of earth on the other side, near the temple, in the mango tope. The largest suttee-tomb contains the ashes of a woman who was burnt in 1825, *i.e.* six years ago. The ashes are always buried near a temple sacred to Bhāwanī, and *never* by any other. Families too poor to raise a tomb of masonry in memory of the burnt-sacrifice, are contented to raise a mound of earth, and place a *kulsa* of red earthenware to mark the spot. [. . .]

The temple of Bhawānī is shaded by a most beautiful peepul-tree, from the centre of which a fākir's flag was flying; it stands in a plantation of mango-trees. I desired an Hindoo, who was present when I sketched the temple, to count the suttee-graves around it. As he counted them, he repeatedly made sālām to each mound. [. . .]

Nov.—My beautiful Arab, Mootee, after taking a most marvellous quantity of blue vitriol and opium, has recovered, but will be unfit for my riding; the sinews of his fore-leg are injured; besides which, he is rather too playful; he knocked down his sā'īs yesterday, tore his clothes to pieces, bit two bits of flesh out of his back, and would perhaps have killed him, had not the people in the bazār interfered and rescued the man. It was an odd freak, he is such a sweet-tempered animal, and I never knew him behave incorrectly before.

We spent the month of December, our hunting season, at Papamhow; and purchased several couple of the Berkeley hounds, from the Calcutta kennel, for the pack at Allahabad. I received a present of an excellent little black horse with a long tail; and, mounted on him, used to go out every day after the jackals and foxes. I am rich in riding-horses, and the dark brown stud Arab Trelawny bids fair to rival Mootee in my affections. Returning from chasing a jackal one evening, it was very dark, and as Captain A—— S—— was cantering his Arab across the parade-ground, the animal put his foot into a deep hole, and fell; our friend thought nothing of it; and refused to be bled; a few days afterwards the regiment quitted Allahabad, and he died the second day, on the march to Benares. He was an ill-fated animal, that little horse of his: they called him an Arab pony, but no good caste animal would have been so vicious; he had one fault, a trick of biting at the foot of his rider—he bit off the toe of his former master, mortification ensued, and the man died. I often wished to mount him, but they would never allow me: the creature was very handsome, and remarkably well formed; doubtless a native would have found unlucky marks upon him—at that time I was ignorant respecting samāt, or unlucky marks on horses.

Chapter 9

Residence at Prāg

"I KEEP WRITING ON UPON THE PRINCIPLE OF A GOOD ECONOMIST,
THAT IT IS A PITY SO MUCH PAPER SHOULD BE LOST, WHICH, LIKE THE
QUEER LITTLE OLD MAN IN THE SONG, 'HAS A LONG WAY TO GO.'"

"WHAT RELIANCE IS THERE ON LIFE?"[1]

"HE WHO HAS ILL-LUCK FOR HIS COMPANION WILL BE BITTEN
BY A DOG ALTHOUGH MOUNTED ON A CAMEL."[2]

Jan. 1829.—In the beginning of this month, having promised to meet Captain A. S——at the races at Ghazeepore, we started by land, having sent tents and provisions by water to await our arrival. A violent headache preventing me from mounting my horse, I proceeded in a pālkee, much against medical advice, and slept half-way to Benares, in our tents.

Rising late the next day, we had a hot ride before reaching the Stanhope, where we learnt that our pitaras had been stolen. My husband rode forward in pursuit of the thieves, leaving me seated by the side of the road; the sun becoming very hot, I got into the buggy, overcome from my recent illness, the sā'īs holding the horse. I was startled from a doze by the sound of the bells of a native cart passing with flags flying; the horse alarmed sprang from the sā'īs's hands, pulling away the reins, which fell to the ground; away galloped the horse, a strong animal fifteen hands high; he looked down the steep ditch on one side the raised road, turned round, looked over the ditch on the other side, made one more sudden turn in alarm, and upset the buggy. I was thrown head foremost through the opening in the back, my limbs remaining under the buggy-hood, which was broken to pieces; the horse fairly kicked himself out of the shafts, and galloped off; I was glad when I found he was free, and knew he could not break my legs, which were still under the hood: at length I dragged them out, with my long habit-skirt, and made an attempt to go after the horse, but was obliged to sit down—blue and yellow suns, stars, and bright objects floated before my eyes—I was unable to stand: my dressing-case having been thrown out of

[1] Oriental proverbs.   [2] Ibid.

the buggy, I drank some *sal volatile*, which took off the giddiness. My husband returned at this moment, and an officer from some tents near at hand came to our assistance. The Stanhope was carried forward by coolies; we had a Calcutta buggy also with us, in which we proceeded. The road was covered with the finest sand, rendering it impossible to see the deep holes in every direction. The horse, a powerful English imported creature, was going very fast, when he put both his fore feet into a deep hole, and came down; the high Calcutta buggy swung forwards with such force I was pitched out over the wheel on my head, and remained insensible for a few seconds. My husband was not thrown out. He was unable to leave the frightened horse; it was a relief when he heard a voice from the dust, saying, "I am not hurt;" a voice he feared he should never hear again. The bruises I had before received, united with this blow on my head, which cut through my riding-hat, made me very nervous; and when at the last stage we had to drive a run-away mare, laid for us by a friend, I really sat in fear and trembling. At last we arrived at Benares. I was carried up-stairs to bed, my limbs being stiff and painful. For ten days I could scarcely move, so much was my body bruised by the iron rail and hood of the buggy, and my right arm was greatly swollen.

My recovery was brought about by having four women to shampoo me for five hours daily, and by going into a vapour-bath belonging to the Rajah of Benares. In the bath the women shampooed, and twisted, and pinched my limbs, until I could walk without assistance—that vapour-bath was a great relief.

One morning the rajah sent me a bouquet of flowers, they were beautifully made of ubruk (talc, mica) and coloured wax, the first I had seen well executed.

My husband at the billiard-table, said: "I am uncertain respecting that stroke, I wish A——S——was here." "Do you not know he is dead?" said his opponent, "he died in consequence of his fall with that Arab pony at Papamhow." We were greatly shocked.

Jan. 29th.—We quitted our kind friends at Benares to return home: ill-luck pursued us—the first stage the horse fell lame, and we reached our tent with difficulty. During the night a heavy storm came on; the tent being old was soon saturated, and the water poured in on our chārpāīs. The horses picketed outside were drenched, they neighed and shook their chains; the sā'īses crept under the corners of the rāwtī, and we had the floorcloth put over us, to protect us from the rain and cold.

The next day we galloped to our second tent, which we found soaked through from the rain of the night. There was the tent, and nothing else. One of the camels having fallen lame, the servants had made it a pretext for not continuing their march, and we were *planté* in the jungle without food, bedding, or warm clothing? A camel-driver caught a chicken, and drawing out a long queer crooked blade, killed it, and dressed an excellent curry in a few minutes; having had no food all day, and much exercise, we devoured it to the last grain of rice. I thought of the saying, "If you ask a hungry man how much two and two make—he answers, 'Four loaves.'"[1] The night was miserable, the wind blowing through the wet canvass; we could not even borrow a blanket from the horses, everything was drenched. A pukka ague and fever was the consequence, which lasted seven or eight days, and returned regularly once every four weeks for three months.

Nor did our misfortunes end here. Much to the surprise of my husband, his Arab Rajah, whom he had had for seven years, threw him over his right shoulder. Rajah was particularly pleased; for having looked at him, he cocked his tail and went off at his best pace towards home. Monsieur was not hurt, and received only a few bruises for his carelessness, which, considering he now weighs fourteen stone, shows that, like Cæsar, he has much respect for his person and can fall in proper form.

[. . .]

The arrival of a friend from England has pleased us greatly. What pleasure reminiscences Etonian and Harrovian give him and the sāhib! "Economy, *esperanza*, and 1833," is our motto. "In five years," says an old Harrovian, "we may hear the bell and going up—sounds worth listening to."

Cicer arietinum (chickweed), is called *arietinum* because the young seed bears a very curious resemblance to a ram's horn. The crops being favourable this year, this chickweed (chāna or gram) was sold in the city one mŭn twenty-two ser per rupee; and in the district, one mŭn thirty-five ser for the same.

March 8th.—At this time my husband was attacked with ague and fever, the consequence of our expedition to Benares.

There is a rumour of a central government being established, the location to be hereabouts, so that Allahabad may again become a city of repute.

We have had much annoyance of late from the servants stealing all sorts of little things, as also wine. Two of the khidmatgārs were the culprits: one has been ratened,[1] and put in irons to work on the road, we could not punish the other, but it was a pleasure to get him out of the house. In India, amongst so many servants, it is very difficult to discover the thief.

---

[1] Oriental Proverbs.

1 ratened, caned.

May 31*st*.—How I rejoice this month is over!—this vile month! It appears almost wicked to abuse the merry merry month of May, so delightful at home, but so hot in India. Mr. M——started from Calcutta to come up dāk on the 7th instant, and died in his pālkee of brain-fever only three days afterwards, in consequence of the intense heat! We spare no expense to keep the house cool, and have fourteen men whose sole business night and day is to throw water on tattīs to cool the rooms; unless the wind blows, the tattīs are useless. The heat makes you as sick as if you were to shut your head up in an oven.

A young bullock was standing in the stable to-day by the side of three horses, a snake bit the animal, and it died in a few minutes; the horses escaped—and so did the snake, much to my sorrow.

July 19*th*.—The other evening Major P——was with us, when Ram Din, a favourite Hindoo servant, brought into the room a piece of cotton cloth containing 150 rupees tightly tied up in it; the man placed it on the table by my side, and retired. Major P——, who thought the cloth looked dirty, took it up, and saying, "Oh the vile rupees!" let it drop upon the ground between his chair and mine. We took tea: and I retired to rest, entirely forgetting the bag of rupees. When I looked for it the following morning, of course it had disappeared. By the advice of the jāmadār of the office we sent for a gosāin, a holy personage, who lived in a most remarkable temple on the ruins of an old well by the side of the Jumna, close to our house. The gosāin came. He collected the Hindoos together, and made pooja. Having anointed a sacred piece of wood[1] with oil and turmeric, and placed it in a hut, he closed the door; and coming forth, said: "To show you that I am able to point out the thief, I have now left a gold ring in front of the idol in that house; go in and worship, every man of you. Each man must put his hand upon the idol. Let one amongst you take the ring, I will point out the man."

The Hindoos looked at him with reverence; they all separately entered the dwelling, and did as they were ordered. The jāmadār performed the same ceremony, although he was a Mussulmān. On their appearing before the gosāin, he desired them all to show their hands, and having examined them with much attention, he exclaimed, looking at the hands of the jāmadār, "You are the thief!" The man held up his hands to heaven, exclaiming, "God is great, and you are a wonderful man! *I*, a Mussulmān, did not believe in your power; your words are words of truth; I took the ring, here it is: if it be your pleasure, you can, doubtless, point out the man who stole the rupees."

[1] Acacia Arabica, or Babool.

The gosāin then told the people, that unless the money were forthcoming the next day, he would come and point out the thief. That evening the jāmadār roamed around the house, calling out in the most dismal voice imaginable, "You had better put back the rupees, you had better put back the rupees." The police came, and wished to carry off Ram Din to prison, because he was the servant who had put the money by my side. The man looked at me. "Is it your will? I am a Rajpoot, and shall lose caste; I have served you faithfully, I am present."

"Who will be security that you will not run away?" said the barkandāz. I replied, "*I* will be his security: Ram Din will remain with us, and when the magistrate sends for him, I will answer for it he will be present." The man's eyes filled with tears: it was the greatest compliment I could pay him: he made a deep sālām, saying, "Mem sāhiba! Mem sāhiba!" in an agitated and grateful tone. The next morning the jāmadār informed me that a bag was on the top of the wardrobe in my dressing-room, and none of the servants would touch it. I went to the spot, and desired Ram Din to take it down.

"This is the cloth that contained the rupees," said the man, "and it has never been opened; I know it by a peculiar knot that I always tie." He opened the bag, and found the whole of the money.

We had reason to believe one of the under bearers committed the theft. The Hindoos have such faith in their gosāins, and their influence over them is so great, they dare not do otherwise than as they are ordered by the holy men. I got back the 15*l.*, and gave 4*l.* to those who had exerted themselves to find it.

The Gosāin's Temple

Just above the Fort of Allahabad, on the banks of the Jumna, close to the Jāmma Musjid, or large mosque, amongst the ruins of the *ancient* city of Prāg, within a Boorj (or Bastion), is an old well, from which the bank has been washed away by the river, and which now stands within the edge of the stream.

The well in the centre of the Boorj descends into the Jumna; over it is built a most peculiar, circular, and singular temple; this and a small square outer building is the residence of the gosāin, who by his incantations, made the servants restore the 150 rupees that had been stolen.

The pillars are peculiar—Ionic—no further ornamental work is visible: perforated stone fills up the openings above: some have been blocked up: the Nagree writing in red letters at the foot of the pillar is recent: several boorj (bastions) beyond this one, which contains the water-gate, have sunk into the river: there were eight originally, seven of which are still visible. Accompanied by a gentleman, I went to sketch it, and asked the gosāin to allow us to see the interior. The holy man made some difficulty in allowing us to enter; sweet words induced him to open the door.

"By sweet words and gentleness you may draw an elephant by a hair."[1]

Within was a small room, in which was the gosāin's bed, and a large green painted chest, iron clamped, on wheels, which, I suppose, contained his valuables: it must have been put together in the room, being too large to have come in through the door-way. In a nitch of the wall was a small brazen image of Krishna, with a smaller one of Rhada, the latter dressed in a full red and yellow petticoat, stretched out like a fan, and many times wider than the height of the idol.

This is the second time I have seen a place consecrated to these images. The worship is very impure, I am told; and, in spite of the holy character of the priest, histories are whispered about which account for the marvellous properties of the seeds of the peepul-tree. Women principally worship at this shrine.

The circular temple above the well, to which there is a grating, contains either the gosāin's money or zenāna, or both: he would not allow us to take a view of the interior. On the outside, at the foot of the temple, is a neglected and broken image, in stone, of Varaha, the avatār of Vishnoo with the head of a boar.

Whilst sketching the temple, we remarked its strong resemblance to the temple of the Sibyl, and were greatly surprised at its Ionic style of architecture.

On my return to England, a gentleman, seeing the sketch, said, "You must have painted from imagination, no such architecture is in the East." This remark annoyed me. I defended the truth and faithfulness of my pencil, and determined, should fate ever carry me back to the ancient city of Prāg, to pay most particular attention to the architecture, and to re-sketch the temple. The mystery of its similarity to that of the Sibyl will be explained hereafter.

I must give a specimen of the natives. I asked the man who has the charge of the rabbits, why a remarkably handsome buck was missing, and a white doe was in its place?

The man vowed that "the day being extremely hot, the sun had turned the black buck white, and had altered the sex also!" I called a chaprāsī, desired him to pay the man's wages, deducting the value of the buck, and turn him out of my service: his penitence and recantation were in vain. "I

[1] Oriental Proverbs.

wish you would give me a beating, and let me remain in your service," said the man. "You may have a beating if you wish it," said I, "but unless it changes your sex, you shall not remain in my service."

"THE DIVER WHO THINKS ON THE JAWS OF THE CROCODILE,
WILL NEVER GATHER PRECIOUS PEARLS."[1]

This saying is very applicable to Europeans in India: the climate is worse than the jaws of the crocodile; and as for the pearls—when large appointments, in the hope of attaining which men have been slaving upon small allowances, fall vacant, the shears are applied, and a reduction of one-third or more follows. It is rumoured, but upon doubtful evidence, that the Governor-general and members of Council determined to sacrifice part of *their* allowances to contribute to the general exigencies of the state, but found *they* were restricted from receiving less by the Act of Parliament, by which their salaries are fixed. The Governor-general, in common parlance, is called "the clipper."

It is to be hoped the Half Batta measure will be abandoned; if it is insisted upon, the experiment will be somewhat perilous. Let the Board of Control look at the numbers carried off by the climate, and they must acknowledge their pay is blood-money. The sipahis are deserting from different stations, eight and nine a day, and some regiments are almost in a state of mutiny. The men desert to Runjeet Singh; and I understand the officers of many regiments will not dine at the Government-house, and only make their appearance when obliged by order. Heaven help those poor fellows who have wives and children to starve on half batta![2]

[1] Oriental Proverbs.

2 Batta: an extra allowance paid when in the field rather than in garrison to cover extra expenses. Bentinck made a new rule that only half batta was to be paid to those regiments stationed within 400 miles of Calcutta. The salary of an officer consisted of a small salary and substantial expenses in the form of tentage, house-rent and batta.

Chapter 10

Sketches at Allahabad

"THE LAMP BURNS NOT BEFORE THE BLACK SNAKE."[1]

Which, like the Burmese idols, is supposed to carry a bright jewel in its head.

1829, *Oct.*—Snakes are very numerous in our garden; the cobra de capello, and the black snake, whose bite is just as mortal. This morning I turned over some tiles with my foot, when a cobra I had disturbed glided into the centre of the heap, where we killed him.

Mohummud said, "Kill snakes, and kill the snake which has two black lines upon its back, and kill the snake called *abter*, on account of its small tail; for verily these two kinds of snake blind the eyes as soon as they are looked at. You must not kill the snakes that live in the houses, because they are not snakes but a kind of genii. Domestic snakes, which are genii, must be warned to depart; if they do not, they are to be killed. The genii are of three kinds, one kind have wings, and fly; another are snakes and dogs; and the third move about from place to place like men."

"But do not hurry in killing them, but say, 'do not incommode me, if you do, I shall kill you.' Then, if it goes away, so much the better; but if not, kill it, because it is an infidel *genius*."

"Kill all snakes, except the small white one, which is not poisonous."[2]

Several were in the stable and hen-house. A snake-charmer came, who offered to fascinate and catch the snakes for me at one rupee a head. He caught one, for which I gave him a rupee; but as I had it killed, he never returned—the charm was broken—it was a tame fangless snake, which he had tried to pass off as the wild one.

We killed three scorpions in the dining-room, of rather large dimensions. Our friend and neighbour had much compassion on frogs. Many an enormous bull-frog he rescued alive from the jaws of the snakes he killed in his garden. The poor frogs lost their defender on his return to England, and we an excellent friend.

During the Burmese war I had presents made me of seven or eight idols;

[1] Oriental Proverbs.   [2] Mishcat ul Masabih.

one was of gold, several of silver; some of black, some of white marble, others of bronze. The soldiers in Burmah opened the heads of many of the large idols, and found jewels within them. I have never disturbed the "reflecting gems" within the brains of my Burmese gods; they may contain, for aught I know, "heaps of gold, inestimable jewels,"—there let them rest.

Oct. 29th.—We drove to the Parade-ground, to view the celebration of the Ram Leela festival. Ram the warrior god is particularly revered by the sipahīs. An annual tamāshā is held in his honour, and that of Seeta his consort. A figure of Rawan the giant, as large as a windmill, was erected on the Parade-ground: the interior of the monster was filled with fire-works. This giant was destroyed by Ram. All sorts of games are played by the sipahīs, on the Parade. Mock fights and wrestling matches take place, and fire-works are let off. Two young natives, about ten or twelve years old, are often attired to represent Ram and Seeta; and men with long tails figure as the army of monkeys, headed by their leader Hŭnoomān.

On dit, the children who personate Ram and Seeta, the handsomest they can select, never live more than a year after the festival—for this I vouch not—it is said they are poisoned.

One ceremony was very remarkable: each native regiment took out its colours and made pooja to the standards, offering them sweetmeats, flowers, rice, and pān, as they do to a god! At Cawnpore I saw the men of the third cavalry riding round the image of the giant, with their colours flying, after having made pooja to them.

At the conclusion of the tamāshā, the figure of Rawan is blown up by the conqueror Ram. At the great Mela at Allahabad, I procured a large marble image of Ram, which came from Jeypore; it is highly gilt and ornamented: in his left hand is the bow of power, and the quiver full of arrows in his right: the trident mark adorns his forehead, and on his head is a crown. See the figure on the left of Ganesh in the frontispiece.

"Ram, the deified hero, was a famous warrior, and a youth of perfect beauty. He was the happy possessor of the divine bow Danush, which the giant Ravuna could not bend, and with which he contested for, and won, the hand of the goddess Seeta. It was ordained, that he only who could bend this bow, and with it shoot a fish, while revolving on a pole, through the left eye, not seeing the fish, but its reflection in a pan of oil, should espouse Seeta. The name of Ram is used beyond the pale of his own sectarists, in supplication and praise."

Rám, rám, is a usual salutation, like our good-morrow, between friends at meeting or parting. It is reverently reiterated at times in aid of abstraction, and in moments of enthusiasm or distress.

On the birthday of this god the Hindoo merchants in general begin their year's accounts; and on this day the gods caused a shower of flowers to fall from heaven.

"Ravuna, a giant who reigned at Ceylon, having seized Hŭnoomān, ordered his tail to be set on fire. The enraged monkey, with his burning tail, leaped from house to house, and set all Lŭnka (Ceylon) on fire; after finishing which, he came to Seeta, and complained that he could not extinguish the fire that had kindled on his tail. She directed him to spit upon it; and he, raising it to his face for this purpose, set his face on fire. He then complained, that when he arrived at home with such a black face, all the monkeys would laugh at him. Seeta, to comfort him, assured him, that all the other monkeys should have black faces also; and when Hŭnoomān came amongst his friends, he found that, according to the promise of Seeta, they had all black faces as well as himself.

"Mŭndodŭrēē, the chief wife of Ravuna the giant, whom Ram had killed, came to Ram weeping; and he, not knowing who she was, gave her this blessing, that she should never become a widow. Finding his mistake, having just killed her husband, he ordered Hŭnoomān continually to throw wood upon the fire, according to a proverb amongst the Hindoos, that as long as the body of the husband is burning, a woman is not called a widow.

"To this day, therefore, Hŭnoomān keeps laying logs on the fire; and every time a Hindoo puts his fingers in his ears and hears a sound, he says he hears the bones of the giant Ravuna burning."[1]

The marks on the foreheads of Ram's followers very much resemble a trident.

At the time of death many Hindoos write the name of Ram on the breast and forehead of the dying person, with earth taken from the banks of the Ganges; and thence those persons after death, instead of being dragged to Yamu, the Holy King, the Judge of the Dead, to receive sentence, immediately ascend to heaven.

The mock fights at the Ram Leela are in remembrance of the time when Hŭnoomān and his monkeys constructed a bridge from the continent of India to Ceylon (Lŭnka), over which Ram's army passed, and rescued the imprisoned Seeta from the hands of the giant Rawan or Ravuna, who had carried her off. Seeta then passed through the ordeal of fire, and by her miraculous incombustibility assured the world of her purity; Ram placed the mālā, the chaplet of marriage, around her neck, and the monkeys capered and gambolled with delight.

[1] Ward on the History, Literature, and Religion of the Hindoos.

The white marble figure in the frontispiece to the left of Ganesh represents Ram, the deified hero, with his bow and quiver. The brass figure in front of the latter is Hŭnoomān, bearing Ram Seeta on his shoulders.

The Board of Works

Nov.—The cold season is a busy time. Having procured a quantity of teak timber and toon wood, we established a Board of Works in the verandah, consisting of five carpenters, two sawyers, two turners, six iron-smiths, one stone-cutter, and one harness-maker. Most excellent and very handsome were the dining-tables, sideboard, horseshoe-table, wardrobes, &c., and a Stanhope made by these men, from our own designs.

The carpenters carve wood extremely well. On my return to England, I saw and admired a round table in a friend's drawing-room; "Do you not remember," said she with surprise, "you made up that table yourself?" On looking at it, I recognized the pedestal and claw carved with broad leaves, copied from a model I made for my carpenter of Ganges mud.

The furniture was of various kinds of wood, as follows:—

Teak sāgūn (tectona grandis) or Indian oak—a fine heavy timber, in colour resembling oak; strong and good wood. The teak I made use of came from Ava, and was brought up from the salt-water lake near Calcutta; good sāgūn was also to be purchased at Cawnpore.

The finest is brought from Java and Ava. I saw *one plank* of Java teak which, even when made up, measured five feet six inches in diameter. It was the top of an oval table. It bears a good polish, and is suited for tables, wardrobes, and the beds of billiard-tables. In the up-country the usual price is one rupee per foot when the plank is one inch in thickness; in Calcutta, the same price when the plank is four inches in thickness. The *general* size of the timber brought from Ava is eighteen inches in breadth.

Sāl, sānkho or sākoo (shorea robusta)—a heavy strong wood, from the up-country; fit for beams of houses, wardrobes, frames, window-frames, kitchen-tables, &c. Price, when thirty feet in length by seventeen inches in breadth, twenty-six rupees; when twenty-one feet in length by twenty-two in breadth, thirty-two rupees. It is sold cheap at Cawnpore in September and October.

Shīsham, sissoo or sesoo (dalbergia sissoo)—from the up-country; fit for tables, chairs, carriage-wheels and bodies; very heavy, takes a good polish, fine grained. Price, eighteen feet in length by fourteen in breadth, thirteen rupees; good for bullock-collars; cheap in September.

Toon—a light soft-grained wood, very much resembling mahogany;

fit for tables, chairs, billiard-table frames, book-cases &c.; reasonable at Cawnpore.

Soondry—comes from Calcutta; the best wood for shafts and carriage-wheels.

Arnoose, or bastard ebony, also called teenoo—a common timber, found on the banks of the Jumna; used for fire-wood; three or four mŭns per rupee. In the centre of the wood the ebony is found, which is lighter, both in colour and weight, than the ebony from the hills (abnoos), which is very heavy, hard, and difficult to cut; also of a good blackness; useful for handles of seals, chess-men, &c.

Cocoa-nut tree, naryul—from Calcutta; also one of the best for shafts; the bark is curious; when petrified and polished it is made into ornaments, brooches, &c.

Sutsaul—something like rosewood; comes from the Nepaul Terāee.

Tindoa—hard, tough, and very good for turning.

Rouswood (rous)—from the hills; extremely delicate and fine grained; turns beautifully; colour light. I procured rous-wood fit for turning in the jungles near Allahabad.

Neem or neemb (melia azadirachta)—extremely heavy and tough; colour light—almost white; turns well.

Korieah—Benares toys are made of this wood: it is beautifully white, fine grained, and delicate; it turns delightfully, and is very light. The toys are lacquered on the lathe by applying sealing-wax to them; the friction warms the sealing-wax, and it adheres. See Appendix.

Mango-wood, amrā, (spondias mangifera)—fit for common work, out-house doors and beams, kitchen-tables, &c.

Babul—a very heavy and extremely hard wood (acacia Arabica).

Patang—a red wood, used in colouring cloths.

Lall chundun—a cedar.

Chucrassy—also walnut-wood from the hills.

From the Soane and Cane rivers we procured about half a bushel of pebbles, consisting of chalcedony, moss-agate, tree and fortification agate, cornelian, cinnamon-stone, goree (a sort of spar); and from Lucnow and Agra, bloodstone, lapis-lazuli, jet, petrified cocoa-nut bark, plum-pudding-stone, fossil-stone, gold-stone, and amethyst.

The tree-agate, or tree-stone, is so called by the natives from the marks on the surface resembling trees and flowers. In other agates the marks lie deep in the stone, in these they are all on the surface, and in grinding and polishing are easily destroyed, unless care be taken not to go too deep; they reminded me of a stone I saw in England, called Mocha-stone, which was set in small brilliants.

The pebbles from the Soane river are generally esteemed more than those of the Cane.

[. . .]

Raj Ghāt is on the banks of the Ganges, about a mile and a half above the Fort of Allahabad, and the village of Daragunge extends along the side of the Mahratta Bund above for some distance. To the right of the spot where travellers land on coming from Benares is a fine building, called a dhrumsālā, or place to distribute alms; it is dedicated to a form of Māhadēo, which stands in the shiwālā, or little temple, above: the form of this octagonal temple, as well as that of a similar one, which stands at the other side of the building, is very beautiful. On the left are the remains of a very large and curious old well. "Why is a woman like a Hindoo temple?"[1]

After sketching this dhrumsālā, we ascended the bank to Daragunge, to see the inner court, and found it filled with elephants, tattoos, cows, and natives. It is used as a sarāe, or abode for travellers. I saw there a most beautiful and exceedingly small gynee (a dwarf cow), with two bars of silver round each of her little legs; she looked so pretty, and was quite tame. Through the doorways of this court you look into the little octagonal temples, and, through their arches, on a fine expanse of the Ganges which flows below.

You cannot roam in India as in Europe, or go into places crowded with natives, without a gentleman; they think it so incorrect and so marvellous, that they collect in crowds to see a beebee sāhiba who is indecent enough to appear unveiled. A riding-habit and hat, also, creates much surprise in unfrequented bazārs, where such a thing is a novelty.

We proceeded through the bustee (village) on foot, and up a dirty alley, through which I could scarcely pass, to the Temple of Hŭnoomān, the black-faced and deified monkey, and found there an enormous image of the god painted red and white, and made either of mud or stone. A great number of worshippers were present. The bearers hold Hŭnoomān in the greatest reverence.

In another apartment were forty or fifty large and small figures, representing Ram and Seeta his consort, with his brother Lutchman, Hŭnoomān, and all his army of monkeys. Seeta was carried off by the giant Ravuna, Hŭnoomān fought for and restored her to Ram, therefore they are worshipped together.

These figures were decorated with coloured cloth and tinsel, much in the same manner in which the saints are clothed in the churches in France. I had never but once before seen idols, in India, tricked out after this fashion.

[1] See Appendix.

Many lamps were burning before the shrine. We were allowed to behold them from the door, but not to enter the apartment.

The evening was very fine; my companion, as well as myself, enjoyed rambling about and exploring such queer, curious, and out-of-the-way places.

Dec. 5th.—Let me record the death of little Jack Bunce, my pet squirrel. On our arrival at Prāg I went into the stable to see a sick horse, and, hearing a chirping noise, looked up, and saw a young squirrel, which, having escaped from its nest, was in great perplexity on its first expedition from home. I caught it. Its eyes were open; but it could not run very fast. For the first week it lived either in my husband's pocket or on my shoulder; if alarmed, it took refuge with him. It became very tame, and never ran away. A gay house with two rooms was built for it. At first it drank milk and ate sweetmeats (pera); as it grew older it had bread, grain, milk, and whatever it pleased during meals, at which time it would quit my shoulder for the table. We caught several young ones, and put them into Jack's cage; he was pleased, and tended them like a little old nurse; but they grew very wild, and we let them go, with the exception of one little female whom Jack reared as his helpmate, and appeared very fond of her; she was very wild, and would not allow me to touch her. They went with me to Lucnow. One night I heard Jack and his wife quarrelling violently—she bit off his beautiful long tail, and Jack killed her for it: the wretches also ate their young one. Jack returned with me, and, to complete his education, I took him to the holy city of Benares, that he might gain absolution for his little improprieties. Never was there so travelled a squirrel! He lived with us three years, always fat, sleek, and merry; and very fond of us, chirping and running to us when we called him; at last he fell ill, and died quickly. Sometimes he would run off into the garden, but when I called him would return, run up my gown to my shoulder, and give a shrill peculiar whistle; he was the largest of the kind I ever saw, and the three streaks down his back were beautiful. Poor little Jack! you were a nice and sensible little animal! The males are more courageous, and more easily tamed, than the females.

At this time the plain in front of the fort, by the avenue on the side of the Jumna, was exceedingly picturesque. It was covered by an encampment awaiting the arrival of the Governor-general. There were assembled 200 elephants, 1000 camels, horses and hackeries, servants and natives without number. A double set of new tents for the Governor-general were pitched on the plain; the tents which were new the year before, and which cost a lac, having been discarded. These new tents, the elephants, camels, horses, and thousands of servants, will cost the Company more than half-batta saves in the course of a year.

News have just arrived that the Directors have rendered all this encampment useless, by sending orders to Lord William Bentinck not to proceed up the country at *their* expense; in consequence Lord William has discharged the people. I am glad they are going away. Last night a friend of ours, who is in tents in our grounds, had his gun and dressing-case stolen, no doubt by thieves from the encampment.

20*th*.—The ashes of a rajah were brought to Prāg this morning to be thrown into the Ganges at the holy junction; they were accompanied by the servants of the rajah, bearing presents to be given, as is the custom, to the Brahmans, amongst which were two remarkably fine Persian horses. One of these horses, a flea-bitten grey from Bokhara, was bought by us from the Brahman to whom it had been presented. On Christmas-day my husband gave me this horse, making my own particular riding-stud amount to a fair number—Mootee, Black Poney, Trelawney, Bokhara. Are ladies in England as fond of their horses as I am? They cannot make pets of them in that country as we can in India.

25*th*.—How many presents I received this day—and such odd ones— the Bokhara grey, a sketch of Lord William Bentinck, Martin's Deluge, a proof-print, a bag of walnuts, a diamond ring, a hill-shawl, two jars of jam, and two bottles of hill-honey! All farewell-gifts from friends bound to England. We spent the evening around the horseshoe-table, the coal fire blazing brightly as we cracked the hill-walnuts and enjoyed the society of our friends. Of all the offerings of that day, the most welcome was a packet of letters from the beloved and absent ones in England. "A letter is half an interview."[1]

[1] Oriental Proverbs.

Chapter 11

Removal to Cawnpore— Confessions of a Thug

"WHAT VARIETY OF HERBS SOEVER ARE SHUFFLED TOGETHER IN THE DISH,
YET THE WHOLE MASS IS SWALLOWED UP IN ONE NAME OF *SALLET*.
IN LIKE MANNER I WILL MAKE A HODGE-PODGE OF DIFFERING ARTICLES."

Jan. 1830.—The failure of Messrs. Palmer and Co., early in this month, caused the greatest consternation in India, and fell most severely on the widows and orphans of military men, who, having left their little portions in Palmer's house, had returned to England.

9th.—My husband gave over charge of his office to Mr. N——, who had returned from the Cape, and we began to speculate as to our destiny.

March 1st.—My husband, having applied to remain up the country, was informed he might proceed to Cawnpore as acting-collector for eight months, on condition that he consented to give up the deputation-allowance, to which he was entitled by the rules of the Civil Service. The conditions were hard, although offered as a personal favour, and were accepted in preference to returning to Calcutta.

Cawnpore, 150 miles from Allahabad, and 50 from Lucnow, a large station, is on a bleak, dreary, sandy, dusty, treeless plain, cut into ravines by torrents of rain; if possible, the place is considered hotter than Prāg.

Like the patriarchs of old we travelled with our flocks and herds, or, rather, we sent them on in advance, and followed dāk.

March 27th.—We quitted Allahabad, and drove the first stage to Allumchund, where we were kindly received by friends. At this place I first remarked the mowa-tree (bassia longifolia). The fruit was falling, and the natives were collecting it to make bazār srāb (ardent spirits). The fruit, which is white, only falls during the day-time; when dried, it is given to cows as cheap food—from it the butter takes a fine yellow colour.

In the evening we proceeded dāk, and arrived the next morning at the house of the judge of Futtehpore. Just before entering his compound, (grounds around a house,) I stopped my palanquin, and desired a bearer to draw me a lota full of water from a well at the road side. The man took the brass vessel, which was fastened to a very long string, and threw it into the well; then drawing it up, he poured the contents on the ground, saying, "A thuggee has been committed, you cannot drink that water. Did you not hear the lota—bump—bump upon a dead body in the well?"[1] I reported the circumstance on my arrival, and not having before heard of the Thugs, was very much interested in the following account of "The Confessions of a Thug."

Copy of "The Confessions of a Thug," from a circular dated August, 1829, sent by the Governor-general to the judges of the different stations on this subject. The reason for the Governor-general sending this circular to all the judges and magistrates, was to induce them to be on the alert after Thugs, in consequence of a party of them having been seized up the country by Captain Borthwick, four of whom turned evidence against the others. They were examined separately, and their confessions compared.

The following is the confession and statement of the principal witness:—

"My father was a cultivator of land in Buraicha and other neighbouring villages, and I followed the same occupation until I entered my thirtieth year, when I joined the Thugs, with whom I have been more or less connected ever since, a period of upwards of thirty years.

"During this time, however, I have not accompanied them on every excursion; but, on the contrary, for intervals of two, three, and even six years, have remained at home and earned a subsistence by cultivating land, so that I have been engaged in only six predatory excursions: four under a leader, since dead, called Oo-dey Singh, and two under my present chief and fellow-prisoner, Mokhun Jemadar.

"Whilst residing at home during the last interval alluded to, I was apprehended on suspicion of being a Thug, but the proofs I adduced of having been for so many years employed in husbandry were the means which restored me to liberty.

"By this event, however, my circumstances became so greatly embarrassed, that I was forced to go to Salany to borrow money from Mokhun Jemadar, who I knew had generally some at command; but he would not agree to relieve my wants except on condition of my engaging to bring my family to Salany and becoming one of his gang. These conditions I was forced by my destitute state to comply with, and I accordingly accompanied him in his last two excursions.

"Oo-dey Singh my former leader was, at the period of my joining his

---

[1] Thuggee has a long history, but it was only in the time of Bentinck that the Thuggee and Dacoity Department was set up under Colonel Sleeman to suppress it.

gang, beyond the prime of life, although, at the same time, active and enter-
prising; but gradually becoming unfit for the exertion required of him by
his situation, and his son Roman being seized, with other Thugs, and cast
into prison at Jubbalpore, he abandoned his former course of life, and
shortly after died.

"At the time I was serving under Oo-dey Singh, tranquillity had not been
established throughout the country, and our excursions were neither carried
to so great a distance, nor were they so lucrative or certain as they have
since been; for in those days travellers, particularly those possessed of much
property, seldom ventured from one place to another unless in large parties,
or under a strong escort; and we ourselves held the Pindaries and other
armed plunderers in as much dread as other travellers.

"About three months after I had joined Mokhun's gang, which consisted
of forty men, we set out from Bundelkund for the Dekkun, this was in the
month of Phagoon Summet, 1883 (about March, 1826). We proceeded by
regular stages, and crossed the Nerbudda at the Chepanair Ghāt, where we
fell in with Chotee Jamadar (a Brahman), who joined us with his gang, the
strength of which was about the same as our own.

"We then continued our course towards Mallygaow, and at Thokur, near
that cantoonment, celebrated the Hooly; after which we resumed our route
and reached Mallygaow, where we struck off by the Nassuk road, intending to turn from Nassuk to Poona and Aurungabad.

"After proceeding a coss or two on this road we met a relation of
Mokhun's, belonging to Oomrao and Ruttyram's gangs, who informed us
that these two leaders with their gangs were near at hand on the Poona
road, engaged in the pursuit of some angriahs with treasure. It was proposed that Mokhun should join them with some of his men, in order to
be entitled to a share of the spoil. Mokhun at first thought of going himself,
but recollecting that Oomrao and himself were not on good terms, he sent
twenty-five men with Chotee Jamadar. On the day following we heard the
business was effected, and that they intended to proceed with Oomrao and
Ruttyram to Bhoorampore, at which place they requested us to meet them.
We accordingly proceeded to that quarter, and found Chotee Jemadar and
his party at Bhoorampore, Oomrao and Ruttyram having returned to their
homes.

"Here we learnt that the angriahs had been attacked and murdered near
Koker (the place where we had celebrated the Hooly), and that no less a
sum than 22,000 rupees was found on their persons in gold, bullion,
mohurs, and pootlies. Of this 6000 rupees had been received as the share
of our two gangs, and was disposed of in the following manner.

"Mokhun received one-third for himself and gang, a third was given to Chotee Jamadar for himself and his gang, and the remainder was reserved for the mutual expenses of the two gangs. Mokhun and Chotee despatched the two-thirds above mentioned to their homes: that sent by the latter reached its destination safely; but one of Mokhun's men in charge of our share having got drunk at Jansy, blabbed that he was a Thug, and returning with others with a large amount of treasure; he was consequently seized by the sirdar of the place, and the money taken from him. We now quitted Bhoorampore, and proceeded to Aurungabad, but, meeting with little or no success, we returned by Dhoolia and Bhopaul to Bundelcund, and reached our several homes before the rains set in. Our next excursion was towards Guzerat, but in this nothing occurred worthy of note.

"I have never, during my connexion with the Thugs, known a single instance of their committing a robbery without the previous destruction of life, which is almost invariably accomplished by strangulation. This is effected either by means of a roomal (handkerchief) or shred of cloth well twisted and wetted, or merely by the hands, though the latter is rarely practised, and only had recourse to from accidental failure in the former and usual mode.

"A preconcerted signal being given, the victim or victims are instantly overpowered, and death, either by the roomal or hands, is the act of a moment. In perpetrating murder it is an invariable rule with the Thugs never, if possible, to spill the blood of their victims, in order that no traces of murder may appear, to awaken suspicion of the deed in the minds of those who may happen to pass the spot, and detection be the consequence. In the hurry in which it is sometimes necessary to dispose of the bodies, holes cannot be dug sufficiently large to contain them in an entire state, particularly when the number of them is great; the bodies are then cut in pieces and packed therein.

"When these holes are near the road side, and especially in an exposed spot, it is usual, after covering them with earth, to burn fires over them, to do away with the appearance of the earth having been newly turned. Murders, in the manner just described, are perpetrated as frequently, and with equal facility and certainty, whilst the victims are walking along the road, as when they have been enticed to our places of encampment, and, unconscious of what is to befal them, are sitting amongst us with every thing carefully and leisurely arranged for their destruction.

"These murders frequently take place near villages where we encamp, and usually during twilight; and always, whilst the business is going on, the hand-drum is beaten and singing commenced, to drown any noise that might be made by the victims.

"The several persons actually engaged commence their operations simultaneously at a preconcerted signal given.

"The signal is an arbitrary one; generally a common, coarse expression is used, not likely to strike the attention of the victims, such as, 'Tumbākoo lao,' (bring tobacco).

"I have never seen the phansy (or noose) made of cord employed for strangling, though I am fully aware of the general supposition, that it is with it that we strangle people; but if such has ever been employed, which I greatly doubt, it has long since been laid aside, for the obvious reason, that if a Thug were seized having it about his person, it would inevitably lead to his detection.

"A direct understanding with the local authorities in Bundelcund is constantly kept up by Oomrao, Mokhun, and all the other leaders and jāmadārs, who on their return from their excursions reside in that part of the country, and these authorities are conciliated and their favour gained by suitable presents.

"Assistance and support from the English authorities, being likewise indispensable, are obtained through artifice. This is effected by means of their emissaries, who by misrepresentation and falsehood, frequently contrive to extricate them from the difficulties in which persons of our habits are constantly involved. A relation of Oomrao's, Motee by name, and Lala Hajain, an inhabitant of Secundra, render important services in this way. Motee, who was himself a Thug formerly, has for some years past discontinued going on predatory excursions. He first brought himself into notice with European gentlemen by informing against a gang, which was seized in consequence, and confined at Jubbulpore, where the greater part still remain.

"Since then Motee has advanced in favour with these gentlemen, who are led to suppose he acts as a check upon the Thugs and other plunderers; at least, he persuades us that such is the case, the consequence of which is, that he exercises great influence over us; making us pay well for his connivance, and the good offices he no doubt frequently performs in our behalf.

"He principally exerts himself in protecting and assisting Oomrao, Ruttyram, Hera Mandeen, and their gangs.

"Lala Hajain, by means of representations to different persons of his acquaintance in the adālut at Cawnpore, renders great assistance to Mokhun in getting him through matters of difficulty. The latter, after his return to Bundelcund from his last excursion but one, when he heard the mishap which had befallen the share of the plunder sent by him to Boorampore, had recourse, as was usual with him, to his patron Lala Hajain. Lala lost no time in waiting on his friend Madee Moonshee, at Cawnpore, to whom he represented matters in such a light, that the moonshee wrote himself, or had instructions sent by his superiors to the Tausy Rajah, intimating that, it having been made known that he, the Rajah, had seized four travellers of respectable and inoffensive character passing through his territories, and plundered them of their property—he was directed to restore them to liberty, with whatever property he had taken from them.

"A day or two before the receipt of the letter containing this order, the Rajah had released Mokhun's men, having first obtained from them an acquittance of the money he had taken; but now, thinking that unless he could prove the men to be Thugs, and that their true characters had been misrepresented, he should get a bad name with Europeans, he immediately sent after them, and had them again apprehended. What became of these men afterwards I have never been able to learn.

"Besides Lala Hajain, who manages matters favourably for him through his acquaintance at the courts and kutcherries at Cawnpore, Etaweh, Humeerpore, Auria, and Mynpoor, Mokhun has a great friend and supporter in the Tauzie Vakeel, Gunesh Lall, who resides at Humeerporah.

"Oomrao may have other patrons besides his relation Motee, who watches over his interests principally at Jubbulpore. Makay Sahib, at Kytah, is a great friend of Motee's, and it was from him that the English pass, which Oomrao showed the horsemen when we were apprehended at Dekhola, was obtained.

"Passing through a country in so numerous a body as our gangs sometimes form, is certainly calculated to awaken suspicion, but when this happens, it is always lulled to rest by our being all prepared with the same story or explanation.

"Few of us carry arms, indeed, amongst fifteen or twenty persons not more than two or three swords may be found.

"When Thugs, though strangers to each other, meet, there is something in their manner which discovers itself; and, to make 'assurance doubly sure,' one exclaims 'Alee khan!' which being repeated by the other party, recognition takes place, but is never followed by a disclosure of past acts.

"In the division of plunder the jāmadārs receive seven and a half per cent., besides sharing equally with the rest of the gang; but, before any division is made, a certain portion is devoted to Bhawānī, our tutelar deity. This applies only to money in gold or silver; for when the plunder consists of diamonds and pearls, the leader draws blood from his hand, and having sprinkled a little over them, the sanction of the goddess to a division is thereby obtained without any other alienation. But the omission of this ceremony, or neglecting, when success attends us, to propitiate a continuance of Bhawānī's favour by laying aside a part of our acquisitions for her service, would, we firmly believe, bring heavy misfortune upon us.

"The office of strangler is never allowed to be self-assumed, but is conferred with due ceremony, after the fitness of the candidate in point of firmness, activity, and bodily strength, has been ascertained, and a sufficient degree of expertness in the use of the roomal has been acquired by long sham practice amongst ourselves.

"When thus qualified, the person on whom the office is to be conferred proceeds to the fields, conducted by his gooroo (spiritual guide), previously selected, who carries with him the roomal (or handkerchief), and anxiously looking out for some favourable omen, such as the chirping of certain birds, or their flight past the right hand, knots the roomal at each end the moment that either occurs, and delivers it to the candidate, imploring success upon him.

"After this they return, when the ceremony is closed by a feast, or distribution of sweetmeats. The seniors only confer this office, generally old Thugs held in some estimation, but who from infirmity or age have ceased to accompany the gangs in their expeditions, and whose chief support is received from the voluntary contributions of those on whom they have conferred the privilege of using the roomal.

"Certain terms, known to ourselves alone, are made use of to distinguish certain circumstances, events, &c., connected with our proceedings: viz.

The persons whose office it is to strangle the victims are called *Luddya*, also *Bullod*.

Those who dig the graves or holes, *Lucka*.

Those who carry away the bodies, *Gutnee Walow*.

A scout or spy, *Tulha*.

A traveller on whom designs are formed, *Betoo*.

If a Musulmān, *Sultan Betoo*.

If a Hindoo, *Bundoo Betoo*.

A murder committed at the halting-place or encampment-ground, *Topa*.

A murder committed whilst the victims are walking along the road—if during the day, *Phoolkee*; if during the night, *Kootul*.

The spot where the bodies are buried, *Kurwa*.

The spot where the murder is committed, *Balee*.

A female victim, *Ecmud*.

A child victim, *Chumota*.

Horse, *Poornkna* or *Pootra*.

Bullock, *Subba*.

Gold, *Sirya*.

Sword, *Lumberee.*
Silver or rupee, *Peeky.*
Matchlock, *Puttakee.*
Gold mohurs, *Tandya.*
Turban, *Kassee.*
A ring, *Pulbya.*
Dhotee, *Kurdhunny.*
Pearls, *Punnyara.*
Diamonds, *Kukreya.*
A knife, *Booky.*
The roomal with which people are strangled, *Phyloo* and *roomal.*
If one person is strangled, it is called *Eloo.*
If two persons are strangled, it is called *Beetsee.*
If three . . . . . . *Singod.*
If four . . . . . . *Bhurra.*
If five . . . . . . *Puckrao.*
If six . . . . . . *Chutroo, &c.*

"These terms are used by the Thugs in all parts of the country. The numerals exclusively apply to travellers, and are used to denote the number that fall into the hands of detached parties."

This is the end of the "Thug's Confession."

The other men, on their examination, acknowledged having murdered a bearer, on whom they found four rupees. They also met with twelve seapoys; eight of the soldiers took one road, and the other four another. The Thugs, therefore, divided into two parties, overtook the seapoys, and killed them all.

One Thug said, that on a certain day eleven men were killed and buried. The other Thug said, that on the same day only seven were strangled: on re-examination he replied, "Yes, it is true I only mentioned seven—there might have been eleven, or more, I cannot remember; we strangled people so constantly, that I took little account of the numbers buried, I only know on that day about seven or eleven were buried."

The Thugs never attack Europeans.

Chapter 12

Arrival at Cawnpore

March 29*th*.—My husband proceeded dāk to Cawnpore, to take charge of his appointment and to engage a house, leaving me with my friends. On one stage of the road he had such a set of coolies, instead of bearers, to his pālkee, that they could not continue to carry it—at last, setting it down, they all ran away, and he had to wait six hours on the road until other bearers came: as this happened during the night, it was of no further consequence than making the latter part of his dāk very hot, as he did not reach his destination until 11 A.M. The bearers on this road are proverbially bad.

Here I saw the first thermantidote, and took a sketch of it, in order to make one for myself. Here, also, I saw the first alligator, a snub-nosed fellow, which was caught in the Jumna, and sent up on a chārpāī. Mr. W——had the kindness to give me skulls of alligators, crocodiles, hyenas, and tigers beautifully prepared, to add to my cabinet of curiosities.

Collecting Persian and Hindostānī proverbs and sayings, and having them cut on seals, was another of my amusements.

April 19*th*.—This day brought a letter, saying a good bungalow had at length been procured, and I started dāk the next day. The judge, that I might meet with no adventures on the road, gave me a guard, which was relieved at the different chaukees, police stations.

A barkandāz, or policeman, and two chaukidārs (watchmen) ran by the side of my palanquin all the way; in consequence I was not detained one moment more than necessary on the road. One of the barkandāz was armed with *two* swords and a great bamboo!

[. . .]

I arrived at Cawnpore at 7 A.M., and was glad to take shelter in my new house, which I found very cool and pleasant, after a hot drive during the last stage in a buggy.

The house, or rather bungalow,[1] for it is tiled over a thatch, is situated in the centre of the station, near the theatre; it stands on a platform of stone

---

[1] Properly Banglā.

rising out of the Ganges, which flows below and washes the walls. The station is a very large one: besides the gentlemen of the Civil Service, there are the artillery, the eleventh dragoons, the fourth cavalry, and three or four regiments of infantry.

The work of this day began by what is really an operation in India, and constantly repeated, that is, washing the hair. My ayha understood it remarkably well; for the benefit of those ladies having beautiful tresses in the East, I give the receipt.[1]

June 9th.—The deaths are numerous in our farm-yard; in such weather it is a matter of surprise that any thing can exist. At 4 P.M. the thermometer outside the verandah, in the sun, stood at 130°; in the shade, at 110°! From this time to the end of August we lost 280 Guinea fowls from vertigo, and three calves also died.

A storm is raging: it arose in clouds of dust, which, sweeping over the river from the Lucnow side, blow directly on the windows of the drawing-room; they are all fastened, and a man at every one of them, or the violence of the wind would burst them open; my mouth and eyes are full of fine sand; I can scarcely write;—not a drop of rain, only the high wind, and the clouds of dust so thick we cannot see across the verandah. I feel rather afraid lest some part of the house, which is not in good repair, should give way if it continue to blow in such gusts. This bay-windowed room feels the whole force of the *tufān*, which is the heaviest I have seen. In Calcutta we had severe storms, with thunder and lightning; here, nothing but clouds of sand—reaching from earth to heaven—with a hot yellow tinge, shutting out the view entirely. The storm has blown for an hour, and is beginning to clear off; I can just see the little white-crested waves on the river beneath the verandah.

In the open air the thermometer stands at 130°; in the drawing-room, with three tattīs up, at 88°. The heat is too oppressive to admit of an evening drive.

A high caste and religious native gentleman, Shah Kubbecroo-deen Ahmud, requested to be allowed to play at chess with me; the natives are passionately fond of the game, which is remarkable, as chess was one of the games forbidden by the prophet. On the arrival of my opponent, I recognized the native gentleman who had entertained me with fire-works at Sahseram. I have spoken of him as of *high caste*—that term is only correct when applied to an Hindoo, Musulmāns have no distinction of caste.

14th.—A tufān, a sand storm, or rather a storm of sand and dust, is now blowing; indeed, a little while ago the darkness was so great from that

[1] See Appendix.

cause, I was obliged to leave off writing, being unable to distinguish the letters.

. [. . .]

If a house has a flat roof covered with flag-stones and mortar, it is called a pukka house; if the roof be raised and it be thatched, it is called a bungalow; the latter are generally supposed to be cooler than the pukka houses. The rooms of our house are lofty and good; the dining-room forty feet by twenty-eight, the swimming-bath thirty feet by twenty-one, and all the other rooms on a suitable scale. There is a fine garden belonging to and surrounding the house, having two good wells, coach-house, stables, cow-house, &c. In India the kitchen and all the servants' offices are detached from the dwelling on account of the heat. We pay 150 rupees a month, about 150 guineas per annum, a heavy rent for an up-country house: the houses are always let unfurnished.

Very fine white grapes are now selling at fourpence-halfpenny per pound. Cawnpore is famous for its fruit-gardens.

The natives are curious people! My ayha, a Musulmāne, asked me to allow her to go to a dinner-party given by some khidmatgārs, friends of hers; and on her return, she said to me, "Mem sāhiba, we have had a very fine khānā (dinner), and plenty to eat—I am quite full;" patting her body with great glee, "but we have had a great quarrel." She then explained that at a native feast every guest sits down in a circle, or in a line, and before each person a freshly gathered leaf is placed as a plate; then the giver of the feast comes round, and puts an equal portion of curry and rice before each guest. When all have been helped, they start fair—and, in general, the host refills all the plates. It sometimes happens that some of the guests eat so fast they get a greater share than the others, this puts the rest into a rage, and they quietly vent their spite by slyly cutting holes in the clothes worn by the great eaters. It happened at this feast that my ayha sat next a man who was helped three times, and I suspect she cut holes in his attire, which caused the disturbance.

During this month of June we have lost two very fine grey carriage-horses, the first we have lost during a residence of nearly eight years in India; they have been poisoned by the grass-cutters for the sake of their skins, each skin being worth about six rupees. The first stage out of Cawnpore is famous as a place where horses die on their march, and hides are there procurable for tanning. The poison is made into small balls, scarcely larger than pills, which are thrown into the manger, or into the grass. In the evening I observed about twenty natives surrounding the entrance-gates, who had come in the hope of carrying the carcase away, to sell the hide, and to feast themselves upon the flesh, for the people of the Jullah or Doom caste eat carrion. They were disappointed in their hope of a repast; we had the horse put into a boat, and sunk in the Ganges.

Women have more influence over men in India than in any other country. All out-door amusements are nearly denied to the latter by the climate, unless before sun-rise or after sun-set; therefore the whole time of military men, generally speaking, is spent in the house, devoted either to music or drawing, which of course they prefer in the society of ladies, or in the study of the languages, or in gaming. The young officers at this station play exceedingly high, ruinously so—two guinea points at short whist, and 100 guineas on the rubber, is not unusual amongst the young men.

Happily the gentlemen in the Civil Service have too much employment to admit of their devoting their time to gambling.

If you ask a native—"Where is your master gone?" if the gentleman be from home, you are sure to receive the answer—"Howā khānā-ke-waste" (to eat the air); this chamelion-like propensity of eating the air is always the object during the early morning ride and the evening drive.

Our servants at present only amount to fifty-four, and I find it quite difficult enough to keep them in order; they quarrel amongst themselves, and when they become quite outrageous, they demand their discharge.

My ayha and the ābdār had a laughable quarrel. She was making herself a pair of Europe chintz pajamas (trousers) such as they usually wear, made very full round the body, and quite tight from the knee to the ancle.

Musulmāne women never wear a petticoat when amongst themselves; it is the badge of servitude, and put on to please European ladies; the moment an ayha gets into her own house, she takes off her full petticoat and the large white mantle (chādar) that covers her head and the upper part of her body, and walks about in the curiously shaped trousers I have described, with a sort of loose jacket of muslin over the upper part, beneath which is the angiya.

The ayha was sitting on her chārpāi (native bed) working away with great eagerness, when her friend the ābdār advised her to make the trousers full to the ankle; and she came to me to give warning to quit my service, vowing revenge upon the ābdār, because nāch women wear trousers of that description. The old ābdār, Sheik-jee, was sitting down very quietly making chapāties (flour-cakes), and smoking his narjil (cocoa-nut shell hooqŭ) at intervals, enjoying the ayha's anger, until she stood up, and, screaming with passion, gave him gālee (abuse); he then flew into a rage, and I had some trouble to restore peace and quietness. Natives seldom, indeed hardly ever, come to blows, but they will go on for hours abusing each other in the grossest language, screaming out their words from passion.

Bishop Heber, who did not understand native character, and possessed much simplicity, was surprised when the up-country natives thus addressed him: "Defender of the poor, peace be unto you! Refuge of the distressed, salāmut"[1] and imagined it was from respect to his holy office. I was playing with the son of the judge, a little fellow of two years old; the child offered to shake hands, and presented his left hand—his native attendant, shocked at what he considered an insult, desired him to give the right hand; the child did so, when the chaprāsī cried out with great pleasure, "Well done! well done! Refuge of the distressed! defender of the poor!"

Ram Din was a Rājput sipahī in the Company's service, from which, after twelve years' service, he obtained his discharge; he was in many engagements. In Calcutta the man came to us, and, making salām, presented his chitthīs (written vouchers of conduct), saying; "Refuge of the distressed, having heard of your great name, I am present to offer my services; I have served the Company faithfully twelve years, I will serve you faithfully." He was a fine native, about six feet high or upwards; he lived with us many years, and had always charge of the boats or the tents when we moved about the country.

A native is very fond of wearing a plain silver ring on the little finger, with a stone on the top, on which is engraved his own name, and sometimes that of the god he particularly worships, if the man be an Hindoo. They usually stamp any petition they may have to send to any gentleman with it, by putting Hindostanī ink on the seal, wetting the paper, and pressing the seal down upon it.[2]

On the signet-ring of the Rājput above mentioned was "Ram Din Mahādeo." The engraver invariably puts the date of the year on the corner of the stone, unless it be expressly forbidden. Engraved on the ruby of a signet-ring, brought to me from Persia, was "Allah, Muhammad, Ali, Fatima, Hussen, Hossein."[3]

The Durwān

What happy wretches the natives are! A man who gets two annas a day (fourpence), can find himself in food, clothing, house, silver finery for his person, and support his wife and children also. My ayha in Calcutta, who received eleven rupees a month, refused any longer to dine with her dear friend the durwān, because, as she expressed it, he was so extravagant and

[1] Oriental Proverbs and Sayings.   [2] See Appendix.
[3] Oriental Proverbs and Sayings.

112

such a glutton he would eat as much as one rupee and a half or two rupees a month; and, as she herself never ate more than one rupee per month, she would no longer go shares in his expenses. The durwān lives at the entrance-gates of his master's house, and is always in attendance to open them; his wages are usually five rupees a month; and he is always on the watch that nothing may be carried away clandestinely.

[. . .]

The durwāns are very fond of brilliant colours, and are generally well dressed; their food consists principally of curry made of kid, fish, chicken, prawns, or vegetables, with a great quantity of Patna rice boiled to perfection, every grain separate, and beautifully white. My ayha brought me one day a vegetable curry of her own making, to show me the food on which she lived with her friend the durwān; it would have been excellent, had it not been made with moota tel, *i.e.* mustard oil.

16*th.*—The native boys whom I see swimming and sporting in the river of an evening, are much better off than the poor people in England. I wish we had some of them here, on whom to bestow a fine cold saddle of mutton. A round of beef would be of importance to them. You may imagine how much must be thrown away, when you cannot with the greatest care, at this season, keep meat good for more than twenty-four hours; and roasted meat will only keep until the next day.

In Calcutta, the tank water being unwholesome to drink, it is necessary to catch rain water, and preserve it in great jars; sixty jars full will last a year in our family. It is purified with alum, and a heated iron is put into it. Here we drink the Ganges water, reckoned the most wholesome in India; it is purified in jars in the same manner. The water of the Jumna is considered unwholesome, and in some parts, my old ābdār declares, it is absolutely poisonous.

We were glad to quit Allahabad, the small-pox having commenced its ravages at that station. On our arrival at Cawnpore, we found it raging still worse; the magistrate took it, and died in three days. Hundreds of children are ill of this disease in the bazār; and the government, in their humanity, have done away with the vaccine department here. Surely it is a cruel act, where there are so many regiments and so many European children, who cannot now be vaccinated. It is very severe, and numbers of adults have been attacked.

In India wax candles are always burned. A bearer will not touch a mould because they say it is made of pig's fat. We burn spermaceti generally. The first time the bearers saw them, they would not touch the spermaceti, and I had great difficulty in persuading them the candles were made from the fat of a great fish. Some bearers in Calcutta will not snuff a candle if it be on the dinner-table, but a khidmatgār having put it on the ground, the bearer will snuff it, when the other man replaces it. In the upper provinces they are not so particular.

One of the grass-cutters has been sent to the hospital, dying, I fear, or fever. Every horse has a sā'īs (groom) and a grass-cutter allowed him: the latter goes out every morning, perhaps some four or five miles, cuts a bundle of grass, and brings it home on his head. The men are exposed to the sun so much, and live so badly, it is no wonder they fall ill of fever; besides which, they are extremely fond of arrak (bazar spirits). Wine they delight in: when the empty bottles are carried from the house to the godown, the grass-cutters often petition to have the dregs of the wine. They pour off into their lotas (brass drinking cups) the remains of all the bottles, mixing beer, sherry, claret, vinegar, hock, champagne, in fact, any thing of which they can find a drop; and then, sitting down, each man drinks a portion and passes the cup to his neighbour, often saying "Bahut achchhā, bahut achchhā," very good, very good, and eagerly looking out for his turn again, and fair play.

I have several times made them put this vile mixture away for another day, or they would have drunk it until the whole was finished.
[. . .]

August 4th.—It is said, the Earl of C———lost 65,000 rupees a short time ago, by forgeries committed in Calcutta: the person at the head of the forgeries was Rajah Buddinath Roy, a native prince in high favour with Lord Amherst; and I rather imagine his lordship has suffered also by the Rajah's forged bills. *On dit,* he used to talk about Christianity as if *in time* he might be converted; he subscribed to schools and missionary societies, and dis-tributed Bibles—the bait took—in return he was allowed such and such honorary attendance, as by the Company's regulations a native may not have without permission. This flattered his pride, and his seemingly reli-gious disposition secured him from suspicion falling upon him as a forger, especially of passing forged bills on the Governor-general. The case is now being tried in Court.

People think of nothing but converting the Hindoos; and religion is often used as a cloak by the greatest schemers after good appointments. Religious meetings are held continually in Calcutta, frequented by people to pray themselves into high salaries, who never thought of praying before.

In India we use no bells to call servants; but as the chaprāsīs are always in attendance just without the door, if you want one, you say "Qui hy?" *i.e.* "is there any one?"—or "Kon hy?"—"who is there?" when a servant appears. For this reason old Indians are called Qui hys.

7th.—The plagues of Egypt were not worse than the plagues of India. Last night the dinner-table was covered with white ants, having wings: these ants, at a certain period after a shower, rise from the earth with four large wings. They fly to the lights, and your lamps are put out in a few minutes by swarms of them: they fall into your plate at dinner, and over your book when reading, being most troublesome. Last night heavy rain fell, and the rooms were swarming with winged-ants, which flew in; their wings fell off almost immediately, verifying the proverb: When ants get wings they die."[1]

To-night we are suffering under a more disagreeable infliction; a quantity of winged-bugs flew in just as dinner was put on the table, the bamboo screens having been let down rather too late. They are odious; they fly upon your face and arms, and into your plate; if you brush them away, they emit such terrible effluvia it is sickening, and yet one cannot bear them to crawl over one's body, as one is at this minute doing on my ear, without pushing them off.

21st.—There has been a great fire in the Fort of Allahabad, and the magazine of gunpowder was with difficulty saved. What an explosion it would have caused had it taken fire!

Oh! how I long for the liberty and freshness of a country life in England—what would I not give for a fine *bracing* air, and a walk by the sea-side, to enable me to shake off this Indian languor, and be myself again! The moon is so hot to-night, I cannot sit on the Terrace; she makes my head ache. A chatr (umbrella) is as necessary a defence against the rays of the moon at the full, as against the sun.

These natives are curious people. Two of our khidmatgārs were looking at the weather; the one said, "It is a good thing that from the pleasure of Allah the rain has been stopped; otherwise, so many houses would have fallen in." The ābdār answered, "Those are the words of an unbeliever." Kaffir ke bat. "You are a Kaffir," exclaimed the first man, in a great rage. It being high abuse to use the term, the ābdār took off his shoe and flung it at the other, on which the first man struck him a good blow with his fist, which cut his cheek open. Here ended the fight—they were both frightened at the sight of blood—it is the only instance we have met with of a native using his fists like an Englishman.

The other affair was this: my sā'īs (groom) had bought some ganja, an intoxicating herb, which he put into his hooqŭ to smoke, and offered it to the other sā'īses. To refuse to smoke from an offered hooqŭ, is a high

[1] Oriental Proverbs.

offence. The sā'īses would not smoke the ganja, abused the man for buying it, and getting intoxicated daily from its effect. He said, "I will not stay in service, if you will not smoke with me." "Well, go and give warning," said the head groom. My sā'īs gave him gālee (abuse); at which the head groom took a stick and beat him. The sā'īs immediately said, "My life be on your head," and running to the well, he let himself drop down into the water; but when at the bottom, he began to halloo for assistance, the well being very deep, and the water also. He was drawn up by ropes. I do not think he meant to kill himself; and yet dropping down such a distance was a great risk. He said, if he had died of the fall, the head groom would have been hung, and he should thus have had his revenge. The next time he plays such a prank, he is to remain at the bottom of the well.

22nd.—They tell me the people in Calcutta are dying fast from a fever resembling the yellow fever. The soldiers, European, here are also going to their graves very quickly; three days ago, six men died; two days ago, six more expired; and one hundred and sixty are in the hospital. The fever, which rages, tinges the skin and eyes yellow; perhaps only the severe bilious fever of India brought on by drinking brandy and arrak, a bazār spirit extremely injurious, to say nothing of exposure to the sun. Almost every evening we meet the two elephants belonging to the hospital carrying each about ten sick men, who are sufficiently recovered to be able to go out "to eat the air," and for exercise; the poor fellows look so wan and ghastly. The sā'īs before-mentioned added the leaves of hemp (cannabis sativa) to his tobacco, and smoked it to increase its intoxicating power. Bhang, an intoxicating liquor, is prepared from the same leaves. Pariah arrak, an inferior sort of spirituous liquor, is sold extremely cheap, from one to four ānās a quart: it is most unwholesome, and mixed with most injurious articles to increase its intoxicating power, such as the juice of the thorn-apple and ganja. There are many kinds of arrak; that distilled from cocoa-nut toddy is, they say, the least injurious. Who can be surprised at the number of deaths that occur amongst men in the habit of drinking this heating and narcotic spirit, called rack by the soldiers? Flax is grown in great quantities in India, but is little used for cloth. Taat, which is made from sunn (hemp), is manufactured into paper. Linseed oil is extracted from the seed, and the remainder, the cake, is given to cows. The waste land in our compound (grounds around the house) was covered with thorn-apple plants. I had them rooted out, leaving only two or three of different kinds in the garden. Abdārs have been known to administer this plant (datura) to their masters in the hooqŭ: an over-dose produces delirium.

There are several species of this beautiful plant:

Common datura	(Datura stramonium), thorn-apple.
Kala datura	(Datura fastuosa), a triple flower of a most beautiful dark purple.
Suffeid datura	(Datura metel), flowers white, hairy thorn-apple.
Another	(Datura ferox), flowers yellow.
Ditto	(Datura canescens), a variety, flowers always single, and of a yellowish white colour.

Qualities, intoxicating and narcotic.—The Mahomedans give kala datura in those violent headaches that precede epilepsy and mania. It produces vertigo when taken in large doses, and has the effect of dilating in a singular manner the pupil of the eye. Some writers call it "*Trompette du jugement*," and "*Herbe aux sorciers.*" The leaves of the datura ferox are sometimes used to make arrak more intoxicating: its seeds produce delirium. Stramonium is an abbreviation of the Greek "Mad apple," on account of the dangerous effects of the fruit of that species. Metel is an Arabic name, and expresses the narcotic effect of the plant.

What can be more wretched than the life of a private soldier in the East? his profession employs but little of his time. During the heat of the day, he is forced to remain within the intensely hot barrack-rooms; heat produces thirst, and idleness discontent. He drinks arrak like a fish, and soon finds life a burden, almost insupportable. To the man weary of the burden of existence, to escape from it, transportation appears a blessing. The great source of all this misery is the cheapness of arrak mixed with datura, and the restlessness arising from the want of occupation; although a library is generally provided for the privates by the regiment.

You at home, who sleep in gay beds of carved mahogany, with handsome curtains, would be surprised at sight of the beds used by us during the hot winds. Four small posts, and a frame, on which very broad tape (newār) is plaited and strained very tight, over this a sītal-pātī, a sort of fine cool Manilla mat, then the sheets, and for warmth, either an Indian shawl, or a rezai, which is of silk quilted with cotton, and very light. We use no mosquito curtains, for each chārpāī is placed just before an open window, with the east wind blowing on it, and a pankhā, with a deep double frill, is in full swing over the beds all night, pulled by a string which passes through a hole in the wall—the wind it creates drives off the musquitoes, and the man who pulls the pankhā is relieved every two hours.

[. . .]

The Governor-general left Calcutta on the 11th inst., and proposes to be at Benares on the 10th December. Lady William Bentinck accompanies him in his tour. They say that she is dreadfully nervous about him. His unpopularity is increasing, and some ill-regulated person, in a moment of disappointment and frenzy, might perhaps cause a scene. The events of the last few years, since Mr. Canning's death, have been astounding. I wonder if there is more room for amazement. I hope his Grace the Duke will not take us under his charge. We are satisfied with King Log, provided he stands in the way of King Stork.

Lord William has been doing away with all the good appointments in the Civil Service; and the army have been cruelly treated, with respect to the half-batta. Perhaps, when the renewal of the Charter is concluded, the Directors will again be enabled to treat those living under their command with the generosity which has ever distinguished them, and which has rendered their service one of the finest in the world.

Chapter 13

Residence at Cawnpore— The Dewālī

1830, *Oct.*—Mooatummud-ood-Dowlah, generally known as Āghā Meer, the deposed Prime Minister to the King of Oude, Ghazee-ood-Deen Hyder, is coming over to Cawnpore; his zenāna, treasures, two lacs of shawls, &c. &c., have arrived on the other bank of the Ganges, escorted by the military.[1] The ex-minister has not yet arrived; and a large detachment of the military from this station has been sent to escort him in safety to the Company's territories.

This morning, from the verandah, I was watching what appeared to be

[1] When Ghazi-uddin Hyder came to the throne Agha Meer became his Prime Minister, but when Nasir-uddin-Hyder succeeded him he put Agha Meer under house arrest. In 1830 the Resident intervened and Agha Meer was freed and escorted across the frontier. Bentinck may have intervened because Agha Meer may have managed a loan which the Company needed in connection with the Burma War.

a number of buffaloes floating down the stream, with their drivers; but, as they approached, found them to be sixteen of Aghā Meer's elephants swimming over.

The distance from the Camp on the opposite side the river to our garden, under which they landed, must be four miles, or more. Elephants swim very low, and put down their trunks occasionally to ascertain if they are in deep water. Their heads are almost invisible at times, and the mahāwats strike them with the ānkus (goad) to guide them.

On reaching the bank just below our verandah, they set up a loud *bellowing*, which was answered by those still struggling to get to land, a work rather difficult to accomplish on account of the rapidity of the river.

What would not the people at home give to see sixteen fine elephants swimming four miles over a rapid river, with their mahāwats on their backs, the men hallooing with all their might, and the elephants every now and then roaring in concert! It was an interesting sight, and my first view of their power in the water.

2nd.—A friend, just returned from the hills, brought down with him some forty Cashmere goats; the shawl goats, such as are found in the hills: they die very fast on quitting the cold regions; he has lost all but three females, which he has given to me; they will scarcely live in this burning Cawnpore.

Report says the Governor-general has put off his journey for a month longer; it is supposed he will, if possible, avoid this large military station; the soldiers are in so discontented a state, he may perchance receive a bullet on parade. The privates here have several times attempted the lives of their officers, by shooting and cutting them down, sometimes upon the slightest cause of complaint, and often without having any to provoke such conduct.

7th.—I have just returned from calling on a friend of mine, and overheard the remarks of a gentleman, who was speaking of her to another; they amused me.

"Really that is a noble creature, she has a neck like an Arab, her head is so well set on!"

Buffaloes from Cawnpore swim off in the early morning in herds to the bank in the centre of the river, where they feed; they return in the evening of their own accord. The other evening I thought a shoal of porpoises were beneath the verandah—but they were buffaloes trying to find a landing-place; they swim so deeply, their black heads are only partly visible, and at a little distance they may easily be mistaken for porpoises.

Sometimes I see a native drive his cow into the river; when he wishes to cross it, he takes hold of the animal by the tail, and holding on, easily crosses over with her; sometimes he aids the cow by using one hand in swimming.

"What is that going down the river?" exclaimed a gentleman. On applying a telescope, we found fifty or sixty buffaloes all in a heap were coming down with the stream, whilst ten natives swimming with them kept thrashing them with long bamboos to make them exert themselves, and keep all together: the natives shouting and urging on the animals, and the buffaloes bellowing at every blow they received. At what a rate they come down! The stream flows with such rapidity during the rains! This is the first time I have seen such a large herd driven in this curious fashion.

Methodism is gaining ground very fast in Cawnpore; young ladies sometimes profess to believe it highly incorrect to go to balls, plays, races, or to any party where it is possible there may be a quadrille. A number of the officers also profess these opinions, and set themselves up as New Lights.

9th.—I was remarking to an officer to-day, I thought it very unlikely any one would attempt the life of the Governor-general. He replied: "The danger is to be feared from the discharged sipahīs, who are in a most turbulent and discontented state. Squadrons of them are gone over to Runjeet Singh,[2] who is most happy to receive well-disciplined troops into his service."

I have just learned how to tell the age of a stud-bred horse. All stud horses are marked on the flank, when they are one year old, with the first letter of the stud and the last figure of the year. Our little mare, Lachhmī, is marked K. 0., therefore she was foaled at Kharuntadee in 1819, and marked in 1820—making her age now eleven years.

Oct. 10th.—I see in the papers—"A member in the House of Commons expressed his satisfaction that so abominable a practice as that of sŭtēē should have been abolished without convulsion or bloodshed. Great credit was due to the noble lord at the head of the Government there, and to the missionaries, to whom much of the credit was owing."

How very absurd all this is, was proved to me by what came to my knowledge at the time of the sŭtēē at Allahabad. If Government at that time had issued the order to forbid sŭtēē, not one word would have been said. The missionaries had nothing to do with it; the rite might have been abolished long before without danger.

Women in all countries are considered such dust in the balance, when their interests are pitted against those of the men, that I rejoice no more widows are to be grilled, to ensure the whole of the property passing to the sons of the deceased.

[2] See note on Runjeet Singh, Chapter 6, note 1.

KANIYAJEE AND THE GOPEES.

Figure 4   Kaniyā-jee and the Gopīs

The Government interferes with native superstition where rupees are in question—witness the tax they levy on pilgrims at the junction of the Ganges and Jumna. Every man, even the veriest beggar, is obliged to give one rupee for liberty to bathe at the holy spot; and if you consider that one rupee is sufficient to keep that man in comfort for one month, the tax is severe.

The Dewālī

16th.—This is the great day of the Dewālī, celebrated by the Hindoos in honour of Kālī, also called Kālee-pooja. This evening, happening to go down to the river just below the verandah to look at a large toon-wood tree lying in a boat, which some people had brought in hopes we should purchase it, my attention was attracted to a vast quantity of lamps burning on Sirsya Ghāt, and I desired the boatmen to row to the place; I had never been on the river before, nor had I seen this ghāt, although only a stone's throw from our bungalow, it being hidden by a point of land.

On reaching the ghāt, I was quite delighted with the beauty of a scene resembling fairy land. Along the side of the Ganges, for the distance of a quarter of a mile, are, I should think, about fifty small ghāts, built with steps low down into the river, which flows over the lower portion of them. Above these ghāts are, I should imagine, fifteen small Hindoo temples, mixed with native houses; and some beautifully picturesque trees overshadow the whole.

The spot must be particularly interesting by daylight—but imagine its beauty at the time I saw it, at the Festival of Lights.

On every temple, on every ghāt, and on the steps down to the river's side, thousands of small lamps were placed, from the foundation to the highest pinnacle, tracing the architecture in lines of light.

The evening was very dark, and the whole scene was reflected in the Ganges. Hundreds of Hindoos were worshipping before the images of Mahadēo and Gŭnéshŭ; some men on the ghāts standing within circles of light, were prostrating themselves on the pavement; others doing pooja standing in the river; others bathing. The Brahmans before the idols were tolling their bells, whilst the worshippers poured Ganges water, rice, oil, and flowers over the images of the gods.

Numbers of people were sending off little paper boats, each containing a lamp, which, floating down the river, added to the beauty of the scene. I saw some women sending off these little fire-fly boats, in which they had adventured their happiness, earnestly watching them as they floated down the stream: if at the moment the paper boat disappeared in the distance the lamp was still burning, the wish of the votary would be crowned with success; but if the lamp was extinguished, the hope for which the offering was made was doomed to disappointment. With what eagerness did many a mother watch the little light to know if her child would or would not recover from sickness! The river was covered with fleets of these little lamps, hurried along by the rapid stream.

The stone ghāts are of all shapes and sizes, built by the Cawnpore merchants according to their wealth. Some are large and handsome—some not a yard in diameter. A good one, with arches facing the water, is put aside for the sole use of the women; and all were most brilliantly lighted. The houses in the city were also gaily illuminated. But to see the Dewālī in perfection, you must float past the temples during the dark hours on Gunga-jee. I was greatly pleased: so Eastern, so fairy-like a scene, I had not witnessed since my arrival in India; nor could I have imagined that the dreary-looking station of Cawnpore contained so much of beauty.

The goddess Kālee, to whom this festival is dedicated, is the black goddess to whom human sacrifices are offered. This evening beholding the pretty and fanciful adorations of the Hindoos, offering rice and flowers, and sending off their floating lamps upon the river, I could scarcely believe the worship could be in honour of Kālee.

I have seen no temples dedicated to her up the country. Her celebrated shrine is at Kāli Ghāt, near Calcutta. A Hindoo often makes a vow, generally to Kālee, that if she will grant his prayer, he will not cut off a particular lock of his hair for so many years; at the end of that time he goes to the shrine, makes pooja, and shaves the lock: at particular times of the year, they say, piles of hair are shaved off at Kālee Ghāt.

When we were residing in Chowringhee we heard of the body of a man, who had been sacrificed to the goddess, having been found before the image at Kālee Ghāt. It was supposed he was some poor wanderer or devotee, possessing no friends to make inquiries concerning his fate. When a victim is sacrificed, it is considered necessary to cut off the head at one blow with a broad heavy axe.

At Benares I purchased thirty-two paintings of the Hindoo deities for one rupee! and amongst them was a sketch of the goddess Kālee.

Phŭlŭ-Hŭrēē

A figure of Kālee, exactly similar to the one purchased at Benares, and attired in the same manner, I saw worshipped at Pārg under the name of Phŭlŭ-hŭrēē (she who receives much fruit). She is worshipped at the total wane of the moon, in the month Jyoishthŭ—or any other month, at the pleasure of the worshipper. Her offerings are fruits especially. Animals are sacrificed in her honour, and Jack-fruit and mangoes are presented to her in that particular month.

The day after the worship the people carried the goddess in state down to the river Jumna, and sank her in its deep waters: the procession was accompanied by the discordant music of tom-toms, &c., and all the rabble of Kydgunge. The image, about three feet in height, dressed and painted, was borne on a sort of platform.

The goddess is represented as a black female with four arms, standing on the breast of Shivŭ. In one hand she carries a scymitar; in two others the heads of giants, which she holds by the hair; and the fourth hand supports giants' heads.

"She wears two dead bodies for ear-rings, and a necklace of skulls. Her tongue hangs down to her chin. The heads of giants are hung as a girdle around her loins, and her jet black hair falls to her heels. Having drunk the blood of the giants she slew, her eyebrows are bloody, and the blood is falling in a stream down her breast. Her eyes are red, like those of a drunkard. She stands with one leg on the breast of her husband Shivŭ, and rests the other on his thigh."

Men are pointed out amongst *other animals* as a proper sacrifice to Kālee: the blood of a tiger pleases her for 100 years; the blood of a lion, a reindeer, or a man, for 1000 years. By the sacrifice of three men she is pleased for 100,000 years.

Kālee had a contest with the giant Ravŭna, which lasted ten years; having conquered him, she became mad with joy, and her dancing shook the earth to its centre. To restore the peace of the world, Shivŭ, her husband, threw himself amongst the dead bodies at her feet. She continued her dancing, and trampled upon him. When she discovered her husband she stood still, horror-struck and ashamed, and threw out her tongue to an uncommon length. By this means Shivŭ stopped her frantic dancing, and saved the universe. When the Hindoo women are shocked or ashamed at anything, they put out their tongues as a mode of expressing their feelings. Nor is this practice confined to the women of the East alone, it is common amongst the lower orders of the English.

18*th*.—Āghā Meer, the ex-minister of Oude, has come over. His train consisted of fifty-six elephants, covered with crimson clothing deeply embroidered with gold, and forty gārees (carts) filled with gold mohurs and rupees.

His zenāna came over some days ago, consisting of nearly 400 palanquins; how much I should like to pay the ladies a visit, and see if there are any remarkably handsome women amongst them!

[. . .]

20*th*.—In the evening I went with Mr. A——to Sirsya Ghāt; whilst we were sketching the mut'hs (Hindoo temples), about fifty women came down, two by two, to the ghāt. After having burnt the corpse of a Hindoo by the side of the Ganges, they came in procession, to lament, bathe, and put on clean garments; one woman walked in front, reciting a monotonous chant, in which the others every now and then joined in chorus, beating their breasts and foreheads in time to the monotonous singing.

They assembled on the steps of the ghāt. Each woman wore a white chudda (in shape like a sheet), which was wrapped so closely around her that it covered her body and head entirely, the eyes alone being visible. Standing on the steps of the ghāt, they renewed their lament; beating their breasts, foreheads, and limbs, and chanting their lament all the time; then they all sat down, and beat their knees with their hands in time to the dirge; afterwards, they descended into the river to bathe and change their clothes; such an assortment of ugly limbs I never beheld! A native woman thinks no more of displaying her form as high as the knee, or some inches above it, than we do of showing our faces. This being rather too great an exhibition, I proposed to my companion to proceed a little further, that the lovely damsels might bathe undisturbed.

25th.—I have been more disgusted to-day than I can express: the cause is too truly Indian not to have a place in my journal; I fancied I saw the corpse of a European floating down the Ganges just now, but, on looking through the telescope, I beheld the most disgusting object imaginable.

When a rich Hindoo dies, his body is burned, and the ashes are thrown into the Ganges; when a poor man is burned, they will not go to the expense of wood sufficient to consume the body. The corpse I saw floating down had been put on a pile, covered with ghee (clarified butter), and fire enough had been allowed just to take off all the skin from the body and head, giving it a white appearance; any thing so ghastly and horrible as the limbs from the effect of the fire was never beheld, and it floated almost entirely out of the water, whilst the crows that were perched upon it tore the eyes out. In some parts, where the stream forms a little bay, numbers of these dreadful objects are collected together by the eddy, and render the air pestiferous, until a strong current carries them onwards. The poorer Hindoos think they have paid all due honour to their relatives when they have thus skinned them on the funeral pile, and thrown them, like dead dogs, into the Ganges.

The Musulmāns bury their dead—generally under the shade of trees, and erect tombs to their memory, which they keep in repair; they burn lights upon the graves every Thursday (Jumarāt), and adorn the tomb with flowers.

[. . .]

Nov. 8th.—My husband received an order to return to Allahabad; this gave us much satisfaction.

17th.—

[. . .]

Another fire has taken place in the fort at Allahabad, and sulphur, valued at two lacs of rupees, melted by the heat, ran over the square like lava; fortunately the fire did not reach the powder magazine. This is the second attempt that has been made within the space of a few weeks to burn the fort; the discharged natives who used to work at the powder mills are supposed to be the persons who kindled the fires.

The damage done by these fires is much greater than the saving which has arisen to Government from cutting the pay of the men, or from dismissing them; so much for economy!

18th.—To-day, our Mug cook died suddenly after a short illness; the corpse will be burned, and the ashes thrown into the Ganges; the man came from Ava. The Mugs are reckoned better cooks than the Musulmāns. He was an excellent *artiste* and a good servant; we shall replace him with difficulty. He professed himself a Hindoo, and during their festivals would give money, and worship according to their fashion.

During the Muharrum he called himself a follower of the prophet; he gave forty rupees to assist in building a Taziya, performed all the ceremonies peculiar to the faithful, and was allowed to be considered a Musulmān for the time; at the conclusion, when the Taziya was thrown into the river, he became a Mug again.

22nd.—With a westerly wind, and the thermometer at 65°, we Indians find it very cold, the contrast to the hot winds is so great. I have worn a shawl all the morning, and to-night, for the first time this year, we have begun fires; and have had the horse-shoe table placed in front of the fireplace, that we may enjoy the warmth during dinner-time. The room looks so cheerful, it puts me into good humour and good spirits; I feel so *English*, without lassitude, so strong and well. My husband has just sallied out in his great coat to take a very long walk; and the little terrier is lying under the table, watching a musk rat, which has taken refuge in a hole under the grate.

26th.—I have just heard of an occurrence at Lucnow, which is in true native style. The Nawāb Hukeem Mehndee Ali Khan, the present minister, poisoned the King of Oude's ear against one of his people by declaring that the man betrayed some state secrets and intrigues; the king accordingly, without judge or jury, ordered the man's head to be fixed, and a heavy weight to be fastened on his tongue until the tongue should be so wrenched from the roots that it should ever after hang out of his mouth. This brutal

punishment was inflicted some two or three months ago, and the poor creature's life has been preserved by pouring liquids down his throat, as, of
course, he is unable to eat at present. They have now discovered the man
is innocent! but what does it avail him? His accuser, the Nawāb Hukeem
Mehndee, is rich; money is power. The king is displeased with the minister, I understand, for his misrepresentations; he is also on bad terms with
the resident,—they do not speak.

Any lady having a horror of the plagues of Egypt would not admire what
is going on at this moment; several lizards are peering about, as they hang
on the window frames, with their bright round eyes; a great fat frog or toad,
I know not which, is jumping across the floor, under the dinner-table; and
a wild cat from the jungles, having come in, has made her exit through the
window, breaking a pane of glass; a musk-rat is squeaking in the next room,
I must go and prevent the little terrier from catching it: I do not like to
see the dog foam at the mouth, which she always does after killing this
sort of rat.

Dec. 1st.—A marriage has taken place this day, between the widow
of the Mug cook, a low caste Hindoo, old and ugly, and one of our
khidmātgars, a Mahommedān. On account of her caste the man cannot eat
with her without pollution; therefore, having taken her to a mosque, and
the kurān having been read before her, she declares herself a convert. The
musulmān servants have dined with her; she is now a follower of the
prophet. They are very fond of making converts, but the Hindoos never
attempt to convert any one; in fact, they will not admit converts to their
faith, nor will they embrace any other religion; here and there a woman
becomes a musulmāne, on her marriage with a man of that faith.

5th.—To-day's news is, that the Governor-general met the 3rd cavalry at
Allahabad, on their march from Cawnpore to Benares. His lordship
reviewed the regiment, and asked the officers to dinner; an invitation they
all refused. This annoyed his lordship very much, being the first display of
resentment manifested towards him on his march by the army, and he
ordered them to dine with him on pain of forfeiting their rank, pay, and
allowances, pending a reference to the Court of Directors. Of course the
officers obeyed *the order*; they were obliged to do so: what an agreeable party
the Governor-general must have had, with guests whom he had forced to
partake of the feast!

Dec. 11th.—I went to the races at sunrise: the first race was between two
beautiful Arabs; Sultan looked so handsome at starting, and shot ahead of
the other, keeping him in the rear until he very nearly gained the stand at
the end of the three miles; of a sudden his speed relaxed, the other horse
came up, and passed the post just before him. Sultan looked wild; the jockey

dismounted; the horse fell, regained his feet three times, reared with pain, and, falling again, died in the space of a minute.

The Cawnpore races have been unfortunate; two years ago, a jockey was thrown, and broke his neck on the spot. Last year, the favourite Arab broke his hind leg and was shot: this year, Sultan has been killed, and two other horses have gone lame.

13th.—I accompanied some ladies to the riding-school of the 11th dragoons, and, being much pleased, requested to be allowed to take lessons with them; afterwards, riding there during those hours that the school was unoccupied by the dragoons, formed one of our greatest amusements. As for the corporal, the roughrider of the 11th dragoons who attends in the riding-school, his affections are quite divided between my horse Trelawny and myself; I heard him say the other day, speaking of the former, "I like that little chap, he looks so *innicent.*"

My sā'īs cannot accomplish putting me on my horse after the English fashion; therefore, he kneels down on one knee, holding the horse in his left hand, and the stirrup in the right; I step from his knee to the stirrup, and take my seat on the saddle; rather a good method, and one of his own invention.

Christmas Day.—The house is gaily decorated with plantain trees, roses, and chaplets of gaudy flowers, but no holly; we miss the holly and misletoe of an English Christmas. The servants are all coming in with their offerings,—trays of apples, grapes, kishmish, walnuts, sugar, almonds in the shell, oranges, &c. The saddler, who is also a servant, has brought five trays in honour of kishmish (Christmas); these presents are rather expensive to the receiver, who returns kishmish bakhshish (Christmas boxes) in rupees; the apples *au naturel*, brought down at this time of the year by the Arab merchants from Cabul, are rather insipid, yet the sight is very grateful to the eye; they are large, fine, and of a roseate hue. The grapes, which are in small round boxes, are picked off the bunch, and placed in layers of cotton. The dates are excellent. Kishmish are small raisins without stones, which have an agreeable acidity; they are known in England as sultana raisins. These Arab merchants bring pattū, pushmeena, cashmere gloves and socks, curiously illuminated old Persian books, swords and daggers, saleb misree, and Persian cats, saffron, and various other incongruous articles, which are all laden on camels, which they bring in strings, in large numbers. The men are fine, hardy, picturesque looking personages, independent in their bearing; and some of the younger ones have a colour on their cheeks like the bright red on their apples. Their complexions are much fairer than any I have seen in India.

Chapter 14

Scenes in Oude

[. . .]

1831. *Jan.* 5*th.*—The view from our verandah is remarkably good; the King of Oude, Ghazee-ood-Deen Hyder, has pitched his tent on the opposite side of the Ganges, and has constructed a bridge of boats across the river. In attendance upon him, they say, there are 2000 elephants, camels, and men in proportionate number; the sides of the river swarm with troops, animals, and tents.

Early on the morning of the 6th, the Governor-general, Lord William Bentinck, arrived at Cawnpore; and her Ladyship received the station. We paid our devoirs; and, in conversation with Lady William on the subject of the zenāna of the King of Oude, I excited her curiosity so much by my account of Tajmahŭl, that I feel convinced she will pay her a visit on her arrival at Lucnow.

7*th.*—We were invited to breakfast with the Governor-general, with whom the King of Oude was to breakfast in state. We rode to the tents— but let me commence the narrative from the dawn of day. Long before sunrise the guns and drums in the king's encampment announced that all were in preparation to cross the bridge of boats. About 7 A.M. an enormous train of elephants, camels, and troops crossed over, brilliantly decorated, and proceeded to the camp of the Governor-general. We then cantered off—I on the Bokhara grey, who became very impetuous; but, although surrounded with elephants, camels, galloping horses, and guns firing, I never lost my courage for an instant: nevertheless, I will play no such game again, it is too hazardous.

Lord William met the king half-way, and having been invited to enter the royal howdah, he took his seat on the king's elephant, and they proceeded together to the breakfast-tent through a street of dragoons, infantry, &c. Lady William, with all her visitors assembled around her, was in the tent awaiting the entrance of the great people; on their arrival, after the usual embracings and forms were over, we proceeded to breakfast.

The whole scene was one of extreme beauty. The magnificent dresses of the natives, the superb elephants, covered with crimson velvet embroidered with gold, the English troops, the happy faces, and the brilliant day, rendered it delightful.

After breakfast Lord William received all visitors who asked for a private audience in a separate tent: my husband made his sālām, and requested permission to visit Lucnow in his Lordship's train; having received a kind affirmative, we returned home.

8*th*.—The Governor-general returned the king's visit, and, crossing the bridge of boats, breakfasted with his majesty on the territories of Oude.

10*th*.—Lady William gave a ball to the station.

11*th*.—His lordship was invited to dinner—and dined with the eleventh dragoons, he being their colonel; the next day the Governor-general's party commenced their march to Lucnow, the king having quitted the day before.

18*th*.—Having sent on our camels and tents beforehand, we started for Lucnow, intending to drive the whole distance in one day, for which purpose we had laid eight buggy horses on the road, the distance being only fifty-five miles.

Going over the sandy bed of the Ganges, the horse being unable to drag the Stanhope, we mounted an elephant, which took us some miles; being obliged to return the elephant, we got into a native cart drawn by bullocks, and so arrived at the spot where the second horse was laid. But the horses found it almost impossible to get through the sand, the country had been so much cut up from the multitudes that had crossed and recrossed it. In consequence night overtook us in the middle of Oude without a tent or food, and a dark night in prospect; whilst debating where to find shelter, we espied a tent in the distance, which proved to be an empty one belonging to a friend of ours, and there we took up our quarters.

A boy came forward, and saying, "I Christian," offered to procure a chicken and give us a curry, which we ate off red earthen dishes, with two bits of bamboo as a knife and fork, after the style of chop-sticks. I must not forget to mention, that after our repast, Christian came forward and repeated the Creed and the Lord's Prayer in Hindostanee; he repeated them like a parrot, but, judging from his answers when questioned, did not appear at all to comprehend his newly-acquired religion.

The sutrāengī, the cotton carpet of the tent, served to defend us from the cold during the night; and the next morning we recommenced our journey, but did not reach Lucnow in time to join the dinner-party at the Residency, to which we were invited to meet Lady William Bentinck.

Our camels, tents, and horses had gone on in advance. On our arrival, I found the camel that carried my trunks had fallen down in crossing part of the river, and both my finery and my journal were soaked in the stream; much damage was done to the wardrobe—and, as for the journal, it was quite mouldy and almost illegible: for the benefit of distressed damsels in a similar predicament, I give a receipt to restore the colour of faded writing, to which I had recourse with good success on this occasion.[1]

18th.—The Governor-general breakfasted with the king. The whole party quitted the Residency on elephants most beautifully clothed, and were met half-way by his majesty. The scene was magnificent. The elephants, the camels, the crowds of picturesque natives, the horsemen, and the English troops, formed a *tout ensemble* that was quite inspiring. The Governor-general got into the king's howdah, and proceeded to the palace, where breakfast was laid in a fine service of gold and silver. After breakfast we proceeded to a verandah to see various fights, and, having taken our seats, the order was given to commence the tamāshā.

The Elephant Fights

The river Goomtee runs in front of the verandah; and on the opposite side were collected a number of elephants paired for the combat. The animals exhibited at first no inclination to fight, although urged on by their respective mahawats, and we began to imagine this native sport would prove a failure.

At length two elephants, equally matched, were guided by the mahāwats on their backs to some distance from each other, and a female elephant was placed midway. As soon as the elephants turned and saw the female they became angry, and set off at a long swinging trot to meet each other; they attacked with their long tusks, and appeared to be pressing against each other with all their might. One elephant caught the leg of the other in his trunk, and strove to throw his adversary or break his fore-leg. But the most dangerous part appeared to be when they seized one another by their long trunks and interlaced them; then the combat began in good earnest. When they grew very fierce, and there was danger of their injuring themselves, fireworks were thrown in their faces, which alarmed and separated them, and small rockets were also let off for that purpose.

The situation of a mahāwat during the fight is one of danger. The year before, the shock of the combat having thrown the mahāwat to the ground, the elephant opposed to him took a step to one side, and, putting his great foot upon him, quietly crushed the man to death!

Sometimes the elephant will put up his trunk to seize his opponent's mahāwat and pull him off: skill and activity are requisite to avoid the danger.

[1] Appendix.

131

The second pair of elephants that were brought in front of the verandah hung back, as if unwilling to fight, for some time; several natives, both on horseback and on foot, touched them up every now and then with long spears to rouse their anger. One of the elephants was a long time ere he could be induced to combat—but, when once excited, he fought bravely; he was a powerful animal, too much for his adversary—for having placed his tusks against the flank of his opponent, he drove him before him step-by-step across the plain to the edge of the river, and fairly rolled him over into the Goomtee. Sometimes a defeated elephant will take to the water, and his adversary will pursue him across the river.

The animals are rendered furious by giving them balls to eat made of the wax of the human ear, which the barbers collect for that purpose!

The hair on the tail of an elephant is reckoned of such importance, that the price of the animal rises or falls according to the quantity and length of the hair on the tail. It is sometimes made into bracelets for English ladies.

A great number of elephants fought in pairs during the morning; but, to have a good view of the combat, one ought to be on the plain on the other side the river, nearer to the combatants; the verandah from which we viewed the scene is rather too distant.

When the elephant fights were over, two rhinoceros were brought before us, and an amusing fight took place between them; they fought like pigs.

The plain was covered by natives in thousands, on foot or on horseback. When the rhinoceros grew fierce, they charged the crowd, and it was beautiful to see the mass of people flying before them.

On the Goomtee, in front of the verandah, a large pleasure-boat belonging to his Majesty was sailing up and down; the boat was made in the shape of a fish, and the golden scales glittered in the sun.

The scene was picturesque, animated, and full of novelty.

In an inclosed court, the walls of which we overlooked, seven or eight fine wild buffaloes were confined: two tigers, one hyena, and three bears were turned loose upon them. I expected to see the tigers spring upon the buffaloes, instead of which they slunk round and round the walls of the court, apparently only anxious to escape. The tigers had not a fair chance, and were sadly injured, being thrown into the air by the buffaloes, and were received again when falling on their enormous horns. The buffaloes attacked them three or four together, advancing in line with their heads to the ground. I observed that when the buffaloes came up to the tiger, who was generally lying on the ground, and presented their horns close to him—if the animal raised his paw and struck one of them, he was tossed in a moment; if he remained quiet, they sometimes retreated without molesting him.

The bears fought well, but in a most laughable style. The scene was a cruel one, and I was glad when it was over. None of the animals, however, were killed.

A fight was to have taken place between a country horse and two tigers, but Lady William Bentinck broke up the party and retired. I was anxious to see the animal, he is such a vicious beast; the other day he killed two tigers that were turned loose upon him.

Combats also took place between rams: the creatures attacked each other fiercely—the jar and the noise were surprising as head met head in full tilt. Well might they be called battering rams!

21st.—We visited Constantia, a beautiful and most singular house, built by General Martine;[1] it would take pages to describe it; the house is constructed to suit the climate; ventilation is carried up through the walls from the ground-floor to the top of the building, and the marble hall is a luxurious apartment. The king having refused to give General Martine the price he asked for Constantia, the latter declared his tomb should be handsomer than any palace in his Majesty's dominions. He therefore built a vault for himself under the house, and there he lies buried; this has desecrated the place, no Musulmān can inhabit a tomb . . .

The house is a large and very singular building; a motto fronts the whole, "*Labore et Constantiâ*,"—hence the name of the house.

Returning from this interesting place, we proceeded on elephants to see the Roomee Durwāza, a gateway built at the entrance of the city, on the Delhi road, by Ussuf-ood-Dowla; it is most beautiful and elegant, a copy of a gate at Constantinople.

Near this spot is the Imām-Bārā, a building almost too delicate and elegant to be described; it contains the tomb of Ussuf-ood-Dowla, the second king of this family.[2] Within the court is a beautiful mosque.

We were delighted with the place and the scene altogether—the time being evening, and the streets crowded with natives.

[. . .]

22nd.—The Governor-general quitted Lucnow at daybreak. On account of some points of etiquette respecting the queenmother and the king's favourite wife, Gosseina, Lady William Bentinck did not visit the royal zenāna.

This day we visited a palace called Padshāh-i-Takht, containing the king's throne and the banquetting-rooms, a delightful place; on quitting it we

[1] Claude Martine, born in Lyons, was sent to Oudh to do survey work and joined the Nawab's service as Superintendent of Artillery and Arsenal; he also speculated in indigo. Constantia became the La Martiniere School at Lucknow.

[2] Asaf udDowlah was in fact the fourth Nawab Wazir of Oudh. The Nawab Wazirs ruled on behalf of the Mughal emperors until in 1819 Ghazi-uddin Hyder took the title of King.

crossed the river to a new house and garden, built by the present king, called Padshāh Bāgh.

[. . .]

23rd.—Mr. M——invited us to quit our tents, and come into the Residency, giving us the apartments vacated by the Governor-general, which are delightful; and here we are installed with some most agreeable people.[3] First and foremost, our kind host the Resident; Mr. G——, the Resident of Nagpore; Mr. H——, the Resident of Delhi;[4] and Col. Gardner, a most charming old gentleman;—but he will require pages to himself, he is one of *many* thousand.

But I can write no more—my aide-de-camp, a young Bhopaul chieftain, is in attendance, to invite me to ride with the Resident. This little native chief is a fine intelligent boy about fourteen years of age; he rides well, on a small horse covered with silver ornaments; and his own dress, with two and sometimes three swords at his waist, is so curious, I should like to have his picture taken. The young chief, with his followers, often attends me on horseback to do my bidding.

The king has a charming park near Lucnow, called Dil-Kushā, or "Heart's Delight," filled with game; deer, nil-gā'ī, antelopes, bears, tigers, peacocks, and game of all sorts; the drive through it is most agreeable, the road being kept constantly watered: the house is good, and very convenient. His Majesty visits the place often for shooting.

Just beyond the park is a second park called Beebeepore, formerly the residence of Mr. Cheery, who was murdered at Benares.

24th.—I took a steam bath in true oriental style, which was very delightful; when the pleasing fatigue was over, I joined a party, and proceeded to Daulut Khāna, a palace built by Ussuf-ood-Dowla, but now uninhabited, except by some of the ladies and attendants of the old king's zenāna.

We went there to see a picture painted in oil by Zoffani, an Italian artist, of a match of cocks, between the Nāwab Ussuf-ood-Dowla and the Resident, Colonel Mordaunt; the whole of the figures are portraits; the picture excellent, but fast falling into decay.

The next place visited was the country-house of one of the richest merchants in India, a place called Govinda Bāgh. It is one of the handsomest houses I have entered, and beautifully furnished, with fine mirrors and lustres; its painted ceilings are remarkably well done, and have a very rich effect; the pillars also in imitation of porphyry look extremely well. The owner, Govind Lall, lives in a mean dirty house, in one of the meanest

---

[3] Thomas Henry Maddock, Resident at Lucknow, 1829–31.
[4] Hawkins, Resident at Delhi 1829 and Acting Resident 1831.

gulīs (lanes) in the city, that his wealth may not attract robbers or cause jealousy.

25th.—My husband accompanied the Resident and a party to breakfast with the King, and I called on my charming friend, Mrs. F——, in cantonments.

In the evening I accompanied the Resident, in his barouche, drawn by four fine horses, round the grounds of Dil-Kushā. The carriage was attended by an escort on horseback; when it passed the guards, arms were presented, and trumpets blown: and sometimes men with baskets of birds running by the side of the carriage, let them fly whenever they caught his eye, in the hope of some reward being thrown to them for having liberated their captives in compliment to the great man.

To release captive birds propitiates the favour of heaven. A great man will release prisoners from jail when he is anxious for the recovery of a relative from illness, or to procure an heir!

The Jānwar Khāna, a menagerie filled with wild beasts, animals of every sort, and birds in profusion, next attracted my attention. You may talk of Le Jardin des Plantes, but the Jānwar Khāna at Lucnow is far better worth visiting. There was an immense Doomba sheep, with *four* horns, and such a tail! perfectly enormous.

We paid a visit to the tomb of Saadut Ulee Khan, the king's grandfather, a beautiful building, near which is the tomb of the begam, both worth seeing.

20th.—I rode with the Resident to his country-house, a short distance from Lucnow, situated in the midst of delightful gardens; there are about twenty of these gardens, filled with fine tanks, wells, and beautiful trees; the Resident contemplates turning them into a park.

28th.—We went over a zenāna garden; the house, dedicated to the ladies, was a good one, situated in a large garden surrounded by a high stone wall. The orthodox height for the four walls of a zenāna garden is, that no man standing on an elephant can overlook them. The building is surrounded with fine trees; and a fountain played before it, in which gold and silver fish were swimming. Near it was an avenue, in which was a swing, the invariable accompaniment of a zenāna garden. The season in which the ladies more particularly delight to swing in the open air is during the rains. I cantered back to the Residency at ten A.M.; the sun was warm, but I thought not of his beams.

After breakfast, I retired to write my journal (knowing how much pleasure it would give her for whom it was kept), although I had that delightful man, Colonel Gardner, to converse with; such a high caste gentleman! how I wish I had his picture! He is married to a native princess, and his granddaughter is betrothed to one of the princes of Delhi. The begam, his wife, is in Lucnow, but so ill that I have been unable to pay my respects to her. Colonel Gardner has promised me, if we will visit Agra or Delhi next year, which we hope to do, he will give me letters of introduction to some of the ladies of the palace, under which circumstances I shall have the opportunity of seeing Delhi to the greatest advantage.

A very fine corps of men, called Gardner's Horse, were raised by him; single-handed nothing can resist them, such masters are they of their horses and weapons. I told him, I was anxious to see good native riding, and feats of horsemanship; he said, "An old servant of mine is now in Lucnow, in the king's service; he is the finest horseman in India. I gave that man 150 rupees a month (about 150 *l.* per annum) for the pleasure of seeing him ride. He could cut his way through thousands. All men who know any thing of native horsemanship, know that man: he has just sent me word he cannot pay his respects to me, for if he were to do so, the king would turn him out of service." I asked why? He answered, "There is such a jealousy of the English at court: as for the king, he is a poor creature, and can neither like nor dislike. Hakīm Mehndie the minister rules him entirely, and he abhors the English."

It is a curious circumstance that many of the palaces in Lucnow have fronts in imitation of the palaces in Naples and Rome, &c.; and the real native palace is beyond in an enclosed space.

Being tired with writing, I will go down and talk to Colonel Gardner; should no men be in the room, he will converse respecting the zenāna, but the moment a man enters, it is a forbidden subject.

Lucnow is a very beautiful city; and the view from the roof of the Residency particularly good.

I am fatigued with my ride through the sun; nevertheless, I will go out on an elephant this evening, and view all the old part of the city. I like this barā sāhib life; this living *en prince*; in a climate so fine as this is at present it is delightful.

The subjects of his Majesty of Oude are by no means desirous of participating in the blessings of British rule. They are a richer, sleeker, and merrier race than the natives in the territories of the Company.

What a delightful companion is this Colonel Gardner! I have had the most interesting conversation with him, which has been interrupted by his being obliged to attend his poor sick wife, as he calls the begam. She is very ill, and her mind is as much affected as her body: he cannot persuade her to call in the aid of medicine. A short time ago, she lost her son, Allan Gardner, aged twenty-nine years: then she lost a daughter and a grandson; afterwards a favourite daughter; and now another young grandson is dan-

Figure 5   Ancient Hindu ruin

gerously ill. These misfortunes have broken her spirit, and she refuses all medical aid. That dear old man has made me weep like a child. I could not bear the recital of his sorrows and sufferings. He said, "You often see me talking and apparently cheerful at the Resident's table, when my heart is bleeding."

We have had a long conversation respecting his own life, and I have been trying to persuade him to write it. He says, "If I were to write it, you would scarcely believe it; it would appear fiction." He is gone to the sick begam. How I long for another *tête à tête*, in the hope of learning his private history!

He must have been, and is, very handsome; such a high caste man! How he came to marry the begam I know not. What a romance his love must have been! I wish I had his portrait, just as he now appears, so dignified and interesting. His partiality flatters me greatly.

Chapter 15

Revelations of Life in the Zenāna

Saadut Khan, known at first under the name of Meer Muhammad Ameen, descended in a direct line from the Imām Mousa Kasim, of the family of Ali, esteemed in Persia as of the highest and most noble extraction. During the civil wars, he quitted Khorasān, his native province, and repaired to Lahore, where he took the name of Saadut Khan. On the accession of Mahmud Shāh, he was created a noble of the empire, and Soobadar of Oude, with the titles of "Pillar of the empire, confident support of the state, Meer Muhammad Ameen Khan, the Glory of War."

Fortune having proved favourable, he sent for his only sister, the widow of a nobleman, Jaafer Beg, and her two sons, and bestowed his only daughter in marriage on the elder brother, the young Nawāb Munsoor Ulee Khan, commonly called Sefdar Jung, who on the death of his uncle was confirmed by the king in his government of Oude. He died in 1756, leaving Soojah-ood-Dowla his son and successor.

Soojah-ood-Dowla, the first prince of the race, died leaving two sons, Ussuf-ood-Dowla and Saadut Ulee Khan. Ussuf-ood-Dowla ascended the masnud; he built Lucnow, and most of the palaces around the city, also the Roomee Durwazah, and the Imām-Bārā; in the latter he was buried.

The Daulut Khāna was also built by him; in it is his picture, by Zoffani. In fact, whenever you ask who built this or that place, the answer is sure to be Ussuf-ood-Dowla.

He died, leaving no issue, and was succeeded by Wuzeer Ulee Khan, an adopted son, but whom he declared to be his own. Mr. Cherry was at this time Resident of Lucnow. Sir John Shore deposed Wuzeer Ulee Khan, on account of his not being the real son of the late king, and raised Saadut Ulee Khan to the throne, the brother of Ussuf-ood-Dowla.

The deposed Wuzeer went to Benares, and attempted to rouse the natives to murder all the English. In pursuance of which plan, Ulee Khan came to Mr. Cherry's house, he being at that time Resident at Benares, and murdered him, while sitting at breakfast. The house of Mr. and Mrs Davis, of the Civil Service, was attacked. Mr. Davis and his wife ran up a narrow winding staircase to the roof of the house, where, with a hog-spear, he

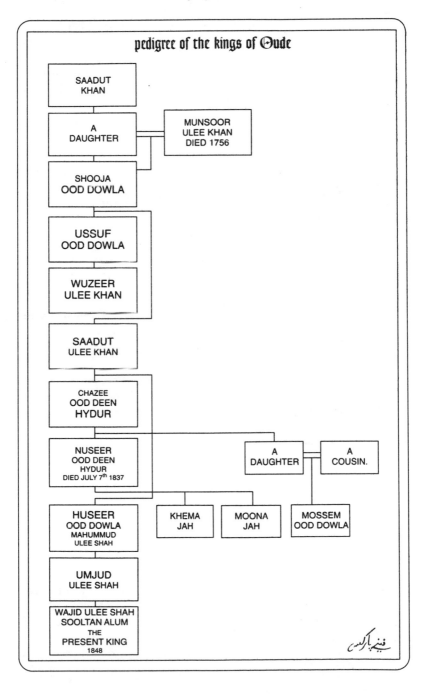

pedigree of the kings of Oude

SAADUT
KHAN

A
DAUGHTER — MUNSOOR
ULEE KHAN
DIED 1756

SHOOJA
OOD DOWLA

USSUF
OOD DOWLA

WUZEER
ULEE KHAN

SAADUT
ULEE KHAN

CHAZEE
OOD DEEN
HYDUR

NUSEER
OOD DEEN
HYDUR
DIED JULY 7th 1837

A
DAUGHTER — A
COUSIN.

HUSEER
OOD DOWLA
MAHUMMUD
ULEE SHAH

KHEMA
JAH

MOONA
JAH

MOSSEM
OOD DOWLA

UMJUD
ULEE SHAH

WAJID ULEE SHAH
SOOLTAN ALUM
THE
PRESENT KING
1848

defended the door of the staircase, and kept his pursuers at bay until the arrival of the military from cantonments. The roof of the house being flat, as is the custom in India, and the narrowness of the winding stair admitting only one person at a time, Mr. Davis was able to defend himself, and killed several of the assailants. Wuzeer Ulee Khan was confined for life in the Fort, in Calcutta, and died a few years ago.

Saadut Ulee Khan, the brother of Ussuf-ood-Dowla, amassed thirteen millions of money, and left the throne to his son, Ghazee-ood-Deen.

The Nāwab Wuzeer, Ghazee-ood-Deen Hydur, assumed the sceptre by the advice of his minister, Āghā Meer. He cast off allegiance to Delhi, and stamped coins in his own name.

The gold mohurs struck by him, bear the following inscription in the Persian character:—

> "Coined in the Royal Treasury of Lucnow, Soubah Oude, in the 3rd year of the great and auspicious reign. Struck in silver and gold, by the grace of God, the giver of all good, by Ghazee-ood-Deen Hydur, the Great Lord, the King of Time."

The crown is placed between two standards, on each of which is a fish: the standards are supported by leopards: beneath the crown is the double-handled dagger, a most formidable weapon; and at the base of the whole are two large fish.

Ghazee-ood-Deen Hydur had no son, and one only daughter, who married her cousin, and had issue Mossem-ood-Dowla, the true heir to the throne; a man whom you may see constantly at the present king's table.

Ghazee-ood-Deen, instead of leaving the throne to his true heir and grandson Mossem-ood-Dowla, left it to Nuseer-ood-Deen Hydur, a boy whom the king declared to be his own son by a slave girl; but who, they say, is in reality the son of a dhobee (washerman) belonging to the palace. This man is the present king of Lucnow. The English are aware of these facts. On the decease of the present king, the succession will be disputed, as he wishes to place a boy, named Khema-jah, on the masnud, instead of his own son, Feredooa Buckht Moona-jah: but for the history of these two boys, I refer you to the lives of the wives of the king.

The Muhammadan law allows an adopted son to take the place of a legitimate son at the pleasure of the parent, by which law Nuseer-ood-Deen Hydur claimed the throne, and put aside Mossem-ood-Dowla, the grandson of Ghazee-ood-Deen Hydur.

29th.—We drove to Barouda, a palace built in the French style; I saw there nothing worthy of remark, but two marble tables, inlaid in the most delicate and beautiful manner with flowers of the convolvulus.

30th.—The Resident and all his party breakfasted with the King on the anniversary of his coronation, which takes place in any month, and on any day, according to his Majesty's pleasure.

During breakfast my attention was deeply engrossed by the prime minister, the Nawāb Mootuzim-ul-Dowla, Mehndee Ulee Khan Bahadur, commonly called Nawāb Hakīm Mehndi.[1] I conversed with him at times, and eyed him well as he was seated next to me, and opposite the King, telling his beads the whole time, for good luck perhaps; his rosary was composed of enormous pearls.

His majesty's hooqŭ was presented to the Nawāb; Lord William Bentinck and the Resident were honoured with the same: it is a great distinction; no subject can smoke, unless by permission, in the royal presence. Hooqŭs are only presented to the Governor-general, the Commander-in-chief, the Resident, and the Bishop of Calcutta—if he likes a pipe.

Numerous histories respecting the prime minister were current in the bazār, far too romantic and extraordinary to be believed, of which the following is a specimen:

"The truth or falsehood of the story rests on the head of the narrator."[1]

"The dagger in his bosom and salutation in his mouth."[2]

The hakīm (physician or learned man) was formerly employed on a salary of about twenty rupees a month. The commencement of his enormous fortune began thus:—He was in tents in the district; a very rich Hindoo was with him, within the (kanāts) canvass walls, with which tents are surrounded. This man was said to have died during the night; his corpse was given to his relations, who were in the camp, to be burned according to Hindoo custom. There were two black marks round the neck of the corpse. It is a custom amongst Hindoos to put sweet-meats into the mouth of a dead body. When they opened the mouth of the corpse for this purpose, within it was found a finger, bitten off at the second joint. On that very night the *confidential servant* of the hakīm lost his finger! The hakīm seized the man's treasure, which laid the foundation of his fortune. He next took into pay a number of thieves and murderers, who made

---

[1] Oriental Proverbs.

[2] Ibid.

[1] In 1827 Hakim Menhdi was made Prime Minister by Nasir-uddin. Bentinck thought highly of him and felt that he would be able to save Oudh. The Resident thus did not interfere in the affairs of state.

excursions, and shared the booty with the hakīm. They say the man's art is such that he keeps in favour both with natives and Europeans, in spite of his crimes.

Having been unable to bring the Resident over to his views, he is his sworn enemy, and would give thousands to any one who would poison him. Many of the servants now standing behind the Resident's chair know the reward they might obtain. They would not poison any dish from which many might eat, the most likely thing in which it would be administered would be coffee or ice!

After breakfast, the King went into the next apartment, where the Resident, with all due form, having taken off the King's turban, placed the crown upon his head, and he ascended the masnud.

Khema-jah, the eldest boy, about fourteen years of age, is an ill-looking low caste wretch, with long, straight, lank hair, coarse, falling lips, and bad teeth. The manners and looks of the boy proclaim his caste. He was the first person presented to his Majesty, and received four or five dresses of honour, made of thick Benares gold and silver kimkhwāb, which were *all* put upon his person one over the other.[2] A jewelled turban was put on his head, and a necklace of pearls and precious stones round his neck; and over all these dresses of honour were placed four or five pairs of Cashmere shawls. A sword, dagger, and shield were given him; an elephant, a horse, and a palanquin. Having made his salām to his majesty, and offered some gold mohurs, he retired.

The younger boy, Feredooa Buckht, a bold and independent child, then came forward and received the same presents in the same style.

The khil'ats (dresses of honour) are sometimes given away to dependents on the same day; this, if known, would be considered an insult.

Then appeared the minister, the Nawāb Hakīm Mehndi: when the first dress of honour was put on him, it being too small, he could only put in one arm; and there he stood shaking, perhaps from an idea of its being a bad omen. The Nawāb prostrated himself before the King, and took off his own turban; his Majesty himself immediately placed a jewelled one on the uncovered head of the minister. Imagine the old man, sinking beneath the weight of years, his head totally bald, and his person overwhelmed with dresses of honour, shawls, and presents, like those before given to the young princes: he trembled so much, the elephant-goad fell from his hand, a sign of his own

---

[2] Dresses of honour, khillats, and other presents such as weapons, horses, elephants, and ornaments were presented to everyone at court according to one's status. These presents were often not of great value. Bishop Heber was presented with a horse at the Delhi court which was later valued at 30 rupees.

fall; and the gold mohurs he attempted to retain in his hands fell at the foot of the throne. The people say there is a prophecy he will come to an untimely end next February:—"A bad omen ought not to be mentioned."[1]

When Mossem-ood-Dowla (the true heir) approached, he was coldly received, and a deep cloud for some time darkened his countenance. Mossem-ood-Dowla is a fine, handsome man, with a keen eye, and a very intelligent, good-natured countenance. It was a painful sight to see him do homage to one who had no right to the throne, but through the power of an unjust law.

I was standing next to the Resident and the Prime Minister, when, during a part of the ceremony, a shower of precious stones was thrown over us; I looked at the Resident, and saw him move his arm to allow the valuables that had fallen upon him to drop to the ground; I imitated his example by moving my scarf, on which some were caught; it would have been *infra dig.* to have retained them; they fell to the ground, and were scrambled for by the natives; the shower consisted of emeralds, rubies, pearls, &c., &c.

A magnifique style of largesse!

After all the dresses of honour had been presented to the different persons, a hār (a necklace of gold and silver tinsel, very elegantly made,) was placed around the neck of each of the visitors; atr of roses was put on my hands, and on the hands of some other visitors, in compliment to the Resident, by his Majesty himself. Pān was presented, and rose water was sprinkled over us; after which ceremonies, we all made our bohut bohut udūb salām[2] to the King of Oude, and took our departure. The gold and silver tinsel hārs have been substituted for strings of pearl, which it was customary to present to visitors, until an order of government, promulgated four years ago, forbade the acceptance of presents.

The Zenāna

"LOVE AND MUSK DO NOT REMAIN CONCEALED."[3]

"WHEREVER THERE IS A FAIRY-FACED DAMSEL, SHE IS ATTENDED BY A DEMON."[4]

The following account of the Begams was given me by one whose life would have paid the forfeit, had it been known he had revealed the secrets of the zenāna; he desired me not to mention it at the time, or he should be murdered on quitting Oude.

[1] Oriental Proverbs.   [2] Most respectful reverence.
[3] Oriental Proverbs.   [4] Ibid.

Sultana Boa

"*The* Queen is the daughter of his Royal Highness Mirza Muhammad Sulimān Shekō, the own brother of the present Emperor of Delhi, Akbar Shāh.

"From the first day after marriage, neglected and ill-treated, she was only allowed, until lately, twenty rupees a day; she has now 2000 rupees a month, but is not permitted to leave her apartments; the servants of her family have all been discharged, and she is in fact a prisoner. Neither the King nor any of his family ever visit her, and no other person is permitted to approach her apartments.

"The lady of the Resident told me, 'She is a great beauty, the handsomest woman she ever saw;' I have seen her sister, and can easily believe she has not exaggerated. The Queen is now about sixteen or seventeen years old (1830), and has been married, I believe, about five years.

"Mirza Sulimān Shekō, the father, lived at Lucnow since the time of Ussuf-ood-Dowla, and was forced by the late King of Oude to give him his daughter in marriage. The *mehn* (dower) of the Princess was settled at five crores,[1] and the father had a grant of 5000 rupees a month, which is not paid; and in June, 1828, the Prince was insulted, and obliged to quit Lucnow with every sort of indignity."

Mulka Zumanee

"The second begam is the wife of Ramzānee, a cherkut or elephant servant, who is now pensioned on thirty rupees a month, and kept in surveillance at Sandee; some time after her marriage the lady proved naughty, and was next acknowledged as the *chère amie* of an itinerant barber; she left him, and took service with Mirza Jewad Ali Beg's family as a servant-of-all-work, on eight anās a month and her food. She was next heard of as a gram-grinder at——serai, where her eldest son, by name Tillooah, was born; her next child was a daughter.

"At this time Moonah Jāh (Feredooa Buckht) was born in the palace; and, amongst others who sought the situation of nurse, Ramzanee's wife attended; she was approved of by the hākims, and was installed nurse to the heir-apparent.

"Her age was then near forty, her size immoderate, her complexion the darkest; but she soon obtained such influence over the King, that he married her, and gave her the title of—(the daughter of the Emperor

[1] A karor is ten millions.

Furrukshere, and the wife of the Emperor Mohummud Shāh,)—Mulka Zumanee! Well may she exclaim, 'Oh Father! I have got into a strange difficulty, I have left off picking up cow-dung, and am employed in embroidery!'[1]

"She has a jagheer of 50,000 rupees a month, and the power of expending 50,000 rupees more from the treasury monthly. Her son Tillooah was about three years of age when she was entertained as nurse, but such was her power, that his Majesty publicly declared himself the father of the boy, and he was in consequence recognised as heir to the crown, with the title of Khema Jāh!"

The King has five queens, although by Mahummadan law he ought only to have four. His Majesty of Oude possesses, to a considerable extent, that peculiarly masculine faculty of retaining the *passion*, and changing the *object.*

He heeds not the proverb, "Do not put your heard into the hands of another."[2]

As far as I recollect the history of his last and favourite wife, it is this:

The Nawāb Hakīm Mehndi, finding his influence less than usual, adopted a Nāch girl as his daughter, because the King admired her, and induced his Majesty to marry her. Her name is Gosseina; she is not pretty, but possesses great influence over her royal lover. This girl, some fourteen months ago, was dancing at the Residency for twenty-five rupees a night: and a woman of such low caste not even a sā'is would have married her. The King now calls the hakīm his father-in-law, and says, "I have married your daughter, but you have not married her mother; I insist on your marrying her mother." The hakīm tries to fight off, and says he is too old; but the King often annoys him by asking when the marriage is to take place.

"There is no bird like a man,"[3] *i.e.* so volatile and unsteady.

The beautiful Tajmahŭl, whom I mentioned in Chapter 8, is entirely superseded by this Gosseina, the present reigning favourite; Tajmahŭl has taken to drinking, and all the King's drunken bouts are held at her house.

When he marched to Cawnpore, he took Tajmahŭl and Gosseina with him, and their retinue was immense. It is said, that the beautiful Timoorian, Sultana Boa, the Princess of Delhi, was so much disgusted at her father's being forced to give her in marriage to Nusseer-ood-Deen Hydur, and looked upon him as a man of such low caste, in comparison

[1] Oriental Proverbs.   [2] Ibid.   [3] Ibid.

with herself, that she never allowed him to enter her palace,—a virgin queen.

Her sister, Mulka Begam, married her first cousin, Mirza Selim, the son of the emperor, Akbār Shah; from whom she eloped with Mr. James Gardner, and to the latter she was afterwards married. This elopement was the cause of the greatest annoyance and distress to Col. Gardner, nor did he grant his forgiveness to his son for years afterwards.

Affairs being in so unpleasant a state at the Court of Lucnow, was the cause of Lady Wm. Bentinck's being unable to visit the zenāna; and after her ladyship's departure, I was prevented going there by the same reason.

One cannot be surprised at a Musulmān's taking advantage of the permission given him by his lawgiver with respect to a plurality of wives.

The Prophet himself did not set the best possible example in his own domestic circle, having had eighteen wives! Nevertheless, his code of laws respecting marriage restricted his followers to four wives, besides concubines.

In a book published in England, it is observed, "there are some instances of remarkable generosity in the conduct of good wives, which would hardly gain credit with females differently educated." This, being interpreted, means, a good wife provides new wives for her husband!

The King is very anxious the Resident should patronize Khema Jāh, his adopted son, and is much annoyed he can gain no control over so independent and noble-minded a man.

Chapter 16

The Return to Allahabad—
Execution of Twenty-Five Thugs

"WHO HAS SEEN TO-MORROW?"

i.e. Enjoy to-day, no one knows what will happen to-morrow.[1]

1831. *Feb.* 1*st*.—We quitted the Residency at Lucnow, feeling greatly gratified by the kindness we had experienced from the Resident, and returned
to Cawnpore.

We now prepared for our removal to Allahabad, the horses and carriages
having been dispatched by land; the furniture, &c., was put into six great
country boats, one of which, an immense 900 mŭn pataila, contained cows,
sheep, goats, besides a number of fowls, guinea-fowls, turkeys, &c.; and on
the top of all was a great thermantidote.

17*th*.—We quitted Cawnpore, and commenced our voyage down the
Ganges.

18*th*.—The low sandbanks in the river swarm with crocodiles; ten are
basking on a bank to the left of our boat, and five or six are just ahead. The
sāhib has fired at them several times, but they are beyond the reach of pistol
shot. They are timid animals; as soon as you approach them they dive down
into the river. We have only seen the long-nosed crocodiles, none of the snub-
nosed alligators. What a monster there is very near us, and such a winsome
wee one by its side! I want a baby crocodile very much for my cabinet.

At Sheorajpore our friends tried to tempt us to remain with them,
showing us a nil-gā'i, a wild boar, hares, black partridges, and the common
grey partridges, that they had shot; and offering us an elephant to enable
us to join the sportsmen the next day.

How much I enjoy the quietude of floating down the river, and admiring the picturesque ghāts and temples on its banks! This is the country of
the picturesque, and the banks of the river in parts are beautiful.

On the morning of our quitting Lucnow, my aide-de-camp, the young
Bhopaul chieftain, was made quite happy by being allowed to make his
salām to his Majesty, who gave him a dress of honour.

[1] Oriental Proverbs.

I can write no more; the sāhib's vessel has lugāoed, that is, has made fast to the bank; I must go out shooting with him, and mark the game.

19th.—We slept off Nobusta; the wind was very high, it blew a gale, but the high bank afforded us protection. Our boats are large, flat-bottomed, shallow, and broad country boats, on each of which a great house is built of bamboo and mats, and the roof is thatched. The interior is fitted up with coloured chintz, like that used for tents. Such unwieldy vessels are very likely to be upset in a storm. The great patailā, which contains the cows, &c., has given us much trouble; she has been aground several times, being, from her height and bulk, almost unmanageable in a strong wind.

It is very cold, the rain is falling fast; all the servants and the crew look so deplorable, and keep their shoulders to their ears. The horses on their march will be exposed to it; they are merely sheltered by a tree at night,— a cold berth for animals accustomed to warm stables.

20th.—This has been a day of rain and contrary wind; we have made but little way, and being unable to reach Mirzapore, have lugāoed off a sand-bank.

[. . .]

24th.—We arrived at Allahabad, and my husband took charge of his appointment. Then commenced dinner-parties given in honour of our return by our old friends at the station.

Am I not happy once more in dear old Prāg? We have no troubles as at Cawnpore; no one poisons our horses; all the people around us appear pleased at our return, and eager to serve us; our neighbours here are friends interested in our welfare. My old carpenters, the saddler, the ironsmith, the painter, the stonecutter, and the sealing-wax-maker, are all in their old nooks in the verandah.

March 1st.—It was so cold we had fires of an evening, which were not discontinued until the 5th of the month.

Our friend Capt. B—— is going home; he will tell those we love of our goings out and comings in, and will be as a connecting link to those, betwixt whom and us this great gulph of distance is fixed. It really requires an exile from home to be able to enjoy its blessings. He will, or ought to run about almost demented for the first year. Heaven prosper the good country! I hope to turn Hampshire hog myself, either here or hereafter, after the Pythagorean system.

The weather is becoming very hot; we are making our house look cool and comfortable, colouring it with French grey, and hanging pankhās in preparation for the hot winds. We hope to feel cool by the aid of a thermantidote, for which we are building a terrace and verandah.

𝔊round 𝔓lan of the 𝔗omb of the 𝔗āj.

Chapter 20

The Great Fair at Allahabad

"TALKING TO A MAN WHO IS IN ECSTACY (OF A RELIGIOUS NATURE PRACTISED OR FEIGNED BY FAKIRS) IS LIKE BEATING CURDS WITH A PESTLE."[1]

1833, *Jan.*—The burā mela at Prāg, or the great fair at Allahabad, is held annually on the sands of the Ganges below the ramparts of the Fort, extending from the Mahratta Bund to the extreme point of the sacred junction of the rivers. The booths extend the whole distance, composed of mud walls, covered with mats, or thatched. This fair lasts about two months, and attracts merchants from all parts of India, Calcutta, Delhi, Lucnow, Jeypore, &c. Very good diamonds, pearls, coral, shawls, cloth, woollens, China, furs, &c., are to be purchased. Numerous booths display brass and copper vessels, glittering in the sun with many brazen idols: others are filled with Benares' toys for children. Bows and arrows are displayed, also native caps made of sable, the crowns of which are of the richest gold and silver embroidery.

The pearl merchants offer long strings of large pearls for sale, amongst which some few are fine, round, and of a good colour. The natives value size, but are not very particular as to colour; they do not care to have them perfectly round, and do not object to an uneven surface. They will allow a purchaser to select the best at pleasure from long strings.

The deep red coral is valued by the natives much more than the pink. I bought some very fine pink coral at the fair: the beads were immense; the price of the largest, eleven rupees per tola; *i. e.* eleven rupees for one rupee weight of coral. The smallest, six or four rupees per tola; it was remarkably fine. Some years afterwards the Brija Bā'ī, a Mahratta lady, a friend of mine, called on me; she observed the long string of fine pink coral around my neck, and said, "I am astonished a mem sāhiba should wear coral; we only decorate our horses with it; that is pink coral, the colour is not good; look at my horse." I went to the verandah; her horse was adorned with a necklace of fine deep red coral. She was quite right, and I made over mine to my grey steed.

Some of the prettiest things sold at the Mela are the tīkas, an ornament

[1] Oriental Proverbs.

181

for the forehead for native women. The tīka is of different sizes and patterns; in gold or silver for the wealthy, tinsel for the poorer classes; and of various shapes. The prettiest are of silver, a little hollow cup like a dew-drop cut in halves: the ornament is stuck with an adhesive mixture on the forehead, just in the centre between the eyebrows. Some tīkas are larger, resembling the *ferronière* worn by European ladies.

The Allahabad hukāks are famous for their imitation in glass of precious stones. I purchased a number of native ornaments in imitation of the jewellery worn by native ladies, which were remarkably well made, and cost only a few rupees. I also bought strings of mock pearls brought from China, that are scarcely to be distinguished from real pearls, either in colour or weight.

The toys the rich natives give their children, consisting in imitations of all sorts of animals, are remarkably pretty; they are made in silver, and enamelled: others are made of ivory very beautifully carved; and for the poorer classes they are of pewter, moulded into the most marvellous shapes.

At this time of the year lākhs and lākhs of natives come to bathe at the junction of the Ganges and Jumna; they unite at the extremity of a neck of land, or rather sand, that runs out just below the Fort. On this holy spot the Brahmans and religious mendicants assemble in thousands. Each fakīr pitches a bamboo, from the end of which his flag is displayed, to which those of the same persuasion resort. Here they make pooja, shave, give money to the fakīr, and bathe at the junction. The clothes of the bathers are put upon charpāis to be taken care of, for so many pāisa. Every native, however poor he may be, pays tribute of one rupee to Government before he is allowed to bathe.

Two boats, by order of Government, are in attendance at this point to prevent persons from drowning themselves or their children. The mere act of bathing in the waters of the Gunga, on a particular day, removes ten sins, however enormous, committed in ten previous births. How much greater must be the efficacy at the junction of the Gunga and Yamuna, which the Saraswati, the third sacred river, is supposed to join underground! The benefits arising from bathing at the lucky moment of the conjunction of the moon with a particular star is very great, or at the time of eclipse of the sun or moon.

The holy waters are convenient for washing away a man's sins, and as efficacious as a pope's bull for this purpose. Groups of natives stand in the river whilst their Brahman reads to them, awaiting the happy moment at which to dip into the sacred and triple waves. They fast until the bathing is over. Suicide committed at the junction is meritorious in persons of a certain caste, but a *sin* for a Brahman!

The holy men prefer the loaves and fishes of this world to the immediate moksh or beatitude, without further risk of transmigration, which is awarded to those who die at the sacred junction.

Bathing will remove sins, gain admittance into heaven, and the devotee will be reborn on earth in an honourable station.

A married woman without children often vows to Gunga to cast her first-born into the river: this in former times was often done at Prāg, it now rarely occurs. If the infant's life is preserved, the mother cannot take it again.

Religious Mendicants

The most remarkable people at this Melā are the religious mendicants; they assemble by hundreds, and live within inclosures fenced off by sticks, a little distance from the booths. These people are the monks of the East; there are two orders of them; the Gosāins, or followers of Shivŭ, and the Byragies, disciples of Vishnoo. Any Mahomedan may become a fakīr, and a Hindoo of any caste, a religious mendicant. The ashes of cow-dung are considered purifying: these people are often rubbed over from head to foot with an ashen mixture, and have a strange dirty white, or rather blue appearance. Ganges mud, cow-dung, and ashes of cow-dung, form, I believe, the detectable mixture.

The sectarial marks or symbols are painted on their faces according to their caste, with a red, yellow, white, or brown pigment, also on their breasts and arms. Their only covering is a bit of rag passed between the legs and tied round the waist by a cord or rope.

One man whom I saw this day at the Melā was remarkably picturesque, and attracted my admiration. He was a religious mendicant, a disciple of Shivŭ. In stature he was short, and dreadfully lean, almost a skeleton. His long black hair, matted with cow-dung, was twisted like a turban round his head,—a filthy jŭta![1] On his forehead three horizontal lines were drawn with ashes, and a circlet beneath them marked in red sanders—his sectarial mark. If possible, they obtain the ashes from the hearth on which a consecrated fire has been lighted. His left arm he had held erect so long that the skin and flesh had withered, and clung round the bones most frightfully; the nails of the hand which had been kept immoveably clenched, had pierced through the palm, and grew out at the back of the hand like the long claws of a bird of prey. His horrible and skeleton-like arm was encircled by a twisted stick, the stem, perhaps, of a thick creeper, the end of which was cut into the shape of the head of the cobra de capello, with its

[1] Braided locks.

hood displayed, and the twisted withy looked like the body of the reptile wreathed around his horrible arm. His only garment, the skin of a tiger, thrown over his shoulders, and a bit of rag and rope at his waist. He was of a dirty-white or dirty-ashen colour from mud and paint; perhaps in imitation of Shivŭ, who, when he appeared on earth as a naked mendicant of an ashy colour, was recognized as Mahadēo the great god. This man was considered a very holy person. His right hand contained an empty gourd and a small rosary, and two long rosaries were around his neck of the rough beads called mundrāsee. His flag hung from the top of a bamboo, stuck in the ground by the side of a trident, the symbol of his caste, to which hung a sort of drum used by the mendicants. A very small and most beautifully formed little gynee (a dwarf cow) was with the man. She was decorated with crimson cloth, embroidered with cowrie shells, and a plume of peacock's feathers as a jika, rose from the top of her head. A brass bell was on her neck, and around her legs were anklets of the same metal. Numbers of fakīrs come to the sacred junction, each leading one of these little dwarf cows decorated with shells, cowries, coloured worsted tassels, peacock's feathers, and bells. Some are very small, about the size of a large European sheep, very fat and sleek, and are considered so sacred that they will not sell them.

Acts of severity towards the body, practised by religious mendicants, are not done as penances for sin, but as works of extraordinary merit, promising large rewards in a future state. The Byragee is not a penitent, but a proud ascetic. These people bear the character of being thieves and rascals.

Although the Hindoos keep their women parda-nishīn, that is, veiled and secluded behind the curtain, the fakīrs have the privilege of entering any house they please, and even of going into the zenāna; and so great is their influence over the natives, that if a religious mendicant enter a habitation leaving his slippers at the door, the husband may not enter his own house! They have the character of being great libertines.

On this day I purchased curious old china dished and brass circular locks of remarkable form. Also some brass idols that are scarce and very valuable. I have a large collection of idols of all sorts and sizes: some have undergone pooja for years, others are new.

[. . .]

Jan. 11*th.*—Some natives are at the door with the most beautiful snakes, two of them very large, and striped like tigers; the men carry them twisted round their bodies, and also round their necks, as a young lady wears a boa; the effect is good. The two tiger-striped ones were greatly admired as a well-matched pair; they are not venomous. A fine cobra, with his great hood spread out, made me shrink away as he came towards me, darting out his forked tongue.

There were also two snakes of a dun yellow colour, spotted with white, which appeared in a half torpid state; the men said they were as dangerous as the cobra. They had a biscobra; the poor reptile was quite lame, the people having broken all its four legs, to prevent its running away. They had a large black scorpion, but not so fine a fellow as that in my bottle of horrors.

The melā is very full; such beautiful dresses of real sable as I have seen to-day brought down by the Moguls for sale! Lined with shawl, they would make magnificent dressing-gowns. I have bought a Persian writing-case, and a book beautifully illuminated, and written in Persian and Arabic: the Moguls beguile me of my rupees.

We are going to a ball to-night at Mr. F——'s, given in honour of Lady Wm. Bentinck, who is expected to arrive this evening.[1] The natives have reported the failure of Messrs. Mackintosh & Co., in Calcutta; I do not think it is known amongst the Europeans here; the natives always get the first intelligence; I will not mention it, lest it should throw a shade over the gaiety of the party. An officer, who got the lākh, and 60,000 rupees also in the lottery last year, passed down the river to-day, to place it in Government security; it is all gone; a note has been despatched to inform him of the failure, and save him a useless trip of eight hundred miles; he lost twenty-five thousand only a few weeks ago, by Messrs. Alexander's failure. Lachhmī abides not in his house.

12th.—The ball went off very well, in spite of Messrs. Mackintosh's failure being known; and people who had lost their all danced as merrily as if the savings of years and years had not been swept away by "one fell swoop!"

20th.—It is so cold to-day, I am shivering; the cocoa-nut oil in the lamps is frozen slightly; this weather is fit for England. I must get all the bricklayer's work over before the hot winds, that I may be perfectly quiet during the fiery time of the year.

21st.—This being a great Hindoo holiday and bathing day, induced me to pay another visit to the fair. Amongst the tamāshā (sport) at the melā, was a Hindoo beggar, who was *sitting upon thorns*, up to his waist in water!—an agreeable amusement. One man played with his right hand on a curious instrument, called a been, while in his left hand he held two pieces of black stone, about the length and thickness of a finger, which he jarred

---

[1] William Fane, brother of Sir Henry Fane the Commander in Chief was the Collector and Deputy Opium Agent at Allahabad in 1829.

together in the most dexterous manner, producing an effect something like castanets, singing at the same time. The passers by threw cowries, pāisa (copper coins), and rice to the man.

I purchased two musical instruments, called surinda, generally used by the fakīrs, most curious things; Hindoo ornaments, idols, china, and some white marble images from Jeypore.

[. . .]

On platforms raised of mud and sand, some ten or twelve missionaries were preaching; every man had his platform to himself, and a crowd of natives surrounded each orator. Seeing one of my own servants, an Hindoo, apparently an attentive listener, I asked the man what he had heard. "How can I tell?" said he; "the English padre is talking." I explained to him the subject of the discourse, and received for answer, "Very well; it is their business to preach, they get pāisa for so doing; what more is to be said?"[2]

A large number of fine marble images having been brought down from Jeypore, for sale at the great fair, I sent a Rajpūt to the owner, and, after much delay and bargaining, became the possessor of the large white marble image of Gŭnéshŭ which adorns the frontispiece. The man had scruples with regard to allowing me to purchase the idol, but sold it willingly to the Rajpūt. In this place, I may as well describe the frontispiece. The history of Gŭnéshŭ is fully related in the Introduction.

[. . .]

Ram, the deified hero, with his bow of marvellous power, stands on the left of the shrine; the image is carved in white marble, painted and gilt, and is twenty-one inches in height.

[. . .]

On the right, Krishnŭ the beloved is playing on his pipe; the figure is of black marble . . .

[. . .]

On the second step of the altar, to the right of Gŭnéshŭ, the first figure, is that of a woman supporting a five-wicked lamp in her hands, which is used in pooja. The figure is of brass, and has a handle to it. The receptacles for oil or ghee are small, and of a mystic shape; a lamp of this description is called pancharty.

Next to this figure, on the same step, are two little chirāghs (lamps), with small cotton wicks; they are lighted; the little cups are of brass. Lamps of

---

[2] The missionaries had been banned until 1813 by the Charter of the Company; it was not until 1835 that there was much missionary activity.

this sort are burned before every shrine; and at the Dewālī, the temples and ghāts are illuminated with thousands of these chirāghs, which are then formed of red pottery.

Next to the lamps is a small lota, for carrying Ganges water, wherewith to bathe the idol.

Near them are two bells, which are used in pooja.

The bell (gant'ha) is essential in holy ceremonies, and is rung at certain times to scare away evil spirits. Bells are much used in and about Hindoo temples, but were rejected by Mahommedans, by order of their prophet, who deemed them relics of superstition. Those used by the Hindoos differ in make according to the deity in whose honour pooja is performed.

The bells are of brass; the handle of one of them is composed of two images of Hŭnoomān back to back; the handle of the other represents Hŭnoomān and Garuda, in the same attitude; on the top of the handle of another the holy cow is *couchant*.

The spouted vessel (jari) holds lustral water, and is of brass.

Next to the jari are three more lamps; and beyond them is a Nāga Linga Nandi, carved in black marble; it represents Nandī the bull kneeling and supporting a Linga on his back, in the centre of which rise Siva's five heads,—four heads supporting the fifth,—over which protrudes the head of a snake. The exterior is beaded; a snake is within it, the tail of which nearly reaches the end of the figure. The scale is too small to allow of a distinct representation.

On the first step of the altar, at the feet of the black marble image of Krishnŭ, is the bull-mouthed shell, which is considered holy, and often placed on a shrine. Shells as well as flowers as used for adornment.

The white conch shell (Sankh) has been described in the Introduction; the sankh or shŭnkhŭ, a shell conferring victory on whomsoever should sound it, was one of the fourteen articles, usually called fourteen gems, that were obtained at the churning of the sea. Shell ornaments worn by females on the wrist are prescribed by the Shastr. At the hour of death, a female leaves her ornaments to whomsoever she pleases; sometimes to her spiritual guide, or to the family priest. A person not bequeathing something to these people is followed to the next world with anathemas.

Next to the conch is a brazen lota, highly polished and engraved; it is used for Ganges water, oil, or ghee; water is always presented to bathe the idol.

The figure adjoining is a brazen image of Devi, a goddess (the term is generally applied to Doorga), but I know not of what particular goddess this is the representation. In her right hand she bears a mirror; in the left, a small lamp of mystic shape, similar to the boat-like argha. She stands upon a tortoise, which is made to contain Ganges water: the head of the tortoise unscrews, to admit the liquid. The Devi is ornamented with necklaces and bracelets; and in her ears are enormously thick ear-rings: to insert them, it is necessary to elongate the lobe of the ear; and having cut in it a slit nearly an inch in length, the end of the ear-ring is inserted. These ear-rings are worn by women of the lower orders, made of bamboo, painted and gilt. Some wear them of pewter, ornamented in colours; and some of the richer classes have them of silver, set with precious stones.

Against the edge of the step next to the Devi is a small circular copper-plate, the edges of which are scalloped. In front of it is another little plate made of brass, of which the interior is engraved.

The lustral spoons are called Sruva and Druva, in Sanscrit: by the Mahrattas and other Hindoos, Pulahi and Atchwan; and have different forms according to the rites or objects of adoration. One of the spoons represents Naga the holy serpent, overspreading Gŭnéshŭ; on the other, the Naga overspreads the image of some deity, of whose name I am ignorant; and on another; the spread hood of the snake appears to cover Hŭnoomān.

Next to the spoon is the argha, a vessel shaped like a boat, used by the Hindoos in lustrations; it is of spout-like form, so that liquids may be poured from it. Lustral ceremonies are deemed very important by Brahmans, and are attended to as prescribed in their books, with the most minute particularity. Images are frequently bathed with water, oil, &c.; indeed, there is no end to lustral ceremonies, and spoons and arghas are therefore in extensive use. In marriage, and in funeral ceremonies, as well as in the Sraddha, funeral obsequies in honour of deceased ancestors, an argha is indispensable.

In the centre of the shrine is a brazen image of Gunga the deified river, which was also procured at this great bathing festival. It represents a woman sitting on an alligator, or the sea animal Mŭkŭrŭ. One hand is open in charity, one forbids fear, one bears a water-lily, and the fourth a lota. She is the daughter of Mount Himavŭt. This idol is rare and valuable. Gunga-jee-ke-jy! "Victory to Gunga-jee!"

Other heathen nations appear to have held certain rivers sacred: hence, Naaman the Syrian said, "Are not Abana and Pharpar, rivers of Damascus, better than all the waters of Israel? May I not wash in them and be clean?"

The Dŭshŭhŭra festival is held in commemoration of Gunga's descent on earth. Crowds of people assemble from the different towns and villages near the river, especially at the most sacred places, bringing their offerings of fruit, rice, flowers, fresh garlands, cloth, sweetmeats, &c. "O goddess! the owl that lodges in the hollow of a tree on thy banks is exalted beyond measure; while the emperor, whose palace is far from thee, though he may possess a million of stately elephants, and may have the wives of millions of conquered enemies to serve him, is nothing."

The next object is a pair of small cymbals, which are sounded by the priest in time to his chanted prayer.

Beyond them is a large highly-ornamented circular brass dish, containing a peealu or brass drinking cup, in which is either oil or holy water: this cup has figures carved upon it. By its side is a small brass plate, filled with rice, which the devotee takes up in the spoon, and puts upon the head of the idol. Various sacred flowers are also carried in the circular dish, to strew over and before the god. In the early morning you often see the Hindoos, both men and women, going to a shrine with a circular brass dish of this description similarly filled.

The next figure is Hunooman, the monkey god, carrying Ram and Seeta on his shoulders in commemoration of his bringing them in safety from Ceylon.

Beyond this figure is a conch shell and another bull-mouthed shell; and thus ends the description of the shrine of Gŭnéshŭ in the frontispiece.

In front of my cabinet stands a very large Brahmanical bull, by name Chamélee, carved in white marble, painted and gilt. A curious Persian writing has just been offered to the Nandī (the bull), which Chamélee has been graciously pleased to accept and add to the cabinet over which he presides.

The image of the sacred bull in black or white marble is worshipped in the temples of the Hindoos.

Chapter 21

The Nut Log

1833, *Feb. 1st.*—The new hounds have just arrived; such little animals by the side of Jan Peter (Trumpeter) and Racer! Out of eight couple there is not a good dog; the gentlemen say three hundred rupees, *i.e.* £30, is a long price for dogs not worth their food, and who would be better out of than in the pack.

At the fair to-day, I purchased a gumuki, a sort of loose bag, the shape of a carpenter's square, large enough to admit the hand at one end, but sewed up at the other. It is made of blue cloth, embroidered with figures of the holy cow. A Hindoo will perform pooja seated on the ground, his right hand passed into a bag of this sort. His hand holds, and he counts most sedulously, a rosary of round beads (mālā), containing in number one hundred and eight, exclusive of connecting beads, differently shaped: the attention is abstractedly fixed on the deity, assisted by the rosary. Sometimes it is composed of amber, sometimes of certain rough berries sacred to the gods. Such rosaries, when used to promote abstraction, are called jap-mālā. During the time, a cloth is bound over his mouth, to prevent the entrance of insects; and he is supposed to be in holy meditation.

Feb. 22nd.—To-day is the Eed: it is customary for the Musulmāns to put on very gay new clothes on this day, and to go to prayers at the Jāmma Musjid, the large mosque on the banks of the Jumna. A camel is often sacrificed on the Buckra Eed, on the idea that the animal will be in readiness to carry the person who offers it over the bridge of Sirraat, safe to heaven. The poorer classes will offer a goat (Buckra), or a sheep, lambs, or kids. This festival is to commemorate Abraham's sacrifice of Isaac. The Musulmāns contend it was Ishmael not Isaac who was the offering.

I have lost my companion, my horse Trelawny: he was so quiet, and good-tempered, and good-looking; he was as pretty a boy as Hindoo or Musulmān might look on in the Central Provinces. Poor Trelawny, Jumna-jee rolls over my good steed! He died this morning of inflammation, caused by some internal injury he received when we were plunging together in the quicksands on the banks of the Ganges.

I am reading Captain Mundy's "Sketches in India," a much more amusing journal than I can write. I have no tigers to kill, no hurdwar to visit; nor have I even seen the taj. His journal is very spirited, very correct, and very amusing; I am pleased to hear the praises bestowed upon it in England.[1]

Have you heard of the Rev. Joseph Wolff? He is a German Jew converted to the faith of Christ: "Unto the Jews a stumbling-block, and unto the Greeks foolishness." He roams about the world in search of the lost tribes of Israel, "preaching Christ, and him crucified," in the churches, and delivering lectures on the subject of the divinity of our Saviour, and his own wanderings. When at Simla, he was with Lord William Bentinck, and preached every Sunday in the presence of the Governor-general, which he would not have been allowed to do had he not been an ordained clergyman. He arrived here three days ago. In the evening he delivered a lecture in the Fort, which was attended by all the inhabitants of Allahabad. Curiosity is, I fear, stronger than religion; for I never before saw the church so crowded.[2]

My husband accompanied me to hear Mr. Wolff. He is a strange and most curious-looking man; in stature short and thin; and his weak frame appears very unfit to bear the trials and hardships to which he has been, and will be, exposed in his travels. His face is very flat, deeply marked with small-pox; his complexion that of dough, and his hair flaxen. His grey eyes roll and start, and fix themselves, at times, most fearfully; they have a cast in them, which renders their expression still wilder. Being a German, and by birth a Jew, his pronunciation of English is very remarkable; at times it is difficult to understand him: however, his foreign accent only gives originality to his lectures, aided occasionally by vehement gesticulation. His voice is deep and impressive; at times, having given way to great and deep enthusiasm, and having arrested the attention of his hearers, he sinks at once down into some common-place remark, his voice becoming a most curious treble, the effect of which is so startling, one can scarcely refrain from laughter. He understands English very well; his language is excellent, but evidently borrowed more from reading than from conversation. He makes use of words never used in common *parlance*, but always well and forcibly applied. He carries you along with him in his travels, presenting before you the different scenes he has witnessed, and pointing out those customs and manners still in use, which prove the truth of Scripture. His

[1] Captain Mundy must have met Fanny Parkes in Lucknow in 1827. His *Pen and Pencil Sketches being the journal of a tour in India* was published in 1832.

[2] Dr Joseph Wolff (1795–1862) had travelled widely and had been received by Ranjit Singh at Amritsar. An account, by Fitzroy Maclean in 1958, was written of his journey to Bokhara, where he tried to rescue two captive Englishmen.

descriptions at times are very forcible, and his account of the lives of St. Augustine and other holy men very interesting.

[. . .]

21st.—We have had heavy storms, with hailstones of most surprising magnitude; I wish the wind would change; the new moon has "the old moon in her arms," and if the wind change not now, we shall still have to endure this dreadful weather. The garden is a cake of parched white earth, all split and cracked.

What plagues these servants are! This morning, one of the cows being very ill, I ordered a mixture for her; at sunset it had not been given to her, because, to use the man's own words, "he wished to send a man into the district, to dig up a *certain sort of rat*, which rat, having been mixed up with hot spices, he would give to the cow, and she would be well!"

Very provoking! the animal will die on account of not having had a proper remedy administered in time. One has to fight against the climate and the servants until one is weary of life.

23rd.—Such a disaster in the quail-house! Through the negligence, or rather stupidity, of the khānsāmān, 160 fat quail have been killed.

June 1st.—The Muharram is over; I am glad of it, it unsettles all the servants so much, and nothing is ever well done whilst they are thinking of the Taziya.

4th.—Last night we drove to the churchyard, to visit the tomb of one of the most charming girls I ever met with, who had departed in her youth and beauty's prime: it was a melancholy visit.

One of the Fitzclarences died at Allahabad, and was buried here, without any name or inscription on the tomb; within the last six months an inscription has been put upon it, by order of Lord William Bentinck.

In the churchyard was a great number of plants of the mādār or ark, (asclepias gigantea,) gigantic swallow-wort. Upon them we found the most beautifully spotted creatures, like enamelled grasshoppers; they appear partial to this plant, the ark; when alive, their spots are most beautiful, in dying, all their brilliancy vanishes. I gathered a quantity of the fine down from the pods of the mādār, and gave it to a gentleman fond of experiments, who says he will weave it as a shawl is woven, and see if it will answer.

[. . .]

The Great Gun at Agra

"The utmost offer that has yet been made for the metal of the great gun is sixteen rupees per maund; it is proposed to put it up now for sale by auction, at the Agra-Kotwallee, in the course of next month; the upset price of the lots to be fourteen ānās per seer.

"The destruction of the Agra gun, our readers are aware, has, for some time past, been entrusted to the executive engineer. As stated in the last *Meerut Observer*, an attempt was made first to saw, and afterwards it was intended to break it to pieces. In the mean time, it is lying, like Robinson Crusoe's boat, perfectly impracticable under the fort. Though there is a tradition in the city of its weight being 1600 maunds, it has not been found, on actual measurement, to contain more than 845 mds. 9 s., which, at the rate of two lbs. to the seer, would be equal to 30 tons, 3 cwt. 2 qrs. 18 lbs. The analysis of the filings made by the deputy Assay Master in Calcutta was, we understand, as

	Copper.	Tin.
1	29.7	7.3
2	92.2	7.8
3	88.3	11.7
Mean	91.06	8.94

"The gun, from its size, is naturally regarded by the native population as one of the lions of our city. Of the Hindoos, too, many are accustomed to address their adorations to it, as they do, indeed, to all the arms of war, as the *roop* of Devee, the Indian Hecate. Beyond this, Hindoo tradition has not invested the gun with any character of mythological sanctity. The antiquaries of our city, indeed, say that it was brought here by the Emperor Acbar, perhaps from the fortress of Chittore. We have, however, ourselves been unable to find any mention of it in *tawareek* of that reign, or of any subsequent period. Among its other just claims to be saved from the hands of the *Thatheras*, we must not forget the fact of its having once fired a shot from Agra to Futtehpoor Sicri, a distance of twenty-four miles. A stone ball now marks the spot where it fell to the student in artillery practice, putting him entirely out of conceit of the vaunted power of Queen Elizabeth's pocket pistol, which we believe can scarcely carry one-third of that distance. The fellow of the Agra gun is stated to be still embedded in the sands of the Jumna.

"Its destruction seems as unpopular with the natives as it is with the European community. Its doom, however, being, we believe, sealed, we are gratified to think that the proceeds of its sale are to be devoted to the erection of a permanent bridge of boats over the Jumna at this city, the estimate for which, the supposed value of the gun, with an advance of one or two years' ferry tolls, is expected to meet. The future surplus funds derived from the bridge will probably, we hear, be expended in forming a new branch road from Raj-ghaut to Mynpoory, to unite with the grand trunk now making between Allahabad and Delhi, under Captain Drummond.

We shall, however, postpone till another opportunity our remarks on this and other plans to improve the means of communication in this quarter."— *Mofussil Achbar.*

"At five o'clock on Wednesday morning, the Great Gun at this place was burst, other means of breaking it up having proved unsuccessful, The gun was buried about twenty feet deep in the ground, and 1000 lbs. of gun-powder was employed for the explosion. The report was scarcely heard, but the ground was considerably agitated, and a large quantity of the earth was thrown on all sides. As far as we can learn, the chief engineer has at length been completely successful. A large portion of the European community and multitudes of natives were present to witness the novel spectacle. The inhabitants of the city were so alarmed, that a considerable portion abandoned their houses, and that part of the town in the vicinity of the Fort was completely deserted."—*Mofussil Achbar, June 29.*

July 18th.—Last night, as I was writing a long description of the tēz-pāt, the leaf of the cinnamon-tree, which humbly pickles beef, leaving the honour of crowning heroes to the *laurus nobilis*, the servants set up a hue and cry that one of our sā'īses had been bitten by a snake. I gave the man a teaspoonful of eau-de-luce, which the khānsāmān calls "Blue-dee-roo," mixed with a little water.[3] They had confined the snake in a kedgeree-pot, out of which he jumped into the midst of the servants; how they ran! The sā'īs is not the worse for the fright, the snake not being a poisonous one; but he says the mem sāhiba has burnt up his interior and blistered his mouth with the medicine. I hope you admire the corruption of eau-de-luce—blue-dee-roo! Another beautiful corruption of the wine-coolers is, soup-tureen for sauterne! Here is a list of absurdities:—

Harrico, harry cook.	Butcher, voucher.
Parsley, peter selly.	Prisoner, bridgeman.
Mignionette, major mint.	Champagne, simkin.
Bubble-and-squeak, dublin cook.	Trumpeter, jan peter.
Decree, diggery.	Brigade major, bridget.
Christmas, kiss miss.	Knole cole, old kooby.

An officer in the 16th Lancers told me he was amused the other day by his servant designating the trumpeter a "poh poh walla."

The gardener has just brought in a handful of the most beautiful *scarlet velvet* coloured insects, about the size of two large peas, but flattish, and commonly found on reddish sandy soil, near grass; these insects are used

---

[3] Eau de luce was made of alcohol, ammonia and oil of amber.

as one of those medicines which native doctors consider efficacious in snake bites: they call them beerbotie; the scientific name is *mutella occidentalis*.

The carpenter, in cutting down the hedge of the garden, found in the babūl and neem-trees such beautiful creatures; they appear to be locusts; the variety and brilliancy of their colours are wonderful. The upper wings are green, lined out with yellow, the under wings scarlet, the body green, yellow, and black: they are most beautifully marked. I have had some prepared with arsenical soap.
[. . .]

Chapter 22

The Cholera

"IT WAS HAMMERED UPON MY FOREHEAD."[1]
i.e. It was my destiny.

"WHERE IS THE USE OF TAKING PRECAUTIONS, SINCE
WHAT HAS BEEN PREORDAINED MUST HAPPEN?"[2]

1833. *Aug. 8th.*—The same terrible weather continues, the thermometer 90° and 91° all day; not a drop of rain! They prophesy sickness and famine; the air is unwholesome; the Europeans are all suffering with fever and ague and rheumatism. The natives, in a dreadful state, are dying in numbers daily of cholera; two days ago, seventy-six natives in Allahabad were seized with cholera—of these, forty-eight died that day! The illness is so severe that half an hour after the first attack the man generally dies; if he survive one hour it is reckoned a length of time.

A brickmaker, living near our gates, buried four of his family from cholera in one day! Is not this dreadful? The poor people, terror-stricken,

[1] Oriental Proverbs.   [2] Ibid.

are afraid of eating their food, as they say the disease follows a full meal. Since our arrival in India we have never before experienced such severely hot winds, or such unhealthy rains.

"Every country hath its own fashions."[1] The Hindoo women, in the most curious manner, propitiate the goddess who brings all this illness into the bazār: they go out in the evening about 7 P.M., sometimes two or three hundred at a time, carrying each a lota, or brass vessel, filled with sugar, water, cloves, &c. In the first place they make pooja; then, stripping off their chādars, and binding their sole petticoat around their waists, as high above the knee as it can be pulled up, they perform a most frantic sort of dance, forming themselves into a circle, whilst in the centre of the circle about five or six women dance entirely naked, beating their hands together over their heads, and then applying them behind with a great smack, that keeps time with the music, and with the song they scream out all the time, accompanied by native instruments, played by men who stand at a distance; to the sound of which these women dance and sing, looking like frantic creatures. Last night, returning from a drive, passing the Fort, I saw five or six women dancing and whipping themselves after this fashion; fortunately, my companion did not comprehend what they were about. The Hindoo women alone practise this curious method of driving away diseases from the bazār; the Musulmānes never. The men avoid the spot where the ceremony takes place; but here and there, one or two men may be seen looking on, whose presence does not appear to molest the nut-brown dancers in the least; they shriek and sing and smack and scream most marvellously.

The moonshee tells me the panic amongst the natives is so great, that they talk of deserting Allahabad until the cholera has passed away.

My darzee (tailor), a fine healthy young Musulmān, went home at 5 P.M., apparently quite well; he died of cholera at 3 P.M., the next day; he had every care and attention. This evening the under-gardener has been seized; I sent him medicine; he returned it, saying, "I am a Baghut (a Hindoo who neither eats meat nor drinks wine), I cannot take your medicine; it were better that I should die." The cholera came across the Jumna to the city, thence it took its course up *one side* of the road to the Circuit Bungalow, is now in cantonments, and will, I trust, pass on to Papamhow, cross the Ganges, and Allahabad will once more be a healthy place.

"Magic is truth, but the magician is an infidel."[2] My ayha said, "You have told us several times that rain will fall, and your words have been true; perhaps you can tell us when the cholera will quit the city?" I told her, "Rain will fall, in all probability, next Thursday (new moon); and if there

[1] Oriental Proverbs.   [2] Ibid.

be plenty of it, the cholera may quit the city." She is off to the bazār with the joyful tidings.

The Muhammadans believe the prayers of those who consult magicians are not accepted, and that rain is given by the favour of God, not by the influence of the moon. Muhammad forbade consulting fortune-tellers, and gave a curious reason why they sometimes hit on the truth. "Aa'yeshah said, 'People asked the Prophet about fortune-tellers, whether they spoke true or not?' He said, 'You must not believe any thing they say.' The people said, 'O messenger of God! wherefore do you say so? because they sometimes tell true.' Then his Highness said, 'Yes; it may be true sometimes, because one of the genii steals away the truth, and carries it to the magician's ear; and magicians mix a hundred lies with one truth.' 'Aa'yeshah said, 'I heard his Majesty say, 'The angels come down to the region next the world, and mention the works that have been pre-ordained in Heaven; and the devils, who descend to the lowest region, listen to what the angels say, and hear the orders pre-destined in Heaven, and carry them to fortune-tellers; therefore they tell a hundred lies with it from themselves.' 'Whoever goes to a magician, and asks him any thing about the hidden, his prayers will not be approved of for forty nights and days.' Zaid-Vin-Rhalid said, 'His Highness officiated as Imām to us in Hudaibiah, after a fall of rain in the night; and when he had finished prayers, he turned himself to the congregation, and said, 'Do ye know what your Cherisher said?' They said, 'God and his messenger know best.' His Highness said, 'God said, Two descriptions of my servants rose this morning, one of them believers in me, the other infidels; wherefore, those who have said they have been given rain by the favour of God, are believers in me, and deniers of stars; and those who have said, we have been given rain from the influence of the moon are infidels, and believers in stars.'" "An astrologer is as a magician, and a magician is a necromancer, and a necromancer is an infidel."[1]

Aug. 17th.—The new moon has appeared, but Prāg is unblessed with rain; if it would but fall! Every night the Hindoos pooja their gods; the Musulmāns weary Heaven with prayers, at the Jamma Musjid (great mosque) on the river-side, near our house;—all to no effect. The clouds hang dark and heavily; the thunder rolls at times; you think, "Now the rain must come," but it clears off with scarcely a sprinkling. Amongst the Europeans there is much illness, but no cholera.

22nd.—These natives are curious people; they have twice sent the cholera over the river, to get rid of it at Allahabad. They proceed after this fashion: they take a bull, and after having repeated divers prayers and ceremonies,

[1] Mishcat ul Masabih.

they drive him across the Ganges into Oude, laden, as they believe, with the cholera. This year this ceremony has been twice performed. When the people drive the bull into the river, he swims across, and lands or attempts to land on the Lucnow side; the Oude people drive the poor beast back again, when he is generally carried down by the current and drowned, as they will not allow him to land on either side.

During the night, my ayha came to me three times for cholera mixture; happily the rain was falling, and I thought it would do much more good than all the medicine; of course I gave her the latter.

Out of sixty deaths there will be forty Hindoos to twenty Musulmāns; more men are carried off than women, eight men to two women; the Musulmāns eat more nourishing food than the Hindoos, and the women are less exposed to the sun than the men.

[. . .]

26th.—I was sitting in my dressing-room, reading, and thinking of retiring to rest, when the khānsāmān ran to the door, and cried out, "Mem Sāhiba, did you feel the earthquake? the dishes and glasses in the almirahs (wardrobes) are all rattling." I heard the rumbling noise, but did not feel the quaking of the earth. About half-past eleven, P.M., a very severe shock came on, with a loud and rumbling noise; it sounded at first as if a four-wheeled carriage had driven up to the door, and then the noise appeared to be just under my feet; my chair and the table shook visibly, the mirror of the dressing-glass swung forwards, and two of the doors nearest my chair opened from the shock. The house shook so much, I felt sick and giddy; I thought I should fall if I were to try to walk; I called out many times to my husband, but he was asleep on the sofa in the next room, and heard me not; not liking it at all, I ran into the next room, and awoke him; as I sat with him on the sofa, it shook very much from another shock, or rather shocks, for there appeared to be many of them; and the table trembled also. My ayha came in from the verandah, and said, "The river is all in motion, in waves, as if a great wind were blowing against the stream." The natives say tiles fell from several houses. A shoeing-horn, that was hanging by a string to the side of my dressing-glass, swung backwards and forwards like the pendulum of a clock. The giddy and sick sensation one experiences during the time of an earthquake is not agreeable; we had one in September, 1831, but it was nothing in comparison to that we have just experienced. Mr. D—— and Mr. C——, who live nearly three miles off, ran out of their bungalows in alarm.

Sept. 5*th.*—The rain fell in torrents all night; it was delightful to listen to it, sounding as it was caught in the great water jars, which are placed all round the house; now and then a badly made jar cracked with a loud report, and out rushed the water, a proof that most of the jars would be full by morning. From the flat clean pukkā roof of the house the water falls pure and fresh; from the thatch of a bungalow it would be impure. To-day it is so dark, so damp, so English, not a glimpse of the sun, a heavy atmosphere, and rain still falling delightfully. There is but little cholera now left in the city; this rain will carry it all away.

Our friend Mr. S—— arrived yesterday: he was robbed ere he quitted Jaunpore of almost all he possessed: the thieves carried off all his property from the bungalow, with the exception of his sola topī, a great broad-brimmed white hat, made of the pith of the sola.

The best sola hats are made in Calcutta; they are very light, and an excellent defence from the sun: the root of which the topī is formed is like pith; it is cut into thin layers, which are pasted together to form the hat. At Meerut they cover them with the skin of the pelican, with all its feathers on, which renders it impervious to sun or rain; and the feathers sticking out beyond the rim of the hat give a demented air to the wearer. The pelicans are shot in the Tarāī.

"Shola (commonly sola), (æschynomene paludosa), the wood of which, being very light and spongy, is used by fishermen for floating their nets. A variety of toys, such as artificial birds and flowers, are made of it. Garlands of those flowers are used in marriage ceremonies. When charred it answers the purpose of tinder."[1]

How dangerous the banks of the river are at this season! Mr. M—— lugāoed his boats under a bank on the Ganges; during the night a great portion of the bank fell in, swamped the dog-boat, and drowned all the dogs. Our friend himself narrowly escaped: his budjerow broke from her moorings, and went off into the middle of the stream.

19*th.*—The weather killingly hot! I can do nothing but read novels and take lessons on the sitar. I wish you could see my instructor, a native, who is sitting on the ground before me, playing difficult variations, contorting his face, and twisting his body into the most laughable attitudes, the man in ecstacies at his own performance!

Consumption of Ice

One of the most striking instances of the enterprise of the merchants of the present age, is the importation of a cargo of ice into India from the distant shores of America; and it is to be hoped, that the experiment having so far succeeded, it will receive sufficient encouragement here to ensure the

[1] Shakespear's Dict.

community in future a constant supply of the luxury. The speculators are Messrs. Tudor, Rogers, and Austin, the first of whom has been engaged for fifteen or twenty years in furnishing supplies of ice to the southern parts of America and the West Indian islands.

The following particulars will furnish an idea of the plan pursued in this traffic, and of the cost incurred in it:—

The ice is cut from the surface of some ponds rented for the purpose in the neighbourhood of Boston, and being properly stowed, is then conveyed to an ice-house in the city, where it remains until transported on board the vessel which has to convey it to its destined market. It is always kept packed in non-conducting materials, such as tan, hay, and pine boards, and the vessel in which it is freighted has an ice-house built within, for the purpose of securing it from the effects of the atmosphere. The expense to the speculators must be very considerable, when they have to meet the charges of rent for the ponds, wages for superintendents and labourers, and agents at the place of sale; erection of ice-houses, transportation of the article from the ponds to the city, thence to the vessel, freight, packing, and landing, and the delivery of the article at the ice-house which has been built for it in Calcutta.

The present cargo has arrived without greater wastage than was at first calculated on, and the packing was so well managed to prevent its being affected by the atmosphere, that the temperature on board during the voyage was not perceptibly altered. This large importation of ice may probably give rise to experiments to ascertain in what way it may be applied to medicinal uses, as it has already elsewhere been resorted to for such purposes; but the chief interest the community generally will take in it, will be the addition it will make to domestic comfort.

[. . .]

All the three Residencies are agog about steam navigation once again.[1] I think there is a fair chance of success, if the whole of the funds are voted in support of the Bombay scheme, by which communication might be established in fifty days; and if the overland dāk from Bombay was put on a more speedy footing, we might hear from England within two months. Nearly £15,000 has been already subscribed, and the work of collection still

---

[1] In 1825 the *Enterprise* sailed to India via the Cape partly by steam and partly by sail, taking four months for the journey. In 1830, it was decided to use the Red Sea route to carry the official mail and the *Hugh Lindsay* steamed from Bombay to Suez taking twenty-two days. The journey continued from Suez to Alexandria by camel and by French ship to Europe. In 1857 a regular service was established by P & O from Southampton to Alexandria; from there passengers travelled by rail to Cairo and by mule to Suez. Within ten years, the Suez Canal was opened.

goes on: the newspapers are flattering the rich baboos, and dependent and independent Rajahs, and some have given their thousands.

The interference with the Company's charter, that people in England may drink their tea cheaper, which result, however, appears doubtful, and that the surplus population may come out to colonize, and *cholerize*, has done the Service no benefit. Economy is still the rage, and we of the present day have nothing to look to but the pension from our Civil Annuity Fund, after twenty-two years' actual residence, of £1000, for which we are to pay one-half, or 50,000 rupees, when we can hoard up as much. The generality of men's lives after twenty-two years' residence, and twenty-five of service, three years of these being allowed for furlough, which few are able to take, is scarcely worth five years' purchase. Numbers, of course, do not live out their time; and if they have subscribed for twenty-one years and eleven months, the whole goes to the fund, principal and interest.

Nov. 3rd.—There are some most wondrous animals called Gungun Medha, or Bāgh-sira, the latter Hindoo word meaning tiger-headed, from the shape of the animal's horrible head. I was told they could be dug out of the sands on the river-side. I therefore sent the jamadar and a cooly across the river this morning, and they brought back eight or nine of these beasts; their wings curl up in a most singular fashion, and make them appear as if they had four curly tails, all close together; their great jawbones are edged like a coarse saw. They are very fierce; they fight, kill each other, and the conqueror eats up his adversary. Their legs and wings are most remarkable. We put two under a wire dish-cover, and they fought fiercely, although, from having been dug up some hours, they were not as active as at first. They bite terribly; it is necessary to seize them by their backs like crabs to avoid a bite.

I had some Sarāta lizards dug out of the sands near the Parade ground; they are not half as curious as these tiger-headed beasts, which are in thousands in the sand-banks, their holes six or seven feet deep. A Rajpūt Rana of high degree has pitched his tents in Alopee Bāgh: nineteen guns were fired in honour of his arrival. This great man has a numerous retinue: to bathe at the sacred junction of the rivers has brought him to Prāg. I drove a young lady through his encampment the other evening; many of his people came out of their tents, and absolutely ran on by the side of our carriage, staring at us as if we were bāgh-siras (grylli monstrosi), or animals as wonderful.

Their astonishment was great, occasioned most likely by the sight of unveiled ladies driving about. Passing through the encampment was a service of danger; it was difficult, in keeping clear of the teeth of the camels, not to run against a number of stalls where cakes and sugar were displayed for sale. No sight do I like better than a native encampment; the groups of strange-looking men, the Arab horses, the camels, elephants, and tents are charming. No country can furnish more or so many picturesque scenes as India.

Dec. 5th.—People talk of wonderful storms of hail. I have just witnessed one so very severe, that had I not seen it, I think I should scarcely have believed it. At ten at night a storm, accompanied by thunder and lightning, came on; the hail fell as thick as flakes of snow,—I can scarcely call it hail, the pieces were ice-bolts. I brought in some which measured four inches and a half in circumference, and the ground was covered some inches deep; it appeared as if spread with a white sheet, when by the aid of the lightning one could see through the darkness around. The old peepul-tree groaned most bitterly, the glass windows were all broken, the tobacco-plants cut down, the great leaves from the young banyan-tree were cut off, and the small twigs from the mango and nīm trees covered the ground like a green carpet. It was a fearful storm. The next morning for miles round you saw the effect of the hail, and in the bazār at eight A.M. the children were playing marbles with the hailstones.

31st.—I trust we have now become *acclimated*, for we have nearly passed through this year,—the most fruitful in illness and death I recollect, both among civilians and soldiers,—without much sickness. I have had fever and ague. My husband has suffered from acute rheumatism, and the little pet terrier, Fury, has been delicate, but we are all now re-established. I am on horseback every morning rejoicing in the cold breezes, feeling as strong and full of spirit as the long-tailed grey that carries me; and Fury is chasing squirrels and ferrets, and putting the farm-yard to the rout.

The Imàms the Leaders of the Faithful

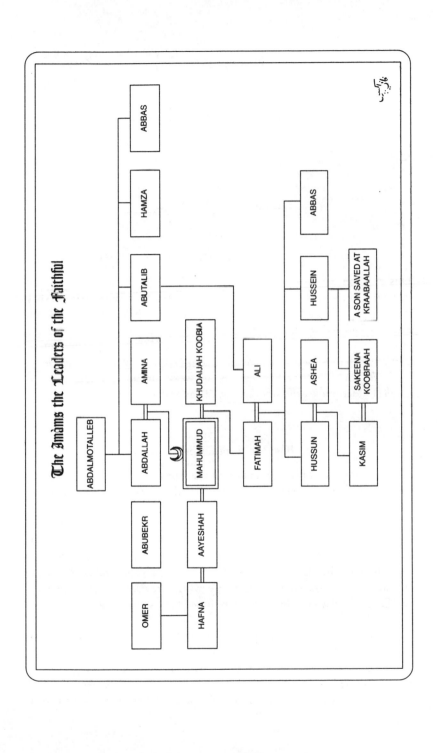

Chapter 23

The Muharram

بسم الله الرحمن الرحيم

"BISM ILLAH UR RAHMAN UR RAHĪM."

"IN THE NAME OF GOD, THE COMPASSIONATE, THE MERCIFUL."

This is written at the commencement of all Persian books and writings; but at the top of the first page of every letter, purwanah, or short writing, they almost invariably put only the letter A or ALIF, which is a symbol of God, and is considered an abbreviation of the whole sentence above. Alif is the first letter in the Arabic and Persian alphabets, and in the representation of numbers it stands for *one*; whence it is also used as a symbol of the Deity; it signifies moreover the first day in the week, or Sunday; and in astronomical descriptions, the sign Taurus of the zodiac.

[...]

The Muharram Ceremony

The ceremony takes place annually on the first day of the moon (Muharram). Their year has twelve moons only, and they do not add a moon every third year, as some persons suppose.

The Imām-bara is expressly built for commemorating the Muharram. In this building the Taziya is placed facing Mecca, with the banners, the sword, the shield, and the bow and arrows supposed to have been used in the battle of Kraabaallah. The most magnificent Taziyas remain in the Imā-bara. The less costly, which are used in the processions on the tenth day, are buried, with funeral rites, in cemeteries named Kraabaallah.

Although the Taziya, the model of their Imām's tomb, at Kraabaallah belongs, by right, only to the Sheas, it is remarkable that many Soonees have Taziyas, and also some Hindoos. My cook, who was a Mug, used to expend sometimes as much as forty rupees on a Taziya of his own; and after having performed all the ceremonies like a good Musúlmān, returned to his original Hindooism, when he had placed his Taziya in the burial-ground, accompanied by rice, corn, flowers, cups of water, &c.

But little or no attention is paid to the models of the Taziya: they are of different forms, and of every variety of material, according to the wealth of the person who sets up this remembrance of Hussein. On the Taziya is placed a small portion of corn, rice, bread, fruits, flowers, and cups of water; this is in accordance with the Musulmān funerals, at which food is invariably conveyed to the tomb with the corpse.

The Taziya displayed by the king of Oude during the Muharram is composed of green glass, with or-molu or brass mouldings. Some are of ivory, ebony, sandal-wood, cedar, &c., or of wrought filligree silver: those for the poor are of coloured tale.

In front of the Taziya two standards are erected, between which are laid strings of the fresh flowers of the sweet-scented bela (jasmine); and a chaunrī, made of the tail of the yāk, fixed in a silver handle, is used to fan away the flies.

When the Taziya is placed in the Imām-bara, the face is turned to Mecca. The institution of carrying the Taziya in procession first took place in the A.H. 352, at Bagdad, under Noez-od-Dowla Dhelmé, and is never omitted in Persia.

Hussein, on his favourite horse Dhul Dhul, was pierced by arrows without number; the animal shared the same fate, ...
....

with the exception of one infant son and the females of the family. ....
....
....
.... [1]

The usual arrangement of the procession is as follows:—In the order of march the elephants first appear, on which men are seated, displaying the consecrated banners, crowned by the spread hand. The banners are of silk, embroidered in gold or silver. The spread hand on the top of them represents five: Muhammad, Fátíma, Ali, Hussun, Hussein; the three fingers, the Caliphas Omer, Osmun, and Abubekr. The Soonees favour the latter; the Sheas uphold Imām Ali. The ends of the banners are fringed with bullion, and they are tied with cords of gold. Then follows the band, which is always in attendance, and is composed of Arab music only.

The jilādār or sword-bearer carries a pole, from which two naked swords, each tipped with a lemon, are suspended from a bow reversed. The arrows

---

[1] Two short passages were omitted here from the 1973 edition.

are fixed in the centre. The sword-bearer is generally dressed in green, the mourning colour of the Syuds. The standard-bearers and a band of musicians attend him, carrying the banner of Hussun and Hussein.

Some men, the mourners of the procession, bear long black poles, on which are fixed very long streamers of black unspun silk, which are intended to represent grief and despair.

The horse Dhul Dhul next appears: in the procession he sometimes bears a Taziya, at other times he is caparisoned as if in readiness for his master. After the Muharram, the animal and all its attire are given to a poor Syud; the bloody horsecloth and the legs stained red, are supposed to represent the sufferings of the animal. The tail and mane are dyed with mehndī or lakh dye. The horse is attended by a man carrying the afthaadah, which is a sun embroidered on crimson velvet, affixed to the end of a long staff, and carried in an elevated position, in order to shelter a man of rank on horseback from the rays of the sun. Men with chaunrīs attend to whisk away the flies from the horse: assa burdars, men with long silver sticks, and sonta burdars, with short silver tiger-headed staffs, walk at the side, and harkāras (running footmen) are in attendance. An embroidered chatr (umbrella) is supported over the head of the horse.

In the cavalcade is a chaunter or reader; he repeats affecting passages descriptive of the death of Hussein, during which time the procession halts for a few minutes, whilst the Musulmāns give way to the most frantic expressions of grief, beating their breasts with violence, throwing dust upon their heads, and exclaiming "Hussun! Hussein! Hussun! Hussein!"

The Paīk, a Fakīr, is a remarkable person, wearing the bow, arrows, sword, pankhā, and chaunrī of the martyred Imām. Some men in the procession carry censers, suspended by chains, which they wave about, and perfume the air with the incense of a sweet-scented resin; rose-water, for sprinkling, is also carried in long-necked bottles, called gulāb-pash.

Then follows the Taziya, attended by its proprietor, his relatives, and friends; it is surrounded by banners, and covered by a canopy upheld by poles supported by men.

A Taziya of shields and swords, each tipped with a lemon or an orange, is carried in procession, and on it are suspended written petitions to Hussun and Hussein, and it is adorned with strings of freshly-gathered jasmine flowers.

The model of the tomb of Kasim is the next object; it is covered with gold brocade, and a canopy is supported over it, the poles carried by men. The palkee of his bride, Sakeena Koobar, follows the tomb; and her chandol, a sort of palanquin.

Then follow trays of mehndi, carried on the heads of men, with presents,

&c., such as are usually sent during the marriage ceremony, with flowers of ubruk.

The charkh-charkhī wālās are numerous; the charkhī is composed of ebony or any hard wood, about the size of a cricketball, divided in halves. Each man has a pair; they are beaten in a particular manner on the flat surface, so as to produce the sound of horses galloping; and where some fifty or one hundred men are engaged in the performance the imitation is excellent.

The females during the battle were perishing of thirst; Abbas, the brother of Hussein, and his standard-bearer, made great efforts to procure water for them, in doing which the former was severely wounded.

Hence the bihishtī with his mashk; and, in remembrance of this event, sherbets are also distributed gratis, in red earthen cups, from temporary sheds; abdār khanas, as they call them by the road-side. The awnings of these sheds are reared on poles, and they are lighted by lamps made of ubruk, or of the skeleton leaves of the peepul-tree. The bihishtī bears the standard of Hussun and Hussein.

The camels carrying the tent equipage and luggage of Hussein represent the style of his march from Medina to Kraabaallah. Sometimes, in pictures, a small Taziya is drawn on the back of a camel, and the animal is represented as issuing from a rocky pass.

Bārkandāz attend, and fire their matchlocks singly and at intervals during the march.

Great sums are expended in charity during this mourning festival, and food is always distributed by the richer Taziyadars during the ten days.

The procession is closed by several elephants, and men seated upon them distribute food and money to the poor.

Natives of all ranks, from the highest to the lowest, walk on the tenth day with their heads uncovered, and without slippers, to the Kraabaallah, whatever may be the distance; and they fast until the third watch has passed, refraining from the hooqŭ, or from drinking water. At the Kraabaallah the funeral ceremony is performed, and the Taziya is committed to the grave with a solemnity equal to that which is observed when their dead are deposited in the tomb. The native ladies within the walls of the zenāna keep the fast with the greatest strictness, and observe all the ceremonies of the Muharram.

A religious man will neither ride nor wear shoes during the Muharram; and a pious Musulmān will neither eat nor drink out of a silver or a gold vessel.

"That person who shall drink out of a silver cup or cup of gold, you may say drinks a draught of hell-fire." Muhammud said, "Do not wear silk clothes nor satin, nor drink out of gold or silver vessels, nor eat out of golden dishes; because these are for the infidels in the world, and for you in futurity."

The lamps, which are made of ubruk (talc), or of the skeleton leaves of the peepul-tree, and lighted up in the houses of the faithful at this time, are beautifully made.

One day, on entering the verandah, my darzee (tailor), a Musulmān of the Shea sect, was sitting on the ground, holding a ghirgit (the scaly lizard, a sort of chameleon,) in one hand, while he beat it with a twig, exclaiming with each stroke he gave the poor little beast, "Ever to be accursed, and never sufficiently to be beaten!" The man was very unwilling to give up his captive, or to desist from putting it to torture; the creature was changing colour at every stroke. I made him release it, and asked him why he had beaten and cursed it so vehemently? The man replied, "Blessed be the spider! ever to be accursed, and never sufficiently to be beaten be the ghirgit! When the Imām, on whom be blessings, hid himself in a well from his pursuers, the spider weaved his web across the mouth of the well, to hide him from his enemies; the ghirgit,—the prying, inquisitive beast!—the ghirgit went to the well, he peered over, he stretched his neck this way, he stretched his neck that way (here he imitated the curious motion of the head natural to the animal); the pursuers were attracted, they observed the ghirgit looking over the well; they imitated his example, they discovered the Imām, they murdered him! Ever to be accursed, never sufficiently to be beaten be the ghirgit!"

Mohammud ordered a chameleon to be killed, and said, "it was a chameleon which blew the fire into which Nimrod threw Abraham." "Whoever shall kill a chameleon at one stroke shall have one hundred good acts written for him; and whoever kills one at two strokes shall have less than one hundred good deeds written for him; and whoever shall kill one by three strokes shall have less written for him than the second."

His Highness forbade the killing of four animals, the ant (before stinging), the bee, the woodpecker, the starling. It is criminal in a Shea, and indeed with Soonees, to kill pigeons, though they are recommended to eat them!

An alligator, seven feet in length, was caught in the Jumna, below our house, a few days ago; I had it prepared with arsenical soap, stuffed, and set out in the verandah, where it grins in hideous beauty, nailed down upon the carpenter's large table, where it will remain until it stiffens into proper form.

My cabinet of curiosities and fondness of horrors ensured many a strange present from absent friends. A small military party were dispatched to capture a mud fort; on reaching the spot no enemy was to be discovered; they entered with all due precaution against ambush; an enormous tiger in a cage was the sole occupant. The tiger was sent down per boat to me,—the first prize of the campaign; on my refusal to accept the animal, he was forwarded to the accoutrement-maker of the officer, in Calcutta, in liquidation of his account! The tiger was sold at length to an American captain for 250 rupees, which just or very nearly paid the expenses of boat-hire, servants, meat, &c., contracted on his the tiger's account. Such changes in his way of life must have puzzled his philosophy; the capture, the Ganges, and sea voyage ending in North America, will give him a queer idea of the best of all possible worlds; but he well deserves it, being a cruel, treacherous, bloodthirsty brute.

My eccentric friend also wrote to say he had at length procured for me an offering after my own heart, an enormous boa constrictor, perfectly tame, so domestic and sweet tempered, that at meals it would cross the room, displaying, as it advanced with undulating motion, its bright-striped and spotted skin, until, having gained your chair, it would coil its mazy folds around you, and tenderly putting its head over your shoulder, eat from your hand!

I was greatly tempted to accept this unique offering. They tell us mankind have a *natural* antipathy to a snake; an antipathy I never shared. I have killed them as venomous reptiles, but have a great fancy for them as beautiful ones. No child dislikes snakes until it is taught to fear them. [. . .]

I have not heard from home for six months, heart-sick with hope deferred. These tardy ships! Will the steam communication ever be established?

"A merry heart doeth good like a medicine, but a broken spirit drieth the bones."

> "I could lie down like a tired child,
> And weep away this life of care,
> Which I have borne, and still must bear."

When shall I feel energy enough to mount my horse again? for three months I have been unable to ride. Nothing is going forward, stupid as possible, shut up all day, languid and weary: this India is a vile country!

"The heart knoweth its own sorrows, and no man interfereth with its joys."

Woe is me that I sojourn in this land of pestilence, that I dwell afar from the home of my fathers!

Chapter 24

The Brahmanical Thread

1834, *June.*—This morning I was on the sofa, fancying myself not quite well, when Ram Din came in with a Brahmanical thread; as soon as I had any thing to amuse me, all my illness vanished; the history thereof is as follows:—The name in common use for what we call the sacred thread is janao; it is not confined merely to Brahmans, for in the Veda called Bhagavat, which relates to Krishnŭ, it is allowed to be worn by three out of the four great tribes into which the Hindoos are divided. The three privileged tribes are the Brahmans, the Chuttri or Rajpūt, and the Khuttri or Vaisya. However, many others now wear the sacred thread who by the Vedas have no right to do so. The janao must be made by the hands of a Brahman; it is worn one month, and then either thrown into the Ganges, or hung upon the sacred peepul-tree, when a fresh one is made. After six years old, a boy may receive the janao, from which time he must observe all the rules respecting eating and drinking, according to the custom of his tribe.

The janao is composed of three threads, each measuring, as the Hindoos say, four less than one hundred—that is, ninety-six—hāt: one hāt is the length measured twice round the breadth of the hand, or one cubit. These three threads are twisted together, and folded into three, then twisted again, making it to consist of nine threads; these are again folded into three, without twisting, and each end fastened with a knot.

It is put over the left shoulder next the skin, and hangs down the right thigh as far as the fingers can reach; two of these threads are worn by a Brahman. After a certain age, if a boy be not invested with the janao, he becomes an outcast.

There are four great tribes amongst the Hindoos, which are subdivided into *innumerable* classes; in the second tribe there are, they say, upwards of five hundred subdivisions!

1st tribe, Brahmans or priests; however, many Brahmans are not priests.

2nd tribe, Chuttri,—Rajpūts, Rajahs, and warriors.

3th tribe, Vaisya or merchants,—artizans, cultivators, &c.

4th tribe, called Soodra,—mechanics, artizans, and labourers: the natural duty of the Soodra is servitude.

Ram Din tells me he more especially worships Krishnŭ: he also makes pooja to Radha, also to Rām; the former the love, the second the warrior god and brother of Krishnŭ. On his forehead, as the mark of his worship, he paints three perpendicular lines, the centre of white, the two others of red clay. Ram Din is of the second tribe, a Rajpūt.

It is scarcely possible to write, the natives are making such a noise overhead, repairing the flat roof of the house, which is made of flag-stones, supported by large beams of wood; over that brick-dust and lime, mixed with water, is laid a foot in depth, which they are now beating down with little wooden mallets, holding one in each hand.

"The sight of a beggar is a request personified."[1] On the plain near the fort, just before you come to the Mahratta Bund, a fakīr had taken up his abode, where abode there was none. Ascetics of the orthodox sect, in the last stage of exaltation, put aside clothing altogether. This man's only *garment* was a chatr (an umbrella made of basket-work), his long hair, matted with cow-dung and ashes, hung in stiff, straight locks nearly to his waist; his body was smeared all over with ashes; he was always on the same spot, sitting doubled up on the ground, and when suffering from illness, a bit of tattered blanket was thrown over his shoulders.

Night and day the fakīr was to be seen, a solitary wretched being, scarcely human in appearance. The passers-by threw cowries and grains of boiled rice to him; sometimes a woman would come and kindle a few bits of charcoal, and then quit him; the hot winds, the rains, the bitter frosty nights of the cold weather, were unheeded; nothing appeared to disturb the devotee. Was his frame insensible to the power of the elements? When I first saw him he had occupied that spot for twelve years, and I know he never quitted it for five years afterwards, until he was consigned to the Ganges on his decease. One night, some thieves demanded rupees of the holy man; he pleaded poverty. "I have killed such a poor man as you, and have got nine mŭns of fat out of him,"[2] said one of the fellows. They beat and tortured the poor wretch until he revealed his secret hoards: he showed them a spot on the plain; they dug up some ghāras (coarse earthen vessels), which contained two thousand rupees! Content with their plunder, they quitted the holy man. The next morning he went to the General Commandant of the garrison, and told his tale, ending by producing seven hundred rupees, which the thieves had not discovered, and requesting the General to place it in security for him! His request having been granted, the fakīr returned to the plain, where he and his chatr remained until his spirit was summoned to the presence of Yamu, the judge of the dead. The

[1] Oriental Proverbs.   [2] Ibid.

211

police did not molest him in the out-of-the-way spot he had chosen for his retreat; they would not have allowed him to roam about the station.

Speaking of this fakīr reminds me I forgot to mention, that, when I visited the fair early in February last, I rode there before sunrise, and was greatly amused. Hundreds of Hindoos were undergoing penance, not for their sins, but for copper coins; some were lying on their backs upon thorns, each with a child upon his breast, asking charity; one man was standing upon one leg, in meditation; he began his penance at sunrise, and ended it at sunset.

We rode down to the water's edge, and saw the Hindoos doing pooja to living cows. One man, the shawl over whose shoulders was tied to the end of the chādar, worn over the head by a woman, came to a cow, the woman following him; he took hold of the cow's tail in his hand, holding in it at the same time the sacred cusa-grass; the woman did the same; the Brahman muttered a prayer, which the man repeated; he then, followed by the woman, walked round the cow many times turning to the left, which having done a certain number of times, he whispered into the cow's right ear; the woman came to the same ear, and also whispered to the cow; which ceremony being accomplished, they were sent into the river to bathe at the junction. The rites I witnessed, are, I believe, a portion of the marriage ceremonies of the Hindūs. The cusa-grass is the poa cynosurides; almost every poem in Sanscrit contains allusions to the holiness of this grass. Some of the leaves taper to a most acute point; it is an Hindoo saying, speaking of a very sharp-minded man, "his intellects are as acute as the point of a cusa leaf."

Some of the marble images at the fair were very fine ones; the price demanded was three hundred rupees, or £30 a-piece.

I received a present this morning of a flying fox, an enormous bat with leathern wings; I had previously thought such creatures were mere fables; the one presented to me is a prepared specimen. The next day, I sent some sipahīs to shoot flying foxes; they found a number in a large tree, and killed two of them; they are such savage, but intelligent-looking animals, curious and wonderful, but disgusting creatures.

During the cold weather I gathered a handful of a very sweet-smelling air-plant on the Mahratta Bund; taking it home, I threw it on the top of a biar-tree (zizyphus jujuba) to see if it would really grow in the air; it died away, as I thought, and I forgot it; the other day, by chance, glancing at the biar-tree, I saw my air-plant in high beauty, covering about two yards of the top of the tree, and hanging in long light green strings, like sea-weed, down towards the ground. The natives call it amur bel, the undying climber, and ākās bel, air creeper; the flowers are white, small, bell-shaped, and five-cleft; the plant leafless; the running stalks greenish yellow, shining, and spreading over the top of a tree like a sheet thrown over it; the scent very fragrant. The ākās nīm is a parasite, growing on nīm-trees: the ākās pussun is the cuscuta reflexa, dodder, or air-plant.

Last month we were unlucky in the farm-yard; forty-seven fat sheep and well-fatted lambs died of small-pox; a very great loss, as to fatten sheep on gram for two or three years makes them very expensive; it is remarkable that none of the goats, although living in the same house, were attacked.

This morning three musk-deer, prepared and stuffed, were shown to me; they are a present for Runjeet Singh, and are now *en route* from Nepal. The men had also a number of musk-bags for the Lion of the Punjab. The hair of the musk-deer is curious stuff, like hog's bristles; and their two tusks are like those of the walrus. Buffon gives an admirable description of this animal. Some time ago a musk-bag was given me as a curiosity; the scent is extremely powerful. The musk-deer is rare and very valuable.

Aug. 9th.—This is a holiday, the nāg-panchamī, on which day the Hindūs worship a snake, to procure blessings on their children; of course, none of the carpenters or the other workmen have made their appearance. The other day, a gentleman, who is staying with us, went into his bathing-room to take a bath; the evening was very dark, and, as he lifted a ghāra (an earthen vessel), to pour the water over his head, he heard a hissing sound among the waterpots, and, calling for a light, saw a great cobra de capello. "Look at that snake!" said he to his bearer, in a tone of surprise. "Yes, sāhib," replied the Hindoo, with the utmost apathy, "he has been there a great many days, and gives us much trouble!"

Sept. 11th.—We purchased a very fine pinnace, that an officer had brought up the river, and named her the Seagull. She is as large as a very good yacht; it will be pleasant to visit those ghāts on the Ganges and Jumna, during the cold weather, that are under the sāhib's control. The vessel is a fine one, and the natives say, "She goes before the wind like an arrow from a bow."

The city of Allahabad, considered as a native one, is handsome: there are but few pukka houses. The rich merchants in the East make no display, and generally live under bamboo and straw. The roads through the city are very good, with rows of fine trees on each side; the drives around are numerous and excellent. There is also a very handsome sarā'e (caravansary), and a bā'olī, a large well, worthy a visit. The tomb and garden of Sultan Khusrau are fine; a description of them will be given hereafter. The fort was built by Akbar in 1581, at the junction of the Ganges and Jumna. Within the fort, near the principal gateway, an enormous pillar is prostrate; the unknown characters inscribed upon it are a marvel and a mystery to the learned, who as yet have been unable to translate them. The bazār at Allahabad is famous for old coins.

Having been requested to contribute to a fancy fair for charitable purposes, I had some sealing-wax made in the verandah, under my own eye; the lākh was brought to me in little cakes from the bazār, enclosed in leaves of the palās or dhāk (butea frondosa), fastened together with wooden pins like long thorns. Many articles are wrapped up in this way in lieu of using paper; and packets of the leaves freshly gathered are to be seen in the shops ready for use. The lākh is the produce of an insect (chermes lacca), in which its eggs are deposited; it is found on the dhāk, the peepul, the banyan, and the biar, as well as on several other trees. The wood and leaves of the dhāk are used in religious ceremonies; the bark is given with ginger in snake bites, and the calyx of the fruit is made into jelly, which has a pleasant acid taste. When the bark is wounded a red juice issues, which soon hardens into a ruby-coloured, brittle, astringent gum; a solution of it in water is of a deep red colour; the addition of a little sal martis changes it into a good durable ink. An infusion of the flowers dyes cotton, which has been steeped previously in a solution of alum, a beautiful bright yellow; a little alkali added changes it to a deep reddish orange. The flowers are papilionaceous, of a deep red, shaded orange and silver, and very numerous. Another species, a large twining shrub, is the butea superba. The leaves are large and fine, and give beautiful impressions when taken off with the preparation of lamp-black and oil. The Chupra lākh is the best for sealing-wax, to which we merely added the colouring. It is very hard and brittle, and will not melt with the heat of the climate. The seal of a letter, stamped on English wax, in which there is always a large portion of resin, often arrives merely one lump of wax, the crest, or whatever impression may have been on the seal, totally obliterated; and the adhering of one seal to another *en route* is often the cause that letters are torn open ere they reach their destination.

Ainslie mentions, "Scarlet was, till of late years, produced exclusively with the colouring matter of the cochineal insect; but it would appear that a more beautiful and lasting colour can be obtained by using the lākh insect."

Oct. 7th.—Yesterday being the Hindoo festival of the Dewalī, a great illumination was made for my amusement; our house, the gardens, the well, the pinnace on the river below the bank of the garden, the old peepul-tree, and my bower, were lighted up with hundreds of little lamps. My bower on the banks of the Jumna-jee, which is quite as beautiful as the "bower of roses by Bendameer's stream," must be described.

It was canopied by the most luxuriant creepers and climbers of all sorts. The ishk-pechā, the "Twinings of Love,"[1] overspread it in profusion; as the slender stems catch upon each other, and twine over an arbour, the leaves, falling back, lie over one another *en masse*, spreading over a broad surface in the manner in which the feathers of the tail of a peacock spread over one another, and trail upon the ground; the ruby red and starlike flowers start from amidst the rich green of its delicate leaves as bright as sunshine. This climber, the most beautiful and luxuriant imaginable, bears also the name of kamalāta, "Love's Creeper." Some have flowers of snowy hue, with a delicate fragrance; and one, breathing after sunset, the odour of cloves!

The doodēya,[2] so called because it gives forth a milky juice, also denominated chābuk churree, from the resemblance of its long slender shoots to a whip, displayed over the bower its beautiful and bell-shaped flowers; it also bears the name of swallow-wort, from the fancied resemblance of its seed-vessels to a swallow flying.

In wondrous profusion, the gāo-pāt, the elephant climber, spread its enormous leaves over the bower; the under part of the leaf is white, and soft as velvet; the natives say it is like the tongue of a cow, whence it derives its name gāo-pāt.[3] In the early morning, or at sunset, it was delightful to watch the humming-birds as they fluttered over and dived into its bell-shaped flowers, seeking nectar; or to see them glancing over the crimson stars of the ishk-pechā. The bower was the favourite resort of the most beautiful butterflies,—those insect queens of Eastern Spring,—not only for the sake of the climbers, but for the blossoms of the Lucerne grass that grew around the spot. Observing one day there were but few butterflies, I asked the reason of the jāmadār? he replied, "The want of rain has killed the flowers, and the death of the flowers has killed the butterflies."

From the topmost branches of the surrounding trees, the moon-flower[4] hung its chaste and delicate blossoms, drooping and apparently withered; but as the night came on they raised their languid heads, and bloomed in beauty.

"The Nymphæa[5] dwells in the water, and the moon in the sky, but he that resides in the heart of another is always present with him."[6] The Nymphæa expands its flowers in the night, and thence is feigned to be in love with the moon. The water-lily as it floats on the stream, luxuriating in

---

[1] Ipomæa quamoclit.　　[2] Asclepias rosea.
[3] Ipomæa speciosa, or convolvolus speciosus; broad-leaved bindweed.
[4] Convolvolus grandiflora.　　[5] Water-lily.　　[6] Oriental Proverbs.

the warmth of the moonbeams, has a powerful rival in the burā luta, the beautiful moon-flower, whose luxuriant blossoms of snowy whiteness expand during the night.

The sorrowful nyctanthes, the harsingahar, is it not also a lover of the moon, its flowers expanding, and pouring forth fragrance only in the night? Gay and beautiful climber, whence your name of arbor tristis? Is it because you blossom but to die? With the first beams of the rising sun your night flowers are shed upon the earth to wither and decay.

The flowers of the harsingahar, which are luxuriously abundant, are collected by perfumers and dyers; the orange-coloured stem of the white corolla is the part used by the latter. The flowers are sold in the bazār, at one and a half or two rupees the sēr. It is one of the most beautiful climbers I have seen.

My humming-birds were sacred; no one dared molest them, not even a rover with a pellet-bow was allowed a shot at my favourites.

Speaking of a pellet-bow, I have seen small birds and butterflies shot with it. One day a gentleman, seeing a pigeon flying across the garden, just above my spaniel's head, brought it down with a pellet. The dog looked up, opened his mouth, and caught the stunned bird as it fell upon him. Ever afterwards, he was constantly in the garden watching the pigeons with his mouth wide open, expecting they also would fall into it!

The bower, which was supported on bamboo posts, was constantly falling in from the havoc occasioned by the white ants. I sent for a hackery (cart) load of the flower-stems of the aloe, and substituted the stems for the bamboos: in consequence, the white ants gave up the work of destruction, having an antipathy to the bitterness of the aloe. It is said the aloe flowers only once in a century; what may be its vagaries in a colder climate I know not; the hedges here are full of the plant, which flowers annually.

I wish I had tried the teeth of the white ants by putting up pillars of stone. An orthodox method of killing these little underminers is by strewing sugar on the places frequented by them: the large black ants, the sworn enemies of the white ants, being attracted by the sugar, quickly appear, and destroy the white ones. The white ants are sappers and miners; they will come up through the floor into the foot of a wardrobe, make their way through the centre of it into the drawers, and feast on the contents. I once opened a wardrobe which had been filled with tablecloths and napkins: no outward sign of mischief was there; but the linen was one mass of dirt, and utterly destroyed. The most remarkable thing is, the little beasts always move under cover, and form for themselves a hollow way, through which they move unseen, and do their work of destruction at leisure. The hollow way they form is not unlike pipe maccaroni in size, and its colour is that of mud. I never saw them in Calcutta; up the country they are a perfect nuisance. The queen ant is a curious creature; one was shown me that had been dug out of an ants' nest: it was nearly four inches long by two in width, and looked something like a bit of blubber. The white ants are the vilest little animals on the face of the earth; they eat their way through walls, through beams of wood, and are most marvellously troublesome. They attack the roots of trees and plants, and kill them in a day or two. To drive them away it is advisable to have the plants watered with hing (assafœtida) steeped in water. If a box be allowed to stand a week upon the floor without being moved, it is likely at the end of that time, when you take it up, the bottom may fall out, destroyed by the white ants. Carpets, mats, chintz, such as we put on the floors, all share, more or less, the same fate. I never saw a white ant until I came to India. They resemble the little white maggots in a cheese, with a black dot for a head, and a pair of pincers fixed upon it.

[. . .]

By the side of the bower are two trees, the roots of which, dug up and scraped, have exactly the appearance and taste of horseradish, and are used on table for the same purpose. The tree grows very quickly; the flowers are elegant, but the wood is only useful for dying a blue colour: the sahjana, hyperanthera moringa, horseradish-tree.

The ichneumons, mungūs, or newalā, were numerous in the garden, lurking in the water-courses; they committed much havoc occasionally in the poultry-yard. A mungūs and a snake will often have a battle royal; if the mungūs be bitten, he will run off, eat a particular plant, and return to the charge. He is generally the conqueror. Never having seen this, I will not vouch for the fact; the natives declare it to be true. The name of the plant has escaped my memory. The newalā may be easily tamed if caught young: I never attempted to keep one in the house, on account of the dogs. The moon-flower is supposed to have virtue in snake bites. I know of no remedy but eau-de-luce applied internally and externally.

I must not quit the garden without mentioning my favourite plants. The kulga, amaranthus tricolor, a most beautiful species of sāg, bearing at the top a head or cluster of leaves of three colours, red, yellow, and green, which have the appearance of the flower: it is very ornamental, and used as spinach (sāg). If the head be broken off, similar clusters form below.

There is another plant, amaranthus gangeticus (lal sāg), or red spinach, which is most excellent; when on table its ruby colour is beautiful, and its agreeable acidity renders it preferable to any other kind of spinach.

The koonch, or goonja (abrus precatorius), is an elegant little plant, of which there is only one species; the seeds, which are smooth, hard, and of

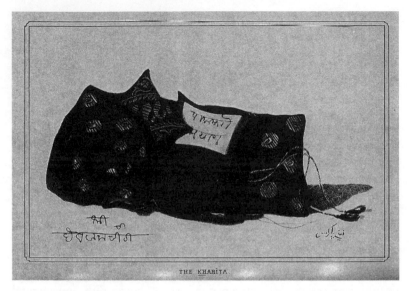

THE KHARĪTA

Figure 7   The Kharīta

a glowing scarlet colour, form the retti weight of the Hindostanī bazārs. The seeds are strung and worn as beads for ornament, and also as rosaries, hence the specific name precatorius.

The rāmturāī, or binda (hibiscus longifolius), adorned the kitchen garden; its corolla is of a beautiful sulphur colour, the interior purple. The pods, when plain boiled, and eaten when quite hot, are excellent; the French use them in soups, and pickle them as capers.

Perhaps a touch of superstition induced me to be careful of a very fine specimen of the salvia Bengalensis, which grew near the bower; or perhaps the well-known verse,

"Cur moriatur homo, cui salvia crescit in horto?"

showing the estimation in which it was held in former days, contributed to the care with which it was preserved. The gardener calls it sistee, perhaps a corruption of sage; and on account of the strong scent of its leaves, it is also called (velāitie kāfūr-ke-pāt), the leaf of the English camphor.

I had a curious plant, which I was told was an air-plant; the natives called it pēr-pāt, or rus-putta: if a leaf dropped on the ground, a little root would strike out on each side of it, and thus a fresh plant would be formed. I buried several leaves, and they took root in that manner. The botanical name of the plant is unknown to me.

218

The hibiscus mutabilis flourished in great perfection: the flowers of this rose hibiscus change their hue in the course of a few hours.

The lajwantee, the sensitive plant, grew in profusion, covered with its tuft-like blossoms, and shrinking from the touch. Near it were some very fine specimens of Bourbon cotton, which flourished admirably; this gossypium differs from the herbaceum, because the down which lines the capsules which contain the seeds is of a brown colour, whereas the down of the common cotton plant, grown in the fields in India, is beautifully white.

A small quantity of the bhuta (zea mays) was in the garden: when the corn had formed, just before it hardened, whilst it was soft, and green, and milky, it was brought to table fried until brown, and eaten with pepper and salt; a most excellent vegetable. It is called common Indian corn; but it appears to me it was very little used for making bread in the Up Country, as I never saw any thing generally used but wheat for the unleavened cakes, which constitute the bread of the natives.

We have the burā shim (dolichus), horse-eye bean; the pods are cut and dressed like French beans, but are inferior; the bean itself is large.

The rut aloe (dioscorea sativa) was not only a most useful vegetable when potatoes were losing their excellence, but the beautiful leaves of this climber were in themselves an ornament. The roots grow to a great size; those the most valued for culinary purposes are a much smaller sort, which, when broken, are perfectly white and milk-like in appearance.

Perhaps one of the best things in the garden was the patūā, the Indian hibiscus; the corolla is sulphur-coloured and reddish purple; the fruit, of a bright red colour, is excellent in tarts; and when made into a jelly, has something of the appearance and, taste of fresh damson cheese; but the patūā jelly is transparent, and its hue brilliant. In the West Indies it is called red sorrel. The bark of the hibiscus cannabinus (hemp-leaved hibiscus), as well as that of the sabdariffa is made into cordage.

Tambācu, Virginian tobacco (nicotiana tabacum), also flourished with us; but that for the hooqŭ was usually procured from Chunar, a place celebrated for the excellence of its tobacco.

Every morning it is the custom of the Mālee (gardener) to appear at breakfast time to present a dālī (a basket of vegetables) and a bouquet of flowers. Amongst the latter many were novelties to an European.

The āgāst (æschynomene grandiflora) was remarkable; the corolla of a most brilliant rose colour; but on some of the trees the flowers were white.

The amultas (cassia fistula) was there, with its long, beautiful, pendant, yellow, and fragrant flowers. The tree is sometimes fifty feet in height, and remarkable for the fruit, which is a brownish-coloured pod, about the thickness of a thumb, and some two feet or more in length; it is divided into numerous cells, upwards of forty, each containing one smooth, oval, shining seed. This pod is called by the natives "Bunda-ke-lāt," the monkey's staff; the seeds are used medicinally, and the pods are for sale in every bazār.

One of the most beautiful of shrubs is the gooltura or gooliturah (Poinciana pulcherrima), *fleur de Paradis*; from the extreme beauty of this flower Burmann gave it the appellation of "crista pavonis flore elegantissimo variegato."

The pomegranate-tree, anār (punica granatum), was abundant; the following description gives a perfect idea of it:—

"The finest fruit is brought from Persia and Cabul: there are two sorts, the sweet and acid pomegranate. Sherbet is made with the fruit; the tree is singularly beautiful, and much cultivated in India. The leaves are of a rich dark green, very glossy, and the tree is adorned at the same time with every variety of bud, bloom, and fruit, in the several stages of vegetation, from the first bud to the ripe fruit in rich luxuriance, and this in succession nearly throughout the year. The bright scarlet colour of the buds and blossoms, which seldom varies in its shade, contrasts beautifully with the glossy dark green of the foliage. There is a medicinal benefit to be derived from every part of this tree, from the root upwards, even to the falling blossoms, which are carefully collected. The rind of the fruit is dried and sold as a medicine, and each part of this tree possesses a distinct medicinal property. The pomegranate was introduced into India from Persia." As a medicine, a decoction of the roots, or of the rind, was of great use in the farm-yard and in the kennel.

Sometimes a small specimen of the kyā-pootie-tree was brought to me (melaleuca kyā-pootie). I regarded it with interest on account of its fragrant oil. There are three varieties of this tree: from the leaf of the smaller, by distillation, the fragrant essential oil is obtained, called by the ignorant cajeput. Mr. Crawford observes in his History of the Indian Archipelago: "The kyā-pootie-trees are gigantic myrtles; the largest sort is a mountain tree, and grows in extensive continuous forests. The smaller, which yields the oil, thrives near the sea-coast, and has got its name from its colour, kāyu-puti, which signifies *white wood*, and hence its appellation arbor alba." The oil is distilled from leaves which have been previously infused in water and left to ferment for a night. The oil I procured in India was limpid, transparent, and of a brilliant emerald green, extremely powerful, and the scent delicious; the bruised leaves also emit a powerful odour.

"The mistress of the night," the polyanthes tuberosa, was in profusion in the garden. It is used in pooja: the natives call it gōl-shub-boo, from shub, night; and boo, scent; because it gives forth its odours during the night.

The kudum (nauclea orientalis) is one of the holiest trees in the opinion of the Hindoos. The flowers have an odour very agreeable in the open air, which the ancient Indians compared to the scent of new wine; and hence they call the plant Halyprya, or beloved of Halim; that is, by the third Ráma, who was the Bacchus of India. The corolla of the kudum-tree is of a pale yellow, and very fragrant; the flowers are borne in round heads, perfectly globular, and covered uniformly with gold-coloured florets. One species, nauclea gambir, is said to yield the gamboge gum of the bazār.

Of all the flowers brought to me, the perfume of the ketgi, keura, or keora (pandanus odoratissimus), was the most overpowering. From the flower of this green-spined screw-tree, arrak and atr are made: the tough fibres of the roots are used by basket-makers, and the roots themselves are used by the Malays as cords. The flowers of the male plant yield the most overpowering fragrance, which is esteemed very highly by the natives.

An atr is also prepared from the mulsari or múlasrí (mimosops elengi). Children eat the fruit of this tree: the flowers are agreeably fragrant in the open air, but the perfume is too strong for an apartment. In the Puranas this tree is called bacula, and placed amongst the flowers of the Hindoo Paradise.

Another remarkable plant was the martynia proboscidea horn-capsuled martynia, called by the natives the insect seed, from the resemblance of the capsule to a horned beetle, if there be a beetle with two curled horns.

Oct.—I have just returned from taking a sketch of the Circuit bungalow; it reminds me of very many pleasant mornings, although to an English ear it may not give an idea of pleasure to rise at three A.M., to take coffee by candlelight, or by the light of the mist in the verandah!—The buggy waiting, the lamps lighted, and the horse covered with a blanket, to keep him from taking a chill.—A drab coat with many capes, a shawl beneath, and another round the neck, a drive of two or three miles by lamp-light. Just as you come up to the dogs, a gentleman comes forward to assist the mem sāhiba from the buggy, saying, "Very cold! very cold! one could not be more delightfully cold in England—half-frozen!" Those fine dogs, Jānpeter, Racer, Merrylass, and the rest of them emerge from the palanquin carriage in which they have been brought to Papamhow, much tāmashā! many jackals! Then the canter through the plantations of Urrah, wet with dew—dew so heavy that the sā'īs wrings out the skirt of the mem sāhiba's habit; nevertheless, the lady and the black pony are very happy. Master General carries his rider in most *jemmy* style; a gallant grey by his side takes beautiful leaps, and the mem sāhiba and her black horse scramble up and down ravines, over which the others leap, and by little *detours* and knowledge of the country, find much amusement in the course of the morning.

All natives, from the highest to the lowest, sport the moustache, and pride themselves upon its blackness. My old khānsāmān, Suddu Khan, whose hair, beard, and moustache were perfectly white, came before me one morning, and making sālām, requested me to allow him some hours' leave of absence to dye his hair. In the evening he was in attendance at table; his hair, beard, and moustache in the most perfect order, and jet black! The 16th Lancers, on their arrival in India, wore no moustache; after the lapse of many years, the order that allowed them the decoration arrived in India, and was hailed with delight by the whole corps. The natives regarded them with much greater respect in consequence, and the young dandies of Delhi could no longer twirl their moustachoes, and think themselves finer fellows than the Lancers. As a warlike appendage it was absolutely necessary; a man without moustachoes being reckoned nā-mard, unmanly. Having been often consulted on the important subject of the best dye, I subjoin a recipe which was given me in the Zenāna.[1] A dandified native generally travels with a handkerchief bound under his chin, and tied on the top of his turban, that the beauty and precision of his beard may not be disarranged on the journey.

Chapter 25

Pilgrimage to the Tāj

"RESOLUTION OVERCOMES GREAT DIFFICULTIES."[1]

[. . .]

Dec. 1834.—To look forward to the cold season is always a great pleasure in India; and to plan some expedition for that period is an amusement

---

[1] See Appendix.

[1] Oriental Proverbs.

during the hot winds and rains. We had often determined to visit the Tāj Mahul at Agra—the wonder of the world.

Our beautiful pinnace was now in the Jumna, anchored just below the house, but the height of the banks and the lowness of the river only allowed us to see the top of her masts. My husband proposed that I should go up the Jumna in her, as far as Agra, and anchor off the Tāj; and promised, if he could get leave of absence, to join me there, to view all that is so well worth seeing at that remarkable place. Accordingly, the pinnace was prepared for the voyage, and a patelī was procured as a cook-boat. Books, drawing materials, and every thing that could render a voyage up the river agreeable, were put on board.[1]

Dec. 9th.—I quitted Prāg: the Seagull spread her sails to the breeze, and, in spite of the power of the stream, we made good way against it: at night we *lugāoed* off Phoolpoor, *i.e.* made fast to the bank, as is always the custom, the river not being navigable during the darkness.

10th.—Saw the first crocodile to-day basking on a sandbank; a great long-nosed fellow, a very Indian looking personage, of whom I felt the greatest fear, as at the moment my little terrier Fury, who was running on the shore with the dāndees, seeing me on deck, swam off to the pinnace. I was much pleased when a dāndee caught her in his arms and put her on the cook-boat.

On the commencement of a voyage the men adorn the bows of the vessel with hārs, (chaplets of fresh flowers,) and ask for money: on days of pooja, and at the end of the voyage, the same ceremony is repeated, and half-way on the voyage they usually petition for a present, a few rupees for good luck.

I must describe the Seagull:—She was built in Calcutta to go to Chittagong, and has a deep keel, therefore unfit for river work, unless during the rains: two-masted, copper-bottomed, and brig-rigged. She requires water up to a man's waist; her crew consist of twenty-two men, one sarang, who commands her, four khalāsīs, who hold the next rank, one gal'haiya, forecastle man (from galahi, a forecastle), fourteen dāndees, one cook and his mate, all Musalmāns; total twenty-two. The crew, particularly good men, came from Calcutta with the pinnace; they cook their own food and eat and sleep on board. My food and that of my servants is prepared in the cook-boat. The food of the dāndees usually consists of curry and rice, or

---

[1] A pinnace was the only keeled boat used for river journeys, and it was not as well-adapted to the shoals and shallows of the Jumna as the flat-bottomed country boats. There were three rooms in the stern, a bedroom, bathroom and living room and an enclosed verandah to provide shade. They were fitted with Pankhas. The crew lived on the roof.

thin cakes of flour (unleavened bread) called chapātīs: the latter they bake on a tawā (iron plate) over the fire, on the bank, and eat whilst hot. It is amusing to see how dexterously they pat these cakes into form, between both hands, chucking them each time into the air: they are usually half an inch in thickness, and the size of a dessert plate.

When these common chapātīs are made thin, and allowed to blow out on the fire until they are perfectly hollow, they are delicious food, if eaten quite hot. Thus made they are much better than those generally put on the table of the sāhib loge (gentry), which are made of fine flower and milk.

Being unable to find a boat for hire that would answer as a cook-boat, the jamadār purchased a patelī, a small boat built after the fashion of a large flat-bottomed patailā, for which he gave eighty rupees; and we proceeded to fit it up, by building a large house upon it of mats and bamboo, thickly thatched with straw. This house was for the cook, the servants, and the farmyard. On the top of it was a platform of bamboos, on which the dāndees (sailors) could live and sleep. The crew consisted of seven men, Hindoos; therefore they always cooked their food on shore in the evening, it being contrary to the rules of their religion to eat on board. The sheep, goats, fowls, provisions, wine, &c. were all in the cook-boat, and a space was divided off for the dhobee (washerman). The number of servants it is necessary to take with one on a river voyage in India is marvellous. We had also a little boat called a dinghee, which was towed astern the pinnace.

This morning we passed Sujawan Deota, a rock rising out of the river, crowned with a temple, a remarkably picturesque spot, and adorned with trees. A pinnace is towed by one thick towing line, called a goon, carried by ten men. Native boats containing merchandize are generally towed by small lines, each man having his own line to himself. The wind having become contrary, the men were obliged to tow her; the goon broke, the vessel swerved round, and was carried some distance down the stream; however, she was brought up without damage, and we moored off Sehoree.

11th.—In passing the Burriaree rocks I felt a strange sort of anxious delight in the danger of the passage, there being only room for one vessel to pass through. The serang, a Calcutta man, had never been up the Jumna; and as we cut through the narrow pass I stood on deck watching ahead for a sunken rock. Had there been too little water, with what a crash we should have gone on the rocks! The river is full of them; they show their black heads a foot or two above the stream that rushes down fiercely around or over them: just now we ran directly upon one. The vessel swerved right round, but was brought up again soon after.

We track or sail from 6 A.M., and moor the boats at 7 P.M. On anchoring off Deeya I received two matchlocks, sent to me by my husband, on account of his having heard that many salt-boats on the Jumna have been plundered lately; the matchlocks are to be fired off of an evening when the watch is set, to show we are on our guard. At night a chaprāsī and two dāndees hold their watch, armed, on deck; and two chaukidārs (watchmen) from the nearest village keep watch on shore. My little fine-eared terrier is on board, and I sleep without a thought of robbery or danger. If you take a guard from the nearest village, you are pretty safe; if not, perhaps the chaukidārs themselves will rob you, in revenge for your not employing them.

Parisnāth

12*th*.—The passage off Mhow was difficult,—rocks and sands. We were on a sandbank several times. The temple of Parisnāth at Pabosa was to me a very interesting object. At Allahabad I procured a small white marble image of this god, and while considering whom it might represent, the moonshee came into the room. The man is a high-church Hindoo: on seeing the image, he instantly covered his eyes and turned away, expressing his disapprobation. "That is the idol Parisnāth," said he, "a man of the pure faith may not look upon it, and will not worship in a temple desecrated by its presence." There are about four hundred heretical Hindoos at Prāg. The image is represented in a sitting posture, not unlike the attitude of the Budha idol of Ava, but from which it differs in the position of the right hand.

[. . .]

13*th*.—Every twelve miles a dārogha comes on board to make salām to the mem sāhiba, and to ask her orders. I send letters to Prāg by this means; the dārogha gives them to our own chaprāsīs, who run with them from station to station. There is no dāk (post) in these parts. The dāroghas bring fish, eggs, kids, any thing of which I am in need; and I pay for them, although they are brought as presents, it being against the orders of Government to receive the gift even of a cabbage or beet-root from a native. The tracking ground was fine; moored off Bhowna.

15*th*.—Strong west wind, very cold: the river broad and deep; the thermometer at 9 A.M. 60°. The darzee in the after-cabin is at work on a silk gown: the weather is just cold enough to render warm attire necessary. The other day I was on deck in a green velvet travelling cap, with an Indian shawl, put on after the fashion of the men, amusing myself with firing with a pellet-bow at some cotton boats *en passant* for tamāshā. Some natives came on board to make salām, and looked much surprised at seeing a ghulel (a pellet-bow) in feminine hands. The cotton boats would not get out of the way, therefore I pelted the manjhīs, (masters, or steersmen) of the vessels, to hasten the movements of the great unwieldy lubberly craft. Of whom can I talk but of myself in this my solitude on the Jumna-jee? Now for the telescope to look out for the picturesque.

17*th*.—Wind strong, cold, and westerly: the stream broad and deep, anchored off Jerowlee in a jungle: just the place for a sportsman. A quantity of underwood and small trees amongst the ravines and cliffs afford shelter for the game. Here you find nil-gā'ī, peacocks, partridge, and quail. Several peacocks were quietly feeding on the cliffs; others roosting on the trees. At this place they told me there is a bura kund, which is, I believe, a well, or spring, or basin of water, especially consecrated to some holy purpose or person; but I did not visit the spot.

20*th*.—Passed Chilla Tara Ghāt and the Cane River, in which agates, cornelians, calcedony, &c., are found. The day was pleasant, the water deep, but there being but little wind we were obliged to track. Moored off Arouwl, at which place the patelī got upon the rocks.

21*st*.—A strong east wind: we had a fine sail, but went aground off Bindour: moored at Serowlee.

22*nd*.—After a very pleasant day, and pretty good sailing, we lugāoed off Humeerpore: during the night we were kept on the *qui vive* by a very severe storm, accompanied by thunder, lightning, and very heavy rain.

23*rd*.—A wretched day; cold, damp, and miserable, a most powerful wind directly against us. To add to the discomfort, we sprang a leak, which gave sixty buckets of water in twenty-four hours. The leak was found under the rudder. We had to take down a part of the aft-cabin, and to take up some boards before we could get at it: and when found, we had nothing on board fit to stop it. At last it was effectually stopped with towels, torn up and forced in tight, and stiff clay beaten down over that. I thought this might last until our arrival at Kalpee, where proper repairs might take place: moored off Bowlee.

25*th*.—Christmas Day was ushered in by rain and hail, the wind high and contrary. At noon the wind decreased, and we got on better, tracking along the banks, with fourteen men on the goon (track-rope). At seven in the evening, just as we had moored, a storm came on, accompanied with the most brilliant forked lightning; and the most violent wind, blowing a gale, united with the strong stream, bearing full down against us. It was really fearful. After a time the vivid and forked lightning became sheeted, and the rain fell, like a second deluge, in torrents. The peals of thunder shook the cabin windows, and all the panes of glass rattled. We had lugāoed off a dry nālā (the bed of a stream); the torrents of rain filled the nālā with water, which poured down against the side of the pinnace with great force and noise. Fearing we should be driven from our moorings by the force of the current, I ran on deck to see if the men were on the alert. It was quite dark: some were on shore taking up the lāwhāsees by which she was secured to the bank; the rest were on deck, trying with their long bamboos to shove her out of the power of the current from the nālā. Having succeeded in this, we were more comfortable. It was out of the question to take rest during such a storm, while there was a chance of being driven from our moorings; and being quite alone was also unpleasant. At length the gale abated, and I was glad to hear only the rain for the rest of the night. Day-light closed my weary eyes: on awaking refreshed from a quiet slumber, I found the Seagull far from Ekouna, near which place we had passed so anxious a night.

26th.—Moored off Kalpee, famous for its crystalized sugar. Here a large budget of letters was brought to me. I remained the whole day at the station to procure provisions and answer the letters. Nor did I forget to purchase tools and every thing necessary for the repair of the leak in the vessel, although we forbore to remove the towels and clay, as she now only made half a bucket in twenty-four hours.

28th.—North-west wind very cold: the river most difficult to navigate in parts; rocky, sandy, shallow. Anchored off Palpoor; found a quantity of river shells; they are not very pretty, but some are curious.

29th.—We were in the midst of great sandbanks, in a complete wilder-ness; the stream was strong and deep, the tracking-ground good; here and there the rocks appeared above water under the high cliffs. Off Belaspoor, on one sandbank, I saw ten crocodiles basking in the sun, all close together; some turtle and great white birds were on a rock near them; on the river's edge were three enormous alligators, large savage monsters, lying with their enormous mouths wide open, eyeing the boats. The men on board shouted with all their might; the alligators took no notice of the shout; the croco-diles, more timid than the former, ran into the water, and disappeared immediately. These are the first alligators I have seen in their own domains; they are very savage, and will attack men; the crocodiles will not, if it be possible to avoid them. I would willingly have taken the voyage for this one sight of alligators and crocodiles in their native wildernesses; the scene was so unusual, so wild, so savage. At sunset, anchored off Gheetamow, and found some shells during my evening ramble.

At the sale of the effects of the late Col. Gough, in Calcutta, was the head of a magar (alligator) of incredible size, caught in the Megna; which, though deficient in not having an under-jaw, was a good weight for a man to carry, stooping to it with both hands. The creeks of a bend of the Sunderbunds, not far below Calcutta, are the places frequented, I hear, by the patriarchs of their race.

The next day we entered a most difficult part of the river; it was impossible to tell in which direction to steer the vessel; rocks on every side; the river full of them; a most powerful stream rushing between the rocks; to add to the danger, we had a strong westerly wind directly in our teeth, which, united to the force of the stream, made us fear the goon might break; in which case we should have been forced most violently against the rocks. We accomplished only one mile in four hours and a half! I desired the sarang to anchor the vessel, and let the men have some rest; they had been fagging, up to their waists in water, all the time, and I wished the wind to abate ere we attempted to proceed further. After the dāndees had dined, we pushed off again. At Kurunka a pilot came on board, which pleased me very much, as it was impossible to tell on which side of the rocks the passage might be: the pilot took us up with great difficulty through the rocks to the land-mark off the bungalow at Badoura; there he requested leave to anchor until the wind might abate; he was afraid to try the stream, it being still stronger higher up. Of course I consented; after which, accompanied by the pilot, I walked some three miles to collect fossil bones; these bones were discovered by the sappers and miners on the river-side, at the little village of Badoura; the bones are petrified, but to what animal they belonged is unknown; some cart-loads of them have been taken to Allahabad, to be shown to the scientific; I brought back five or six of the bones we found at the place. A short time ago this part of the river was impassable; the Company sent sappers and miners, who, having surrounded each rock with a fence that kept out the water, blew them up, and made a passage down the centre of the river; of course this was a work of time; the fences were then removed, and the stream flowed unconfined. Large boats can now go up and down in safety, if they know the passage. The next morning the pilot accompanied us as far as Merapoor, when he made his salām, and returned to the sappers' and miners' bungalow. The river now became good and clear; we encountered no more difficulties, and moored quietly off Seholee at six in the evening.

1835, *Jan.* 1*st.*—New Year's Day was as disagreeable as Christmas Day; cold, frosty; a wind in our teeth; rocks and crocodiles. My pet terrier was taken ill; with difficulty she was brought through the attack; poor little Poppus,—she has a dozen names, all of endearment. Passed Juggermunpoor, where the fair for horses is held.

2*nd.*—A fair wind brought us to the Chumbal river. The fort and Hindoo temple of Bhurrage are very picturesque objects. This is one of the most difficult passes on the river, on account of the sand banks, and the power of the stream from the junction of the Jumna and Chumbal. I am directed not to stop a moment for any thing but letters on my way to Agra; on my return I shall go on shore (D.V.), and visit all the picturesque places I now behold merely *en passant*. The Chumbal is a beautiful river; never was a stream more brilliant or more clear; the water, where it unites with the Jumna, is of a bright pellucid green.

From the force of the united streams we had great difficulty in passing the junction; the wind dropped, and we could not move the pinnace on the towing-rope; we sent a hawser in the dinghee to the opposite shore, and then, with the united force of the crews of both vessels, hauled the pinnace across the junction into the quiet waters of the Jumna; it was 6 P.M. ere this was effected. Whilst the people anchored, and got the cook-boat over, I walked to a beautiful Hindoo temple, close to the river's edge. The fort beyond put me in mind of Conway Castle; the towers are somewhat similar: on my return I must stop and sketch it. A wealthy native has sent to petition *an audience*; he is anxious to make salām to the mem sāhiba. I have declined seeing him, as we must start at daybreak; but have told him on my return I shall stay a day or two at this picturesque place, and shall then be happy to receive his visit.

Nothing is so shocking, so disgusting, as the practice of burning bodies; generally only half-burning them, and throwing them into the river. What a horrible sight I saw to-day! crowds of vultures, storks, crows, and pariah dogs from the village glutting over a dreadful meal; they fiercely stripped the flesh from the swollen body of the half-burned dead, which the stream had thrown on a sand bank; and howled and shrieked as they fought over and for their fearful meal!

How little the natives think of death! This morning, when I was on deck, the body of a woman floated by the pinnace, within the reach of a bamboo; she was apparently dead, her long black hair spread on the stream; by the style of the red dress, she was a Hindoo; she must have fallen, or have been thrown into the river. I desired the men to pull the body to the vessel's side, and see if she might not be saved. They refused to touch it even with a bamboo; nobody seemed to think any thing about it, further than to prevent the body touching the vessel, should the stream bring it close to the side. One man coolly said, "I suppose she fell into the river when getting up water in her gharā" (earthen vessel)!

How easily a murdered man might be disposed of! On account of the expense of fuel, the poorer Hindoos only slightly burn the bodies of the dead, and then cast them into the river; by attiring the corpse after the fashion of a body to be burned, and throwing it into the stream, it would never attract attention; any native would say, "Do not touch it, do not touch it; it is merely a burnt body."

This life on the river, however solitary, is to me very agreeable; and I would proceed beyond Agra to Delhi, but that I should think there cannot be water enough for the pinnace; with a fair wind there is much to enjoy in the changing scene, but tracking against a contrary one is tiresome work.

3rd.—A most unpleasant day; we were aground many times, contending against the stream and a powerful wind. The new goon broke, and we were at last fixed most firmly and unpleasantly on a bank of sand; in that position, finding it impossible to extricate the pinnace, we remained all night.

4th.—We were obliged to cut our way through the sandbank to the opposite shore, a distance of about a quarter of a mile; this took twelve hours to accomplish; the anchor was carried to a distance with a chain cable, and there dropped; and the pinnace was pulled by main force through the sand, where there was not water enough to float her. When out of it, we came upon a stream that ran like a torrent, aided by a most powerful and contrary wind. To remain where we were was dangerous; the men carried a thick cable in the dinghee to the shore, made it fast, and were pulling the vessel across; when half-way, just as we thought ourselves in safety, the cable broke, the pinnace whirled round and round like a bubble on the waters, and was carried with fearful velocity down the stream. The sarang lost all power over the vessel, but, as last, her progress was stopped by being brought up fast on a sandbank. By dint of hard work we once more got the cable fastened to the opposite shore, and carried her safely to the other side; where, to my great delight, we anchored, to await the decrease of the wind, that howled through the ropes as though it would tear them from the masts.

Thinking the vessel must have received a violent strain under all the force she had endured, we opened the hold, and found she had sprung a leak, that bubbled up at a frightful rate; the leak was under planks it was impossible to remove, unless by sawing off two feet from three large planks, if we could procure a saw; such a thing could not be found. I thought of a razor, the orthodox weapon wherewith to saw through six-inch boards, and get out of prison; no one would bring forward a razor. At length I remembered the very small fine saw I make use of for cutting the soap-stone, and, by very tender and gentle usage, we at length cut off the ends of the planks, and laid open the head of the leak, under the rudder, below water-mark. Here the rats and white ants had been very busy, and had worked away undisturbed at a principal beam, so that you could run your fingers some inches into it. With a very gentle hand the tow was stuffed in, but as we stopped the leak in one part, it sprang up in another; all day long we worked incessantly, and at night, in despair, filled it up with stiff clay. I went to rest, but my sleep was disturbed by dreams of water hissing in mine ears, and that we were going down stern foremost. During the night I called up the men three times to bale the vessel; she gave up quantities of water. We anchored off Mulgong.

5th.—Detained by the strong and contrary wind; the leak still gave up water, but in a less quantity; and it was agreed to leave it in its present condition until we could get to Etaweh. I was not quite comfortable, knowing the state of the rotten wood, and the holes the rats had made, through which the water had bubbled up so fast. The next day, not one drop of water came from the leak, and the vessel being quite right afterwards, I determined not to have her examined until our arrival at Agra, and could never understand why she did not leak.

9th.—Ever since the 4th we have had the most violent and contrary winds all day; obliged generally to anchor for two hours at noon, it being impossible to stem the stream, and struggle against the wind; most disagreeable work; I am quite tired and sick of it. Thus far I have borne all with the patience of a Hindoo, the wish to behold the Tāj carrying me on. It is so cold, my hand shakes, I can scarcely guide my pen; the thermometer 50° at 10 A.M., with this bitter and strong wind. I dare not light a fire, as I take cold quitting it to go on deck; all the glass windows are closed,— I have on a pair of Indian shawls, snow boots, and a velvet cap,—still my face and head throb with rheumatism. When on deck, at mid-day, I wear a sola topī, to defend me from the sun.

This river is very picturesque; high cliffs, well covered with wood, rising abruptly from the water: here and there a Hindoo temple, with a great peepul-tree spreading its fine green branches around it: a ruined native fort: clusters of native huts: beautiful stone ghāts jutting into the river: the effect greatly increased by the native women, in their picturesque drapery, carrying their vessels for water up and down the cliffs, poised on their heads. Fishermen are seen with their large nets; and droves of goats and small cows, buffaloes, and peacocks come to the river-side to feed. But the most picturesque of all are the different sorts of native vessels; I am quite charmed with the boats. Oh that I were a painter, who could do justice to the scenery! My pinnace, a beautiful vessel, so unlike any thing else here, must add beauty to the river, especially when under sail.

Aground on a sandbank again! with such a wind and stream it is not pleasant—hardly safe. What a noise! attempting to force her off the bank;

it is terribly hard work; the men, up to their waists in water, are shoving the vessel with their backs, whilst the wind and stream throw here back again. Some call on Allah for aid, some on Gunga, some on Jumna-jee, every man shouting at the height of his voice. What a squall! the vessel lies over frightfully. I wish the wind would abate! forced sideways down on the sandbank by the wind and stream, it is not pleasant. There! there is a howl that ought to succeed in forcing her off, in spite of the tufān; such clouds of fine sand blowing about in every direction! Now the vessel rocks, now we are off once more,—back we are again! I fancy the wind and stream will have their own way. Patience, mem sāhiba, you are only eight miles from Etaweh: when you may get over those eight miles may be a difficult calculation. The men are fagging, up to their breasts in the river; I must go on deck, and make a speech. What a scene! I may now consider myself really in the wilderness, such watery *waists* are spread before me!

The Mem Sāhiba's Speech

"Ari! Ari! what a day is this! Ahi Khudā! what a wind is here! Is not this a tufān? Such an ill-starred river never, never did I see! Every moment, every moment, we are on a sandbank. Come, my children, let her remain; it is the will of God,—what can we do? Eat your food, and when the gale lulls we may get off. Perhaps, by the blessing of God, in twelve months' time we may reach Etaweh."

After this specimen of eloquence, literally translated from the Hindostanee in which it was spoken, the dāndees gladly wrapped their blankets round them, and crept into corners out of the wind, to eat chabenī, the parched grain of Indian corn, maize. Could you but see the men whom I term my children! they are just what in my youth I ever pictured to myself canni-bals must be: so wild and strange-looking, their long, black, shaggy hair matted over their heads, and hanging down to their shoulders; their bodies of dark brown, entirely naked, with the exception of a cloth round the waist, which passes between the limbs. They jump overboard, and swim ashore with a rope between their teeth, and their towing-stick in one hand, just like dogs,—river dogs; the water is their element more than the land. If they want any clothes on shore they carry them on the top of their heads, and swim to the bank in that fashion. The mem sāhiba's river dogs; they do not drink strong waters; and when I wish to delight them very much, I give them two or three rupees' worth of sweetmeats, cakes of sugar and ghee made in the bazār; like great babies, they are charmed with their *meetai*, as they call it, and work away willingly for a mem sāhiba who makes presents of sweetmeats and kids.

Saw the first wolf to-day; I wish we were at Etaweh,—to anchor here is detestable: if we were there I should be reading my letters, and getting in supplies for Agra. How I long to reach the goal of my pilgrimage, and to make my salām to the "Tāj beebee ke rauza," the mausoleum of the lady of the Tāj!

Chapter 26

Pilgrimage to the Tāj

"HE WHO HAS NOT PATIENCE POSSESSES NOT PHILOSOPHY".[1]

"Whether doing, suffering, or forbearing,
You may do miracles by persevering."

1835, *Jan.* 10*th.*—Ours is the slowest possible progress; the wind seems engaged to meet us at every turn of our route. At 3 P.M. we lugāoed at Etaweh; while I was admiring the ghāts, to my great delight, a handful of letters and parcels of many kinds were brought to me. In the evening, the chaprāsī in charge of my riding horses, with the sā'īses and grass-cutters who had marched from Allahabad to meet me, arrived at the ghāt. The grey neighed furiously, as if in welcome; how glad I was to see them!

In a minute I was on the little black horse; away we went, the black so glad to have a canter, the mem sāhiba so happy to give him one: through deep ravines, over a road through the dry bed of a torrent, up steep cliffs; away we went like creatures possessed; the horse and rider were a happy pair. After a canter of about four miles it became dark, or rather moonlight, and I turned my horse towards the river, guided by the sight of a great cliff, some 150 or 200 feet high, beneath which we had anchored. I lost my way,

[1] Oriental Proverbs.

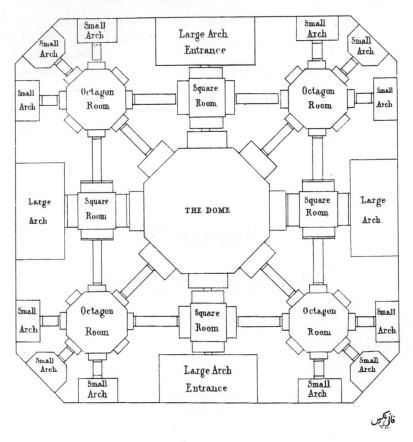

Ground Plan of the Tomb of the Táj.

Figure 8   Ground-plan of the Tomb of the Tāj

but turned down a bridle road in the bed of a ravine, which of course led somewhere to the river. I rode under a cliff so high and overhanging, I felt afraid to speak; at last we got out of the cold and dark ravine, and came directly upon the pinnace. I had met, during my ride, two gentlemen in a buggy; one of them, after having arrived at his own house, returned to look for me, thinking I might turn down by mistake the very road I had gone, which at night was very unsafe, on account of the wolves; but he did not overtake me.

The next morning he called on me, and brought me a letter from a relative; therefore we were soon acquainted, and agreed to have a canter, when the sun should go down. He told me, on his way down, the police had brought him a basket, containing half the mangled body of a child; the wolves had seized the poor child, and had devoured the other half the night before, in the ravines. It was fortunate I did not encounter a gang of them under the dark cliff, where the black horse could scarcely pick his way over the stones.

11*th*.—I rode with Mr. G——through the ravines and the Civil Station, and saw many beautiful and picturesque spots. We returned to the pinnace; he came on board, and we had a long conference. It was not to be marvelled at that the mem sāhiba talked a great deal, when it is considered she had not spoken one word of English for thirty-three days; then she did talk!—ye gods! how she did talk! Mr. G——offered to send armed men with me if I felt afraid, but I declined taking them; and he promised to forward my letters by horsemen every day, to meet the pinnace. Nothing can be greater than the kindness one meets with from utter strangers in India. He gave my husband and me an invitation to pay him a visit on our way back, which I accepted for the absent sāhib.

I was amused by an officer's coming down to the river, which he crossed; he then mounted a camel, and his servant another; he carried nothing with him but some bedding, that served as a saddle, and a violin! In this fashion he had come down from Sabbatoo, and was going, *viâ* Jubbulpore, across to Bombay! thence to sail for England. How charmingly independent! It is unusual for a gentleman to ride a camel; those who *understand* the motion, a long swinging trot, say it is pleasant; others complain it makes the back ache, and brings on a pain in the liver. At Etaweh every thing was to be had that I wished for; peacocks, partridges, fowls, pigeons, beef, were brought for sale; atr of roses, peacocks' feathers, milk, bread, green tea, sauces; in short, food of every sort. I read and answered my letters, and retired to rest perfectly fagged.

12*th*.—At daybreak the pinnace started once more for Agra,—once more resumed her pilgrimage; it is seventy-two miles by the road from Etaweh; how far it may be by this twisting and winding river remains to be proved. For some days two bird-catchers (chirī-mārs) have followed the pinnace, and have supplied me with peacocks; to-day they brought a hen and three young ones; they also brought their nets and the snares with them, which I had seen them use on shore. The springes are beautifully made of buffalo-horn and catgut. I bought one hundred and six springes for catching peacocks, cyrus, wild ducks, &c., for four rupees, and shall set them in the first jungle we meet. I set them immediately in the cabin, and caught my own two dogs: it was laughable to see the dismay of the dogs, nor could I help laughing at my own folly in being such a child. My head began to throb bitterly, and I spent the rest of the day ill in bed.

[. . .]

17*th*.—An acquaintance, the Hon. Mrs. R——, has just arrived at Allahabad from England; nothing could exceed her astonishment when she heard I had gone up the Jumna alone, on a pilgrimage of perhaps two months or more to see the Tāj, not forced to make the voyage from necessity. I have books, and employments of various sorts, to beguile the loneliness; and the adventures I meet with, give variety and interest to the monotony of life on the river. Could I follow my own inclinations, I would proceed to Delhi, thence to the Hills, and on to the source of the Jumna; this would really be a good undertaking. "Capt. Skinner's Travels," which I have just read, have given me the most ardent desire to go to the source of the Jumna.[1]

[. . .]

19*th*.—We arrived at the city of Betaizor, which is built across the bed where the Jumna formerly flowed. The Rajah Buddun Sing built this ghāt, and very beautiful it is; a perfect crowd of beautiful Hindoo temples clustered together, each a picture in itself, and the whole reflected in the bright pure waters of the Jumna. I stopped there for an hour, to sketch the ghāt, and walked on the sands opposite, charmed with the scene,—the high cliffs, the trees; no Europeans are there,—a place is spoiled by European residence. In the evening we anchored off the little village of Kheil: rambling on the river's bank, I saw five peacocks in the shimoul (the silk-cotton tree), and called Jinghoo Bearer, who ran off to fetch a matchlock, which he loaded with *two* bullets; the birds were so unmolested, they showed no fear when I went under the tree with the dogs, and only flew away when Jinghoo fired at them; the report aroused two more peacocks from the next tree; a flock of wild geese, and another of wild ducks, sprang up from the sands; and the solitary chakwā screamed āw! āw! The shimoul is a fine high-spreading tree, the flower a brilliant one; and the pod contains a sort of silky down, with which mattresses and pillows are often stuffed. The natives object to pillows stuffed with silk-cotton, saying it makes the head ache. The large silk-cotton tree (bombax ceiba) is the seat of the gods who superintend districts and villages; these gods, although minor deities, are greatly feared. Punchaits, or native courts of justice, are held beneath the shimoul, under the eye of the deity in the branches. There are fields of kāpās, the common white cotton plant, (gossypium herbaceum,) on the side of the river; the

---

[1] Capt. John Skinner: *Excursions in India, including a walk over the Himalaya Mountains to the Sources of the Ganges and the Jumna,* 1833.

cotton has just been gathered; a few pods, bursting with snowy down, are hanging here and there, the leavings of the cotton harvest: the plant is an annual. In my garden at Prāg are numerous specimens of the Bourbon cotton, remarkably fine, the down of which is of a brown colour.

I have met hundreds of enormous boats, laden with cotton, going down to Calcutta, and other parts of the country; they are most remarkably picturesque. I said the report startled the solitary chakwā. The chakwā is a large sort of reddish-brown wild duck (anas cæsarca), very remarkable in its habits. You never see more than two of these birds together; during the day they are never separate,—models of constancy; during the night they are invariably apart, always divided by the stream; the female bird flies to the other side of the river at night, remains there all solitary, and in the morning returns to her mate, who during the livelong night has been sitting alone and crying āw! āw! The male calls āw! some ten or twelve times successively; at length the female gives a single response, "nā'ich!" Leaving the people, some cooking and some eating their dinners, I rambled on alone, as was my custom, to some distance from the boats, listening to and thinking of the chakwā. The first man who finished his meal was the dhobee, a Hindoo, and he started forth to find me. I questioned him respecting the birds, and he spake as follows: "When the beautiful Seeta was stolen away from the god Rām, he wandered all over the world seeking his love. He asked of the chakwā and his mate, 'Where is Seeta, where is my love, have you seen her?' The chakwā made answer, 'I am eating, and attending to my own concerns; trouble me not, what do I know of Seeta?' Rām, angry at these words, replied, 'Every night henceforth your love shall be taken from you and divided by a stream; you shall bemoan her loss the livelong night; during the day she shall be restored.'

"He asked of the stars, 'Where is Seeta?' the silent stars hid their beams. He asked of the forest, 'Where is my beloved?' the forest moaned and sighed, and could give him no intelligence. He asked of the antelope, 'Where is she whom I seek, the lost, the beloved?' The antelope replied, 'My mate is gone, my heart is bowed with grief, my own cares oppress me. Her whom you seek mine eyes have not beheld.'"

It is true the birds invariably live after this fashion: they are great favourites of mine, the chakwās; and I never hear their cry but I think of Seeta Rām.

21st.—The wind westerly and bitterly cold. Loon or noon, from which salt is made, is in large quantities on the river-side. We lugāoed at Aladīnpoor, the village of Ullah-o-deen, or Aladdin, as you call it; and I can think of nothing but his wonderful lamp. I walked through the village; the moment the people caught sight of me and the chaprāsīs, away they ran and hid themselves. In the middle of the village we found some young men sitting on the ground round a fire, warming their hands over the blaze: they did not show any fear, like the rest of the villagers, and I talked to them for some time. They pointed out their fields of the castor-oil plant, all nipped by the frost. I requested them to let me buy a couple of kids to give to the dāndees, a kid feast would warm them such a cold evening. This morning I saw men brushing what is called noon off the clayey banks of the river: they steep it in water, then boil it, when a very good salt is produced. We sometimes use it at table. A poor man in this way brushes up a little noon, and makes enough for his own consumption, which is of great advantage to him. The natives consume salt in large quantities.

All day long I sit absorbed in modelling little temples, or ghāts, or some folly or another, in khuree, a sort of soap-stone. I can scarcely put it aside, it fascinates me so much. I cannot quit my soap-stone. Any thing I see, I try to imitate; and am now at work on a model of the bā'olī (great well) at Allahabad. Captain K—— gave me a tomb he had modelled in soap-stone, and some tools. I copied it, and have since modelled a temple on a ghāt and the bā'olī aforesaid; the stone is easily cut with a saw, or with a knife, and may be delicately carved. That bought in the bazār at Allahabad, weighing two or three sēr, is generally of a darkish colour, because the men who bring it from the Up Country often use it to form their chūlees (cooking places) on the road; it becomes discoloured by the heat. A relative sent me some khuree (soap-stone) from a copper mine hill, near Baghesur on the road to Melun Himalaya, which is remarkably pure and white.

A great deal of the clayey ground on the river's edge that we have passed to-day looks like a badly frosted cake, white from the loon or noon. A little more work at the soap-stone, and then to rest.

23rd.—I could scarcely close my eyes during the night for the cold, and yet my covering consisted of four Indian shawls, a rezaī of quilted cotton, and a French blanket. A little pan of water having been put on deck, at 8 A.M. the ayha brought it to me filled with ice. What fine strong ice they must be making at the pits, where every method to produce evaporation is adopted! I am sitting by the fire for the first time. At 8 A.M. the thermometer was 46°; at 10 A.M. 54°. The dāndees complain bitterly of the cold. Thirteen men on the goon are fagging, up to their knees in water, against the stream and this cold wind; this twist in the river will, however, allow of half an hour's sail, and the poor creatures may then warm themselves. I will send each man a red Lascar's cap and a black blanket, their Indian bodies feel the cold so bitterly. When the sails are up my spirits rise; this tracking day by day against wind and stream so many hundred miles is tiresome work. My solitude is agreeable, but the tracking detestable. I must go on deck, there is a breeze, and enjoy the variety of having a sail. At Pukkaghur eight peacocks were by the river-side, where they had come for water; on our approach they moved gently away. They roost on the largest trees they can find at night. I have just desired three pints of oil to be given to the dāndees, that they may rub their limbs. The cold wind, and being constantly in and out of the water, makes their skin split, although it is like the hide of the rhinoceros; they do not suffer so much when their legs have been well rubbed with oil. What a noise the men are making! they are all sitting on the deck, whilst a bearer, with a great jar of oil, is doling out a chhattak to each shivering dāndee.

[. . .]

26*th*.—This morning from the cliff the white marble dome of the Tāj could just be discerned, and we made salām to it with great pleasure. The pinnace anchored below Kutoobpoor, unable to proceed in consequence of another great sandbank, a quarter of a mile broad. The sarang says, "To attempt to cut through this on a chain-cable would draw every bolt and nail out of her frame." The Ghāt Mānjhī is of the same opinion. I have been out in the dinghee sounding, and, fearless as I am, I dare not attempt cutting through such a bank; it would injure the vessel. There are two more sandbanks besides this ahead. It is folly to injure the pinnace, and I have made up my mind to quit her. Is it not provoking, only sixteen miles from Agra, and to be detained here? I have written to the Hon. H. D—— to request him to send down my horses; they must have arrived long ago, and a palanquin: his answer, I must await with due patience. What a pity I am not a shot! I saw three deer yesterday whilst I was amusing myself in an original fashion, digging porcupines out of their holes, or rather trying to do so, for the dogs found the holes; but the men could not get the animals out of them. Picked up a chilamchī full of river-shells. Before us are thirteen large boats aground on this sandbank. In the evening I took a long walk to see the state of another shallow ahead, which they say is worse than the one we are off. Six of the great cotton boats have cut through the sand; perhaps they will deepen the channel, and we shall be able to pass on tomorrow. There are peacocks in the fields: what a pity my husband is not here, or that I am not a shot!

27*th*.—Not being satisfied to quit the pinnace without having inspected the river myself, I went up to Bissowna in the patelī this morning, and found it would be utter folly to think of taking the Seagull further; besides which, it is impossible. I might upset her, but to get her across a bank half a mile in length is out of the question. The water in the deepest parts is only as high as a man's knee, and she requires it up to the hip-bone. It is very provoking—I am tired of this vile jungle—nothing to look at but the vessels aground; besides which, the noise is eternal, night and day, from the shouts of the men trying to force their boats off the sand into deeper water.

28th.—My riding horses having arrived, I quitted the pinnace, desiring the sarang to return to Dharu-ke-Nuggeria, and await further orders.

I sent off the cook-boat and attendants to Agra, and taking my little pet terrier in my arms cantered off on the black horse to meet the palanquin a friend had sent for me. Late at night I arrived at Agra, found a tent that had been pitched for me within the enclosure of the Tāj, in front of the Kālūn Dāwāzā or great gateway, and congratulated myself on having at length accomplished the pilgrimage in a voyage up the Jumna of fifty-one days! Over-exertion brought on illness, and severe pains in my head laid me up for several days.

Chapter 27

The Tāj Mahul

"I have paid two visits to Agra since I returned from Lucnow, and thought of you and the sāhib whilst admiring the Tāj. Do not, for the sake of all that is elegant, think of going home without paying it a visit. I shall, with great delight, be your cicerone in these regions: if you put it off much longer (if alive), I shall scarce be able to crawl with old age. Do not think of quitting India; it is a country far preferable to the cold climate, and still colder hearts of Europe."

W. L. G——, Khasgunge.

1835, *Jan.*—I have seen the Tāj Mahul; but how shall I describe its loveliness? its unearthly style of beauty! It is not its magnitude; but its elegance, its proportions, its exquisite workmanship, and the extreme delicacy of the whole, that render it the admiration of the world. The tomb, a fine building of white marble, erected upwards of two centuries ago, is still in a most wonderful state of preservation, as pure and delicate as when first erected. The veins of grey in the marble give it a sort of pearl-like tint, that adds to, rather than diminishes its beauty. It stands on a square terrace of white marble, on each angle of which is a minaret of the same material. The whole is carved externally and internally, and inlaid with ornaments formed of blood-stones, agates, lapis lazuli, &c. &c., representing natural flowers. The inscriptions over all the arches are in the Arabic character, in black marble, inlaid on white. The dome itself, the four smaller domes, and the cupolas on the roof, are all of the same white marble carved beautifully, and inlaid with flowers in coloured stones.

[. . .]

This magnificent monument was raised by Shāhjahān to the memory of his favourite Sultana Arzumund Bānoo, on whom, when he ascended the throne, he bestowed the title of Momtâza Zumâni (the Most Exalted of the age).

On the death of Shāhjahān, his grandson Alumgeer placed his cenotaph in the Tāj, on the right hand, and close to that of Arzumund Bānoo; this is rather a disfigurement, as the building was intended alone for the Lady of the Tāj, whose cenotaph rests in the centre. Formerly, a screen of silver and gold surrounded it; but when Alumgeer erected the tomb of Shāhjahān by the side of that of the Sultana, he removed the screen of gold and silver, and replaced it by an octagonal marble screen, which occupies about half the diameter of the building, and encloses the tombs. The open fretwork and mosaic of this screen are most beautiful: each side is divided into three panels, pierced and carved with a delicacy equal to the finest carving in ivory; and bordered with wreaths of flowers inlaid, of agate, bloodstone, cornelian, and every variety of pebble. I had the curiosity to count the number contained in one of the flowers, and found there were seventy-two; there are fifty flowers of the same pattern. The cenotaphs themselves are inlaid in the same manner; I never saw any thing so elegant; the tombs, to be properly appreciated, must be seen, as all the native drawings make them exceedingly gaudy, which they are not. The inscriptions on both are of black marble inlaid on white, ornamented with mosaic flowers of precious stones.

The first glance on entering is imposing in the extreme: the dim religious light, the solemn echoes,—at first I imagined that priests in the chambers above were offering up prayers for the soul of the departed, and the echo was the murmur of the requiem. When many persons spoke together it was like thunder,—such a volume of powerful sounds; the natives compare it to the roar of many elephants. "Whatever you say to a dome it says to you again."[1] A prayer repeated over the tomb is echoed and re-echoed above like the peal of an organ, or the distant and solemn chant in a cathedral.

Each arch has a window, the frames of marble, with little panes of glass, about three inches square. Underneath the cenotaphs is a vaulted apartment, where the remains of the Emperor and the Sultana are buried in two sarcophagi, facsimiles of the cenotaphs above. The crypt is square, and of plain marble; the tombs here are also beautifully inlaid, but sadly defaced in parts by plunderers. The small door by which you enter was formerly of solid silver: it is now formed of rough planks of mango wood.

It is customary with Musulmāns to erect the cenotaph in an apartment over the sarcophagus, as may be seen in all the tombs of their celebrated men. The Musulmāns who visit the Tāj lay offerings of money and flowers, both on the tombs below and the cenotaphs above; they also distribute money in charity, at the tomb, or at the gate, to the fakīrs.

The Sultana Arzumund Bānoo was the daughter of the vizier, Asaf-jāh; she was married twenty years to Shāhjahān, and bore him a child almost every year; she died on the 18th July, 1631, in childbed, about two hours after the birth of a princess. Though she seldom interfered in public affairs, Shāhjahān owed the empire to her influence with her father: nor was he ungrateful; he loved her living, and lamented her when dead. Calm, engaging, and mild in her disposition, she engrossed his whole affection; and though he maintained a number of women for state, they were only the slaves of her pleasure. She was such an enthusiast in Deism, that she could scarcely forbear persecuting the Portuguese for their supposed idolatry, and it was only on what concerned that nation she suffered her temper, which was naturally placid, to be ruffled. To express his respect for her memory, the Emperor raised this tomb, which cost in building the amazing sum of £750,000 sterling. The death of the Sultana, in 1631, was followed by public calamities of various kinds. Four sons and four daughters survived her,—Dara, Suja, Aurunzebe, and Morâd: Aurunzebe succeeded to the throne of his father. The daughters were, the Princess Jahânārā (the Ornament of the World), Roshenrāi Begam (or the Princess of the Enlightened Mind), Suria Bânū (or the Splendid Princess), and another, whose name is not recorded. Arzumund Bānoo was the enemy of the Portuguese, then the most powerful European nation in India, in consequence of having accompanied Shāhjahān to one of their settlements, when she was enraged beyond measure against them, for the worship they paid to images.

[1] Oriental Proverbs.

Such is the account given of the Most Exalted of the Age; but we have no record of her beauty, nor have we reason to suppose that she was beautiful. She was the niece of one of the most celebrated of women, the Sultana of Jahāngeer, whose titles were Mher-ul-nissa (the Sun of Women), Noor-mâhul (the Light of the Empire), and Noor-jahān (Light of the World).

Noorjahān was the sister of the Vizier Asaf-jāh, and aunt to the lady of the Tāj. Many people, seeing the beauty of the building, confuse the two persons, and bestow in their imaginations the beauty of the aunt on the niece. Looking on the tomb of Shāhjahān, one cannot but remember that, either by the dagger or the bow-string, he dispatched all the males of the house of Timūr, so that he himself and his children only remained of the posterity of Baber, who conquered India.

In former times no Musulmān was allowed to enter the Tāj, but with a bandage over his eyes, which was removed at the grave where he made his offerings. The marble floor was covered with three carpets, on which the feet sank deeply, they were so soft and full. Pardas (screens) of silk, of fine and beautiful materials, were hung between all the arches. Chandeliers of crystal, set with precious stones, hung from the ceiling of the dome. There was also one chandelier of agate and another of silver: these were carried off by the Jāt Suruj Mul, who came from the Deccan and despoiled Agra.

It was the intention of Shāhjahān to have erected a mausoleum for himself, exactly similar to the Tāj, on the opposite side of the river; and the two buildings were to have been united by a bridge of marble across the Jumna. The idea was magnificent; but the death of Shāhjahān took place in 1666, while he was a prisoner, and ere he had time to complete his own monument.

The stones were prepared on the opposite side of the Jumna, and were carried off by the Burtpoor Rajah, and a building at Deeg has been formed of those stones. A part of the foundation of the second Tāj is still standing, just opposite the Tāj Mahul.

An immense space of ground is enclosed by a magnificent wall around the Tāj, and contains a number of elegant buildings, surrounded by fine old trees, and beds of the most beautiful flowers; the wall itself is remarkable, of great height, of red stone, and carved both inside and outside. [. . .]

Feb. 1*st.*—A fair, the mela of the Eed, was held without the great gateway; crowds of gaily-dressed and most picturesque natives were seen in all directions passing through the avenue of fine trees, and by the side of the fountains to the tomb: they added great beauty to the scene, whilst the eye of taste turned away pained and annoyed by the vile round hats and stiff attire of the European gentlemen, and the equally ugly bonnets and stiff and graceless dresses of the English ladies. Besides the melā at the time of the Eed, a small fair is held every Sunday evening beyond the gates; the fountains play, the band is sent down occasionally, and the people roam about the beautiful garden, in which some of the trees are very large and must be very ancient.

A thunderbolt has broken a piece of marble off the dome of the Tāj. They say during the same storm another bolt fell on the Mootee Masjid, in the Fort, and another on the Jamma Musjid at Delhi.

The gardens are kept in fine order; the produce in fruit is very valuable. A great number of persons are in attendance upon, and in charge of, the tomb, the buildings, and the garden, on account of the Honourable Company, who also keep up the repairs of the Tāj.

At this season the variety of flowers is not very great; during the rains the flowers must be in high perfection. The mālī (gardener) always presents me with a bouquet on my entering the garden, and generally points out to my notice the wallflower as of my country, and not a native of India.
[. . .]

I laid an offering of rupees and roses on the cenotaph of Arzumund Banoo, which purchased me favour in the eyes of the attendants. They are very civil, and bring me bouquets of beautiful flowers. I have stolen away many times alone to wander during the evening in the beautiful garden which surrounds it. The other day, long after the usual hour, they allowed the fountains to play until I quitted the gardens.

Can you imagine any thing so detestable? European ladies and gentlemen have the band to play on the marble terrace, and dance quadrilles in front of the tomb! It was over the parapet of this terrace a lady fell a few months ago, the depth of twenty feet, to the inlaid pavement below. Her husband beheld this dreadful accident from the top of the minaret he had just ascended.

I cannot enter the Tāj without feelings of deep devotion: the sacredness of the place, the remembrance of the fallen grandeur of the family of the Emperor, and that of Asaf Jāh, the father of Arzumund Banoo, the solemn echoes, the dim light, the beautiful architecture, the exquisite finish and delicacy of the whole, the deep devotion with which the natives prostrate themselves when they make their offerings of money and flowers at the tomb, all produce deep and sacred feelings; and I could no more jest or indulge in levity beneath the dome of the Tāj, than I could in my prayers.

The Kalun Darwāza

The gateway to the garden is very grand; it is of red stone, inlaid with marble, and surmounted by a row of little marble cupolas.

Through a magnificent pair of brass gates you enter a dome, fifty feet in diameter, through which you pass on to the Tāj. The spandrils of all the arches are filled up with elegantly-arranged groups of flowers; there are also broad inscriptions running round the greater arches, both at the gate and the Tāj.

The approach is from the south, through the grand gateway of the garden; up the whole length of which, in the centre of fine trees, is a line of beautiful fountains; the vista is finished by the Tāj. At the end of this fountain-adorned avenue, you ascend by a hidden staircase of twenty solid blocks of marble, and arrive on the terrace above, formed of the same material, from which you go on to the interior of the Tāj, which is an octagon, surmounted by a dome seventy feet in diameter. The lower range of arches has an entablature, which is filled with extracts from the Kur'ān inlaid in black marble.

The Tāj was twelve years in building; two lākhs per annum were allowed to keep it in order, and support the establishment of priests and servants. It is situated on the western bank of the Jumna, three miles from the town of Agra; it is nineteen yards square; and the dome about seventy feet in diameter: the stones used in the mosaic are:—

1 Lapis Lazuli.	8 Plasma, or quartz, or chlorite.
2 Jasper.	9 Yellow and striped marbles.
3 Heliotrope.	10 Clayslate.
4 Calcedony agate.	11 Nephrite.
5 Calcedony.	12 Shells—limestone, yellow, and
6 Cornelians.	variegated.
7 Moss agate.	

[. . .]

A single flower in the screen sometimes contains one hundred stones, exactly fitted, forming a correct representation; many hundred flowers have equal numbers. It is impossible to estimate the cost: the most valuable materials were furnished by the sūbadārs of provinces.

Tavernier, who saw this building commenced and finished, asserts, that it occupied twenty thousand men for twenty-two years. The mausoleum itself, and all the buildings that pertain to it, cost 3,17,48026,—three crore, seventeen lākhs, and forty-eight thousand and twenty-six rupees; or, £3,174,802,—three millions, one hundred and seventy-four thousand, eight hundred and two pounds sterling. Colonel Sleeman, in his "Rambles of an Indian Official," remarks,—"This magnificent building, and the palaces at Agra and Delhi, were, I believe, designed by Austin de Bordeux, a Frenchman of great talent and merit, in whose ability and integrity the Emperor placed much reliance. He was called by the natives Oostan Eesau Nadir ol Asur, the Wonderful of the Age; and, for his office of nuksha nuwees, or plan-drawer, he received a regular salary of one thousand rupees a month, with occasional presents, that made his income very large. He died at Cochin, on his way back from Goa, whither he had been sent by the Emperor; and is supposed to have been poisoned by the Portuguese, who were extremely jealous of his influence at court. Oostan Eesau, in all the Persian accounts, stands among the salaried architects.

Beyond the gate, *outside* the walls, is the tomb of the Simundee Begam, built by Shāhjahān; the place is in ruins. A cowherd feeds his cattle on the marble pavement within the tomb; and sacrilegious hands have picked out all the precious stones with which the white marble sarcophagus was inlaid. The same royal coronet adorns this grave: the masjid, close to it, which is in ruins, is of carved red granite, ornamented with white marble, and surmounted by three white marble domes. The tomb is of red granite, with a white marble dome.

Beyond the outer gate, to the right, is a masjid belonging to the tomb of the Fathīpooree Begam, built of red carved granite, now in ruins: within, a number of young natives were winding and twisting silk; the bright red and golden-coloured silks gleamed in the light,—a curious contrast to the ruin of sober red granite.

A short distance beyond is the Sitee Khānam, which, as well as the masjid opposite, was built by Shāhjahān; it is of red granite, the dome is also of the same material,—unlike the other tombs, of which the domes are of white marble: the interior is of white marble, and contains the graves of two sisters. The graves are of slightly-carved white marble, with coronets of an inferior sort carved on the upper slab; probably they were attendants or dependents on the Begam.

The erection of the Tāj was the most delicate and elegant tribute, and the highest compliment, ever paid to woman.

And now adieu!—beautiful Tāj,—adieu! In the far, far West I shall rejoice that I have gazed upon your beauty; nor will the memory depart until the lowly tomb of an English gentlewoman closes on my remains.

Chapter 28

Pleasant Days in Agra

1835, *Feb. 3rd.*—I visited the Fort: one I particularly admire; it is perfectly native. An engineer will perhaps say it wants the strength of an European fortification. An admirer of the picturesque, it pleases me better than one more regularly and scientifically built. There are two gateways; the principal one is called the Delhi Gate, and to the second, named after the Rajah Umrāo Sing, is attached a tradition. Akbar demolished the old Fort of Agra, and replaced it in four years by one of red freestone. It contains innumerable buildings of high interest, among which, its brightest ornament, is the

Mootee Masjid, the Mosque of Pearl

From the gate of entrance you do not expect to see much, the mosque being completely hidden by a high screen of stone. Having passed the gate, you find yourself in a court of marble one hundred and fifty feet square. On the opposite side is the mosque itself; its seven arches of Gothic mould are surmounted by three domes, of oval form, and nine cupolas; the interior is formed of arches, three in depth. The mosque fills up one side of the court; on the right and left are ranges of arcades and two gateways. It is built entirely of white marble, finely carved; the arches are deeply scalloped, and extremely beautiful. Next to the Tāj, I prefer the Mootee Masjid to any building I have seen. It was built by Shāhjahān, and completed in the year 1656. It is in good repair, but is seldom used as a place of worship. It has no ornamental work in mosaic of precious stones, but is elegant and lovely in its simplicity.

The Jahāngeeree Mahul, or palace of Jahāngeer, which is in the Fort, was built by Akbar; the whole is of red freestone, richly carved, but greatly in decay. I viewed this palace with the greatest interest, thinking it might be the one in which Jahāngeer confined the beautiful Mher-ul-Nissa, the Sun of Women, for four years, ere she became his favourite sultana. History relates, that Selim, the son of Akbar, in his youth, ere he took the pompous title of Jahāngeer, the Conqueror of the World, beheld and became enamoured of Mher-ul-Nissa, the betrothed of Sher Afgan, a Turkomanian

247

nobleman of high renown, whom she afterwards married. He was a man who had served with great reputation in the wars of Akbar, and was dignified by the title of Sher Afgan, or the Overthrower of the Lion.

The passion which Jahāngeer had repressed returned with redoubled violence when he mounted the throne, and after several ineffectual attempts to take the life of Sher Afgan, he at length succeeded. The brave man, after a noble resistance, fell, six balls having entered his body. The officer who, by the command of the Emperor, had committed this murder, hastened to the house of Sher Afgan, and sent Mher-ul-Nissa, with all imaginable care, to Delhi. The Emperor's mother received her with great tenderness, but Jahāngeer refused to see her; probably remorse had taken possession of his soul. Be that as it may, he gave orders to shut her up in one of the worst apartments of the palace. He would not deign to behold her; and, contrary to his usual munificence to women, he allowed her but fourteen ānās, less than two shillings a day, for the subsistence of herself and some female slaves. This coldness, unless the offspring of remorse, was unaccountable towards a woman whom he had passionately loved when not in his power.

Mher-ul-Nissa was a woman of haughty spirit, and disappointment preyed upon her mind; she trusted to the amazing power of her own beauty, which, to conquer, required only to be seen; as the Emperor persisted in his refusal to see the widow of Sher Afgan, she had recourse to the following expedient: to raise her own reputation in the palace, and to support herself and her slaves with more decency than the scanty pittance allowed her would admit, she called forth her invention and taste, in working some pieces of admirable tapestry and embroidery, in painting silks with exquisite delicacy, and in inventing female ornaments of every kind; these articles were carried by her slaves to the different apartments of the zenāna, and to the harems of the great officers of state. They were bought with the greatest avidity; nothing was fashionable amongst the ladies of Agra and Delhi but the work of her hands. She accumulated by this means a considerable sum of money, with which she repaired and beautified her apartments, and clothed her slaves in the richest tissues and brocades; whilst she herself affected a very plain and simple dress.

In this situation the widow of Sher Afgan continued for four years, without having once seen the Emperor. Her fame reached his ears from every apartment of the zenāna, and from all quarters: curiosity vanquished his resolution; he resolved to surprise her, and suddenly and unexpectedly entering her apartments, found every thing so elegant and magnificent that he was struck with amazement. But the greatest ornament of the whole was the beautiful Mher-ul-Nissa herself, in a plain dress of white muslin, whilst

her slaves were attired in rich brocades. She received the Emperor with
the usual salām, touching first the ground, and then her forehead, with
her right hand; she was silent, and stood with downcast eyes. Jahāngeer
remained equally silent for some time, in admiration of her stature, shape,
beauty, grace, and that inexpressible voluptuousness of mien, he found
impossible to resist.

On recovering from his confusion, he seated himself; and, placing her
by his side, inquired, "Why this difference between the Sun of Women and
her slaves?" She very shrewdly replied, "Those born to servitude must dress
as it shall please those whom they serve; these are my servants, and I lighten
the burthen of bondage by every indulgence in my power: but I, who
am your slave, O Emperor of the World, must dress according to your
pleasure, and not my own." In spite of the sarcasm, Jahāngeer, greatly
pleased, took her in his arms; and the next day a magnificent festival was
ordered to be prepared, for the celebration of his nuptials with the widow
of Sher Afgan. Her name was changed by edict into Noor-Mahul, the Light
of the Harem. The Emperor's former favourites vanished before her, and
during the rest of the reign of Jahāngeer she held the chief power in
the empire. Her father was raised to the office of vizier, and her two brothers to the first rank of nobility; one of whom, Asaf-jāh, was the father
of the Lady of the Tāj. Although Mher-ul-Nissa was anxious to become
the Empress, she was innocent of any participation in the murder of
her husband, Sher Afgan. A second edict changed her name to Noor-jahān,
or Light of the World; to distinguish her from the other wives of the
Emperor, she was always addressed by the title of Shahee or Empress. Her
name was joined with that of the Emperor on the current coin; she was the
spring that moved the great machine of state. Her family took rank immediately after the princes of the blood; they were admitted at all hours into
the presence, nor were they secluded from the most secret apartments of
the zenāna. During an insurrection, it is mentioned, that the Shahee,
mounted on an elephant, plunged into the stream, with her daughter by
her side; the latter was wounded in the arm, but Noor-jahān pressed
forward; three of her elephant-drivers were successively killed, and the elephant received three wounds on the trunk; in the mean time she emptied
four quivers of arrows on the enemy. The Rajpūts pressed into the stream
to seize her, but the master of the household, mounting the elephant, turned
him away, and carried her out of the river, notwithstanding her threats
and commands. Such is the history that is recorded of the Light of the
World, which imparted a strong interest to my visit to the Jahāngīree Palace.
Noor-jahān had one child, a daughter, by Sher Afgan, but no offspring by
Jahāngeer.

The Selīm Ghar

The Selīm Ghar was formerly a large building, but the outer part has been pulled down by the Honourable Company. One centre room of red granite still remains, in the style of the Jahāngīree Palace; it was built by Akbar, and, no doubt, was called Selīm Ghar after his son, ere he took the title of Jahāngeer.

The Palace in the Fort

Contains magnificent buildings, which are all of white marble, and were erected by Shāh-jahān. The dewanī-khas, or hall of private audience, is a noble structure; the arches are beautiful; so is the building, which is of the same material, inlaid with coloured stones. In the interior, the roof and sides are beautifully and delicately ornamented with the representations of various flowers, beautifully combined, and formed of precious stones; the whole of the ornaments are also richly gilt. The apartments of the zenāna, which adjoin this building, are of white marble, exquisitely carved, and inlaid with precious stones, in the style of the mosaic work at the Tāj. These apartments were converted into a prison for Shāh-jahān, during the latter part of his reign. The central room is a fountain, which plays in, and also falls into a basin of white marble, inlaid with the most beautiful designs, so that the water appears to fall upon brilliant flowers.

The Noor-jahān burj, or turret of Noor-jahān, is of the same exquisitely carved marble, inlaid in a similar manner. In an apartment on the opposite side of the court the same style is preserved; the water here falls over an inlaid marble slab, which is placed slanting in the side of the wall, and, being caught, springs up in a fountain.

Some wretches of European officers—to their disgrace be it said—made this beautiful room a cook-room! and the ceiling, the fine marbles, and the inlaid work, are all one mass of blackness and defilement! Perhaps they cooked the sū'ar, the hog, the unclean beast, within the sleeping apartments of Noor-jahān,—the proud, the beautiful Sultana![1]

In this turret I took refuge for some time, from the heat of the noon-day sun. What visions of former times passed through my brain! How I pictured to myself the beautiful Empress, until her portrait was clear and well defined in my imagination: still, it bore an European impress. I had never entered the private apartments of any native lady of rank, and I longed

---

[1] The Company's troops captured the Fort from the Mahrattas under Scindia in 1803 and occupied it for several months.

to behold one of those women of whose beauty I had heard so much; I had seen two paintings of native women, who were very beautiful; but the very fact that these women had been beheld by European gentlemen, degraded them to a class respecting which I had no curiosity. I was now in the deserted zenāna of the most beautiful woman recorded in history; and one whose talents and whose power over the Emperor, made her, in fact, the actual sovereign; she governed the empire from behind the parda. The descendants of Jahāngeer, in their fallen greatness, were still at Delhi; and I determined, if possible, to visit the ladies of the royal zenāna now in existence.

The zenāna masjid, a gem of beauty, is a small mosque, sacred to the ladies of the zenāna, of pure white marble, beautifully carved, with three domes of the same white marble.

[. . .]

I have just returned from an expedition that has taken a marvellous hold of my fancy. Yesterday Mr. C——said that, if I would promise to pay the Shīsha-Mahal[1] a visit, he would have it lighted up: the apartments are usually only lighted up to satisfy the curiosity of the Governor-general. I went with pleasure; the place was illuminated with hundreds of little lamps: there was not time to have the water raised from the river, or we should have seen the effect of the sheets of water pouring over and beyond the rows of lights in the marble niches. After viewing the Shīsha-Mahal, the effect of which was not as good as I had imagined it would be, Mr. C——asked me if I should like to see the apartments under ground, in which the padshah and his family used to reside during the hot winds. We descended to view these tykkanahs and the steam-baths belonging to them. Thence we went by the aid of lighted torches to view a place that made me shudder. An officer examining these subterranean passages some time ago, observed, that he was within the *half* of a vault of an octagon shape, the other half was blocked up by a strong, but hastily formed wall. Tradition amongst the natives asserted, that within the underground passages in the Fort, was a vault in which people had been hanged and buried, but no one could say where this vault was to be found.

The officer above-mentioned, with great toil and difficulty, cut through a wall *eight feet in thickness*, and found himself in an inner vault of large dimensions, built of stone, with a high and arched roof. Across this roof was a thick and carved beam of wood, with a hole in its centre, and a hook, such as is used for hanging people. Below and directly under this hole in

[1] House of glass.

the beam, and in the centre of the vault, was a grave; this grave he opened, and found the bangles (ornaments for the arms) of a woman. Such is the place I have just visited. My blood ran cold as I descended the steps, the torches burning dimly from the foulness of the air, and I thought of the poor creatures who might have entered these dismal passages, never to revisit the light of day. I crept from the passage through the hole which had been opened in the thick wall, and stood on the ransacked grave, or perhaps graves of secret murder. Close to this vault is another of similar appearance; the thickness of the wall has baffled the patience of some person who has attempted to cut through it; however, the officers who were with me this evening say they will open it, as well as a place which they suppose leads to passages under the city. An old sergeant who has been here thirty years, says he once went through those passages, but the entrance has subsequently been bricked up, and he cannot discover it: the place which it is supposed is the blocked-up entrance, through which he passed, will, they say, be opened to-morrow. Having seen this spot of secret murder and burial, I can believe any of the horrible histories recorded in the annals of the padshahs: only imagine the entrance having been blocked up by a wall *eight* feet in thickness!

Quitting the Fort, we drove to the Tāj: the moon was at the full, adding beauty to the beautiful; the Tāj looked like fairy frost-work, yet so stately and majestic. And this superb building—this wonder of the world—is the grave of a woman, whilst only a short distance from it, is the vault of secret murder,—the grave also of a woman! What a contrast! How different the destiny of those two beings! The grave of the unknown and murdered one only just discovered amidst the dismal subterraneous passages in the Fort: the grave of the other bright and pure and beautiful in the calm moonlight. The damp, unwholesome air of the vaults is still in my throat; we were some time exploring and hunting for the passage, which, they say, leads to the temple of an Hindoo, who lives in the Tripolia; he will suffer no one to enter his temple, and declares the devil is there *in propria persona.*

When I retired to rest on my charpāī, I found it difficult to drive away the fancies that surrounded me.

The walls of the Fort, and those buildings within it that are of carved red freestone, were built by Akbar: the marble buildings were erected by Shāhjahān.

The seat of the padshah is an immense slab of black marble, the largest perhaps ever beheld; it was broken in two by an earthquake. A Burā Bahādur, from this throne of the padshah, exclaimed, "I have come, not to succeed Lord Auckland, but Akbar!" The convulsion of the earth, that split in two the throne of black marble, could not have astonished it more than this modest speech—Allāhu Akbar![2]

In front, and on the other side of the court, is the seat of the vizier; a slab of white marble. The seat on which the padshah used to sit to view the fights of the wild beasts in the court below, is one of great beauty; the pillars and arches, of the most elegant workmanship, are beautifully carved; the whole plain and light.

The steam-baths are octagonal rooms below, with arched roofs; three of these rooms are of white marble, with inlaid marble pavements; and there is a fountain, from which hot water springs up from a marble basin. The baths in the apartments below the palace, which most probably belonged to the zenāna, were broken up by the Marquis of Hastings: he committed this sacrilege on the past, to worship the rising sun; for he sent the most beautiful of the marble baths, with all its fretwork and inlaid flowers, to the Prince Regent, afterwards George the Fourth.

Having thus destroyed the beauty of the baths of the palace, the remaining marble was afterwards sold on account of Government: most happily, the auction brought so small a sum, it put a stop to further depredations.

At sunrise, from the Bridge of Boats, nothing can be more beautiful than the view up and down the river: there are an hundred domed bastions jutting out from the banks amid the gardens and residences of the nobles of former days: the Fort, with its marble buildings, peeping over the ramparts; the custom house, and many other prominent objects; form a magnificent *tout ensemble*.

[. . .]

19*th*.—My husband having arrived dāk, with great delight I accompanied him to visit the Fort, and displayed for his benefit all my recently-acquired knowledge.

Secundra

As the burial-place of Akbar Shāh, this is the most interesting spot near Agra; and I accepted an invitation to spend the day there with much pleasure. The tomb is on the Delhi road, about seven miles from Agra; we drove there in the early morning. It is situated in a fine piece of park-like ground, encompassed by a high wall, filled with noble trees and fountains,—a quadrangle of forty acres. To this enclosure there are four gateways; the principal gateway is of red granite, richly carved, inlaid with ornaments in white marble, with inscriptions in the Persian character in black marble. The form

---

[2] Lord Ellenborough, Governor General 1842–44 was noted for his bombast.

of the gateway is reckoned very fine, and likely to be durable. It is very lofty, and the roof is ornamented by four shattered white marble minarets, one at each angle, which are all broken off about the centre; this appears like the effect of time or storm, but I have some idea that they were left in this unfinished state, for some particular reason.

Having passed the gateway, you proceed to the mausoleum, a magnificent pile of red granite, erected by Jahāngeer in memory of his father; the design of the building is most remarkable, and consists of a series of terraces, rising one above the other, until finished by one of white marble; all the arches of which are filled with lattice-work of different patterns. The terraces are ornamented with numberless small turrets, of the most beautiful shape; their domes of white marble, with the exception of eight, which are covered with enamelled porcelain.

[. . .]

Our tents having been pitched under one of the fine trees in the garden, we partook of a most luxurious tiffin; and the wine, which was iced to perfection, proved very acceptable after the fatigues of the day.

In the cool of the evening we visited the tomb of Miriam Zumanee, one of the wives of Akbar: it is a large building of carved red granite, half a mile from the Emperor's monument. The sarcophagus is below; the cenotaph, of plain white marble, above in the open air; and the structure is ornamented with turrets of red granite. The whole is rapidly falling to decay.

Driving to Secundra, I observed two of the Kos Minār, which were erected by Akbar, at a distance of every two miles on the road from Agra to Delhi; one of them was in a very perfect state of preservation. As they will be mentioned hereafter, I will close this account of a pleasant day in the East.

Chapter 29

Revelations of Life in the Zenāna

"WHOEVER HATH GIVEN HIS HEART TO A BELOVED OBJECT,
HATH PUT HIS BEARD INTO THE HANDS OF ANOTHER."[1]

1835, *Feb.*—Khasgunge, the residence of my friend Colonel Gardner, is sixty miles from Agra: he wrote to me expressing a wish that I should visit him, and regretting he was too unwell to meet me at Agra, and conduct me to his house. I was delighted to accept the invitation, particularly at this time, as he informed me a marriage was to take place in his family which might interest me.

His grand-daughter, Susan Gardner, was on the eve of marriage with one of the princes of Delhi, and he wished me to witness the ceremony. I was also invited to pay a visit *en route* to his son, Mr. James Gardner, who was married to a niece of the reigning emperor, Akbar Shāh.

Was not this delightful? All my dreams in the Turret of Noor-māhāl were to be turned into reality. I was to have an opportunity of viewing life in the zenāna, of seeing the native ladies of the East, women of high rank, in the seclusion of their own apartments, in private life: and although the emperors of Delhi have fallen from their high estate, they and their descendants are nevertheless Timoorians and descendants of Akbar Shāh.

I know of no European lady but myself, with the exception of one, who has ever had an opportunity of becoming intimate with native ladies of rank; and as she had also an invitation to the wedding we agreed to go together.

21st.—We started dāk for Kutchowra, the residence of Mr. James Gardner. This is not *that* Kutchowra which yearly used to bring such treasure into the Company's coffers in boat-loads of cotton; but that Kutchowra which stopped and fought Lord Lake, and killed the famous Major Nairn of tiger-killing memory.[1]

---

[1] Oriental Proverbs.

[1] In Lt. J. Pester's account of *War and Sport in India 1802–5*, he remarks "Nairne was probably the only man that was every known to spear a tiger on horse-back. Lord Lake shot the tiger, after it was about to spring on Nairne, and sent the tiger's skin and the broken spear to the Prince of Wales."

We arrived at noon the next day; Mr. James Gardner, whom I had never seen before, received us with much pleasure; his countenance reminded me of his father, whom, in manner, he greatly resembled; he was dressed in handsome native attire, a costume he usually wore.

His grounds contain two houses; the outer one, in which he receives visitors and transacts business, and the second, within four walls, which is sacred to the Begam, and has its entrance guarded night and day.

Mr. James Gardner married Nuwāb Mulka Humanee Begam, the niece of the emperor Akbar Shāh, and daughter of Mirza Sulimān Shekō (the brother of the present emperor), who lives at Agra.

I was taken to the zenāna gates, when three very fine children, the two sons and a daughter of Mr. James Gardner, and the princess, in their gay native dresses of silk and satin, embroidered in gold and silver, ran out to see the new arrival. They were elegant little creatures, and gave promise of being remarkably handsome. I was surprised to see the little girl at liberty, but was informed that girls are not shut up until they are about six years old, until which time they are allowed to run about, play with the boys, and enjoy their freedom. Quitting the palanquins, we walked across the court to the entrance of the zenāna; there we took off our shoes and left them, it being a point of etiquette not to appear in shoes in the presence of a superior; so much so, that Mr. Gardner himself was never guilty of the indecorum of wearing shoes or slippers in the presence of his wife.

The Begam was sitting on a charpāī when we entered the apartment; when Mrs. B—— presented me as the friend of Col. Gardner, she shook hands with me, and said, "How do you do, kŭrow?"—this was all the English she could speak. The Begam appeared ill and languid: perhaps the languor was the effect of opium. I had heard so much of Mulka's wonderful beauty, that I felt disappointed: her long black and shining hair, divided in front, hung down on both sides of her face as low as her bosom, while the rest of her hair, plaited behind, hung down her back in a long tail.

Her dress consisted of silk pājāmas (full trowsers), over which she wore a pair of Indian shawls, and ornaments of jewellery were on her hands and arms. *En passant*, be it said that *ladies* in the East never wear petticoats, but full pājāmas: the ayhas, who attend on English ladies in the capacity of ladies' maids, wear the petticoat; but it is a sign of servitude, and only worn to satisfy the ideal delicacy of English ladies, who dislike to see a female servant without a petticoat. The moment an ayha quits her mistress, and goes into her own house, she pulls off the petticoat as a useless incumbrance, and appears in the native trowsers which she always wears beneath it.

The room in which the Begam received us was the one in which she usually slept; the floor was covered with a white cloth. She was sitting on a charpāi (a native bed); and as the natives never use furniture, of course there was none in the room.

Two or three female attendants stood by her side, fanning her with large feather fans; the others drove away the mosquitoes and flies with chaunrīs made of peacocks' feathers, which are appendages of royalty.

Some opium was brought to her; she took a great bit of it herself, and put a small bit, the size of half a pea, into the mouth of each of her young children; she eats much opium daily, and gives it to her children until they are about six years old.

Native ladies, when questioned on the subject, say, "It keeps them from taking cold; it is the custom; that is enough, it is the custom."

If a native lady wish to keep up her reputation for beauty, she should not allow herself to be seen under the effect of opium by daylight.

When the Princess dismissed us from her presence, she invited us to pay her a visit in the evening; Mrs. B——, with whom she was very intimate, and to whom she was very partial, said,—"I trust, Mulka Begam, since we are to obey your commands, and pay you a visit this evening, you will put on all your ornaments, and make yourself look beautiful." The Begam laughed, and said she would do so. On our quitting the apartments, she exclaimed, "Ah! you English ladies, with your white faces, you run about where you will, like dolls, and are so happy!" From which speech I conjecture the princess dislikes the confinement of the four walls. She always spoke urdū (zaban-i-urdū), the court language, which is Hindostanee, intermixed largely with Persian; her manners were very pleasing and very ladylike. So much for the first sight of the Princess Mulka Begam.

The history I heard in the zenāna is as follows: Mulka Begam, the wife of Mirza Selīm, the brother of Akbar Shāh, was on a visit to her sister, the beautiful Queen of Oude; his Majesty fell in love with Mulka, and detained her against her will in the palace; Col. Gardner, indignant at the conduct of the King, brought Mulka from Lucnow, and placed her in his own zenāna, under the care of his own Begam. Marriages are generally dependant on geographical position; the opportunity Mr. James Gardner had of seeing the Princess, added to he extreme beauty, and the romance of the affair, was more than he could withstand; he carried her off from the zenāna.[2] Col. Gardner was extremely angry, and refused to see or

---

[2] Sleeman in his *Rambles and Recollections of an Indian Official* gives a somewhat different account of James' elopement. He says: "When the King of Oudh refused to give up Mulka Begum, her father, Mirza Suliman Sheko, got his old friend Colonel Gardner, to come and plead his cause. The king gave the young woman up, but stopped the father's pension and ordered him and his family out of Oudh. He set out with Colonel Gardner and his

communicate with his son; they lived in the jungle for nearly two years. One day, Mr. James Gardner, who had tried every method to induce his father to be reconciled to him in vain, seeing him in a boat, swam after him, and vowed, unless Col. Gardner would take him into the boat, he would perish: Colonel Gardner remained unmoved, until, seeing his son exhausted, and on the point of sinking, paternal feelings triumphed; he put forth his hand, and saved him. "Whatever a man does who is afflicted with love, he is to be excused for it."[1]

"Durd ishk-e kushīdu'um ki m' purs
Zahir hijree chushīdu'um ki m' purs"

"Hum ne dil sunum ko dya
Phir kissee ko kya?"

"I have felt the pain of love, ask not of whom:
I have felt the pangs of absence, ask not of whom:"

"I have given my heart to my beloved,
What is that to another?"

Mulka was divorced from Mirza Selīm, and legally married to her present husband. We dined with Mr. Gardner in the outer house; the dinner was of native dishes, which were most excellent. During the repast, two dishes were sent over from the Begam, in compliment to her guests, which I was particularly desired to taste, as the Timoorian ladies pride themselves on their cookery, and on particular occasions will superintend the making of the dishes themselves; these dishes were so very unlike, and so superior to any food I had ever tasted, that I never failed afterwards to partake of any dish when it was brought to me, with the mysterious whisper, "It came from within." It would be incorrect to say, "The Begam has sent it;" "It came from within," being perfectly understood by the initiated.

In the evening we returned to the zenāna, and were ushered into a long and large apartment, supported down the centre by eight double pillars of handsome native architecture. The floor of the room was covered with white cloth; several lamps of brass (chirāgh-dāns) were placed upon the ground, each stand holding, perhaps, one hundred small lamps. In the centre of the

daughter on the road to Delhi, when news was brought that she had run off from the camp with James, who had accompanied his father to Lucknow. The Prince and the Colonel rode after them, but soon gave up the chase in despair. Suliman Sheko insisted on the Colonel immediately fighting him, after the manner of the English, with swords or pistols, but was soon persuaded that the honour of the House of Timur would be better preserved by allowing the offending pair to marry."

[1] Oriental Proverbs.

room a carpet was spread, and upon that the gaddī and pillows for the Begam; the gaddī or throne of the sovereign is a long round pillow, which is placed behind the back for support, and two smaller at the sides for the knees; they are placed upon a small carpet of velvet, or of kimkhwāb (cloth of gold); the whole richly embroidered and superbly fringed with gold. Seats of the same description, but plain and unornamented, were provided for the visitors. A short time after our arrival, Mulka Begam entered the room, looking like a dazzling apparition; you could not see her face, she having drawn her dopatta (veil) over it; her movements were graceful, and the magnificence and elegance of her drapery were surprising to the eye of a European.

She seated herself on the gaddī, and throwing her dopatta partly off her face, conversed with us. How beautiful she looked! how very beautiful! Her animated countenance was constantly varying, and her dark eyes struck fire when a joyous thought crossed her mind. The languor of the morning had disappeared; by lamplight she was a different creature; and I felt no surprise when I remembered the wondrous tales told by the men of the beauty of Eastern women. Mulka walks very gracefully, and is as straight as an arrow. In Europe, how rarely—how very rarely does a woman walk gracefully! bound up in stays, the body is as stiff as a lobster in its shell; that snake-like, undulating movement,—the poetry of motion—is lost, destroyed by the stiffness of the waist and hip, which impedes the free movement of the limbs. A lady in European attire gives me the idea of a German mannikin; an Asiatic, in her flowing drapery, recalls the statues of antiquity.

I had heard of Mulka's beauty long ere I beheld her, and she was described to me as the loveliest creature in existence. Her eyes, which are very long, large, and dark, are remarkably fine, and appeared still larger from being darkened on the edges of the eyelids with soorma: natives compare the shape of a fine eye to a mango when cut open. Her forehead is very fine; her nose delicate, and remarkably beautiful,—so finely chiselled; her mouth appeared less beautiful, the lips being rather thin. According to the custom of married women in the East, her teeth were blackened, and the inside of her lips also, with missee (antimony); which has a peculiarly disagreeable appearance to my eye, and may therefore have made me think the lower part of her countenance less perfectly lovely than the upper: in the eye of a native, this application of missee adds to beauty. Her figure is tall and commanding; her hair jet black, very long and straight; her hands and arms are lovely, very lovely.

On the cloth before Mulka were many glass dishes, filled with sweetmeats, which were offered to the company, with tea and coffee, by her attendants. Mulka partook of the coffee; her hooqŭ was at her side, which she smoked now and then; she offered her own hooqŭ to me, as a mark of favour. A superior or equal has her hooqŭ in attendance, whilst the bindah khāna furnishes several for the inferior visitors. Mrs. Valentine Gardner, the wife of Colonel Gardner's brother, was of the party; she lives with the Begam.[3]

Mulka's dress was extremely elegant, the most becoming attire imaginable. A Musalmānī wears only four garments:—

Firstly, the angīya: a boddice, which fits tight to the bosom, and has short sleeves; it is made of silk gauze, profusely ornamented.

Secondly, the kurtī: a sort of loose body, without sleeves, which comes down to the hips; it is made of net, crape, or gauze, and highly ornamented.

Thirdly, pājāmas: of gold or crimson brocade, or richly-figured silk; made tight at the waist, but gradually expanding until they reach the feet, much after the fashion of a fan, where they measure eight yards eight inches! a gold border finishes the trowser.

Fourthly, the dopatta: which is the most graceful and purely feminine attire in the world; it is of white transparent gauze, embroidered with gold, and trimmed with gold at the ends, which have also a deep fringe of gold and silver.

The dopatta is so transparent it hides not; it merely veils the form, adding beauty to the beautiful, by its soft and cloud-like folds. The jewellery sparkles beneath it; and the outline of its drapery is continually changing according to the movements or coquetry of the wearer. Such was the attire of the Princess! Her head was covered with pearls and precious stones, most gracefully arranged: from the throat to the waist was a succession of strings of large pearls and precious stones; her arms and hands were covered with armlets, bracelets, and rings innumerable. Her delicate and uncovered feet were each decorated with two large circular anklets composed of gold and precious stones, and golden rings were on her toes, In her nose she wore a n'hut, a large thin gold ring, on which was strung two large pearls, with a ruby between them. A nose-ring is a love token, and is always presented by the bridegroom to the bride. No single woman is allowed to wear one.

In her youth Mulka learned to read and write in Persian, but since her marriage has neglected it. Music is considered disgraceful for a lady of rank, dancing the same—such things are left to nāch women. Mulka made enquiries concerning the education of young ladies in England; and on hearing how many hours were devoted to the piano, singing, and dancing,

---

[3] Valentine Gardner was the Colonel's half-brother. In the family-history which Fanny provides, he is married to Alaida Scott, but this is obviously a different, Indian, wife.

she expressed her surprise, considering such nāch-like accomplishments degrading.

A native gentleman, describing the points of beauty in a woman, thus expressed himself:

"Barā barā nāk, barā barā ānkh, much jaisa chānd, khūb bhāri aisa." A very very large nose, very very large eyes, a face like the moon; very very portly, thus!—stretching out his arms as if they could not at their fullest extent encircle the mass of beauty he was describing!

When a woman's movements are considered peculiarly graceful, it is often remarked, "She walks like a goose, or a drunken elephant." "One must behold Lailī with the eyes of Majnūn."[1]

Mr. Gardner has a fine estate at Kutchowra, with an indigo plantation: his establishment is very large, and completely native. I imagine he is greatly assisted in the management of his estate by the advice of the Begam: with the exception of this, she appears to have little to amuse her. Her women sit round her working, and she gives directions for her dresses. Eating opium and sleeping appear to occupy much of her time. Sometimes her slaves will bring the silver degchas and hāndīs (small caldrons and cooking pots) to her, and, guided by her instructions, will prepare some highly-esteemed dish, over charcoal in a little moveable fire-place, called an angethī.

Her husband, who is very proud of her, often speaks of her being a descendant of Timur the Tartar. Timurlane, as we call him, which is a corruption of Timurlung, or the lame Timur: he was a shepherd, and as he sat on the mountain one day watching his flocks, a fakīr came up, who, striking him on the leg, said, "Arise, and be King of the World." He did so, but was lame ever after from the blow. The Timoorians are remarkable for their long, large, and fine eyes. English dresses are very unbecoming, both to Europeans and Asiatics. A Musulmanī lady is a horror in an English dress; but an English woman is greatly improved by wearing a native one, the attire itself is so elegant, so feminine, and so graceful.

Mr. Gardner gave me a room within the four walls of the zenāna, which afforded me an excellent opportunity of seeing native life. At first the strong scent of atr of roses was quite overpowering, absolutely disagreeable, until I became reconciled to it by habit.

The Muhammadans, both male and female, are extremely fond of perfumes of every sort and description; and the quantity of atr of roses, atr of jasmine, atr of khas-khās, &c., that the ladies in a zenana put upon their garments is quite overpowering.

The prophet approved of scents: "Next to women he liked horses, and

[1] Oriental Proverbs.

next to horses perfumes." Ja'bir-bin-Samurah said, "I performed noon-day prayer with his majesty; after that, he came out of the masjid; and some children came before him, and he rubbed their cheeks in a most kind manner with his blessed hand, one after another. Then his majesty touched my cheek, and I smelt so sweet a smell from it, that you might say he had just taken it out of a pot of perfumes."

Mulka Begam, and all the females in attendance on her, stained their hands and feet with menhdī. Aa'yeshah said, "Verily, a woman said, 'O prophet of God! receive my obedience.' He said, 'I will not receive your profession, until you alter the palms of your hands; that is, colour them with hinà; for without it one might say they were the hands of tearing animals.'" Aa'yeshah said, "A woman from behind a curtain made a sign of having a letter; and his highness drew away his hand and said, 'I do not know whether this is the hand of a man or a woman.' The woman said, 'It is a woman's.' His highness said, 'Were you a woman, verily you would change the colour of your nails with hinà.'"

To the slave girls I was myself an object of curiosity. They are never allowed to go beyond the four walls, and the arrival of an English lady was a novelty. I could never dress myself but half a dozen were slily peeping in from every corner of the pardas (screens), and their astonishment at the number and shape of the garments worn by a European was unbounded!

Ladies of rank are accustomed to be put to sleep by a slave who relates some fairy tale. To be able to invent and relate some romantic or hobgoblin adventure, in an agreeable manner, is a valuable accomplishment. I have often heard the monotonous tone with which women of this description lulled the Begam to sleep. To invent and relate stories and fables is the only employment of these persons. The male slaves put their masters to sleep in the same fashion.

Native beds (charpāī) are about one foot high from the ground; people of rank have the feet of these couches covered with thick plates of gold or silver, which is handsomely embossed with flowers. A less expensive, but still a very pretty sort, are of Bareilly work, in coloured flowers; some are merely painted red, green, or yellow; and those used by the poor are of plain mango wood. From the highest to the lowest the shape is all the same, the difference is in the material and the workmanship; no posts, no curtains. The seat of the bed is formed of newār (broad cotton tape), skilfully interlaced, drawn up tight as a drum-head, but perfectly elastic. It is the most luxurious couch imaginable, and a person accustomed to the charpāī of India will spend many a restless night ere he can sleep with comfort on an English bed.

A Musalmānī lady will marry an English gentleman, but she will not permit him to be present during the time of meals. Mr. Gardner and Mulka have three children, two boys and a girl; they are remarkably handsome, intelligent children, and appeared as gay and happy as possible. They always wore rich native dresses,—a most becoming style of attire. The name of the eldest is Sulīman, the second is William Linnæus, and the little girl is called Noshaba Begam.

When I retired to my charpāī, my dreams were haunted by visions of the splendour of the Timoorians in former days; the palace at Agra, and the beautiful Begam with whom I had spent the evening.

23rd.—Mr. Gardner proposed a chītā or cheeta hunt: he had a fine hunting leopard; we went out to look for antelopes; the day was very hot, we had no success, and returned very much fagged; Mrs. B—— was laid up in consequence with an ague. There was a fine elephant at Kutchowra, a great number of horses, and a few dogs.

The next morning I spent an hour with the Begam, and took leave of her; it is difficult to find her awake, she sleeps so much from opium. If you call on a native lady, and she does not wish to receive a visitor, the attendants always say. "The lady is asleep,—" equivalent to Not at home. Sometimes she employs herself in needle-work, and her attendants sit around, and net kurtīs for her on a sort of embroidery frame.

It may be as well to remark, that the opium given by the Begam to her children was remarkably fine and pure; grown in her own garden, and collected daily from incisions made in the pod of the deep red poppy.

On my departure, the Begam presented me with a beautifully embroidered batū'ā (a small bag) full of spices; it was highly ornamented, and embroidered in gold and silver, interwoven with coloured beads.

She wished me to put on churees, which are bracelets made of *sealing-wax*, ornamented with beads; they are extremely pretty, but of little value. I consented, and the churees were put on in this manner: a churee, having been cut open with a hot knife, it was heated over a charcoal fire, opened a little—just enough to allow it to pass over the arm; it was then closed, and the two ends were united by being touched with a hot knife. I wore these churees until they broke and dropped off, in memory of my first visit to the zenāna.

Chapter 30

Life in the Zenāna, and Chītā Hunting

"THE DURWESH MAY SLEEP UNDER THE SAME BLANKET,
BUT TWO KINGS CANNOT EXIST IN ONE KINGDOM."[1]

"A CONTEMPORARY WIFE, THOUGH A HOORI, IS WORSE THAN A SHE DEVIL."[2]

1835, *Feb.*—When a woman of rank marries, two female slaves are given with her, who are also the wives of her husband: this is so completely a custom it is never omitted: nevertheless, "The very voice of a rival wife is intolerable."[1]

A number of women are considered to add to a man's dignity: they add to his misery most decidedly. This custom being more honoured in the breach than the observance, was not put in force at the marriage of Mr. Gardner with Mulka Begam. "The malice of a fellow-wife is notorious."[3] It would only be surprising if such were not the case. "A contemporary wife is intolerable, even in effigy."[4] In native life the greatest misery is produced from a plurality of wives: they, very naturally, hate each other most cordially, and quarrel all day. The children, also, from their cradles are taught to hate the children of the other wives; nevertheless, the following extract proves, that *she* is considered a wife worthy of praise, who loves the offspring of her husband and another woman:—

"A woman may be married by four qualifications; one, on account of her money; another, on account of the nobility of her pedigree; another, on account of her beauty; the fourth, on account of her faith: therefore, look out for a religious woman; but if you do it from any other consideration, may your hands be rubbed in dirt."—"The world and all things in it are

---

[1] Oriental Proverbs.   [2] Ibid.   [3] Ibid.   [4] Ibid.

[1] In *Slavery Days in Old Calcutta*, Vol. II of 1908 Syed Hussain reports that slavery was an established institution in India and the Company sanctioned its continuance. The family of robbers were sold as slaves. However, in the general anti-slavery campaigns in 1811, the importation of slaves from Arabia was stopped and in 1833 the British government formally abolished slavery.

valuable; but the most valuable thing in the world is a virtuous woman."—
"The best women, that ride on camels, I mean the women of Arabia, are
the virtuous of the Koreish; they are the most affectionate to infants,
whether they be their own or their husband's by other women; and they
are the most careful of their husband's property." The proverb is at variance
with the opinion of the prophet, since the former asserts, "A contemporary
wife may be good, but her child is bad."[1] As the means of power over their
husbands, native women value their children very much, and are miserable
if they have none.

A zenāna is a place of intrigue, and those who live within four walls
cannot pursue a straight path: how can it be other-wise, where so may con-
flicting passions are called forth? If a man make a present to one wife, he
must make a similar offering to all the rest, to preserve peace and quietness. The wives must have separate houses or apartments; were it not so,
they would agree as well as caged tigers. The kur'ān permits a Musalmān
to have *four* wives; the proverb says, "The man is happy who has no she
goat."[2] Atàa records, that the prophet had *nine* wives; and from Safíah,
who was the last of them who died, he wished to be divorced; but she said,
"Keep me with your wives, and do not divorce me, peradventure I may be
of the number of your wives in paradise."

Some authorities assert, that the prophet had eighteen wives: Atàa only
mentions nine. To recompense his warlike followers for allowing them only
four wives each, he gives them the mutâh marriage for any period they may
choose with the wives of their enemies taken in battle.

In the beginning of Islàm, the followers of the prophet, the shì'as were
allowed to marry for a limited time; this temporary marriage was called
mutâh. "Verily the prophet prohibited, on the day of the battle of Khaiber,
a mutâh marriage, which is for a fixed time, and he forbade the eating
of the flesh of the domestic ass." "His highness permitted, in the year in
which he went to Awtas, mutâh for three days; after which he forbade it."
At length a revelation came down which rendered every connexion of the
sort unlawful for the faithful, "excepting the captives which their right
hands possess."

If a woman of high rank and consequence has no heir, this farce is often
played. The lady appears to expect one; she is fattened up in the same
curious manner in which they fatten their horses: five or six low caste
women, who really expect children about the same time, are secreted in the
zenāna: when one of them is delivered of a son, the Begam takes it, the
farce of an accouchement is acted, and the child is produced as the heir;

[1] Oriental Proverbs.   [2] Ibid.

265

the real mamma has 500 rupees (£50) given her,—and perhaps a dose of poison to secure her silence.

The father of Mulka Begam, the Huzūr Mirza Sulimān Shekō, the brother of the present Emperor of Delhi, resides at Agra, on a pension from Government; he has children innumerable, all young princes and princesses; there are, it is said, some forty of his children now alive, proud and poor. By Mulka's first marriage with Mirza Selīm, the second son of the present King of Delhi, she had three children. The first wife of the King of Oude is a sister of Mulka's, and is reckoned more beautiful than even Mulka herself.

24th.—We drove over to Khāsgunge, Colonel Gardner's residence, thirteen miles, over roads that were hardly passable. On our arrival, we found our dear friend seated on the steps in front of his house, with many gentlemen, both English and native, around him. I thought I had never seen so dignified and graceful a person; he was dressed in a lubāda of red figured Indian shawl, the rest of the dress was English, but the style of the lubāda was particularly good, and suited to an old man; his half brother, Mr. Valentine Gardner, was with him, also an old nawāb from Cambay.[2]

Colonel Gardner has a fine estate at Khāsgunge; the outer house is dedicated to his friends and English acquaintance; within four high walls is the barā-deri, or pavilion, in the centre of the zenāna gardens, in which his begam resides.

Apartments were given to my husband and me in the outer house, where the English visitors resided. The dinners at first consisted of European, as well as native dishes; but the latter were so excellent, I soon found it impossible to partake of dishes dressed after the English fashion; and as all the guests were of the same opinion, Colonel Gardner had the kindness to banish European dishes from the table.

I must not forget to mention the arwarī fish, the finest and most delicious I ever tasted; the Kālā-naddī is famed for its arwarī, a sort of mullet; the fish delights to bask in the sun, floating on the surface of the water. Colonel Gardner kept two shīkarees (native sportsmen), for the purpose of shooting these fish; one man fired, and the other instantly plunged into the water, and brought out the fish that were killed or stunned. The Musalmāns

[2] The Nawabs of Cambay were descended from the governors appointed by Akbar when he conquered Gujerat in 1572 from among the nobles who accompanied him from Agra. When the Mahrattas partitioned Gujerat, the Nawabs resisted their claim to tribute. By the Treaty of Bassein 1802 Cambay ceded to the British and became a feudatory.

object to eating fish having no scales; such fish was also forbidden to the Jews.

In the evening, the native mimics came to perform before us; they imitated Europeans very well, and mimicked the gentlemen of the party. A pūtlī-nāch was afterwards brought forward; I was surprised to see the natives, young and old, so eager and fond of this absurdity, until Colonel Gardner said, "The natives are madly fond of this pūtlī-nāch; indeed, it is all the English have left them of their former glory. You see, represented by puppets, Shāhjahān and all his Court and Durbar: one puppet is brought forward, and the manager, whilst it bows to the audience, relates the whole history of the minister whom it represents; giving a true account of his pedigree, riches, influence, &c. At this moment, standing behind my chair, at a salary of four rupees a month, is the lineal descendant of one of the first lords in the Court of Shāhjahān. The managers of the show mix up infinite wit with their relation of events, and sarcasms on the English."

After this explanation, I could see the reason of the fondness of the old natives for this puppet-show, which before, in my ignorance, I had not comprehended. One by one every puppet is brought forward, and its history recounted. This evening fatigued me a good deal; we sat under the verandah to see the sights, the glare of the torches was painful to my eyes, and the noise made my head ache.

27th.—A lynx (the caracal), the property of Colonel Gardner, a most extraordinary looking beast, killed a goa samp: I was told, the animal catches crows by springing several feet into the air after them as they rise from the ground.

The cheeta, or chītā, (hunting leopard), killed two antelopes: some nāch girls danced and sang in the evening, and thus closed the day.

My husband, who had accompanied me to Khāsgunge, now took leave of Colonel Gardner, and returned to Allahabad, leaving me with our dear friend to witness the Muhammadan marriage ceremonies. My husband quitted us with regret, being obliged to depart on account of the expiration of his leave of absence.

Colonel Gardner married Nawab Matmunzel ool Nissa Begam, of the Cambay family; she resides in the house or pavilion within the four walls, with her relatives, attendants, and slaves. This morning the Begam sent word she would receive visitors in the evening; Colonel Gardner took me over, and introduced me to her as his adopted daughter; she rose and embraced me, putting her cheek to mine on each side the face, after the fashion of the French, and her arms around me: having received her guests,

267

she sat down on her gaddī of purple velvet, embroidered with gold; and we seated ourselves on plain white gaddīs on either side.

The Begam is a very lively little old woman; she was magnificently dressed in pearls, diamonds, and emeralds,—as many as it was possible to put on her little body; she wore a peshwāz, or very short full gown, with a tight body, made of red and gold Benares tissue; this is a dress of state; pigāmās of silk; and, over all, a dopatta of red and gold Benares tissue, which, as she sat, covered her entirely; and she looked more like a lump of glittering gold and crimson and pearls, than a living woman. A golden hooqŭ, with four nā'echas (snakes) was placed before her on a hooqŭ carpet of raised flowers, curiously cut out in paper. The room was covered with a carpet, over which white cloths were spread after the usual fashion, and the lamps all stood on the ground.

At the other end of the room sat fourteen slave girls, belonging to the Begam, who played on different instruments, whilst one or two of them nāched before us.

The ladies of the family were seated on the Begam's left hand.

There was Hinga Beebee Sāhiba, the widow of Allan Gardner, the eldest son of Colonel Gardner; her eldest daughter, Hirmooze, married Mr. Stuart William Gardner, an officer in the 28th Native Infantry, and son of Admiral Francis Gardner, a relative of Colonel Gardner's.

Her second daughter, Susan, generally called Shubbeah Begam, was not present; being engaged to be married to a young Prince of Delhi, she was kept in pārda. At her feet were the two daughters of James Gardner by a former marriage; the eldest, Alaida (the Morning Star), about fifteen years old, very fair, with a round pretty face; but her great charm was a remarkably sweet and interesting manner; she of them all was the one whom Colonel Gardner best loved; and indeed she was a sweet girl. Her younger sister (the Evening Star) was darker than Alaida, pretty and lively. They, like the Begam, had Tartar faces, in which the eyes are wide apart; but were both, nevertheless, very pretty and interesting girls.

Two English gentlemen, who were fond of native life, and fascinated with Khasgunge, requested me to mention to Colonel Gardner their wish to become of his family; I did so. Colonel Gardner replied, "Shubbeah is engaged to the Prince:" but, said I, "Do you think she likes him?" "How little you know of the natives!" he replied; "it would be considered the greatest indelicacy for a girl to prefer one man to another, or to have seen the man to whom she is to be united. Tell Mr.——I am flattered by his wish to be of my family, and would willingly give him my grand-daughter, but the Begam is bent on this *grand alliance*, as *she* considers it: I have withheld my consent for years; 'The house may be filled with the falling of drops;'[1] *i.e.* continual dripping wears away stones. She has carried the point. I have been happy in my marriage, but I would not advise an European gentleman to marry a native lady. With respect to the proposals of the other gentleman, in a worldly point of view it would be a good match; but I do not like the man; I cannot bestow upon him the Morning Star."

Bānā Beebee Sāhiba was also there; in her younger days she must have been pretty; her liveliness she still retained.[3]

The guests smoked the hooqŭ, and ate pān; some very delicate pān was prepared for me, of which I partook for the first time, and rather liked it.

At the end of the evening, the Begam gave her guests liberty to depart; pān and atr of roses were presented to us; rose-water was sprinkled over us; we made salām in due form, and returned to the outer house.

The Begam has a guard of honour of forty men, who live at the entrance of the zenāna, and guard the gateway night and day.

I must not forget the old Nawāb of Cambay, the uncle of the Begam; he is quite a character, and a very singular one; he has visited England; he used to dine at the table with us, and would take sherry with the guests. When a lady was at table he would take sherry; if gentlemen only were present, the sherry was discarded for brandy: one day I observed he drank some white spirit, and found it was a strong spirit he himself distilled from different flowers: to my surprise, he used also to play backgammon. Natives have names and titles innumerable, of which his are a good specimen: Fakhr-ul-dawla Moomtaj ul Moolk Nawab Meer Momun Khan Bahadur Delme Delawor Jung.

Colonel Gardner's name is William Linnæus, so called after his godfather, the great botanist; he is himself an excellent botanist, and pursues the study with much ardour. His garden at Khāsgunge is a very extensive and a most delightful one, full of fine trees and rare plants, beautiful flowers and shrubs, with fruit in abundance and perfection; no expense is spared to embellish the garden: in the centre is a delightful pavilion, under the shade of fine trees. It is one of the pleasures of the Begam and her attendants to spend the day in that garden: guards are then stationed around it, to prevent intrusion. She is herself extremely fond of flowers, and, although not a botanist, after the European fashion, she knows the medicinal qualities of all the Indian plants, and the dyes that can

[1] Oriental Proverbs.

[3] Banu Bibi was James Gardner's first wife and the mother of the two girls, Alaida and Evening Star.

be produced from them; and this knowledge is of daily account in the zenāna.

March 1st.—Took a gallop on a fine English horse, Rattler by name; being accustomed to ride Arabs, this great monster appeared like a frisky mountain under me.

2nd.—Mr. James Gardner invited us to return to his house at Kutchowra, that we might enjoy chītā hunting. We drove over, and in the evening some nāch women exhibited before us for our amusement.

3rd.—In the early morning I mounted a white pony, and we all rode out eight miles to breakfast in a tent which had been sent out over night. After breakfast the party got into the buggies.

We went directly across the country; there were no roads,—over banks, and through ditches, where it appeared a miracle we were not upset. We came to a deep, narrow, stone water-course: my companion said, "If you will get out of the buggy, I will leap the mare over; if I attempt to walk her over, she will be sure to get her foot in, and break her leg." I got out accordingly; away went the mare; she took a leap at the drain, and carried the buggy over in excellent style. Buggies in India have the remarkable faculty of leaping, being accustomed to such freaks.

We arrived at the estate of a native gentleman, called Petumber, where, on the plain, we saw a herd of about three hundred antelopes, bounding, running, and playing in the sunshine; and a severe sun it was, enough to give one a brain fever, in spite of the leather hood of the buggy. The antelopes are so timid, they will not allow a buggy to come very near the herd; therefore being determined to see the hunt, we got out of the carriage and mounted upon the hackery (cart) on which the cheetā was carried, without even an umbrella, lest it should frighten the deer. The cheetā had a hood over his eyes and a rope round his loins, and two natives, his keepers, were with him.

I sat down by accident on the animal's tail:—O-o-o-wh, growled the cheetā. I did not wait for another growl, but released his tail instantly. The bullock hackery was driven into the midst of the herd. The bandage was removed from the eyes of the cheetā, and the cord from his body: he dropped from the cart and bounded, with the most surprising bounds, towards an immense black buck, seized him by the throat, flung him on the ground, and held him there. The keepers went up, they cut the buck's throat, and then they cut off the haunch of the hind leg, and, dipping a wooden spoon into the cavity, offered it full of blood to the cheetā. Nothing but this would have induced the cheetā to quit the throat of the buck. He followed the men to the cart, jumped upon it, drank the blood, and the men then put his bandage over his eyes. The haunch was put into the back of the cart, the reward for the animal when the hunting was over. The herd had passed on; we followed, taking care the wind did not betray our approach. The cheetā was leaning against me in the hackery, and we proceeded very sociably. Another herd of antelopes went bounding near us, the cheetā's eyes were unbound again, and the rope removed from his loins; a fine buck passed, we expected he would instantly pursue it as usual, but the animal turned sulky, and instead of dropping down from the hackery, he put both his fore-paws on my lap and stood there two or three seconds with his face and whiskers touching my cheek. O-o-o-wh—O-o-o-wh, growled the cheetā!—my heart beat faster, but I sat perfectly quiet, as you may well imagine, whilst I thought to myself, "If he seize my throat, he will never leave it until they cut off my hind quarter, and give him a bowl of blood!" His paws were as light on my lap as those of a cat. How long the few seconds appeared whilst I eyed him askance! Nor was I slightly glad when the cheetā dropped to the ground, where he crouched down sulkily and would not hunt. He was a very fine-tempered animal, but they are all uncertain. I did not like his being quite so near when he was unfastened and *sulky*.

The next time I took care to get off the cart before the creature was freed from restraint. It is painful to witness a cheetā hunt, the beautiful antelope has so little chance of escape.

[. . .]

Mulka Begam sometimes goes out cheetā hunting in a native carriage, drawn by two magnificent bullocks, adorned with crimson housings, and their horns covered with plates of gold.

In this manner the princess can behold the sport, and enter into the amusement, while she is completely secluded from the profane eye of man.

271

Chapter 31

Fathīpoor Sicri and Colonel Gardner

1835, *March.*—The wedding having been deferred for a short time, I took the opportunity of returning dāk to Agra, having promised Colonel Gardner to be at Khāsgunge again in time to witness the ceremony. All this time my pretty pinnace had been awaiting my arrival. I determined to send her back to Allahabad with the cook-boat, and she sailed immediately. I also sent back the carriage and horses, keeping the buggy, Bokharu, the grey and black horse, to accompany me to Khāsgunge. The dāk trip gave me a severe cough and cold, and on my reaching Agra I was little fit for exertion. However, a party was proposed to visit Fathīpoor Sicri, formerly the residence of Akbar Shāh; my curiosity prevailed, and, notwithstanding my illness, I consented to accompany them.

11*th.*—Chār vajr, barī fajr, *i.e.* four o'clock A.M., I was ready to start: the party of four dwindled to two, the others being laid up with influenza, and unable to quit their beds. My relative, Mr. D——, drove me over: tents and provisions had been sent on before. In spite of my illness I was delighted with Fathīpoor Sicri. The gateway, with its superb flight of steps, is a beautiful object; it is built on a fine commanding site. The buildings, which are very extensive, are on high ground; and from an immense quarry on the spot, they daily convey quantities of stone to all parts of India. The Fort of Agra is built of this stone.

Before I say more of the place, I must relate an anecdote of the founder.

Akbar Shāh was extremely unhappy and deeply grieved at being childless. Hearing of the fame of a fakīr who lived at Fathīpoor Sicri, and of the wonderful birth of a child to a couple of poor manufacturers of pottery ware, who lived at that place, from the power of the prayers of the holy man: hearing all this, he determined to make a pilgrimage to Fathīpoor; *àpropos*, the house of the kumhār (potter) and his descendants are still shown to visitors. Akbar commenced his hājī (pilgrimage), but, like all the race of Timur, being rather lame, he found two miles a day (one kos) as much as he could accomplish; therefore, at every day's resting-place he ordered a kos minār to be erected, which now serve as mile-stones. Two of these minārs I saw between Agra and Secundra on my visit to his tomb, as before-mentioned. On his arrival at Sicri, he consulted the holy man Shāh Selīm Cheestie; and, in pursuance of his advice, the Empress, the Jodh Bā'ī, was brought to live at Fathīpoor. She was the daughter of Oodi Sing of Jodhpoor. Her zenāna, inclosed within four walls, is still to be seen. The prayers of the holy man were heard, and the Jodh Bā'ī presented Akbar with a son, who, in honour of *the saint, I suppose*, was called Selīm, which name was afterwards almost forgotten in the appellation of Jahāngeer, the Conqueror of the World. In the Fort of Agra there are still the remains of the Selīm Ghar built by Akbar.[1]

The Emperor, charmed at the birth of a son, bestowed lands and showered rupees upon the sagacious fakīr; and the greatest ornament of the place is,

The Tomb of Shaikh Selīm Cheestie

This beautiful mausoleum, in the centre of the quadrangle, is still in a state of the most perfect preservation; it is of white marble; the open work of the screen is of the most exquisite workmanship. The descendants of the shaikh still live at Sicri, and gain large sums by showing the tomb of the holy man, whose name is held in the highest veneration. The coffin, containing the mortal remains of the saint, is within the building, and is covered with a large pall of silk and brocade. When speaking of the shaikh they continually denominated him Shāh Selīm Cheestie.

[. . .]

The mosque within the quadrangle was finished in 1576, and Akbar's three sons were born in the houses of the saint.

A very intelligent person, by name Bisharut Ali, who acted as cicerone, was much pleased to show off the place, and relate his wonderful stories. Amongst other traditions, he told me that, "in former times, Fathīpoor Sicri was infested with wild beasts, and the people who came to see the saint marvelled he was not afraid to live in such a wilderness; the next day, they found a lion and a wolf at the holy man's door; the lion walking up and down and keeping guard, and the wolf brushing away the dust and dirt before the habitation of the saint"—with his tail, I suppose, for they say

---

[1] Akbar, who had no surviving son, went on a pilgrimage to the holy man Sheikh Selim Chishti who lived at Sikri and brought the Empress Jodhbhai, his Rajput wife, to the place. Jodhbai had a son who was named Selim after the saint (afterwards taking the name Jehangir). Akbar founded the city of Sikri in 1569 and later named it Fatehpur Sikri (City of Victory) after his conquest of Gujerat.

nothing of a broom. This Bisharut Ali is a pensioner on three rupees eight ānās a month; his profile, and that of Mulka Begam's, who is a descendant of Akbar's, were so much alike, that I could not help asking him if he were of Selīm Cheestie's family? He replied, "No; my ancestor was the teacher (oostād) of the saint!"

There is much to visit at this place: the mosque, the numerous tombs, and also a very curious building, in which the council of the nation was held.

The place that most interested my imagination was the Temple of Magic, in which Akbar used to study. How much the Emperor, who was greatly addicted to the art, must have been interested in casting the nativity of the *sons of his pilgrimage*, and in the important task of selecting fortunate names!

On the birth of the heir, the City of Victory must have resounded with the roar of cannon, in honour of the happy event; even the poorest Musulmān testifies his rejoicing on such an occasion by firing off a matchlock; but should the offspring be a girl, the cannon is silent, and no matchlocks are in requisition. There are five different modes of naming children, two of which are as follow:—

Sometimes the infant obtains the name of some one of the family, as that of the parent's father, (it is not customary among Musulmāns to give their own names to their children,) the grandfather, great-grandfather, or the tutelary saint venerated in the family; hence the name of Selīm was given to the first-born of the Emperor.

"Amongst some people it is customary to choose a name from among those that begin with the same letter which is found at the commencement or termination of the name of the planet in whose hour the child is born. In order to ascertain this, it is requisite to consult the horoscope of nativity."[1] The planets, seven in number,—namely, the Sun, Venus, Mercury, the Moon, Saturn, Jupiter, and Mars, are supposed to preside over the twenty-four hours of the day and night, and to exert many favourable and unfavourable influences on the human race. With what anxiety must the great magician Akbar have consulted the horoscope, to ascertain under the reign of what particular planet his son was born! With what care he must have cast his nativity, and thereby predicted his future destiny!

The ladies of the zenāna were not only followers of the prophet, but Rajpūtnees were admitted, Akbar considering it good policy to marry the daughter of a subjugated Hindoo prince. Beauty, also, was and is sufficient to give the possessor a chance of gaining the rank of Begam. I went over the zenāna with much interest, and thought of the innumerable ceremonies that must have been observed within its walls.

[1] Qanoon-e-Islam.

Particular rites take place on the fortieth day after the birth of a child, which is esteemed an important festival; the mother is then allowed to touch the kurān, and enter the masjid. In fancy, I beheld the Jodh Bā'ī taken out into the air, with the "child of the pilgrimage" in her arms, that she might count a few stars; after which, according to Muhammadan custom, her attendants would shoot off two arrows into the air.

With what care the Emperor must have selected verses from the kurān, to engrave in the Arabic character upon tablets, called tawīzī; destined to adorn the person of the infant prince, and to guard him as a spell! These tablets, which are of gold or silver, are strung on a long cord of gold thread, and suspended over one shoulder of a child, crossing his body, and hanging down on the other side below the hip.

The pachīsī-board gives one a glimpse of the manner in which the great Akbar spent his time amongst his lady-loves; the pachīsī-board is in an open court of the zenāna; the squares of the board are formed of coloured marbles, and on so large a scale, that women were used as *counters*. Imagine the great Akbar playing at pachīsī with eight cowries, and sixteen ladies of the zenana squatting down on the squares of the board as counters! Jīta rako Akbar!

The game is played with eight cowries, or with three long narrow dice, and so named from the highest throw, which is twenty-five. The shape of the board is a cross, covered with squares, alternately of a different colour. The natives have them made of red and purple cloth, which can be folded up, and easily carried about; they are passionately fond of this game, and play it at the Dewālī. The counters are sixteen in number, in sets of four, each set of a different colour.

Adjoining the temple of the magician is the anannās-i-ghur, built in the shape of a pine-apple (anannās), as the natives aver.

The taksāl (the mint) is at this place; in it rupees were first coined; unlike the circular rupees of the present day, those coined by Akbar are square; he also coined square gold mohurs, and eight ānā pieces of the same form. The square rupee, if *without a blemish*, is reckoned of great value; it is used in conjuring the truth out of thieves, who are much afraid of it, and often confess the truth from a belief in its virtue.

If a rich native can obtain one of Akbar's rupees, or, what is better, an akbārābādee gold mohur, he puts it away with his hoard of riches, firmly believing that by its virtue robbers will be prevented from discovering his gold. There is an old saying, "To get possession of the wealth without disturbing the snake that guards it."[1] The square rupee appears to act

[1] Oriental Proverbs.

chaukidar as well as the snake. An akbārābādee rupee and an eight ānā piece were procured at Sicri, and added to my museum. The mint has been dug up in every direction by treasure-hunters.

[. . .]

The tomb of the Jhod Bā'ī, who was a Rajpootnee daughter of the Hindoo chief of Jhodpore, by tradition beautiful and amiable, is still to be seen on the Chand-maree, the artillery practice ground, a few miles from Fathīpoor Sicri. It was in ruins, but still you could trace its form and dome. Some artillery officers, out of pure idleness and ignorance, I suppose, about a year ago, blew up the dome of this tomb by way of getting rid of some damaged powder! The sacrilege of destroying the tomb of the mother of Jahāngeer, and the wife of Akbar Shāh!

[. . .]

The influenza having attacked our party, and my having fallen ill from being drenched in a severe storm, on my return to Agra, which increased the cough and cold from which I was suffering, prevented our prosecuting the tour we had planned for visiting Deeg, Burtpore, and other remarkable places.

[. . .]

I greatly wished Colonel Gardner would consent to tell me the history of his remarkable life, which I was anxious to write down from his dictation.[2] One evening he said, "Merā Betee, (my child) when in Holkar's service, I was employed as an envoy to the Company's forces, under Lord Lake, with instructions to return within a certain time; my family remained in camp. Suspicion of treachery was caused by my lengthened absence, and accusations were brought forward against me at the Darbār, held by Holkar on the third day following that on which my presence was expected. I rejoined the camp while the darbār was still assembled; on my entrance, the Mahārāj, in an angry tone, demanded the reason of the delay; which I gave, pointing out the impossibility of a speedier return. Holkar exclaimed, in great anger, 'Had you not returned this day, I would have levelled the khanats of your tents.' I drew my sword instantly, and attempted to cut his highness down, but was prevented by those around him; and ere they had recovered from the amazement and confusion caused by the attempt, I rushed from the tent, sprang upon my horse, and was soon beyond reach of the pursuers."

---

[2] Gardner's father served in America from 1767–82 and there married the daughter of Col. Robert Livingstone of New York. Their son joined the British Army in 1783 as an ensign and came to India in 1796; two years later he resigned his commission and entered the service of Holkar, the Mahratta chieftain.

To account for Colonel Gardner's indignation, it must be remembered, that the kanāts are walls of canvas, that surround the tents of the ladies of the zenāna; to have thrown down those screens, and to have exposed women within parda to the gaze of men, would have been an insult for which there could be no atonement. Colonel Gardner's high spirit was as prompt to avenge the threat as it would have been willing to take the life of Holkar, had he intruded on the privacy of the Begam's apartments.

Through the influence of friends, the Princess and her family were allowed, unmolested, to quit Holkar's dominions, and rejoin her husband.

The account Colonel Gardner gave me of his marriage with the Begam was this: —

"When a young man, I was entrusted to negotiate a treaty with one of the native princes of Cambay. Darbārs and consultations were continually held; during one of the former, at which I was present, a parda (native curtain) near me was gently moved aside, and I saw, as I thought, the most beautiful black eyes in the world. It was impossible to think of the treaty; those bright and piercing glances, those beautiful dark eyes, completely bewildered me.

"I felt flattered that a creature so lovely as she of those deep black, loving eyes must be, should venture to gaze upon me; to what danger might not the veiled beauty be exposed, should the movement of the parda be seen by any of those at the darbār! On quitting the assembly I discovered that the bright-eyed beauty was the daughter of the Prince. At the next darbār, my agitation and anxiety were extreme again to behold the bright eyes that had haunted my dreams by night, and my thoughts by day! The parda again was gently moved, and my fate was decided.

"I demanded the Princess in marriage; her relations were at first indignant, and positively refused my proposal; however, on mature deliberation, the ambassador was considered too influential a person to have a request denied, and the hand of the young Princess was promised. The preparations for the marriage were carried forward; 'Remember,' said I, 'it will be useless to attempt to deceive me; I shall know those eyes again, nor will I marry any other.'

"On the day of the marriage I raised the veil from the countenance of the bride, and in the mirror that was placed between us beheld the bright eyes that had bewildered me; I smiled,—the young Begam smiled also."

Such was Colonel Gardner's account of the first time he beheld his bride. Well might she smile when she gazed upon that noble countenance!
[. . .]

16*th*.—My affairs at Agra having come to a conclusion, and the pinnace, carriage, and horses being on their way home, I once more turned my steps to Khāsgunge, and arrived there dāk, accompanied by a friend, who was extremely anxious to see the marriage ceremony, although all that the eye of a man is permitted to behold is the tamāshā that takes place without the four walls. All that passes within is sacred.

On my arrival the whole party at Khāsgunge were going out to tents by the Ganges to hunt wild boars and otters; to shoot crocodiles, floriken, black partridge, and other game. Even for people in good health it was, at that season of the year, a mad expedition, and I declined going; I longed indeed to accompany them, but my cold and cough were so severe I was forced to give up the idea.

18*th*.—My dear Colonel Gardner, seeing how ill I was, said, "You will never recover, my child, in the outer house; I will give you a room in the inner one, and put you under the care of the begam; there you will soon recover." He took me over to the zenāna; the begam received me very kindly, and appointed four of her slaves to attend upon me, and aid my own women. They put me immediately into a steam-bath, shampooed, mulled, and half-boiled me; cracked every joint after the most approved fashion, took me out, laid me on a golden-footed bed, gave me sherbet to drink, shampooed me to sleep, and by the time the shooting party returned from the Gunga, I had perfectly recovered, and was able to enter into all the amusement of seeing a Hindostanee wedding.

I must here anticipate, and remark that Suddu Khan, our excellent little khansaman, died in June, 1841. He had been ill and unable to attend for months. There is a story, that being in an hummām, he received some injury in the spine while being shampooed and joint-cracked by a barber, who placed his knee to his back, and then forcibly brought his two arms backwards. The story says poor Suddu fainted, and the barber was so much alarmed, he fled, and has never been seen since at Cawnpore, where the scene took place.

Chapter 32

The Marriage

"TO DRESS ONE'S OWN DOLL."[1]

Spoken of a father who defrays the whole expense of his daughter's marriage, her dress, ornaments, &c., without any charge to the bridegroom or his family.

"HE WHO BUILDS A HOUSE AND TAKES A WIFE HEAPS SEVENTY AFFLICTIONS ON HIS HEAD."[2]

1835, *March* 18*th*.—Before entering on a description of the marriage ceremonies, it may be as well to explain the singular manner in which Colonel Gardner's family has intermarried with that of the Emperor of Delhi.

William Gardner, Esq., of Coleraine, left a son.

William Gardner, Esq., Lieut.-Colonel in the 11th regiment of Dragoons. He married Elizabeth, daughter of Valentine Farrington, Esq., and had issue Valentine, born 1739, Allan, and other children. Allan was created a baronet, and afterwards elevated to the peerage in Ireland in 1800; and created a peer of the United Kingdom, 1806.

Valentine, the eldest son, a Major in the army, married, first, Alaida, daughter of Robert Livingstone, Esq., by whom he had a son, William Linnæus, Captain in the army; and, secondly, Frances, daughter of Samuel Holworthy, Esq., by whom he had another son, Valentine.

Colonel William Linnæus Gardner married Nawab Matmunzelol-Nissa Begam Delme, and by her had two sons, Allan and James, and a daughter; the last mentioned died young.

Allan, the eldest son, married Beebee Sāhiba Hinga, and left one son, Mungo, who died young, and two daughters, Hirmoozee and Susan. Hirmoozee married her relative, Stewart William Gardner, Esq., son of Rear-Admiral Francis Gardner, the brother of Allan Hyde Lord Gardner. Susan, . the second daughter, or Shubbeah Begam as she is called, is the one whose marriage is on the *tapis*.

James Gardner, the second son of Colonel William Linnæus Gardner,

[1] Oriental Proverbs.   [2] Ibid.

married, first, Beebee Sāhiba Banoo, by whom he had one son, Hinga, and two daughters, Alaida, the Morning Star, and the Evening Star. He married, secondly, Mulka Humanee Begam, and by her had four children, two sons and two daughters: Sulimān and William Linnæus; Nashaba Begam, and another girl.

Mirza Sulimān Shekō, son of Shāh Allum, the late Emperor of Delhi, and brother of Akbar Shāh, the present Emperor, has a numerous family. Two of the daughters were celebrated for their beauty: one of them, Mulka Humanee Begam, married her cousin, Mirza Selīm, the son of Akbar Shāh, from whom she was divorced: she married, secondly, Mr. James Gardner. Sultana Bōa, the other daughter, married Nusseer-ood-Deen Hydur, the King of Oude. Mirza Unjun Shekō, son of Mirza Suliman Shekō, and half-brother of Mulka Begam, is engaged to Susan Gardner, as before-mentioned.

Colonel Gardner was exceedingly unwilling to allow of the marriage of his grand-daughter with the young prince, but the old Begam, his wife, had set her heart upon it. He would rather have seen her married to a European gentleman; but the Begam, who is an adopted daughter of the Emperor of Delhi, is delighted with the match,—in *her* eyes a fine alliance.

I must describe the bride, Susan Gardner, or, as she is called in the zenāna, Shubbeah Begam, every lady having her name and title also. She had been cried up by the people at Agra as a great beauty, and Colonel Gardner had received several proposals for her, both from European and native gentlemen. She was also described as very accomplished for the inhabitant of four walls, being able to read, and write, and keep accounts with gram. She is about twenty years of age, very old for a bride in this country, where girls marry at eleven or twelve, and the proverb describes them as "shrivelled at twenty."

My surprise was great when I saw her in the zenāna. Her complexion is pale and sallow, her face flat, her figure extremely thin, and far from pretty. Her flatterers called her "so fair!" but she has not the fairness of a European, or the fine clear brown of some Asiatic ladies: her manners were also admired, but I did not like them, nor did she move stately as an elephant, an epithet applied to a woman having a graceful gait.

Unjun Shekō, the bridegroom, who is about twenty years of age, is a remarkably handsome man; his black curling hair hangs in long locks on each side his face; his eyes very large, long, and bright; his features fine; his complexion a clear brown; his figure the middle size; and like all natives, he wore a beard, moustache, and whiskers. His three brothers, who came to the wedding with him, are ugly, low caste looking men. Unjun's manners are good, theirs are cubbish. For four or five years he has been trying to bring about this marriage; but Colonel Gardner opposed it on account of his extravagance. His father, Sulimān Shekō, has refused to give one rupee to the young couple, so that the whole expense of the wedding falls upon Colonel Gardner: he pays for both sides. The young prince has only an allowance of 100 rupees a month! Natives, especially native women, are curious beings; the whole pride of their lives consists in having had a grand wedding: they talk of it, and boast of it to the hour of their death. Colonel Gardner said, "If I were to give Shubbeah the money that will be fooled away in display at this marriage, I should make her miserable; she would think herself disgraced; and although by custom she is not allowed to stir from her room, or to see the sight, still it will charm her to hear the road was lighted up for so many miles, the fireworks were so fine and the procession so grand! She would have this to talk of in preference to the money, even if she were forced to deprive herself of half her food all her life; she is a pakkā Hindostānee!" They were horrified at my description of an English marriage. A carriage and four, attended by five or six other carriages, made a good wedding; when the ceremony had been performed by the padre, the bride and bridegroom drove away: no procession, no fireworks; the money put in the banker's hands, the parents gave a dinner and ball, and all was finished.

The Begam was in a perfect agony from morning till night, lest any one thing should be forgotten,—lest any, even the smallest gift might be omitted; if it were, the people would say, "What a shabby wedding!" and, in spite of all the expense, she would lose her good name.

It would be utterly impossible for me to recount the innumerable ceremonies performed at the wedding of a Muhammadan; the following are a few of the most remarkable.

March 12th.—The ceremonies began: In the first place, the bridegroom's party, consisting of Mr. James Gardner, Mulka Begam, Mrs. B——, and Mr. V——, went into tents four miles distant; while the bride's party, consisting of Colonel Gardner, his Begam, the bride, and myself, remained at Khāsgunge. We had also, in the outer house, Mr. Valentine Gardner, a party of English gentlemen, and the old Nawab of Cambay. It appeared curious to me to sit down to dinner with these gentlemen, who were all attired in native dresses, and do the honours, at times when my dear Colonel Gardner was too unwell to quit the zenāna, and join the dinner party in the outer house. The turban is not a necessary appendage to Asiatic attire; in all friendly or familiar intercourse the skull cap is worn,—the turban in company; it is disgraceful to uncover the head.

But to return to my story. About 3 P.M., Mulka Begam came in procession to bring the bride's dress, which is a present from the bridegroom. The procession consisted of elephants, raths (four-wheeled native carriages drawn by bullocks), palanquins, led horses, &c.; and one hundred trays, carried on men's heads, containing the dress for the bride, sweetmeats, and basun (flour of gram), wherewith to wash the lady. Mulka Begam came in a covered palanquin, screened from the gaze of men.

I, as in duty bound, had made my salām to Shubbeah Begam, and was in attendance in the zenāna, to receive the bridegroom's party.

"Women of the lower class, on entering the female assembly, must not say 'salām;' if the hostess be a lady of rank, they perform kudumbosee (the ceremony of kissing the feet) to her, and merely make salām to the rest. When going away they request permission, in the same way as the men in the male assembly, and take their departure.

"Kudumbosee, or the ceremony of kissing the feet, is, rather, to touch the feet of the hostess with the right hand, and then kiss the latter, or, more generally, make salām with it; while her ladyship, scarce allowing it to be done, out of politeness and condescension, withdraws her foot; and, taking hold of her hands, says, 'Nay, don't do that!' or 'Enough!' 'Long may you live!' 'Come, be seated!' Or, if she be married, 'May God render your *sohag* durable!' *i.e.* May God preserve your husband: if he be dead, 'May God cause your end to be happy!'

"The men of the better ranks of society, however, when coming in or going away, say, 'Salām, bundugee tuslemat!' *i.e.* 'My blessing, service, or salutation to you!' according to the rank of the lady of the house.

"The salām made by females is not like that of the males—touching the forehead with the right hand—but it consists in touching the *puttee*, or hair above the right temple."[1]

Speaking of men entering a zenāna, the place is considered so sacred, that, in a native family, only the nearest male relatives, the father and grandfather, can unrestrainedly obtain admission; the uncles and brothers only on especial occasions. The bride was once allowed to be seen by the brothers of Mirza Selīm, her betrothed husband; but he requested that no other persons but Colonel and Mr. James Gardner might behold her, and said, after marriage, he should not allow her to be seen even by his own brothers.

The trays containing the presents, brought in procession from the Prince, were received by the female slaves, conveyed by them into the zenāna, and placed before Colonel Gardner's Begam and the Princess Mulka. It is a custom never to send back an empty tray; if money be not sent, part of the contents of the tray is left, fruit, flowers, &c. The presents were displayed on the ground before the bride, who was sitting on a charpāī, wrapped in

[1] Qanoon-e-islam.

an Indian shawl, hiding her face, and sobbing violently; I thought she was really in distress, but found this violent sorrow was only a part of the ceremony. Mulka Begam took a silver bowl, and putting into it sandalwood powder and turmeric and oil, mixed it up, whilst both she and Colonel Gardner's Begam repeated with great care the names and titles on both sides; it being unlucky if any name be forgotten, as any evil that may chance to befall the bride hereafter would be occasioned by forgetfulness, or mistaking the name over this oily mixture. The bride was then rubbed from head to foot with it; how yellow it made her, the turmeric! The natives say it makes the skin *so beautiful, so yellow,* and so soft: it certainly renders the skin deliciously soft, but the yellow tinge I cannot admire. After this operation was performed, all the mixture was scraped up, put into the bowl, and mixed with more oil, to be sent to the Prince, that his body might be rubbed with it—this is considered a compliment!

The bridal dress was then put on Shubbeah; it was of yellow gauze, trimmed with silver; the pajamas of red satin and silver. The faces of the attendants were smeared by way of frolic with the oily mixture, and the bridegroom's party returned to their tents. I must not forget to mention that from the moment the bride is rubbed with this turmeric, she is a prisoner for ten days; not allowed to move from her charpāī, on which she sits up or sleeps. Twice a day she is rubbed with almond soap, mixed with turmeric, &c. All this time she is never allowed to bathe; She is fed on sweetmeats, and not allowed to touch acids, or vinegar, &c: even pān is almost denied; but I fancy, without it an Asiatic lady would fret herself to death. And in this horrible state, a girl is kept during all the gaiety of the wedding; never allowed to move; to make her skin soft and yellow, and to render her sweet-tempered, I suppose, by feeding her with lumps of sugar!

As soon as the bridegroom's party were gone, Colonel Gardner requested me to go in procession, with his pretty grand-daughter, Alaida (the Morning Star), to the Prince's tents, to escort the dress of the bridegroom, sent as a present by the bride. We went accordingly in full procession, as described before, taking back the oily mixture. Mulka Begam received us at the Prince's tent; he was placed on a silver footstool; Mulka took off his upper dress, and rubbed his face and arms with the mixture; she then arrayed him in a dress of yellow and orange muslin, a red turban, and red silk pajamas, in which attire he looked very handsome.

Before him sat three women, the Domnee, playing and singing bridal songs; I saw the Prince turn very red; he looked at the women, and said something in a low tone to Mulka Begam, who answered,—"The mem sāhiba knows they are singing gālee (abuse); but she does not understand

Hindostanee sufficiently to comprehend their songs." The language of the songs is complete *slang*. Yellow powder, mixed with water, was then thrown in frolic at all the people; I made my sālam, quitted the tent, and finding a gentleman in waiting ready to drive me back, returned to Colonel Gardner's, leaving the rest of the party to play and sing all night. Thus ended the first day of the ceremonies.

At the festival of the Hūlī, which is particularly dedicated to Krishnŭ, images of the deity are carried about on elephants, horses, in palkees, &c. The songs are exclusively in honour of Krishnŭ, and hailing the return of the season, personified under the name of Vasanta, generally pronounced Bessant. Kama, the god of love, is the son of Krishnŭ.

The Hoolī was celebrated by the natives with due glee; they threw abeer (red powder) into each other's faces, and then squirted orange-coloured water over it; people were also sent on April-fool errands. Colonel Gardner avoided appearing amongst the people during this festival, and I imitated his example. The orange-coloured water is tinged with the flowers of the dhāk tree; the abeer is flour made from the singharra (water nut), and dyed with red sanders; the roots of the singharra are loosened by means of ropes fastened between two boats, with several men in each; and iron prongs are used in collecting them.

I mentioned to Colonel Gardner the songs of the women, the Domnee, who were in the tent, and the distress of the Prince. He said, "When marriages are negotiating, in particular, they are of the most unchaste description; they are admitted on such occasions, but the nāch girls never; the songs of the Domnee are indecent beyond the conception of an European."

Nāch women dance and sing before men, and are not allowed to enter zenānas of respectability; but in all great establishments, such as Colonel Gardner's, and that of his son, the slave girls are formed into sets of dancing girls, to sing and play for the amusement of the Begams.

Colonel Gardner remarked, "The songs of the nāch girls are never indecent, unless 'by particular desire,' and then in representing the bearer's dance,—a dance which is never performed before ladies."

[. . .]

The Sāchak

"WHEN THERE IS A MARRIAGE THEY MAY SING ALL NIGHT."[1]

March 28th.—The bride is denominated dulhān on the day of Sāchak, and the bridegroom dūlha. The poor dulhān is kept in strict parda on her

[1] Oriental Proverbs.

charpāī; the dūlha ought by law to be equally confined, but he generally
contrives to amuse himself during the time. After the bride and bridegroom
had been rubbed a certain number of days with the oily mixture, the time
appointed for the second day's ceremonies arrived; which is called the
Sāchak. Mulka Begam and the prince arrived in procession. The bridegroom's party were dressed out in all their bravery. The party of the bride
wore their old clothes, and looked as deplorable as possible. This was
according to custom, and therefore strictly observed. On this day it is the
fashion for the bride's mother to appear in an undress, and even that soiled!
The procession consisted of elephants in all their crimson and gold trappings, led horses, English and Arab; nalkīs, a sort of litter used by people
of rank, palanquins, and raths, (native bullock carriages,) &c. A number of
men dressed up as horses were prancing about, kicking and playing antics,
and two hundred gharās (earthen vessels) filled with sweetmeats, which
looked very gay from being covered with silver-leaf, were carried on the
heads of two hundred men.

The platforms for the nāch women were the most curious part of
the procession, they are called takhti-rawān, a sort of travelling throne,
formed of bamboo, square in form, over which was spread an awning ornamented with crimson, and gold, and silver, and supported by four bamboos,
one at each angle of the platform. On each travelling throne sat a native
musician, playing on a kettle-drum, and before him danced two nāch
women; the girls twirled and nāched with all their might and skill. The
platforms were *carried on the heads* of a number of men in the procession,
and had a curious and singular effect; the situation was a very unsteady one
for the dancing girls, one of whom became giddy and tumbled down upon
the heads of the crowd of people below. In this fashion ten stands, containing twenty nāch girls and ten musicians, were carried on men's heads
to the sound of kettle-drums. When Mulka had brought in the procession,
and the company were seated, atr of sandal-wood was put on each person's
face, and a necklace of silver tissue around their necks. The same three vile
old women began their songs of abuse; abusing the prince, the Begams,
and myself; but as it was the custom, no one could be angry. I could only
guess the sort of abuse; I could not understand it, never having heard it
before. The prince's yellow dress, now quite dirty, was on him still; according to custom, *over* it was put on a dress of cloth of gold and crimson.
In front of his turban the jewelled jika was placed, and on his arms valuable bazubunds—armlets of precious stones. All this time the poor little
bride was kept in her oily attire on her charpāī, and not allowed to stir. She
only heard the noise and uproar of the procession. Mulka's dress was very
elegant.

The Menhdī—the Third Day

29th.—The menhdī is the tree, Lawsonia inermis, from the leaves of which the hinnā dye is produced: the leaves are gathered and pounded; when put on the hands and feet, and allowed to remain an hour or two, it produces a dark brownish red dye, which is permanent for four or five months; the hands and feet, both of men and women, thus dyed are reckoned beautiful. It is remarkable that female mummies have the nails stained with menhdī.

A number of trays of this prepared menhdī were carried on men's heads, covered with embroidered velvet; they were sent from the bride to dye the bridegroom. This was the grand display on the part of the bride's friends; who all, dressed in all their most costly attire, went, at eleven at night, in procession from Khāsgunge to the Prince's tents. The road was enclosed with bamboo screens, all lighted up with thousands of small lamps; fireworks were let off in profusion, and the triumphal arches across the road were all illuminated; five thousand torches were carried by men, to light the procession. The Begam herself was there in her nālkee, the curtains all down and fastened; the ladies in a long line of native carriages, called raths; the boys in different sorts of native palkees; the men, handsomely dressed, on elephants. I went in an amārī, on an elephant; the amārī is a litter with two seats, covered by two canopies; when the seat on an elephant is open, without a canopy, it is called a howdah. Mr. T——, a friend, accompanied me; we sat in the front seat, and a native gentleman occupied the seat at the back. The elephant was a very large one; we were a great height from the ground, and had a good view, being above the smoke of the blue lights. The native gentleman amused us by his astonishment at Mr. T——'s not being a married man; my friend told him he wished to marry, but how could he without seeing the lady? The Asiatic said that was impossible; but could he not depend on his female friends to see and select for him? Mr. T——deputed me to select a wife for him; the native gentleman thought him in earnest, and said, when every thing was arranged, I might show Mr. T——her picture before they were married. In this manner weddings are made up; it would be the height of indelicacy to suppose a girl could have a choice, she marries just any one whom her friends select. The led horses, in their gay native caparison, looked so well amongst the blue lights; and the handsomest of all was Candidate, an imported English horse, formerly the property of Major P——; Rattler, another English horse, sixteen hands high, whom I had ridden several times, was also there. They were so quiet and well-behaved in the crowd and amongst the fireworks, much more quiet than the native horses.

The ten platforms, containing the twenty nāch girls and the kettle-drum players carried on men's heads were also there. The effect of the gay dresses of the women, as they twirled and attitudinized was good by torch-light. Some of the girls, who were horrors by daylight, looked pretty by the artificial light, at a distance. It took two hours to go with the procession the four miles, through the village of Khāsgunge to the tents. All the inhabitants were either on the road or on the roofs of their houses, and we were attended by thousands of people: such a crowd, we could scarcely move forwards. On our arrival at the tents we found Mulka Begam's tent prepared for the reception of the females of our party. It was in utter darkness. In front fine bamboo screens were let down, which, inside, were covered with thin white muslin. Through this parda, from the inside of the tent, you could see what was going on without, where every thing was brilliantly lighted, whilst we were in complete darkness. From without you could not see into the tent in the slightest degree. These screens are called pardas, and the women who live within them, parda nishīn, secluded behind the curtain. In front of the tent was pitched a very large shamiyana, a canopy, supported on every side by high poles; white cloths were spread on the ground. In the centre was seated the young Prince on his gaddī (throne of the sovereign), most beautifully dressed, and looking very handsome. His four ill-looking brothers were next to him. On a plain gaddī, by his side, sat Colonel Gardner and myself, and all the English and native gentlemen were seated on either side. In front, were one hundred nāch women, the best to be procured, brought, at an immense expense, from great distances; six or eight of these girls danced at a time, and were relieved by another set. Around were countless numbers of natives, in all their gayest dresses: and still further back were many elephants, on which people had mounted to get a sight of the tamāshā. When the preparations within were ready, Colonel Gardner took me, his son, and the five princes, within the tent; a parda (screen) was drawn across part of the tent, behind which were some native ladies, whom it would have been improper the men should have seen, they not being their relatives. The Prince was placed on a low silver seat, and fed with sugar; the amusement appeared to be, as you offered the sugar, and the Prince attempted to take it in his mouth, to snatch away your hand. The ladies behind the parda also put forth their hands to feed him with sugar; he tried to catch their hands, and having succeeded in catching the hand of one of the girls who was teazing him, he tried to draw off her ring, and in the struggle she was nearly pulled through the parda!

A silver bason was brought, and from it, Mulka Begam, Alaida, and her sister, the Evening Star, put the menhdī on the Prince's hands and feet, and washed it off with water, which they poured from a silver vessel, of the most classical and beautiful shape I almost ever beheld. A turban of green and gold, ornamented with brilliants and precious stones, was placed on his head; he was then dressed in a dress of kimkhwab (gold brocade), a red and gold kamarband, and green pājāmas; and a ring and armlets of great value and beauty were also put upon him. Sherbet was given to him, and all the guests, to drink, and their mouths were wiped with a sort of napkin of red and gold cloth by the cup-bearer.

Into the sherbet tray each guest put a gold mohur, the perquisite of the girls who had put the menhdī on the Prince. Afterwards, a slave-girl brought a silver vessel with water; water was poured over the hands of the guests, each of whom put four or five rupees into the bowl; this was given the Domnee, the same three old women who in one corner were singing all the time. Necklaces of the fresh flowers of the yellow jasmine were thrown over the neck of the prince and the guests. After these ceremonies were completed, the prince and Colonel Gardner quitted the tent. I remained with the Begam. A ceremony was then performed that surprised me considerably; the native ladies laughed, and appeared to think it high tamāshā.

It was now dinner time, being midnight. The inner pardas of the tent were let down, and lights were brought in. A white cloth was spread on the ground in front of the Begam's gaddī, upon which eight large round dishes of earthenware were placed. These were filled with boiled rice mixed with almonds and many good things, very pleasant food. These dishes are always prepared at Asiatic weddings, as bride-cake is always an attendant on the same ceremony in Europe. The rice was piled up high, and silvered all over with silver leaf, and a tuft of silver ornamented the top. Silvered food is much used by natives; and in helping a dish, if you wish to pay a compliment, you send as much gold and silver leaf as you can. At weddings the food is served in earthen vessels, instead of the silver vessels commonly used, because, when the repast is over, the remainder of it, vessels and all, are given away.

Of course, according to Asiatic custom, we all sat on the ground. The Begam said, "What shall we do? we have no knives and forks for the bībī sāhiba." I assured her my fingers were more useful than forks. She sent me a large dish, well filled and well silvered. I bowed over it, saying in an undertone to myself, "Jupiter omnipotens digitos dedit ante bidentes." The Begam *explained* to the guests, "English ladies always say grace before meals." After holding forth my right hand to have water poured upon it, I boldly dipped my fingers into the dish, and contrived to appease my hunger very comfortably, much to the amusement of the Asiatic ladies: but I found I could not get my fingers half so far into my mouth as they contrived to do; certainly the mode is ungraceful, but this may be prejudice. I looked

at Mulka Begam, how far she pushed her delicate fingers down her throat—
wah! wah!

"The prophet used to eat with three fingers, the thumb, the forefinger,
and the middle finger; and after eating he used to lick his blessed fingers
before touching any thing else." The prophet said, "Repeat the name of
God, and eat with your right hand; the devil has power over that meat
which is eaten without remembering the name of God." "Verily God is
pleased with a servant who eats a mouthful and says God's praise, and drinks
a draught of water, and says God's praise." "When any one of you eats, he
must do it with his right hand; and when any one of you drinks, he must
take hold of his water-pot with the right hand, because the devil eats and
drinks with his left."

After the repast silver vessels were handed round, and our mouths and
fingers underwent ablution. Besan, the flour of gram, as good for the
purpose as almond-paste, was presented to each guest; with it the grease
was removed from the fingers, and water was poured over them.

Necklaces most beautifully made of silver tissue were now given to the
whole of the company, both within and without the tent; the lights were
carried away, a portion of the parda was removed, and we, unseen, could
then observe what was going on without the tent, the nāching, and the
company. Seeing the Begam apparently fatigued, I requested she would give
me my dismissal, which, having received, I made my salām and returned
to Colonel Gardner, with whom I sat looking at the nāch until 3 P.M.,
at which hour the prince, by taking his departure, broke up the assembly.
"On retiring, the senior guest, addressing the host, says, 'Be pleased to,
or will you, give us leave, or permission, to depart?' Adding, 'May God
bless and prosper you! I have made a hearty meal, or dined heartily (orig.
eaten a belly full)!' To which the other replies, 'It is the will of God and
Muhammad,' i.e. not mine; or, 'Very well:' 'Certainly.' Then the whole
company rise, calling out, 'As salām alaikum!' 'Peace be unto you,' and
take their departure."[1] I returned to Khāsgunge in a palanquin, in which
I slept all the way home, being fatigued and overcome with the exertions
of the day.

It was a sight worth seeing; the thousands of well-dressed natives in picturesque groups, and the dancing girls under the brilliantly illuminated
trees. I was delighted to sit by my dear Colonel Gardner, and to hear his
explanations. In conversation he was most interesting, a man of great intelligence, and in mind playful as a child. I often begged him to write his life,
or to allow me to write it at his dictation. The description of such varied

[1] Qanoon-e-islam.

scenes as those through which he had passed would have been delightful; and he wrote so beautifully, the work would have been invaluable. He used to tell me remarkable incidents in his life, but I never wrote them down, feeling that unless I could remember his language, the histories would be deprived of half their beauty. I have never described Mr. James Gardner, his son. He is a remarkably shrewd, clever, quick man. He has never been in England: he commenced his education at a school in Calcutta; and the remainder he received at home, from Colonel Gardner and his friend Mr. B——. Persian he reads and writes as fluently as a native, and transacts all his business in that language. He is very quick, and so deep, they say he even outwits the natives. He is very hospitable—expert in all manly exercises—a fine horseman—an excellent swordsman—skilled in the lance exercise—an admirable shot with the bow and arrow—excels in all native games and exercises. I fancy the Begam, his mother, would never hear of her son's going to England for education; and to induce a native woman to give way to any reasons that are contrary to her own wishes is quite out of the power of mortal man. A man may induce a European wife to be unselfish and make a sacrifice to comply with his wishes, or for the benefit of her children. A native woman would only be violent, enraged, and sulky, until the man, tired and weary with the dispute and eternal worry, would give her her own way. Such at least is my opinion from what I have seen of life within the four walls of a zenāna. James Gardner is most perfectly suited to the life he leads: the power of the sun does not affect him so much as it does other people: he rides about his estates and farms all day: he has a great number of villages of his own, of which he is lord and master, and is able to conduct his affairs and turn his indigo and farming to profit. In all this he is assisted by the advice of Mulka Begam, to whom the natives look up with the highest respect. She is a clever woman, and her word is regarded as law by her villagers and dependents.

Chapter 33

The Burāt

"THE NUPTIAL PROCESSION IS PROPORTIONED TO
THE RANK OF THE BRIDEGROOM."[1]

1835, *March 30th.*—Colonel Gardner said to me, "The bridegroom will come to-night to carry away his bride; it is an old Tartar custom for the man to fight for his wife, and carry her away by force of arms; this is still retained. I shall have the doors of the gateway barred at the entrance; and the soldiers on the prince's arrival, after refusing to admit him, will at length allow him to enter, if he give them some gold mohurs. We, of the bride's party, are not to join in the procession, but you may go out on an elephant provided you put no gay trappings upon him; and you can look on and say, 'What a paltry procession, not half as fine as ours last night!' this is the custom (dastūr). I will go in my tanjan and stand at one side." This was the grand day of all: the prince and his party came at night; the village through which they passed was illuminated, as well as the road and the triumphal arches; they were accompanied by bands of music and flags innumerable; at every halt fireworks were let off, while blue lights added a picturesque effect to the scene. The prince rode at the head of the procession on an Arab covered with embroidered trappings; on each side, the animal was decorated with the white tails of the yāk; and over all was thrown an ornamental armour made of flowers. On the head of the Arab was a jika, an ornament from which arose a heron's plume, of which each feather was tipped with gold; his neck, the bridle, and the crupper were adorned with ornaments and golden chains. According to etiquette, an attendant on foot by the side of the horse carried an āftābī, a sun embroidered on velvet attached to a staff, gaily ornamented and carried in an elevated position: it is used as a protection from the rays of the sun, and also as a point of dignity. Another carried a magnificent chatr, umbrella of silk, embroidered with gold, a mark of royalty. In Oude the king alone is entitled to the chatr, with the exception of the resident and his assistant. Then followed the elephants, and friends, and attendants on horseback,

[1] Oriental Proverbs.

palanquins and native carriages of many descriptions: the procession was interspersed with the platforms containing dancing girls, carried by men, and a number of horses, English, Arab, and country, were led by their grooms. Innumerable torches flared in every direction, and chirāghs, small lamps fixed on ladders, were carried horizontally by the attendants. Artificial trees made of wax, coloured paper, and shola, decorated with gold and silver leaf, mica, and coloured foil, were carried by men in great number, and added a strangely Asiatic effect to the whole, as the blue lights fell upon them.

When the procession arrived at the entrance to Colonel Gardner's estate, the doors of the gateway were found closed, and the prince was refused admittance; but after a mock fight, he was allowed to pass through into the grounds. The Begam would not have omitted a Timūrian custom for the world. The dress of the bridegroom consisted entirely of cloth of gold; and across his forehead was bound a sort of fillet (sihrā) made of an embroidery of pearls, from which long strings of gold hung down all over his face to his saddle-bow; and to his mouth he kept a red silk handkerchief closely pressed to prevent devils entering his body! In this heavy dress of gold the prince did not look to advantage.

I went out with two gentlemen, on a very shabbily-dressed elephant; we stopped by the roadside, and had a good view of the procession. One of the party, Mr. F——, attired most becomingly in the native fashion, mounted on a handsome white Arab, caparisoned in purple and gold, looked like a picture in a fairy tale, as he rode amongst the blue lights; his plain dress of fine white dacca muslin, with a white muslin turban, and a handsome black Indian shawl, put round his waist coxcomically in native style, was in very good taste. We remained about an hour viewing the scene,—the effect was excellent; even the old Nawāb of Cambay came out in a tanjan, and looked happy and well pleased. On looking for Colonel Gardner, I saw the dear old man seated on the side of a well, in darkness, and quite removed from the crowd, looking on and smiling at the foolery. Perhaps his thoughts reverted to his own marriage, when he had undergone the same ceremonies: I asked him how he could have endured such folly? He answered, "I was young then; and in love, I would have done or promised any thing."

A very large shamiyāna (awning) was pitched before Colonel Gardner's house; the ground beneath it was spread with white cloths, on which was placed the Prince's gaddī, of velvet, embroidered with gold. An immense number of native gentlemen, wedding guests, were present; they came from their tents, which were all pitched on the estate around the house. During the last two days of the wedding, every man, woman, child, horse, elephant, and servant were fed at Colonel Gardner's expense, and an immense outlay it must have been; my jamadār came to me, and said, "For the next two days your horses and servants will be fed by Colonel Gardner; do not object to it, it would bring ill-luck on the wedding; it is the custom (dastūr)." It is also the custom to sit up the whole night on this occasion; to beguile the time, a great number of brilliant ātāshbāzī (fireworks) were let off, which were fixed in the grounds in front of the house. The dancing girls descended from the platforms on which they had been carried, assembled under the shamiyāna, and sang and attudinized the whole night, one set relieving the other. The Prince seated himself on his gaddī, and the contract of marriage was read to him; it was written in Persian on beautifully illuminated parchment, for which Colonel Gardner paid duty 450 rupees, that is, £45.

Previous to the signature, it was necessary to gain the formal consent of the bride; for which purpose, Mr. James Gardner took the kāzī (native judge), and two of his native officers, with Mrs B—— and myself, into the zenāna. We stood in an empty room, adjoining that in which were the bride and the Begam, her grandmother; between us was the parda; we could hear, but not see. The kāzī said, "Is Shubbeah Begam present?" "Yes." "Does Shubbeah Begam give her free consent to marry Mirza Unjun Shekō?" An answer was made, but in so low a tone, it was more like a murmur.

Mr. Gardner said, "You are witnesses, and have heard her give her consent." I replied, "No; I heard a murmur, but know not what it meant."

The Begam then said, "It is the custom for the bride, from modesty, to be unable to answer; but I, her grandmother, say 'Yes' for her."

The kāzī said, "Mirza Unjun Shekō will settle seven lākh of rupees upon her."

The Begam answered, "We forgive him two lākh, let him settle five."

A lady laughed, and whispered to me, "The young Prince has not five cowries of his own."

If the bride were to give her consent in words, she would be disgraced for ever as an impudent good-for-nothing; after repeated demands, and sometimes *pinchings*, her voice is heard in a sort of *hem*, which, it is taken for granted, means "Yes."

A certain number of lumps of sugar were then sent from the bride to the Prince, and we returned to see him sign the contract.

The kāzī having taken off the veil of gold tissue, and the fillet, that were around the head of the bridegroom, requested him to repeat after him, in Arabic, a portion of some of the chapters in the Kur'ān, and, having

293

explained the contract, asked him if he consented to it; to which he answered in the affirmative; after which the kāzī offered up a supplication in behalf of the betrothed pair; and several other ceremonies were performed.

The contract, a most curious document, was then read aloud; the Prince, having listened attentively, signed it; and several English gentlemen added their names as witnesses, to make it as binding as possible.

The dowry is made high as the *only* security the wife has that her husband will not turn her away as soon as he gets tired of her.

Colonel Gardner then took the contract, and said, "I shall keep this in *my* possession." I asked him "Why?" He said, "It is generally kept by the bride; as long as she has it the husband behaves well; for a few months he treats her kindly, and she becomes fond of him; he coaxes her out of the contract, or he finds out where she hides it and steals it; when once he has got it into his possession he swears she gave it up willingly, and the contract is void."

During the time we were signing the contract, a different scene was going on within the zenāna.

The Prince sent the n'hut (the nose-ring) to the bride, which is equivalent to putting the wedding-ring on the finger in Europe; it was a large thin hoop of gold, and a ruby between two pearls was strung upon it. On receiving it, the bride was taken from her charpāī, on which she had reposed during all the preceding days of this ceremony, in her yellow dress and oily paste, and was bathed. What a luxury that bath must have been, after so many nights and days of penance! She was then dressed in her handsomest attire, richly embroidered garments, and an immense number of jewels; but not one atom of this costume was visible, for *over all* was placed a large square of cloth of silver, and *over that* another large square, formed of cloth of gold, which covered her entirely from head to foot, face and all. Over her forehead was bound the same sort of fillet (sihrā) as the Prince wore, composed of strings of pearls and strings of gold, which hung down over the veil so that she could not see, and could scarcely breathe.

When the guns fired at the signing of the contract, the Prince ate the lumps of sugar that had been sent him by the bride; he then arose, and, quitting the male assembly, went into the zenāna, where he was received by the Begam and her guests, and seated on a gaddī. Soon after Mr. James Gardner appeared with the bride in his arms; he carried her from her own room, according to custom, and placed her on the gaddī, by the side of the Prince.

There she sat, looking like a lump of gold; no one could have imagined a human being was under such a covering; with difficulty she was kept from fainting, the heat was so excessive. Her lips and teeth had been blackened for the first time with misī, and gold and silver dust had been thrown over her face!

Surma (collyrium) also had been applied to her eyelids, at the roots of the lashes, by means of a piece of silver or lead, made in the shape of a probe without the knob at the end. The ladies in attendance on the young Begam then performed innumerable ceremonies; they fed the Prince with sugar-candy, and sifted sugar through his hands; they put a lump of sugar on the head of the bride, off which he took it up in his mouth, and ate it; sugar was placed on her shoulders, on her hands, on her feet, and it was his duty to eat all this misrī off all those parts of her body. The bride's slipper was concealed under rich coverings, and the grand art appeared to be to make the Prince eat the sugar-candy off the shoe!

The Kur'ān was produced, and some parts of it were read aloud; a large Indian shawl was then spread over the heads of the bride and bridegroom, as they sat on the floor, and the shawl was supported like a canopy by the ladies in attendance. A looking-glass was put into the hands of the Prince, he drew the veil of the bride partly aside, and they beheld each other's faces for the first time in the looking-glass! At this moment, had any false description of the bride been given to the bridegroom, he had the power of saying, "I have been deceived, the face I see is not the face that was pourtrayed to me; I will not marry this woman." However, the Prince looked pleased, and so did she, for I saw her smile at this important moment; at which time I particularly observed the expression of their countenances. The Prince took up his bride in his arms,—the golden lump I before described,—and placing her on a silver charpāī, sat down by her side, and fanned her carefully. The poor girl was almost stifled beneath the gold and silver coverings, that oppressed but did not adorn her. By this time the night had nearly passed away; the remainder was taken up with tedious and trivial ceremonies; at last morning dawned, and at 11 A.M. the dowry was counted, and made ready to carry away.

When the moment arrived for the Prince to carry off his bride, the whole of the women in the zenāna came round her, and cried and wept with all their might and main; even those who did not regret her departure cried and wept most furiously. Colonel Gardner was sitting there, looking pale and miserable; when he embraced his grand-daughter, whom he loved, the old man trembled in every limb, the tears dropped from his eyes, and he could scarcely stand. He called the Prince to him, and told him that, accord-

295

ing to his treatment of his child should be his own conduct towards him; that if he made her happy he should want for nothing; but if he made her unhappy he would make him miserable. Colonel Gardner then said to me, "When I gave her sister to young Gardner I knew she would be happy; but this poor girl, who may prophesy her fate? However, she wished it; her mother and the Begam had set their hearts upon it; and you know, my betī (my child), women will have their own way."

Although Colonel Gardner always called me his child, and treated me as such, my title in the zenāna was "Fanī Bhū'a," because his son usually addressed me as "*Sister* of my Father."

When it was announced that the procession was ready, the Prince took the bride up in his arms, in her lump-like position, and carried her to her palanquin, the purdas of which were then let down, and fastened outside with gold and silver cords.

This taking up a girl who is sitting on the floor in your arms, and carrying her away without touching the ground with your knees, and without any assistance from another person, is a difficult affair to accomplish; to fail in doing it would be deemed unlucky. The bridegroom performed it very cleverly.

The Prince, in the dress in which he arrived, attended the palanquin on horseback; and the whole of the bride's dower followed in procession, carried on the heads of men, and displayed to view. One golden-footed bed, and one silver-footed charpāī; a number of large trunks, covered with red cloth, containing cashmere shawls and ready-made clothes, sufficient to last for one year; and unmade clothes, and pieces of kimkhwab, gold and silver tissues, silks, and pieces of India muslin, enough to last for three years. I saw a large pile of pājāmas for the bride put into one of the trunks, considered sufficient for the wear of a year; besides which, forty pieces, consisting of coloured silks and gold brocades, for the same article of dress, were sent unmade, and deemed sufficient for three years to come. Two elephants, several horses, a very handsome bilee for the lady herself, and several raths for the ladies in attendance upon her; as also a palanquin. Then came, carried on trays, dishes of various sorts, for the household, which were made of pure silver; ewers and chilamchīs of the same; also for the cook-room, every article in iron or copper necessary for the establishment of a newly-married couple; and all these things were of the best description. The jewels for the bride, which were very handsome and very valuable, were carried in state, together with a pāndan for holding betel, and all the ingredients for pān; another box, with partitions for spices, cardamums, &c.; a misī-dān for holding misī (a powder made of vitriol, &c.), with which they tinge the teeth of a black colour; a surmā-dān, for holding surmā (the collyrium which they apply to the eyes, to give them a brilliant appearance); an atr-dān, a gulabpash (for sprinkling rosewater); and every article for the toilet of an Asiatic lady. Quilts, mattresses, pillows, carpets, boxes, lamps; in fact, an endless list; besides male and female slaves, to attend on the newly-married people. A Kur'ān, for the bridegroom, was also carried in procession.

Every thing necessary for the use of a native lady is sent on such an occasion, and these articles are provided for years; head and heel ropes for the horses, and even wooden pegs to secure them, and the bullocks, are sent with the lady, that nothing may be wanting.

[. . .]

By the time the procession had quitted the gates of the zenāna, I was very glad to return to my own rooms to bathe preparatory to breakfast. I had eaten nothing during the night but cardamums and prepared betel-nut: had smoked a little of Colonel Gardner's hooqŭ, and had drank nothing but tea. Mr. Gardner prepared some pān for me in a particular fashion: I ate it, and found it very refreshing. Pān, so universally eaten in India, is made of the leaf of the piper betel, a species of pepper plant, called pān supéarie and betel-nut; but this betel-nut is not the nut of the piper betel, but of the areca catechu, a palm fifty feet in height. The betel-nut is cut up in small bits and wrapped up in the pān-leaf with lime cuttie, which is a bitter gum resin, an astringent vegetable extract, the produce of a species of mimosa (chadira) catechu Japonica; called kuth by the natives, and some slaked lime, or chunā. Pān at marriage feasts is tied up in packets of a triangular shape, and covered with gold and silver leaf and enamelled foil of bright colours: the lime cuttie dyes the gums and tongue a deep red.

I was quite fresh and free from headache: had I sat up all night in England, where we eat supper, it would have made me ill. Colonel Gardner came in to breakfast, and kissing me on the forehead, said, "Mera betī (my child), you are less fatigued than any one." The Prince lived with his bride at the tents for three days, after which they returned to Colonel Gardner's to perform the final ceremony of playing the chāotree.

Chapter 34

The Chāotree

"ONE SNAKE HAS BIT THEM ALL."[1]

"THE PRINCESS HAS GROWN FOOLISH, SHE PELTS HER OWN
RELATIONS WITH SWEETMEATS, OTHERS WITH STONES."[2]

"THEY HAVE SCATTERED DATŪRA (THORN APPLE) IN THE AIR."[3]

i.e. the people are all gone mad.

1835, *April 2nd.*—The chāotree was to be played this day, it being the finale
of the wedding. When the Prince and Shubbeah arrived at Khāsgunge they
came into the zenāna, and were seated on the gaddī; a large number of
trays, containing fruits and vegetables of every description, fresh from the
garden, were placed before them, with sugar, &c. Shubbeah had divested
herself of her bridal attire, and wore the peshwāz, the court dress of Delhi,
which was made of Benares tissue of gold and silver, and she wore all her
jewels. Nine fruits of different sorts were wrapped in a cloth, and suspended
round her waist by her attendants; it had a curious effect, because the whole
was placed beneath her garments; she arose, encumbered with these fruits,
and made salām to each of the four corners of the room. Her hair was then
decked with natural flowers, her face having previously been covered with
silver dust; and she and the Prince were both fed with sugar off a rupee. A
stick, ornamented with silver tissue, was given to him, and another to her,
with which they pretended to beat each other; these silver wands were presented to all the ladies, and wands covered with flowers were given to the
slaves. For some days before the chāotree, the Begam had been employed
in teaching the ladies in the zenāna and the slave girls a particular dance,
the ancient Princess herself dancing with them, with a silver wand in her
hand. I mentioned this to Colonel Gardner; he said, "It is very remarkable
that, at weddings, all the ladies of this family perform this particular nāch,
but at no other time do they dance; it would lower their dignity". This is
an old Tartar dance, and always performed at weddings amongst the

[1] Oriental Proverbs.   [2] Ibid.   [3] Ibid.

Timūrians; it is the dastūr. The tamāshā consisted in beating each other with these silver sticks, and throwing handfuls of fruits, of turnips, of oranges, of pomegranates, in fact, any thing that could be seized from the trays, at each other; the slaves joining in the fun, breaking the glass windows by accident, and doing much damage. The more you pelt a person, the greater the compliment; sharp jealousy was created in many a breast this day, the source of much anxiety afterwards. This is called playing the chāotree, and finishes the ceremonies of the wedding.

Soon after, a woman came in, with a large basket full of chūrīs for the arms (bracelets), which were made of rings of glass, ornamented with beads. Every body at the wedding, from the Begam to the youngest slave, had chūrīs put on their arms; I was also decorated. These rings are extremely small; to put them on requires considerable art, it being necessary to mull the hand, and render it very pliant, before it can pass through so very small a circumference as that of the churee.

Thus ended the wedding of Prince Unjun Shekō and Shubbeah Begam. They quitted their tents, and went to reside at a pretty little fort and indigo factory, the property of Colonel Gardner, at Moreechee.[1]

The dūlhān (bride) visits her mother on the four first Fridays after her marriage, on each of which the dūlhā (bridegroom) is bribed with a full suit.

"A marriage may be celebrated with a mŭn of rice as well as a mŭn of pearls."[1]

Another wedding immediately began, that of Jhanee Khanum, an adopted daughter of Colonel Gardner's, a slave girl; but I did not stay to witness it, having before seen the grand display.

It is the custom in the zenāna for every young lady to adopt the child of a slave, which serves as a doll, an amusement for her. Shubbeah had an adopted child, for whom she will have eventually to provide; and every lady in the zenāna had an adopted daughter of the same description. The slaves are a set of the most idle, insolent, good-tempered, thievish, laughing girls I ever saw. I should think, counting babies, slaves and all, there must have been two hundred souls within the four walls of Colonel Gardner's zenāna.

The prince allowed his brothers to see the bride the day of the wedding, but said he should not allow them to see her in future. A native woman thinks this sort of jealousy very flattering, and prides herself upon it.

The mother of Shubbeah was the happiest of the happy: in her idea, her

---

[1] Oriental Proverbs.

[1] Subbeah and Mirza Unjun Sheko had a daughter Jane, who in 1879 married her cousin Alan Hyde Gardner, son of Hurmoozee and Stewart William Gardner.

child had made the finest match in the world, by marrying a prince of the house of Delhi, although she was brought up a Christian, he a follower of the prophet. Her other daughter was happily married, her husband being very fond of native life and native customs.

At noon all the slave girls came for their dinners; each had given her a great chapāttī (cake of flour) as large as a plate, and this was filled brim full from two great vessels of curry and rice. This repast took place again at eight in the evening. One day, just as they were beginning their meal, I sat down in the verandah and played an Hindostanee air on a sitar (a native instrument made of a goord); up started all the slaves in an instant and set to, dancing with their food in their hands and their mouths full! Each slave girl carried her curry and rice on the wheaten cake, which was about the size of a plate, and used it as such; until having eaten the contents she finished with the cake. In spite of their dexterity in putting the food down their throats without dropping the rice or soiling their dresses, the fingers retain a considerable portion of the yellow turmeric and the greasy ghee! They eat custards, rice, and milk, and more fluid food with the hand, sucking the fingers to clean them, and afterwards wipe them dry with a chapātī! They were merry, and fat, and happy, unless the Begam happened to catch one out in a theft, when the other girls punished her. Some of the slaves were pretty girls, and great favourites. To show how little they had to do, the following anecdote may suffice. A pretty slave girl was sitting by my bedside; I held out my hand, and desired her to shampoo it: the girl's countenance became clouded, and she did not offer to do it—her name was Tara (the Star). "Why do you not mull my hand, Tara?" said I. "Oh," she replied, "I never mull the hand; the other girls do that; I only mull the Colonel Sāhib's eye-brows. I can take the pain from them when he is ill;—that is my duty. I will not shampoo the hand." I laughed at her description of the work that fell to her lot as a slave, and said, "Well, Tara, mull my eye-brows; my head aches;" with the greatest good-humour she complied, and certainly charmed away the pain. It is the great luxury of the East.

I might have lived fifty years in India and never have seen a native wedding. It is hardly possible for a European lady to be present at one. Alaida and her sister the Evening Star learnt to read and write Persian; a very old moonshee was allowed to teach them. Musulmānī ladies generally forget their learning when they grow up, or they neglect it. Every thing that passes without the four walls is reported to them by their spies: never was any place so full of intrigue, scandal, and chit-chat as a zenāna. Making up marriages is their great delight, and the bustle attendant on the ceremonies. They dote upon their children, and are so selfish they will not part from them to allow them to go to school, if it be possible to avoid it. The girls, of course, never quit the zenāna. Within the four walls surrounding the zenāna at Khāsgunge is a pretty garden, with a summer-house in the centre; fountains play before it, and they are fond of spending their time out of doors. During the rains they take great delight in swinging under the large trees in the open air. They never ride on horseback, or go on the water for pleasure. They are very fond of atr of all sorts, the scent of which is overpowering in their houses. They put scented oil on their hair; to eau-de-Cologne and lavender-water they have the greatest aversion, declaring it to be gin, to drink! The prophet forbade all fermented liquors, after a battle which he nearly lost by his soldiers getting drunk, and being surprised.

The old Begam said to Colonel Gardner, "They are curious creatures, these English ladies; I cannot understand them or their ways,—their ways are so odd!" And yet the Begam must have seen so many European ladies, I wonder she had not become more reconciled to our *odd ways*.

The conduct that shocked them was our dining with men not our relations, and that too with uncovered faces. A lady's going out on horseback is monstrous. They could not comprehend my galloping about on that great English horse, just where I pleased, with one or two gentlemen and the coachman as my attendants. My not being afraid to sleep in the dark without having half a dozen slave girls snoring around me, surprised them. My remaining *alone* writing in my own room; my not being unhappy when I was alone,—in fact, they looked upon me as a very odd creature. It was almost impossible to enjoy solitude, the slave girls were peeping under the corner of every parda. Some one or other was always coming to talk to me; sometimes asking me to make up a marriage! If a native lady is relating a story, and you look incredulous, she exclaims, "I swear to God it is true!" They are very fond of this exclamation. One day, in the gardens, I was talking to Tara, the pretty slave girl, when she darted away over the poppy beds, screaming out, "I swear to God there is a ripe poppy-head!" and she came back with her ripe poppy-head, out of which she beat the seeds on the palm of her hand, and ate them. She then brought some more for me, which I ate in her fashion. The half-ripe seeds of the poppy eaten raw, and fresh gathered, are like almonds; they do not intoxicate. "Remember," said Tara, "after dinner you shall have a dish sent you; partake of it, you will like it." It is made thus; gather three or four young poppy-heads when they are full of opium, and green; split each head into four parts, fry them in a little butter, *a very little*, only just enough to fry them, with some pepper and salt—send them to table, with the dessert. The flavour is very pleasant, and if you only eat enough, you will become as tipsy as mortal may desire. We had them often at Colonel Gardner's; and I have felt rather sleepy from eating them. The old nawab was in his glory when he had two or three spoonfuls of these poppy-heads in his plate, one of which is a good dose. I was so fond of the unripe seeds, that I never went into the garden, but the mālī brought me ten or twelve heads, which I usually finished at once. There were some beds of the double red poppy, especially set apart for the Begam, the opium from that poppy being reckoned the finest; a couple of lumps of opium were collected, and brought in daily. Colonel Gardner said to me, "The Begam is perplexed; she wants to know how you, a married woman, can have received the gift of a nose-ring from a gentleman not your husband? She says the nose-ring is the bridal ring. She is perplexed." I had differed in opinion with a gentleman: he said, "I will bet you a nose-ring you are in the wrong." The native jewellers had been at the house that morning showing their nose-rings, and other native ornaments. I accepted the bet, and was victorious: the gentleman presented me with a nose-ring, which I declined, because its value was one hundred and sixty rupees, *i.e.* £16. "I will accept the n'hut I have won, but it must be one from the bazār, which will be an exact imitation of this ring, and will cost one rupee and a half." It was accordingly procured for me. The Begam having heard this story was perplexed until it was explained to her, that I was not going to marry the gentleman, and had only accepted the nose-ring to make a native dress perfect.

Three of the slave girls, wishing to see the world, I suppose, went to the Begam, and asked her to give them to me. She laughed and told me their request.

Science has not yet entered the confines of the zenāna; nature and superstition reign supreme; nevertheless, native women suffer less on the birth of a child than the women of Europe. The first nourishment given an infant medicinally is composed of umaltass (cassia fistula) sugar, aniseed water, and russote, from a colt just born! Native women do not approve of flannel for infants, thinking it excites the skin too much.

[. . .]

Sons are of inestimable value; the birth of a daughter is almost a calamity; but even the mother blest with a son is not likely to remain long without a rival in the heart of her husband, since ninety-nine out of a hundred take new wives; besides the concubines given by the mother before marriage!

When a Muhammadan has sworn to separate himself from his wife, she retires to her own apartments, and does not behold her husband for four months; if they are not reconciled by the end of that time, all their ties are broken; the woman recovers her liberty, and receives, on quitting the house, the property settled on her by the contract of marriage. The girls follow the mother, the boys remain with the father. The husband cannot send her from his house until the expiration of the four months.

One day Colonel Gardner was ill; he was in the large garden without. The Begam begged me to go to him; she *dared not* leave the zenāna, even to assist her husband, who was so ill that his attendants had run in for aid! I went to him. After a time he was better, and wished to return to the house; he leaned on my shoulder for support, and led the way to the burial-ground of his son Allan, just without the garden. He sat down on a tomb, and we had a long conversation; "If it were not for old age, and the illness it brings on," said he, "we should never be prepared, never ready to leave this world. I shall not last long; I shall not see you again, my betī; I wish to be buried by the side of my son; but I have spoken to James about it. The poor Begam, she will not survive me long; mark my words,—she will not say much, but she will take my death to heart, she will not long survive me: when her son Allan died she pounded her jewels in a mortar." Shortly afterwards we returned to the house.

It may appear extraordinary to an European lady that the Begam, in her affliction, should have pounded her jewels in a mortar: ornaments are put aside in times of mourning; and jewellery with native ladies is highly prized, not merely for its own sake—that of adding to their beauty, but as a proof of the estimation in which they are held by their husbands. If a man be angry with his wife, he will take away her jewels, and not allow her to wear them; if pleased, it is his delight to cover her with the most valuable ornaments, precious stones set in pure gold. The quantity and value of the jewellery thus ascertains the rank to which a lady is entitled in this sort of domestic "order of merit;" the women pride themselves upon this adornment, and delight in jewellery as much as the men of England in stars and garters.

A lady wears slippers only out of doors, and puts them off on entering the house; the slippers are of various forms and patterns; some of them are square at the toes, and have iron heels. "She combs his head with the iron heel of her slipper," is applied to a woman who domineers over her husband. The slippers for the ladies are of cloth, of the gayest colours, ornamented with embroidery of gold and silver, adorned with seed pearls, and with beetle wings, which are worked into flowers upon the cloth, and cover the long peak that turns up over the toes.

Stockings are never worn; but I have seen little coloured socks, made of the wool of Cashmir, worn at times during the cold season. The ankles of a native lady are decorated with massive rings, called kurrā; those worn by the Begam were of gold, thickly studded with jewels; the ladies had them of solid embossed gold; and for the slaves, they were of solid silver. These rings are generally hexagonal or octagonal, of an equal thickness throughout, and terminated by a knob at each end. The gold or the silver of which they are composed being pure metal, they may be opened sufficiently to be put on or off at pleasure; the ends being brought together by the pressure of the hand.

Another ornament consists of a great number of small bells, ghoonghroo, strung on a cord, and worn around the ankle, hanging to the heel. It is reckoned very correct to wear these tinkling bells; if a native wishes to praise a woman most highly, he says, "She has never seen the sun, she always wears bells."

In lieu of this string of bells, another ornament is often worn, called pāezēb, which consists of heavy rings of silver, resembling a horse's curb chain, but much broader, set with a fringe of small spherical bells, all of which tinkle at every motion of the limb; and all the toes are adorned with rings, some of which are furnished with little bells; such rings are called ghoongroodar chhallā. The ladies wear their dresses, unless they be grand dresses for occasions of state, until they are dirty; perhaps for five or six days together; the dresses are then thrown away, and they put on new attire.

5th.—I took leave of my dear Colonel Gardner, and quitted him with a heavy heart, for I saw how feeble his health had become, how necessary quiet and attention were for him, and I knew that, left to the care of natives, his comfort would be little considered.

After my departure, I heard he endured much annoyance from domestic concerns, and that it was too much for his feeble health. He suffered greatly from asthma and violent headaches, and had only recently recovered from an attack of paralysis. I was strongly tempted to return to Khāsgunge when I heard of his illness, but was deterred from a feeling of delicacy: an adopted child has a right to a portion of the inheritance, and my presence might have caused the ladies of the zenāna to imagine a sinister motive influenced me.

A gentleman who was with him afterwards told me,—"During his last illness, Colonel Gardner often spoke of you in terms of the greatest affection, and expressed many times his wish for your presence; I did not write to tell you so, because the hot winds were blowing, and the distance some five or six hundred miles."

Had he only written to me, I would have gone dāk to Khāsgunge immediately; what would the annoyance of hot winds or the distance have been, in comparison with the satisfaction of gratifying the wish of my departing friend? I had lived for weeks in his house, enjoying his society, admiring his dignified and noble bearing, and listening with delight to the relation of his marvellous escapes and extraordinary adventures. His chivalric exploits and undaunted courage deserve a better pen than mine, and he alone was capable of being his own historian.

Colonel Gardner told me, if I ever visited Delhi, he would give me an introduction to the Nawāb Shah Zamānee Begam, the Emperor's unmarried sister; who would show me all that was worth seeing in the zenāna of the palace of the King of Delhi. This pleased me greatly; so few persons ever have an opportunity of seeing native ladies.

On the 29th of the following July my beloved friend, Colonel Gardner, departed this life at Khāsgunge, aged sixty-five. He was buried, according to his desire, near the tomb of his son Allan. From the time of his death the poor Begam pined and sank daily; just as he said, she complained not, but she took his death to heart; she died one month and two days after his decease. Native ladies have a number of titles; her death, names, and titles were thus announced in the papers:— "On the 31st of August, at her residence at Khāsgunge, Her Highness Furzund Azeza Zubdeh-tool Arrakeen Umdehtool Assateen Nuwab Mah Munzil ool Nissa Begam Dehlmī, relict of the late Colonel William Linnæus Gardner."

[. . .]

The sums of money and the quantity of food distributed by Colonel Gardner's Begam in charity was surprising; she was a religious woman, and fulfilled, as far as was in her power, the ordinances of her religion. The necessity of giving alms is strongly inculcated. "To whomsoever God gives wealth, and he does not perform the charity due from it, his wealth will be made into the shape of a serpent on the day of resurrection, which shall not have any hair upon its head; and this is a sign of its poison and long life; and it has two black spots upon its eyes; and it will be twisted round his neck, like a chain, on the day of resurrection: then the serpent will seize the man's jawbones, and will say, 'I am thy wealth, from which thou didst not give in charity; I am thy treasure, from which thou didst not separate any alms.' After this the prophet repeated this revelation. 'Let not those who are covetous of what God of his bounty hath granted them, imagine that their avarice is better for them: nay, rather it is worse for them. That which they have covetously reserved shall be bound as a collar about their necks on the day of resurrection.'"

Chapter 35

The Mahratta Queen

1835, *April 6th.*—I arrived at Fathīghar, at the house of a relative in the Civil Service, the Judge of the Station, and agent to the Governor-general. After a hot and dusty dāk trip, how delightful was the coolness of the rooms, in which thermantidotes and tattīs were in full force! As may be naturally supposed, I could talk of nothing but Khāsgunge, and favoured the party with some Hindustanī airs on the sitar, which I could not persuade them to admire; to silence my sitar a dital harp was presented to me; nevertheless, I retained a secret fondness for the native instrument, which recalled the time when the happy slave girls figured before me.

Having seen Musulmānī ladies followers of the Prophet, how great was my delight at finding native ladies were, at Fathīghar, worshippers of Ganesh and Krishn-jee!

Her Highness the Bāiza Bā'ī, the widow of the late Mahārāj Dāolut Rāo Scindia, was in camp at this place, under the care of Captain Ross. Dāolut Rāo, the adopted son and grandnephew of Mahadajee Scindia, contested with the Duke of Wellington, then Sir Arthur Wellesley, the memorable field of Assaye. On the death of Scindia, by his appointment, the Bāiza Bā'ī, having become Queen of Gwalior, ruled the kingdom for nine years. Having no male issue, her Highness adopted a youth, called Jankee Rāo, a distant relative of Scindia's, who was to be placed on the masnad at her decease.[1]

A Rajpoot is of age at eighteen years: but when Jankee Rāo was only fourteen years old, the subjects of the Bā'ī revolted, and placed the boy at the head of the rebellion. Had her Highness remained at Gwalior she would have been murdered; she was forced to fly to Fathīghar, where she put herself under the protection of the Government. Her daughter, the Chimna

---

[1] The Mahrattas were the last major native force in India to be defeated by the British. Mahadaji Sindhia of Gwalior was the most forceful chief of the eighteenth century. By the time Daulat Rao succeeded him in 1794, the decline of the Mahrattas had begun. Daulat Rao married the Baiza Bai, daughter of Shirji Rao Ghatgay, in 1798, when he was eighteen years old. It was Marquis Wellesley (1776–1842) who seriously weakened Mahratta power during his period as Governor-General of Bengal from 1797 to 1805.

Rājā Sāhib, a lady celebrated for her beauty, and the wife of Appa Sāhib, a Mahratta nobleman, died of fever, brought on by exposure and anxiety at the time she fled from Gwalior, during the rebellion. It is remarkable, that the ladies in this family take the title of *Rājā*, to which Sāhib is generally affixed. Appa Sāhib joined the Bāiza Bā'ī, fled with her, and is now in her camp at Fathīghar. The rebellion of her subjects, and her Highness being forced to fly the kingdom, were nothing to the Bā'ī in comparison to the grief occasioned her by the loss of her beloved daughter, the Chimna Rājā.

Her grand-daughter, the Gaja Rājā Sāhib, is also living with her; she has been married two years, but is alone, her husband having deserted her to join the stronger party.

The Bā'ī, although nominally free, is in fact a prisoner; she is extremely anxious to return to Gwalior, but is prevented by the refusal of the Government to allow her to do so; this renders her very unhappy.

8th.—The Brija Bā'ī, one of her ladies, called to invite the lady with whom I am staying to visit the Mahārāj in camp; and gave me an invitation to accompany her.

12th.—When the appointed day arrived, the attendants of her Highness were at our house at 4 A.M., to escort us to the camp.

It is customary for a visitor to leave her shoes outside the parda, when paying her respects to a lady of rank; and this custom is always complied with, unless especial leave to retain the shoes has been voluntarily given to the visitor, which would be considered a mark of great kindness and condescension.

We found her Highness seated on her gaddī of embroidered cloth, with her grand-daughter the Gaja Rājā Sāhib at her side; the ladies, her attendants, were standing around her; and the sword of Scindia was on the gaddī, at her feet. She rose to receive and embrace us, and desired us to be seated near her. The Bāiza Bā'ī is rather an old woman, with grey hair, and *en bon point*; she must have been pretty in her youth; her smile is remarkably sweet, and her manners particularly pleasing; her hands and feet are very small, and beautifully formed. Her sweet voice reminded me of the proverb, "A pleasant voice brings a snake out of a hole."[1] She was dressed in the plainest red silk, wore no ornaments, with the exception of a pair of small plain bars of gold as bracelets. Being a widow, she is obliged to put jewellery aside, and to submit to numerous privations and hardships. Her countenance is very mild and open; there is a freedom and independence in her air that I greatly admire,—so unlike that of the sleeping, languid, opiumeating Musalmānīs. Her grand-daughter, the Gaja Rājā Sāhib, is very young;

[1] Oriental Proverbs.

her eyes the largest I ever saw; her face is rather flat, and not pretty; her figure is beautiful; she is the least little wee creature you ever beheld. The Mahratta dress consists only of two garments, which are, a tight body to the waist, with sleeves tight to the elbow; a piece of silk, some twenty yards or more in length, which they wind around them as a petticoat, and then, taking a part of it, draw it between the limbs, and fasten it behind, in a manner that gives it the effect both of petticoat and trowsers; this is the whole dress, unless, at times, they substitute angiyas, with short sleeves, for the tight long-sleeved body.

The Gaja Rājā was dressed in purple Benares silk, with a deep gold border woven into it; when she walked she looked very graceful, and the dress very elegant; on her forehead was a mark like a spear-head, in red paint; her hair was plaited, and bound into a knot at the back of her head, and low down; her eyes were edged with surma, and her hands and feet dyed with hinnā. On her feet and ancles were curious silver ornaments; toe-rings of peculiar form; which she sometimes wore of gold, sometimes of red coral. In her nostril was a very large and brilliant n'hut (nose-ring), of diamonds, pearls, and precious stones, of the particular shape worn by the Mahrattas; in her ears were fine brilliants. From her throat to her waist she was covered with strings of magnificent pearls and jewels; her hands and arms were ornamented with the same. She spoke but little,—scarcely five words passed her lips; she appeared timid, but was pleased with the bouquet of beautiful flowers, just fresh from the garden, that the lady who presented me laid at her feet on her entrance. These Mahrattas are a fine bold race; amongst her ladies in waiting I remarked several fine figures, but their faces were generally too flat. Some of them stood in waiting with rich Cashmere shawls thrown over their shoulders; one lady, before the Mahārāj, leaned on her sword, and if the Bā'ī quitted the apartment, the attendant and sword always followed her. The Bā'ī was speaking of horses, and the lady who introduced me said I was as fond of horses as a Mahratta. Her Highness said she should like to see an English lady on horseback; she could not comprehend how they could sit all crooked, all on one side, in the side-saddle. I said I should be too happy to ride into camp any hour her Highness would appoint, and show her the style of horsemanship practised by ladies in England. The Mahārāj expressed a wish that I should be at the Mahratta camp at 4 A.M., in two days' time. Atr, in a silver filagree vessel, was then presented to the Gaja Rājā; she took a portion up in a little spoon, and put it on our hands. One of the attendants presented us with pān, whilst another sprinkled us most copiously with rose-water: the more you inundate your visitor with rose-water, the greater the compliment.

This being the signal for departure, we rose, made our bahut bahut adab salām, and departed, highly gratified with our visit to her Highness the ex-Queen of Gwalior.

14*th.*—My relative had a remarkably beautiful Arab, and as I wished to show the Bā'ī a good horse, she being an excellent judge, I requested him to allow me to ride his Arab; and that he might be fresh, I sent him on to await my arrival at the zenāna gates. A number of Mahratta horsemen having been despatched by her Highness to escort me to the camp, I cantered over with them on my little black horse, and found the beautiful Arab impatiently awaiting my arrival.

[. . .]

I mounted him, and entering the precincts of the zenāna, found myself in a large court, where all the ladies of the ex-Queen were assembled, and anxiously looking for the English lady, who would ride crooked! The Bā'ī was seated in the open air; I rode up, and, dismounting, paid my respects. She remarked the beauty of the Arab, felt the hollow under his jaw, admired his eye, and, desiring one of the ladies to take up his foot, examined it, and said he had the small, black, hard foot of the pure Arab; she examined and laughed at my saddle. I then mounted, and putting the Arab on his mettle, showed her how English ladies manage their horses. When this was over, three of the Bāiza Bā'ī's own riding horses were brought out by the female attendants; for we were within the zenāna, where no man is allowed to enter. The horses were in full caparison, the saddles covered with velvet and kimkwhab and gold embroidery, their heads and necks ornamented with jewels and chains of gold. The Gaja Rājā, in her Mahratta riding dress, mounted one of the horses, and the ladies the others; they cantered and pranced about, showing off the Mahratta style of riding. On dismounting, the young Gaja Rājā threw her horse's bridle over my arm, and said, laughingly, "Are you afraid? or will you try my horse?" Who could resist such a challenge? "I shall be delighted," was my reply. "You cannot ride like a Mahratta in that dress," said the Princess; "put on proper attire." I retired to obey her commands, returning in Mahratta costume, mounted her horse, put my feet into the great iron stirrups, and started away for a gallop round the enclosure. I thought of Queen Elizabeth, and her stupidity in changing the style of riding for women. *En cavalier*, it appeared so safe, as if I could have jumped over the moon. Whilst I was thus amusing myself, "Shāh-bāsh! shāh-bāsh!" exclaimed some masculine voice; but who pronounced the words, or where the speaker lay *perdu*, I have never discovered.

"Now," said I to the Gaja Rājā, "having obeyed your commands, will you allow one of your ladies to ride on my side-saddle?" My habit was put on one of them; how ugly she looked! "She is like a black doctor!" exclaimed one of the girls. The moment I got the lady into the saddle, I took the rein in my hand and riding by her side, started her horse off in a canter; she hung on one side, and could not manage it at all; suddenly checking her horse, I put him into a sharp trot. The poor lady hung half off the animal, clinging to the pummel, and screaming to me to stop; but I took her on most unmercifully, until we reached the spot where the Bāiza Bā'ī was seated; the walls rang with laughter; the lady dismounted, and vowed she would never again attempt to sit on such a vile crooked thing as a side-saddle. It caused a great deal of amusement in the camp.

[. . .]

The Mahratta ladies live in parda, but not in such strict seclusion as the Musalmānī ladies; they are allowed to ride on horseback veiled; when the Gaja Rājā goes out on horseback, she is attended by her ladies; and a number of Mahratta horsemen ride at a certain distance, about two hundred yards around her, to see that the kurk is enforced; which is an order made public that no man may be seen on the road on pain of death.

The Hindoos never kept their women in parda, until their country was conquered by the Muhammadans; when they were induced to follow the fashion of their conquerors; most likely, from their unveiled women being subject to insult.

The Bāiza Bā'ī did me the honour to express herself pleased, and gave me a title, "The Great-aunt of my Grand-daughter," "Gaja Rājā Sāhib ki par Khāla." This was very complimentary, since it entitled me to rank as the adopted sister of her Highness.

A part of the room in which the ex-Queen sits is formed into a domestic temple, where the idols are placed, ornamented with flowers, and worshipped; at night they are lighted up with lamps of oil, and the priests are in attendance.

The Mahratta ladies are very fond of sailing on the river, but they are equally in parda in the boats as on shore.

The next day the Bāiza Bā'ī sent down all her horses in their gay native trappings, for me to look at; also two fine rhinoceroses, which galloped about the grounds in their heavy style, and fought one another; the Bā'ī gave five thousand rupees (£500) for the pair; sweetmeats and oranges pleased the great animals very much.

When Captain Ross quitted, her Highness was placed under the charge of the agent to the Governor-general. I visited the Bā'ī several times, and liked her better than any native lady I ever met with.

A Hindoo widow is subject to great privations; she is not allowed to wear gay attire or jewels, and her mourning is eternal. The Bāiza Bā'ī always slept on the ground, according to the custom for a widow, until she became very ill from rheumatic pains; after which she allowed herself a hard mattress, which was placed on the ground; a charpāī being considered too great a luxury.

She never smoked, which surprised me: having seen the Musalmānī ladies so fond of a hooqŭ, I concluded the Mahratta ladies indulged in the same luxury.

The Mahratta men smoke the hooqŭ as much as all other natives; and the Bā'ī had a recipe for making tobacco cakes, that were highly esteemed in camp. The cakes are, in diameter, about four inches by one inch in thickness; a small quantity added to the prepared tobacco usually smoked in a hooqŭ imparts great fragrance; the ingredients are rather difficult to procure.

Speaking of the privations endured by Hindoo widows, her Highness mentioned that all luxurious food was denied them, as well as a bed; and their situation was rendered as painful as possible. She asked me how an English widow fared?

I told her, "An English lady enjoyed all the luxury of her husband's house during his life; but, on his death, she was turned out of the family mansion, to make room for the heir, and pensioned off; whilst the old horse was allowed the run of the park, and permitted to finish his days amidst the pastures he loved in his prime." The Hindoo widow, however young, must not marry again.

The fate of women and of melons is alike. "Whether the melon falls on the knife or the knife on the melon, the melon is the sufferer."[1]

We spoke of the severity of the laws of England with respect to married women, how completely *by law* they are the slaves of their husbands, and how little hope there is of redress.

You might as well "Twist a rope of sand,"[2] or "Beg a husband of a widow,"[3] as urge the men to emancipate the white slaves of England.

"Who made the laws?" said her Highness. I looked at her with surprise, knowing she could not be ignorant on the subject. "The men," said I; "why did the Mahārāj ask the question?" "I doubted it," said the Bā'ī, with an arch smile, "since they only allow themselves one wife."

"England is so small," I replied, "in comparison with your Highness's Gwalior; if every man were allowed four wives, and obliged to keep them separate, the little island could never contain them; they would be obliged to keep the women in vessels off the shore, after the fashion in which the Chinese keep their floating farmyards of ducks and geese at anchor."

[1] Oriental Proverbs.   [2] Ibid.   [3] Ibid.

"Is your husband angry with you?" asked the Brija, the favourite attendant of her Highness. "Why should you imagine it?" said I. "Because you
have on no ornaments, no jewellery."

The Bāiza Bā'ī sent for the wives of Appa Sāhib to introduce them to
me. The ladies entered, six in number; and walking up to the gaddī, on
which the Bā'ī was seated, each gracefully bowed her head, until her forehead touched the feet of her Highness. They were fine young women, from
fifteen to twenty-five years old. The five first wives had no offspring; the
sixth, who had been lately married, was in expectation of a bābā.

Appa Sāhib is the son-in-law of the ex-Queen; he married her daughter,
the Chimna Bā'ī, who died of fever at the time they were driven out of
Gwalior.

[. . .]

Chapter 36

The Nawab Hakīm Menhdī

1835, *April* 15*th*.—I received an invitation to pay my respects to the Begam
Moktar Mahal, the mother of the Nawab of Fathīgar; she is connected with
Mulka Begam's family, but very unlike her, having none of her beauty, and
not being a lady-like person. Thence we went to the grandmother of the
Nawab, Surfuraz Mahal, in the same zenāna. They were in mourning for a
death in the family, and wept, according to dastūr (custom), all the time I
was there: they were dressed in plain white attire, with no ornaments; that
is their (mátim) mourning. The young Nawab, who is about twelve years
old, is a fine boy; ugly, but manly and well-behaved.

The Nawab Mootuzim Adowlah Menhdī Ali Khan Bahādur, commonly
called Nawab Hakīm Menhdī, lives at Fathīgar; he was unwell, and unable

to call, but he sent down his stud to be shown to me, my fondness for horses having reached his ears.

22nd.—I visited a manufactory for Indian shawls, lately established by the Hakīm to support some people, who, having come from Cashmir, were in distress; and as they were originally shawl manufacturers, in charity be gave them employment. This good deed is not without its reward; three or four hundred workmen are thus supported; the wool is brought from Cashmir, and the sale of the shawls gives a handsome profit. I did not admire them; they are manufactured to suit the taste of the English, and are too heavy; but they are handsome, and the patterns strictly Indian. Colonel Gardner's Begam said to me one day, at Khāsgunge, "Look at these shawls, how beautiful they are! If you wish to judge of an Indian shawl, shut your eyes and feel it; the touch is the test of a good one. Such shawls as these are not made at the present day in Cashmir; the English have spoiled the market. The shawls made now are very handsome, but so thick and heavy, they are only fit for carpets, not for ladies' attire."

26th.—The Nawāb Hakīm Menhdī called, bringing with him his son, a man about forty years of age, called "The General." He invited me to pay him and the Begam a visit, and wished to show me his residence.

29th.—We drove to the Nawāb's house, which is a good one; he received us at the door, and took *my* arm, instead of giving me his. He is a fine-looking old man, older than Colonel Gardner, whom in style he somewhat resembles; his manners are distinguished and excellent. He wore an embroidered cap, with a silver muslin twisted like a cord, and put around it, as a turban; it was very graceful, and his dress was of white muslin. The rooms of his house are most curious; more like a shop in the China bazār, in Calcutta, than any thing else; full of lumber, mixed with articles of value. Tables were spread all down the centre of the room, covered with most heterogeneous articles: round the room were glass cases, full of clocks, watches, sundials, compasses, guns, pistols, swords; every thing you can imagine might be found in these cases.

The Hakīm was making all due preparation for celebrating the Muharram in the most splendid style; he was a very religious man, and kept the fast with wonderful strictness and fortitude. A very lofty room was fitted up as a Taziya Khāna, or house of mourning; from the ceiling hung chandeliers of glass of every colour, as thickly as it was possible to place them, all the length of the spacious apartment; and in this room several taziyas, very highly decorated, were placed in readiness for the ceremony. One of them was a representation of the Mausoleum of the Prophet at Medina; another the tomb of Hussein at Karbala; a third, that of Kasīm; and there was also a most splendid Burāk, a fac-simile of the winged horse, on which the Prophet made an excursion one night from Jerusalem to Heaven, and thence returned to Mecca. The angel Gabriel acted as celestial sā'īs on the occasion, and brought the animal from the regions above. He must have been a fiery creature to control that winged horse; and the effect must have been *more* than picturesque, as the Prophet scudded along on a steed that had the eyes and face of a man, his ears long, his forehead broad, and shining like the moon; eyes of jet, shaped like those of a deer, and brilliant as the stars; the neck and breast of a swan, the loins of a lion, the tail and the wings of a peacock, the stature of a mule, and the speed of lightning!— hence its name Burāk.

In front of the taziyas and of the flying horse were a number of standards; some intended to be fac-similes of the banner ('alam) of Hussein: and others having the names of particular martyrs. The banners of Alī were denominated, "The Palm of the Hand of Alī the Elect;" "The Hand of the Lion of God;" "The Palm of the Displayer of Wonders;" and "The Palm of the Disperser of Difficulties." Then there was the "Standard of Fatima," the daughter of the Prophet, and wife of Alī; also that of Abbās-i-'alam-dār, the standard-bearer; with those of Kasīm, Alī-akbar, and others; the banner of the twelve Imāms; the double-bladed sword of Alī; and the nal-sāhib. There was also the neza, a spear or lance dressed up with a turban, the ends flying in the air, and a lime fixed at the top of it; emblematic, it is said, of Hussein's head, which was carried in triumph through different cities, by the order of Yuzeed, the King of Shawm.

The nal-sāhib is a horse-shoe affixed to the end of a long pole; it is made of gold, silver, metals, wood, or paper, and is intended as an emblem of Hussein's horse.

The 'Alam-i-Kasīm, or Standard of Kasīm the Bridegroom, is distinguished by its having a little chatr in gold or silver, fixed on the top of it. All these things were collected in the long room in the house of the Nawāb, ready for the nocturnal perambulations of the faithful.

After the loss of the battle of Kraabaallah, the family of Hussein were carried away captive with his son Zein-ool-Abaīdīn, the only male of the race of Alī who was spared, and they were sent to Medina. With them were carried the heads of the martyrs; and that of Hussein was displayed on the point of a lance, as the cavalcade passed through the cities. In consequence of the remonstrances and eloquence of Zein-ool-Abaīdīn, the orphan son of Hussein, the heads of the martyrs were given to him; and forty days after the battle they were brought back to Kraabaallah, and buried, each with its own body; the mourners then returned to Medina, visited the tomb of the Prophet, and all Medina eventually became subject to Zein-ool-Abaīdīn.

Alī, the son-in-law of Muhammad, was, according to the Shī'as, the direct successor of the Prophet; they not acknowledging the other three caliphs; but, according to the Sunnīs, he was the fourth Khalifa, or successor of Muhammad.[1]

The Muharram concludes on the fortieth day, in commemoration of the interment of the martyrs at Kraabaallah, the name of a place in Irāk, on the banks of the Euphrates, which is also—and, perhaps, more correctly—called Karbalā. At this place the army of Yuzeed, the King, was encamped; while the band of Hussein, including himself, amounting only to seventy-two persons, were on the other side of an intervening jungle, called Mareea.

The Nawāb is a very public-spirited man, and does much good; he took me over a school he founded, and supports, for the education of native boys; showed me a very fine chīta (hunting leopard), and some antelopes, which were kept for fighting. For the public benefit, he has built a bridge, a ghāt, and a sarā'e, a resting-place for travellers; all of which bear his name.

The Begam, having been informed that I was with the Nawāb, sent to request I would pay a visit to the zenāna, and a day was appointed in all due form.

May 3rd.—The time having arrived, the Nawāb came to the house at which I was staying, to pay me the compliment of escorting me to visit the Begam. The Muharram having commenced, all his family were therefore in mourning, and could wear no jewels; he apologized that, in consequence, the Begam could not be handsomely dressed to receive me. She is a pretty looking woman, but has none of the style of James Gardner's Begam; she is evidently in great awe of the Hakīm, who rules, I fancy, with a rod of iron. The rooms in the zenāna are long and narrow, and supported by pillars on the side facing the enclosed garden, where three fountains played very refreshingly, in which golden fish were swimming. The Begam appeared fond of the fish, and had some beautiful pigeons, which came to be fed near the fountains; natives place a great value upon particular breeds of pigeons, especially those obtained from Lucnow, some of which bring a very high price. It is customary with rich natives to keep a number of pigeons; the man in charge of them makes them manœuvre in the air by word of command, or rather by the motions of a long wand which he carries in his hand, and with which he directs the flight of his pigeons; making them wheel and circle in the air, and ascend or descend at pleasure. The sets of pigeons consist of fifty, or of hundreds; and to fly your own in mock battle against the pigeons of another person is an amusement prized by the natives.

[1] The Sunnis and the Shias are the two major divisions of traditional Islam.

315

Several large glass cases were filled in the same curious manner as those before mentioned; and the upper panes of the windows were covered with English prints, some coloured and some plain. The Hakīm asked me if I did not admire them? There was Lord Brougham;[2] also a number of prints of half-naked boxers sparring; Molineux and Tom Cribb, &c., in most scientific attitudes; divers characters of hunting celebrity; members of Parliament in profusion; and bright red and blue pictures of females, as Spring, Summer, Autumn, and Winter:—a most uncouth collection to be displayed around the walls of a zenāna! I was surprised to see pictures in the house of a man considered to be so religious as the Nawāb; because the Prophet said, "Every painter is in hell-fire, and God will appoint a person at the day of resurrection, for every picture he shall have drawn, to punish him in hell. Then, if you must make pictures, make them of trees, and things without souls." "And whoever draws a picture will be punished, by ordering him to blow a spirit into it; and this he can never do; and so he will be punished as long as God wills."

"The angels do not enter the house in which is a dog, nor into that in which are pictures."

I spent an hour in the zenāna, talking to the old Nawāb; the Begam scarcely ventured to speak. He took me over her flower garden, and made me promise I would never pass Fathīghar without paying him a visit. I told him that when the rains arrived, I should come up in the pinnace, having promised to revisit my relatives, when I should have the pleasure of seeing him and the Begam again. He pressed me to stay and see the ceremonies of the Muharram; I regretted extremely I was obliged to return home, being very anxious to see the mourning festival celebrated in all state.

I happened to wear a ferronière on my forehead; it amused the Begam very much, because it somewhat resembled the tīka worn by the women of the East.

His first Begam, to whom he was much attached, died: he sent her body to Mekka: it went down at sea. This was reckoned a great misfortune, and an omen of ill luck. Four years afterwards he married the present Begam, who was slave girl to the former.

Between the pauses in conversation the Nawāb would frequently have recourse to his rosary, repeating, I suppose, the ninety-nine names of God, and meditating on the attributes of each. In the Qanoon-e-islam it is mentioned, "To read with the use of a tusbeeh (or rosary) is meritorious; but it

---

[2] Henry Peter, Lord Brougham (1778–1868) was a Whig politician, orator, wit and man of fashion. He was Lord Chancellor of England from 1830 to 1834.

is an innovation, since it was not enjoined by the prophet (the blessing and peace of God be with him!) or his companions, but established by certain mushaeks (or divines). They use the chaplet in repeating the kulma (confession of faith) or durood (blessing), one, two, or more hundred times." On the termination of my visit to the zenāna, the Nawāb re-escorted me to the house of the friend with whom I was staying.

For the first time, I saw to-day a person in a burkā walking in the street; it was impossible to tell whether the figure was male or female; the long swaggering strut made me suppose the former. A pointed crown was on the top of the head, from which ample folds of white linen fell to the feet, entirely concealing the person. Before the eyes were two holes, into which white net was inserted; therefore the person within could see distinctly, while even the colour of the eyes was not discernible from without. The burka'-posh, or person in the burka', entered the house of the Nawāb. The dress afterwards was sent me to look at, and a copy of it was taken for me by my darzī (tailor). It is often worn by respectable women, who cannot afford to go out in a palanquin, or in a dolī.

The Hakīm was fond of writing notes in English, some of which were curious. When the office of Commissioner was done away with, he thought the gentleman who held the appointment would be forced to quit Fathīghar. The old Hakīm wrote a singular note, in which was this sentence: "As for the man who formed the idea of doing away with your appointment, my dear friend, may God blast him under the earth." However, as the gentleman remained at Fathīghar, and the Government bestowed an appointment equally good upon him, the Hakīm was satisfied. On my return to Allahabad, he wrote to me, and desired me "not to bury his friendship and affection in oblivion."

4th.—Paid a farewell visit to her Highness the ex-Queen of Gwalior, in the Mahratta Camp, and quitted Fathīghar dāk for Allahabad. A brain fever would have been the consequence, had I not taken shelter during the day, as the hot winds were blowing, and the weather intensely oppressive; therefore I only travelled by night, and took refuge during the day.

5th.—I stopped duing the day at the house of a gentleman at Menhdī Ghāt, which was built by the Nawāb, as well as the sarā'e at Naramhow, which also bears his name. From this place I sent to Kannouj for a quantity of chūrīs, *i.e.*, rings made of sealing-wax, very prettily ornamented with gold foil, beads, and colours: the old woman, who brought a large basketful for sale, put a *very expensive* set on my arms; they cost four ānas or three pence! The price of a very pretty set is two ānas. My host appeared surprised; he must have thought me a Pakka Hindostanī. Kannouj is famed for the manufacture of chūrīs. I wore the bracelets for two days, and then broke them off, because the sealing-wax produced a most annoying irritation of the skin.

6th.—I spent the heat of the day with some kind friends at Cawnpore, and the next dāk brought me to Fathīpoor. The day after, I spent the sultry hours in the dāk bungalow, at Shāhzad-poor; and the following morning was very glad to find myself at home, after my long wanderings. The heat at times in the pālkee was perfectly sickening. I had a small thermometer with me, which, at 10 A.M., often stood at 93°; and the sides of the palanquin were hot as the sides of an oven. The fatigue also of travelling so many nights was very great; but it did me no harm.

I found Allahabad greatly altered; formerly it was a quiet station, it had now become the seat of the Agra Government, and Mr. Blunt, the Lieut.-Governor, was residing there.[3] I had often heard Colonel Gardner speak in high praise of this gentleman, who was a friend of his. My time was now employed in making and receiving visits, and going to parties.

13th.—At the house of Mr. F——I met the Austrian traveller, Baron H——; he requested to be allowed to call on me the next day to see my collection of curiosities.[4] He pronounced them very good, and promised to send me some idols to add to them. I gave him a set of Hindoo toe-rings, the sacred thread of the Brahmans, and a rosary, every bead of which was carved with the name of the god Rām. Men were deceivers ever; the promised idols were never added to my collection. The Lieut.-Governor's parties, which were very agreeable, rendered Allahabad a very pleasant station.

---

[3] In 1834 the North Western provinces were separated from Bengal, to lighten the work of the Government, and Allahabad became their capital until it was replaced by Agra in 1836.

[4] Baron von Hugel, whose *Travels in Kashmir and the Punjab* were published in 1845.

Chapter 37

A Voyage on the Ganges

Aug. 2nd.—I went to the melā (fair) held within the grounds at Papamhow. To this place we had sent the pinnace, the Seagull; and on the 10th of the month my husband accompanied me two days' sail on my voyage, to revisit my relations at Fathīghar, after which, he returned to Allahabad, leaving me and the great spaniel Nero to proceed together. The daily occurrences of this voyage may be omitted, only recording any adventure that occurred during the course of it. The stream is so excessively powerful, that at times, even with a fine strong breeze and thirteen men on the towing-line, we are forced to quit the main stream, and proceed up some smaller branch, which occasions delay.

[. . .]

16*th.*—Anchored at Maigong in rather a picturesque spot, close to a satī mound. By the side of the mound I saw the trunk of a female figure beautifully carved in stone. The head, arms, and part of the legs had been broken off. They said it was the figure of a satī. At the back of the mound was a very ancient banyan-tree; and the green hills and trees around were in all the freshness and luxuriance of the rainy season.

The next morning, to my surprise, on going into the large cabin to breakfast, there was the figure of the headless satī covered with flowers, and at the spot where feet *were not*, offerings of gram, boiled rice, &c., had been placed by some of the Hindoo dāndees. "How came you possessed of the satī?" said I. "The mem sāhiba admired her, she is here." "Chorī-ke-mal nā'īch hazm hota," "Stolen food never digests," *i.e.*, "Ill deeds never prosper, the poor people will grieve for the figure; tell the sarang to lower sail and return her to them." "What words are these?" replied the sarang, "we are miles from the spot; the satī has raised the wind." The headless lady remained on board.

As we passed the residence of Rājā Budannath Singh, he came out with his family on three elephants to pay his respects, thinking my husband was on board. The ladies were peeping from the house-top. The pinnace passed in full sail, followed by ten immense country boats full of magazine stores, and the cook boat. Being unable at night to cross those rivers, we anchored on the Oude side.[1] I did not much admire being in the domains of the King of Lucnow instead of those of the Company; they are a very turbulent set, those men of Oude, and often pillage boats. The vicinity of the Rājā's house was some protection. Rām Din had the matchlocks of the sipahī guard fired off by way of bravado, and to show we were armed; the lathīs (bamboos) were laid in readiness, in case of attack: the watch was set, and, after these precautions, the mem sāhiba and her dog went to rest very composedly.

22*nd.*—Not a breath of air! a sun intensely hot; the river is like a silver lake; but over its calm the vessel does *not* glide, for we are fast on a sandbank! Down come the fiery beams; several of the servants are ill of fever. Heaven help them; I doctor them all, and have killed no one as yet! My husband will fret himself as he sits in the coolness of the house and thinks of me on the river. The vessel was in much difficulty this morning; the conductor of some magazine boats sent forty men and assisted her out of it. Lucky it was that chance meeting with the conductor in this Wilderness of Waters! One is sure to find some one to give aid in a difficulty, no doubt through the power of the satī, whom they still continue to adorn with fresh flowers.

25*th.*—After a voyage of fifteen days and a half I arrived at Cawnpore; coming up the reach of the Ganges, in front of Cantonments, a powerful wind was in our favour. The Seagull gallantly led the way in front of the twelve magazine boats: a very pretty sight for the Cawnporeans, especially as a squall overtook us, struck us all into picturesque attitudes, and sunk one of the magazine boats, containing 16,000 rupees worth of new matchlocks. When the squall struck the little fleet, they were thrown one against another, the sails shivered, and the centre boat sank like a stone. Being an eye-witness of this scene, I was afterwards glad to be able to bear witness, at the request of the conductor, to his good conduct, and the care he took of the boats, when called upon by the magistrate of the place.

28*th.*—Anchored off Bittoor on the opposite side. I regretted being unable to see the place and Bajee Row, the ex-Peshwā, who resides there on an allowance of eight lākh per annum. In 1818, he submitted to the Company, abdicated his throne, and retired to Bittoor for life.[2] It would

---

[1] Oudh was an independent state until 1856, when it was annexed by the British on the grounds of mismanagement. The hostility this caused was one of the main reasons for the outbreak of the Indian Revolt of 1857.

[2] The nominal head of the leading Mahratta families was the Peshwa, based at Poona. When the chief of one of the clans, Holkar, attacked and defeated the Peshwa Baji Rao II in 1802, the latter sought protection from the British. Their intervention defeated the entire Mahratta confederacy by 1818.

have given me pleasure to have seen these Mahrattas; but the channel of
the stream forced me to go up the other side of the river.

The Government wish the Bāiza Bā'ī to live at Benares on six lākh a year;
but the spirited old lady will not become a pensioner, and refuses to quit
Fathīghar. She has no inclination, although an Hindoo, to be satisfied with
"A little to eat and to live at Bunarus,"[1] especially as at this place she is no
great distance from her beloved Gwalior.

Sept. 2nd.—A day of adventures. Until noon, we battled against wind
and stream: then came a fair wind, which blew in severe squalls and storms.
Such a powerful stream against us; but it was fine sailing, and I enjoyed it
very much. At times the squalls were enough to try one's courage. We passed
a vessel that had just broken her mast: the stream carried us back with violence, and we ran directly against her; she crushed in one of the Venetian
windows of the cabin, and with that damage we escaped. Two men raising
the sail of another vessel were knocked overboard by the squall, and were
carried away with frightful velocity, the poor creatures calling for help: the
stream swept them past us, and threw them on a sandbank—a happy escape!

Anchored at Menhdī ghāt; the moon was high and brilliant, the wind
roaring around us, the stream, also, roaring in concert, like a distant water-
fall; the night cold and clear, the stars bright and fine; but the appearance
of the sky foretold more wind and squalls for the morrow. I had no idea,
until I had tried it, how much danger there was on the Gunga, during the
height of the rains; in this vessel I think myself safe, but certainly I should
not admire a small one. All the vessels to-day were at anchor; not a sail
was to be seen but the white sails of the Seagull, and the dark ones of the
cook boat, the latter creeping along the shore, her mānjhī following very
unwillingly.

My sarang says the quantity of sail I oblige him to carry during high
winds, has turned "his stomach upside down with alarm."

3rd.—For some hours the next morning the gale continued so violently,
we could not quit the bank; a gentleman came on board, and told me, by
going up a stream, called the Kalī Nadī, I should escape the very powerful
rush of the Ganges; that I could go up the Nadī twenty miles, and by a
canal, cut in former days, re-enter the Ganges above.

I asked him to show me the ruins of Kannouj; we put off; it was blowing
very hard: at last we got out safely into the middle of the stream. About a
mile higher up, we quitted the roaring and rushing waters of the Ganges,
and entered the placid stream of the Kalī Nadī. Situated on a hill, most
beautifully wooded, with the winding river at its feet, stands the ancient

[1] Oriental Proverbs.

city of Kannouj; the stream flowing through fine green meadows put me in mind of the Thames near Richmond. In the Ganges we could scarcely stem the current, even though the wind, which was fair, blew a gale; in the Nadī we furled every sail, and were carried on at a good rate, merely by the force of the wind on the hull of the vessel, and the non-opposition of the gentle stream. My friend told me he had once thrown a net across the Kalī Nadī, near the entrance, and had caught one hundred and thirty-two great rhoee fish. On the hill above stands the tomb of Colonel——; who, when Lord Lake's army were encamped here on their road to Delhi, attempted on horseback to swim the Nadī, and was drowned.

In the history of Kannouj, it is said, "Rustum Dista, King of the Persian province of Seistan, conquered India; he, for his great exploits, is styled the Hercules of the East; unwilling to retain so distant an empire as a dependent on Persia, he placed a new family on the throne. The name of the Price raised to the empire by Rustum was Suraja, who was a man of great abilities, and restored the power of the empire. This dynasty commenced about 1072 years before the Christian æra, and it lasted two hundred and eighty-six years. It is affirmed by the Brahmins, that it was in the time of this dynasty that the worship of emblematical figures of the Divine attributes was first established in India."

The Persians, in their invasions, they say, introduced the worship of the sun, fire, and the heavenly bodies; but the mental adoration of the Divinity, as the one Supreme Being, was still followed by many.

The great city of Kannouj was built by one of the Surajas, on the banks of the Ganges; the circumference of its walls is said to have been nearly one hundred miles. It contained thirty thousand shops, in which betel-nut was sold; and sixty thousand bands of musicians and singers, who paid a tax to Government. In A.D. 1016, the King of Ghizni took Kannouj, "a city which, in strength and structure, might justly boast to have no equal, and which raised its head to the skies."[3] It is said, "The Hindostanee language is more purely spoken in Kannouj than in any other part of India."

We anchored; and after tiffin, Mr. M—— accompanied me to see the tombs of two Muhammadan saints, on the top of the hill. Thence we visited a most singular Hindoo building, of great antiquity, which still exists in a state of very tolerable preservation; the style of the building, one stone placed on the top of another, appeared to me more remarkable than any

---

[3] In 997 AD the Turkish chieftain Mahmud became Amir of Ghazni in Afghanistan. He embarked on a policy of raiding the rich and disunited kingdoms of India. Palaces and temples in the entire Western half of the subcontinent were looted and desecrated, while great caravans with plunder were sent back to Ghazni. The most notorious raid was that of the shrine of Somnath in Kathiawar.

architecture I had seen in India. A further account of this ancient building, with a sketch annexed, will be given in a subsequent chapter.

The fort, which is in ruins, is on a commanding spot; the view from it all around is beautiful. The people sometimes find ancient coins amongst the ruins, and jewels of high value; a short time ago, some pieces of gold, in form and size like thin bricks, were discovered by an old woman; they were very valuable. The Brahmans brought to us for sale, square rupees, old rupees, and copper coins; but none of them were Hindoo; those of copper, or of silver, not being more than three hundred years old, were hardly worth having. I commissioned them to bring me some gold coins, which are usually genuine and good. A regular trade is carried on at this place in the fabrication of silver and copper coins, and those of a mixed metal. The rose-water of Kannouj is considered very fine; it was brought, with other perfumed waters, for sale; also native preserves and pickles, which were inferior. To this day the singers of Kannouj are famous. I am glad I have seen the ruins of this old city, which are well worth visiting; I did not go into the modern town; the scenery is remarkably pretty. I must revisit this place on my black horse; there are many parts too distant from each other for a walk; I returned very much fatigued to the pinnace. A great many Hindoo idols, carved in stone, were scattered about in all directions, broken by the zeal of the Muhammadans, when they became possessed of Kannouj. I shall carry some off should I return this way.

5th.—A hot day, without a breath of air, was followed by as hot a night, during which I could not close my eyes; and a cough tore my chest to pieces.

When we lugāoed, I saw two fires by the side of the stream; from one of which they took up a half-burned body, and flung it into the river. The other fire was burning brightly, and a Hindoo, with a long pole, was stirring it up, and pushing the corpse of his father, or whoever the relation was, properly into the flames, that it might all consume. The nearest relation always performs this ceremony. The evening had gathered in darkly; some fifteen black figures were between us and the sunset, standing around the fire; the palm-trees, and some huts, all reflected in the quiet stream of the Kalī Nadī, had a good effect; especially when the man with the long pole stirred up his bāp (father), and the flames glowed the brighter.

I was glad to get away, and anchor further on, the smell on such occasions being objectionable; it is a horrible custom, this burning the corpse; the poor must always do it by halves, it takes so much wood to consume the body to ashes.

The sirdar-bearer of an officer died; the gentleman desired a small present might be given to his widow, in aid of the funeral. At the end of the month, when the officer's accounts were brought to him for settlement, he found the following item, "For roasting sirdar-bearer, five rupees!"

Some Hindoos do not burn their dead; I saw a body brought down to the river-side this evening, by some respectable-looking people; they pushed the corpse into the stream, and splashed handfuls of water after it, uttering some prayer.

6th.—After fighting with the stream all day, and tiring the crew to death on sandbanks, and pulling against a terribly powerful current, we were forced back to within two miles of our last night's anchorage; we have happily found a safe place to remain in during the night; these high banks, which are continually falling in, are very dangerous. Fortunately in the evening, assisted by a breeze, we arrived at the canal; and having passed through it quitted the Kalī Nadī, and anchored in the deep old bed of the Ganges.

7th.—With great difficulty we succeeded in bringing the pinnace to within three miles of Fathīghar, where I found a palanquin in waiting for me; the river being very shallow, I quitted the vessel, and, on my arrival at my friend's house, sent down a number of men to assist in bringing her up in safety.

Chapter 38

The Mahratta Camp

1835, *Sept. 8th.*—A deputation arrived from her Highness the Bāiza Bā'ī, claiming protection from the Agent to the Government, on account of a mutiny in her camp. She was fearful of being murdered, as her house was surrounded by three hundred and fifty mutinous soldiers, armed with matchlocks and their palitas ready lighted. The mutineers demanded seven months pay; and finding it was not in her power to give it to them, they determined to have recourse to force, and seized her treasurer, her paymaster, and four other officers. These unfortunate men they had made prisoners for seven days, keeping them secured to posts and exposed the whole day to the sun, and only giving them a little sherbet to drink. The Agent to the Government having called out the troops, marched down with them to the Mahratta Camp, where they seized the guns.

The mutineers would not come to terms, or lay down their arms. The troops spent the night in the Camp; at daybreak they charged into the zenāna compound, killed eight mutineers, and wounded nine: the guns were fired at the Mahratta horsemen, who were outside; after which the men laid down their arms, and tranquillity was restored.

The magistrate of the station, who had gone in with the troops, was engaged with two of the mutineers, when all three fell into a well; a Mahratta from above having aimed his spear at him, an officer struck the weapon aside and killed the assailant; the spear glanced off and only inflicted a slight wound. The moment Colonel J——charged the mutineers in the zenāna compound, they murdered their prisoners, the treasurer and the paymaster, in cold blood; the other four officers escaped in the tumult. The greater part of her Highness's troops being disaffected, they could not be trusted to quell the mutiny; she was therefore compelled to ask for assistance. It was feared her troops, which amounted to eighteen hundred, might attempt to plunder the city and station, and be off to Gwalior; and there being only two hundred of the Company's troops, and three guns at Fathīghar, the military were sent for from other stations, and a large body of police called out. The Bāiza Bā'ī despatched a lady several times to say she wished me to visit her; this was during the time she was a prisoner in her house, surrounded by the mutineers with their matches lighted. The agent for the Government would not allow me to go, lest they should seize and keep me a prisoner with the Bā'ī's officers. I was therefore obliged to sent word I could not obey the commands of her Highness on that account.

Emissaries from Gwalior are at the bottom of all this. The camp was in great ferment yesterday: it would be of no consequence, if we had a few more troops at the station; but two hundred infantry are sad odds against eighteen hundred men, one thousand of whom are horsemen; and they have three guns also.

17th.—Infantry have come in from Mynpooree and cavalry from Cawnpore, therefore every thing is safe in case the Mahrattas should mutiny again.

24th.—The Governor-General's agent allowed me to accompany him to the camp. He took some armed horsemen from the police as an escort in case of disturbance. The Bāiza Bā'ī received me most kindly, as if I were an old friend. I paid my respects, and almost immediately quitted the room, as affairs of state were to be discussed. The Gaja Rājā took me into a pretty little room, which she had just built on the top of the house as a sleeping-room for herself. Her charpāī (bed) swung from the ceiling; the feet were of gold, and the ropes by which it swung were covered with red velvet and silver bands. The mattress, stuffed with cotton, was covered with red and blue velvet: the cases of three large pillows were of gold and red kimkhwab; and there were a number of small flat round pillows covered with velvet. The counterpane was of gold and red brocade. In this bed she sleeps, and is constantly swung during her repose. She was dressed in black gauze and gold, with a profusion of jewellery, and some fresh flowers I had brought for her were in her hair. She invited me to sit on the bed, and a lady stood by swinging us. The Gaja Rājā has a very pretty figure, and looked most fairy-like on her decorated bed. When the affairs of state had been settled, we returned to the Bā'ī. Rose-water, pān, and atr of roses having been presented, I took my leave.

28th.—I was one of a party who paid a visit of state to her Highness. Nothing remarkable occurred. As we were on the point of taking our departure, the Bā'ī said she had heard of the beauty of my pinnace, and would visit it the next morning. This being a great honour, I said I would be in attendance, and would have the vessel anchored close to the Bā'ī's own ghāt, at which place she bathes in the holy Ganges. On my return home, a number of people were set hard to work, to fit the vessel for the reception of the Bā'ī. Every thing European was removed, tables, chairs, &c. The floors of the cabins were covered with white cloth, and a gaddī placed in each for her Highness.

29th.—The vessel was decorated with a profusion of fresh flowers; she was drawn up to the ghāt, close to a flight of steps; and the canvas walls of tents were hung around her on every side, so that no spectators could see within. The sailors all quitted her, and she was then ready to receive the ladies of the Mahratta camp. Although I was at the spot at 4 A.M., the Bā'ī and hundreds of her followers were there before me. She accompanied me on board with all her ladies, and on seeing such a crowd in the vessel, asked if the numbers would not sink her. The Bā'ī admired the pinnace very much; and observing the satī, which stood in one corner of the cabin, covered with flowers, I informed her Highness I had brought the headless figure to *eat the air* on the river; that Ganges water and flowers were daily offered her; that her presence was fortunate, as it brought an easterly wind. The Bā'ī laughed; and, after conversing for an hour, she quitted the vessel, and returned to her apartment on the ghāt. The Gaja Rājā and her ladies went into the inner cabin; Appa Sāhib, the Bā'i's son-in-law, came on board with his followers, the vessel was unmoored, and they took a sail on the river. The scene was picturesque. Some hundreds of Mahratta soldiers were dispersed in groups on the high banks amongst the trees; their elephants, camels, horses, and native carriages standing near the stone ghāts, and by the side of white temples. The people from the city were there in crowds to see what was going forward. On our return from the excursion on the river, I accompanied the Gaja Rājā to the Bā'i; and, having made my salām, returned home, not a little fatigued with the exertion of amusing my guests. During the time we were on the water, Appa Sāhib played various Hindostanee and Mahratta airs on the sitar. It must have been a great amusement to the zenāna ladies, quite a gaiety for them, and a variety in their retired mode of life. They were all in their holiday dresses, jewels, and ornaments. Some wore dresses of bright yellow, edged with red, with black Cashmere shawls thrown over their shoulders; this costume was very picturesque. The Gaja Rājā wore a dress of black and gold, with a yellow satin tight body beneath it; *enormous* pearls in profusion, ornaments of gold on her arms, and silver ornaments on her ankles and toes; slippers of crimson and gold.

Oct. 2nd.—The Ganges at Farrukhabad is so full of sandbanks, and so very shallow, that fearing if I detained the pinnace, I might have some chance of being unable to get her down to Cawnpore, I sent her off with half the servants to that place to await my arrival; I shall go dāk in a palanquin, and the rest of the people can float down in the cook boat.

7th.—I called on the Bā'i; and while she was employed on state affairs, retired with the Gaja Rājā to the pretty little room before mentioned. There I found a Hindoo idol, dressed in cloth of gold, and beads, lying on the floor on a little red and purple velvet carpet. Two other idols were in niches at the end of the room. The idol appeared to be a plaything, a doll: I suppose, it had not been rendered sacred by the Brahmans. An idol is of no value until a Brahman dip it, with divers prayers and ceremonies, into the Gunga; when this ceremony has been performed, the spirit of the particular deity represented by the figure enters the idol. This sort of baptism is particularly expensive, and a source of great revenue to the Brahmans. The church dues fall as heavily on the poor Hindoo, as on the people of England; nevertheless, the heads of the Hindoo church do not live in luxury like the Bishops.

The fakīr, who from a religious motive, however mistaken, holds up both arms, until they become withered and immovable, and who, being, in consequence, utterly unable to support himself, relies in perfect faith on the support of the Almighty, displays more religion than the man, who, with a salary of £8000 per annum, leaves the work to be done by curates, on a pittance of £80 a year.

The Gaja Rājā requested me to teach her how to make tea, she having been advised to drink it for her health; she retired, changed her dress, returned, took her tea, and complained of its bitter taste.

"I am told you dress a camel beautifully," said the young Princess; "and I was anxious to see you this morning, to ask you to instruct my people how to attire a sawārī camel." This was flattering me on a very weak point: there is but one thing in the world that I *perfectly* understand, and that is, how to dress a camel.

"I hope you do not eat him when you have dressed him!" said an English gentleman.

My relative had a fine young camel, and I was not happy until I had superintended the making the attire, in which he—the camel, not the gentleman—looked beautiful! The Nawāb Hakīm Menhdī, having seen the animal, called, to request he might have similar trappings for his own sawārī camel; and the fame thereof having reached the Mahratta camp, my talents were called into play. I promised to attend to the wishes of the Gaja Rājā; and, returning home, summoned twelve mochīs, the saddlers of India, natives of the Chamar caste, to perform the work. Whilst one of the men smokes the nārjīl (cocoa-nut pipe), the remainder will work; but it is absolutely necessary that each should have his turn every half-hour, no smoke,—no work.

Five hundred small brass bells of melodious sound; two hundred larger ditto, in harmony, like hounds well matched, each under each; and one large bell, to crown the whole; one hundred large beads of imitative turquoise; two snow-white tails of the cow of Thibet; some thousands of cowries, many yards of black and of crimson cloth, and a number of very long tassels of red and black worsted. The mochīs embroidered the attire for three days, and it was remarkably handsome. The camel's clothing being ready, it was put into a box, and the Gaja Rājā having appointed an hour, I rode over, taking it with me, at 4 A.M.

In the court-year of the zenāna, I found the Bā'ī, and all her ladies; she asked me to canter round the enclosure, the absurdity of sitting on one side a horse being still an amusing novelty.

The Bā'ī's riding horses were brought out; she was a great equestrian in her youthful days, and, although she has now given up the exercise, delights in horses. The ladies relate, with great pride, that, in one battle, her Highness rode at the head of her troops, with a lance in her hand, and her infant in her arms![1]

A very vicious, but large and handsome camel was then brought in by the female attendants; he knelt down, and they began putting the gay trappings upon him; his nose was tied to his knee, to prevent his injuring the girls around him, whom he attempted to catch hold of, showing his great white teeth; if once the jaw of a camel closes upon you, he will not relinquish his hold. You would have supposed they were murdering, not dressing the animal; he groaned and shouted as if in great pain, it was piteous to hear the beast; and laughable, when you remembered it was the "dastūr;" they always groan and moan when any load is placed on their backs, however light. When the camel's toilet was completed, a Mahratta girl jumped on his back, and made him go round the enclosure at a capital rate; the trappings were admired, and the bells pronounced very musical.

[. . .]

The finest young sawārī camels, that have never been debased by carrying any burthen greater than two or three Persian cats, are brought down in droves by the Arabs from Cabul; one man has usually charge of three camels; they travel in single file, the nose of one being attached to the crupper of another by a string passed through the cartilage. They browse on leaves in preference to grazing. It was a picturesque scene, that toilet of the camel, performed by the Mahratta girls, and they enjoyed the tāmāsha.

I mentioned my departure was near at hand; the Bā'ī spoke of her beloved Gwalior, and did me the honour to invite me to pay my respects there, should she ever be replaced on the gaddī. She desired I would pay a farewell visit to the camp three days afterwards. After the distribution, as usual, of betel leaves, spices, atr of roses, and the sprinkling with rose-water, I made my salām. Were I an Asiatic, I would be a Mahratta.

The Mahrattas never transact business on an unlucky day; Tuesday is an

---

[1] Another woman traveller, Frances Isabella Duberly, describes meeting the Baiza Bai at the age of seventy, "apparently as energetic as in the days of her fiery and intriguing youth". Duberly relates a snatch of their conversation: " 'Could I ride on horseback?' 'Had I seen a European battle between the English and the Ruski?' [the reference is to the Crimean War] 'Ay,' she said, her dark eyes dilating as she spoke, 'I, too, have ridden at a battle: I rode when Wellesley Sahib drove us from the field, with nothing but the saddles on which we sat' " (Frances Isabella Duberly (1859) *Campaigning Experiences in Rajpootana and Central India, during the Suppression of the Mutiny, 1857–1858*, Smith, Elder & Co., London, pp. 154–7).

unfortunate day, and the Bā'ī, who was to have held a durbār, put it off in consequence. She sent for me, it being the day I was to take leave of her; I found her looking grave and thoughtful, and her sweet smile was very sad. She told me the Court of Directors had sent orders that she was to go and live at Benares, or in the Deccan; that she was to quit Fathīghar in one month's time, and should she refuse to do so, the Governor-General's agent was to take her to Benares by force, under escort of troops that had been sent to Fathīghar for that purpose. The Bā'ī was greatly distressed, but spoke on the subject with a command of temper, and a dignity that I greatly admired. "What must the Mahāraj do? Cannot this evil fate be averted? Must she go to Benares? Tell us, Mem sāhiba, what must we do?" said one of the ladies in attendance. Thus called upon, I was obliged to give my opinion; it was an awkward thing to tell an exiled Queen she must submit,—"The cudgel of the powerful must be obeyed."[1] I hesitated; the Bā'ī looked at me for an answer. Dropping the eyes of perplexity on the folded hands of despondency, I replied to the Brija, who had asked the question, "Jiska lāthī ooska bhains,"—*i.e.* "He who has the stick, his is the buffalo!"[2] The effect was electric. The Bāiza Bā'ī and the Gaja Rājā laughed, and I believe the odd and absurd application of the proverb half reconciled the Mahāraj to her fate.

I remained with her Highness some time, talking over the severity of the orders of Government, and took leave of her with great sorrow; the time I had before spent in the camp had been days of amusement and gaiety; the last day, the unlucky Tuesday, was indeed ill-starred, and full of misery to the unfortunate and amiable ex-queen of Gwalior.

---

[1] Oriental Proverbs. [2] Ibid.

Chapter 39

The Mahrattas at Allahabad

1835, *Oct.*—One day I called on the Begam, the mother of the young Nawāb of Farrukhabad, and found her with all her relations sitting in the garden; they were plainly dressed, and looked very ugly. For a woman not to be pretty when she is shut up in a zenāna appears almost a sin, so much are we ruled in our ideas by what we read in childhood of the hoorīs of the East.

One morning, the Nawāb Hakīm Menhdī called; his dress was most curious; half European, half Asiatic. The day being cold, he wore brown corduroy breeches, with black leather boots, and thick leather gloves; over this attire was a dress of fine white flowered Dacca muslin; and again, over that, a dress of pale pink satin, embroidered in gold! His turban was of gold and red Benares tissue. He carried his sword in his hand, and an attendant followed, bearing his hooqŭ; he was in high spirits, very agreeable, and I was quite sorry when he rose to depart. In the evening, he sent down a charming little elephant, only five years old, for me to ride; which I amused myself with doing in the beautiful grounds around the house, sitting on the back of the little beauty, and guiding him with cords passed through his ears.

The next evening the Nawāb sent his largest elephant, on which was an amārī,—that is, a howdah, with a canopy,—which, according to native fashion, was richly gilt, the interior lined with velvet, and velvet cushions; the elephant was a fast one, his paces very easy, and I took a long ride in the surrounding country.

[. . .]

15*th.*—Having despatched the pinnace to await my arrival at Cawnpore, I started dāk for that place, which I reached the next day, after a most disagreeable journey; I was also suffering from illness, but the care of my kind friends soon restored me to more comfortable feelings.

22*nd.*—I accompanied them to dine with the Nawāb Zulfecar Bahādur, of Banda. The Nawāb is a Muhammadan, but he is of a Mahratta family, formerly Hindoos; when he changed his religion, and became one of the faithful, I know not. Three of his children came in to see the company; the

Wanderings of a Pilgrim

Wanderings of a Pilgrim

two girls are very interesting little creatures. The Nawāb sat at table, partook of native dishes, and drank sherbet when his guests took wine. The next day, the Nawāb dined with the gentleman at whose house I was staying, and met a large party.

24th.—I quitted Cawnpore in the Seagull, and once more found myself on the waters of the Gunga: a comet was plainly visible through a glass; its hazy aspect rendered it a malignant-looking star. The solitude of my boat is very agreeable after so much exertion.

[. . .]

26th.—Here are we,—that is, the dog Nero and the Mem sāhiba,—floating so calmly, and yet so rapidly, down the river; it is most agreeable; the temples and ghāts we are now passing at Dalmhow are beautiful; how picturesque are the banks of an Indian river! the flights of stone steps which descend into the water; the temples around them of such peculiar Hindoo architecture; the natives, both men and women, bathing or filling their jars with the water of the holy Gunga; the fine trees, and the brightness of the sunshine, add great beauty to the scene. One great defect is the colour of the stream, which, during the rains, is peculiarly muddy; you have no bright reflections on the Ganges, they fall heavy and indistinct.

28th.—Lugāoed the pinnace in the Jumna, beneath the great peepul in our garden, on the banks of the river.

31st.—Dined with Mr. Blunt, the Lieutenant-Governor; and the next day a lancet was put into my arm, to relieve an intolerable pain in my head, brought on by exposure to the sun on the river.

Nov. 6th.—The Lieutenant-Governor gave a farewell ball to the Station, on resigning the appointment to Mr. Ross. The news arrived that her Highness the Bāiza Bā'ī, having been forced to quit Fathīghar, by order of the Government, is on her march down to Benares; at which place they wish her to reside. Una Bā'ī, one of her ladies, having preceded her to Allahabad, called on me, and begged me to take her on board the Calcutta steam-vessel, an object of great surprise to the natives.

9th.—The gentlemen of the Civil Service, and the military at the Station, gave a farewell ball to the Lieutenant-Governor; I was ill, and unable to attend. Oh! the pain of rheumatic fever! The new Lieutenant-Governor arrived; he gave a few dinners, and received them in return; after which Allahabad subsided into its usual quietude, enlivened now and then by a Bachelor's Ball.

1836, Jan. 16th.—The Bāiza Bā'ī arrived at Allahabad, and encamped about seven miles from our house, on the banks of the Jumna, beyond the city. A few days after, the Brija Bā'ī, one of her ladies, came to me, to say her Highness wished to see me; accordingly I went to her encampment. She

332

was out of spirits, very unhappy and uncomfortable, but expressed much pleasure at my arrival.

Feb. 5th.—Her Highness requested the steam-vessel should be sent up the river, opposite her tents; she went on board, and was much pleased, asked a great many questions respecting the steam and machinery, and went a short distance up the river. Capt. Ross accompanied her Highness to Allahabad, and remained there in charge of her, whilst her fate was being decided by the Government.

9th.—The Bā'ī gave a dinner party at her tents to twenty of the civilians and the military; in the evening there was a nāch, and fireworks were displayed; the ex-Queen appeared much pleased.

There is a very extensive enclosure at Allahabad, called Sultan Khusrū's garden; tents had been sent there, and pitched under some magnificent tamarind trees, where a large party were assembled at tiffin, when the Bā'ī sent down a Mahratta dinner, to add to the entertainment. In the evening, her two rhinoceroses arrived; they fought one another rather fiercely; it was an amusement for the party. Captain Ross having quitted Allahabad, Mr. Scott took charge of her Highness.

March 1st.—The Brija Bā'ī called to request me to assist them in giving a dinner party to the Station, for which the Bāiza Bā'ī wished to send out invitations; I was happy to aid her. The guests arrived at about seven in the evening; the gentlemen were received by Appa Sāhib, her son-in-law; the ladies were ushered behind the parda, into the presence of her Highness. I have never described the parda which protects the Mahratta ladies from the gaze of the men: In the centre of a long room a large curtain is dropped, not unlike the curtain at a theatre, the space behind which is sacred to the women; and there the gaddī of the Bā'ī was placed, close to the parda; a piece of silver, about six inches square, in which a number of small holes are pierced, is let into the parda; and this is covered on the inside with white muslin. When the Bā'ī wished to see the gentlemen, her guests, she raised the bit of white muslin, and could then see every thing in the next room through the holes in the silver plate—herself unseen. The gentlemen were in the outer room, the ladies in the inner. Appa Sāhib sat close to the parda; the Bā'ī conversed with him, and, through him, with some of the gentlemen present, whom she could see perfectly well.

Dancing girls sang and nāched before the gentlemen until dinner was announced. Many ladies were behind the parda with the Bāiza Bā'ī, and she asked me to interpret for those who could not speak Urdu. I was suffering from severe rheumatic pain in my face; her Highness perceiving it, took from a small gold box a lump of opium, and desired me to eat it, saying, she took as much herself every day. I requested a smaller portion;

she broke off about one-third of the lump, which I put into my mouth, and as it dissolved the pain vanished; I became very happy, interpreted for the ladies, felt no fatigue, and talked incessantly. Returning home, being obliged to go across the country for a mile in a palanquin, to reach the carriage, the dust which rolled up most thickly half choked me; nevertheless, I felt perfectly happy, nothing could discompose me; but the next morning I was obliged to call in medical advice, on account of the severe pain in my head, from the effect of the opium.

The table for dinner was laid in a most magnificent tent, lined with crimson cloth, richly embossed, and lighted with numerous chandeliers. The nāch girls danced in the next apartment, but within sight of the guests; her Highness and her grand-daughter, from behind the parda, looked on. About two hundred native dishes, in silver bowls, were handed round by Brahmans; and it was considered etiquette to take a small portion from each dish. On the conclusion of the repast, the Governor-General's agent rose, and drank her Highness's health, *bowing to the parda*; and Appa Sāhib returned thanks, in the name of the Bā'ī. The dinner and the wines were excellent; the latter admirably cooled. Fireworks were let off, and a salute was fired from the cannon when the guests departed. Her nephew was there in his wedding dress—cloth of gold most elaborately worked. The Bā'ī expressed herself greatly pleased with the party, and invited me to attend the wedding of her nephew the next day, and to join her when she went in state to bathe in the Jumna. I was very glad to see her pleased, and in good spirits.

March 4th.—This being the great day of the wedding, at the invitation of the Bā'ī we took a large party to the camp to see the ceremonies in the cool of the evening. Having made our salām to her Highness, we proceeded with the Gaja Rājā Sāhib to the tents of the bride, which were about half a mile from those of the bridegroom. The ceremony was going on when we entered. The bridegroom, dressed in all his heavy finery, stood amongst the priests, who held a white sheet between him and the bride, who stood on the other side, while they chanted certain prayers. When the prayers were concluded, and a quantity of some sort of small grain had been thrown at the lady, the priest dropped the cloth, and the bridegroom beheld his bride. She was dressed in Mahratta attire, over which was a dopatta of crimson silk, worked in gold stars; this covered her forehead and face entirely, and fell in folds to her feet. Whether the person beneath this covering was man, woman, or child, it was impossible to tell: bound round the forehead, outside this golden veil, was a sihrā, a fillet of golden tissue, from which strings and bands of gold and silver fell over her face. The bridegroom must have taken upon trust, that the woman he wished to marry was the one concealed under these curious wedding garments. It was late at night; we all returned to the Bā'ī's tent, and the ladies departed, all but Mrs Colonel W——and myself; the Gaja Rājā having asked us to stay and see the finale of the marriage. The young Princess retired to bathe, after which, having been attired in yellow silk, with a deep gold border, and covered with jewels, she rejoined us, and we set out to walk half a mile to the tents of the bride; this being a part of the ceremony. The Gaja Rājā, her ladies, and attendants, Mrs W——, and myself, walked with her in parda; this is, the canvas walls of tents having been fixed on long poles so as to form an oblong inclosure, a great number of men on the outside took up the poles and moved gently on; while we who were inside, walked in procession over white cloths, spread all the way from the tent of the Bā'ī to that of the bride. It was past 10 P.M. Fireworks were let off, and blue lights thrown up from the outside, which lighting up the procession of beautifully dressed Mahratta ladies, gave a most picturesque effect to the scene. The graceful little Gaja Rājā, with her slight form and brilliant attire, looked like what we picture to ourselves a fairy was in the good old times, when such beings visited the earth. At the head of this procession was a girl carrying a torch; next to her a nāch girl danced and figured about; then a girl in the dress of a soldier, who carried a musket and played all sorts of pranks. Another carried a pole, on which were suspended onions, old shoes, and all sorts of queer extraordinary things to make the people laugh. Arrived at the end of our march, the Gaja Rājā seated herself, and water was poured over her beautiful little feet. We then entered the tent of the bride, where many more ceremonies were performed. During the walk in parda, I looked at Mrs W——, who had accompanied me, and could not help saying, "We flatter ourselves we are well dressed, but in our hideous European ungrace-ful attire we are a blot in the procession. I feel ashamed when the blue lights bring me out of the shade; we destroy the beauty of the scene."

I requested permission to raise the veil and view the countenance of the bride. She is young, and, for a Mahratta, handsome. The Bā'ī presented her with a necklace of pure heavy red gold; and told me she was now so poor she was unable to give her pearls and diamonds. New dresses were then pre-sented to all her ladies. We witnessed so many forms and ceremonies, I cannot describe one-fourth of them. That night the bridegroom took his bride to his own tents, but the ceremonies of the wedding continued for many days afterwards. I returned home very much pleased at having wit-nessed a shādī among the Hindoos, having before seen the same ceremony among the Muhammadans.

The ex-Queen had some tents pitched at that most sacred spot, the Treveni, the junction of the three rivers; and to these tents she came down continually to bathe; her ladies and a large concourse of people were in attendance upon her, and there they performed the rites and ceremonies. The superstitions and the religion of the Hindoos were to me most interesting subjects, and had been so ever since my arrival in the country. Her Highness was acquainted with this, and kindly asked me to visit her in the tents at the junction whenever any remarkable ceremony was to be performed. This delighted me, as it gave me an opportunity of seeing the worship, and conversing on religious subjects with the ladies, as well as with the Brahmans. The favourite attendant, the Brija Bā'ī never failed to call, and invite me to join their party at the time of the celebration of any particular rite. At one of the festivals her Highness invited me to visit her tents at the Treveni. I found the Mahratta ladies assembled there: the tents were pitched close to the margin of the Ganges, and the canvas walls were run out to a considerable distance into the river. Her Highness, in her usual attire, waded into the stream, and shaded by the kanāts from the gaze of men, reached the sacred junction, where she performed her devotions, the water reaching to her waist. After which she waded back again to the tents, changed her attire, performed pooja, and gave magnificent presents to the attendant Brahmans. The Gaja Rājā and all the Mahratta ladies accompanied the ex-Queen to the sacred junction, as they returned dripping from the river, their draperies of silk and gold clung to their figures; and very beautiful was the statue-like effect, as the attire half revealed and half concealed the contour of the figure.

15th.—The hot winds have set in very powerfully; to-day I was sent for by the Bāiza Bā'ī, who is in tents; great sickness is prevalent in the camp, and many are ill of cholera.

22nd.—Sir Charles Metcalfe arrived to reside at Allahabad, on his appointment to be Lieutenant-Governor of Agra.[1] The hot winds are blowing very strongly; therefore, with tattīs, the house is cool and pleasant; while, out of doors, the heat is excessive. Her Highness, having been unable to procure a house, still remains encamped; the heat under canvas must be dreadful.

May 1st.—She sent for me, and I found the Gaja Rājā ill of fever, and suffering greatly from the intense heat.

May 9th—Was the Sohobut Melā, or Fair of Kites, in Alopee Bāgh; I went to see it; hundreds of people, in their gayest dresses, were flying kites in all directions, so happily and eagerly; and under the fine trees in

[1] Sir Charles Metcalfe (later Lord Metcalfe) had been Resident at Delhi and Hyderabad, and acting Governor-General. On his resignation from the Company's service in 1843 he became Governor-General of Canada.

the mango tope, sweetmeats, toys, and children's ornaments, were displayed in booths erected for the purpose. It was a pretty sight, that Alopee ke Melā.

The kites are of different shapes, principally square, and have no tails; the strings are covered with mānjhā, a paste mixed with pounded glass, and applied to the string, to enable it to cut that of another by friction. One man flies his kite against another, and he is the loser whose string it cut. The boys, and the men also, race after the defeated kite, which becomes the prize of the person who first seizes it. It requires some skill to gain the victory; the men are as fond of the sport as the boys.

The string of a kite caught tightly round the tail of my horse Trelawny, and threatened to carry away horse and rider tail foremost into mid-air! The more the kite pulled and danced about, the more danced Trelawny, the more frightened he became, and the tighter he tucked in his tail; the gentleman who was on the horse caught the string, and bit it in two, and a native disengaged it from the tail of the animal. A pleasant bite it must have been, that string covered with pounded glass! Yah! yah! how very absurd! I wish you had seen the tamāshā. In the evening we dined with Sir Charles Metcalfe; he was residing at Papamhow. He told me he was thinking of cutting down the avenue of nīm trees (melia azadirachta), that led from the house to the river; I begged hard that it might be spared, assuring him that the air around nīm trees was reckoned wholesome by the natives, while that around the tamarind was considered very much the contrary. In front of my rooms, in former days, at Papamhow, was a garden, full of choice plants, and a very fine young India-rubber tree; it was pleasant to see the bright green of the large glossy leaves of the caoutchouc tree, which flourished so luxuriantly. In those days, many flowering trees adorned the spot; among which the katchnar (bauhinia), both white and rose-coloured and variegated, was remarkable for its beauty. Sir Charles had destroyed my garden, without looking to see what trees he was cutting down; he had given the ruthless order. I spoke of and lamented the havoc he had occasioned; to recompense me, he promised to spare the avenue; which, when I revisited it years afterwards, was in excellent preservation.

14th.—The Bāiza Bā'ī sent for me in great haste; she was in alarm respecting the Gaja Rājā, who was ill of epidemic fever. Having lost her daughter, the Chimna Bā'ī, of fever, when she was driven out of Gwalior by her rebellious subjects, she was in the utmost distress, lest her only remaining hope and comfort, her young grand-daughter, should be taken from her. I urged them to call in European medical advice; they hesitated to do so, as a medical man might neither see the young Princess, nor feel her pulse. I drove off, and soon returned with the best native doctress to be procured; but, from what I heard at the consultation, it may be presumed her skill is not very great.

The Nawāb Hakīm Menhdī is very ill; I fear his days are numbered.

The murder of Mr. Frazer, by the Nawāb Sumshoodeen, at Delhi, who bribed a man called Kureem Khan to shoot him, took place when I was at Colonel Gardner's; no one could believe it when suspicion first fell upon the Nawāb; he had lived on such intimate terms with Mr. Frazer, who always treated him like a brother. The Nawāb was tried by Mr. Colvin, the judge, condemned and executed. The natives at Allahabad told me they thought it a very unjust act of our Government, the hanging the Nawāb merely for bribing a man to murder another, and said, the man who fired the shot ought to have been the only person executed. On Sunday, the 13th March, 1835, Kureem Khan was foiled in his attempt on Mr. Frazer's life, as the latter was returning from a nāch, given by Hindoo Rāo, the brother of the Bāiza Bā'ī. He accomplished his purpose eight days afterwards, on the 22nd of the same month. In the Hon. Miss Eden's beautiful work, "The Princes and People of India," there is a sketch of Hindoo Rāo on horseback; his being the brother of the Bāiza Bā'ī is perhaps his most distinguishing mark; I have understood, however, he by no means equals the ex-Queen of Gwalior in talent.[2]

June 7th.—Sir Charles Metcalfe gave a ball to the station: in spite of all the thermantidotes and the tattīs it was insufferably hot; but it is remarkable, that balls are always given and better attended during the intense heat of the hot winds, than at any other time.

9th.—The Bāiza Bā'ī sent word she wished to see me ere her departure, as it was her intention to quit Allahabad and proceed to the west: a violent rheumatic headache prevented my being able to attend. The next morning she encamped at Padshah Bāgh, beyond Allahabad, on the Cawnpore road, where I saw her the next evening in a small round tent, entirely formed of tattīs. The day after she quitted the ground and went one march on the Cawnpore road, when the Kotwal of the city was sent out by the magistrate to bring her back to Allahabad, and she was forced to return. Her grand-daughter is very ill, exposed to the heat and rains in tents. I fear the poor girl's life will be sacrificed. Surely she is treated cruelly and unjustly.

---

[2] The Hon. Emily Eden (1797–1869) and her sister Frances accompanied their brother, George Lord Auckland during his term as Governor-General of India from 1836 to 1842. He is mainly known for his role in the disastrous First Afghan War (1838–42) which ended in a catastrophe for the British troops. Emily Eden's diary *Up the Country* was published in 1866 and has become one of the best-known memoirs of colonial India ever since. It describes their two-and-a-half year goodwill tour up the country, undertaken in a lavish style. It was during this tour that Fanny Parkes met the Eden sisters.

THREE SATĪS AND A MANDAP NEAR GHAZĪPŪR.

Figure 9   Three Satīs and a Mandap near Ghazīpur

She who once reigned in Gwalior has now no roof to shelter her: the rains have set in; she is forced to live in tents, and is kept here against her will,— a state prisoner, in fact.

The sickness in our farm-yard is great: forty-seven gram-fed sheep and lambs have died of small-pox; much sickness is in the stable, but no horse has been lost in consequence.

25th.—Remarkably fine grapes are selling at one rupee the ser; *i.e.*, one shilling per pound. The heat is intolerable; and the rains do not fall heavily, as they ought to do at this season. The people in the city say the drought is so unaccountable, so great, that some rich merchant, having large stores of grain of which to dispose, must have used *magic* to keep off the rains, that a famine may ensue, and make his fortune!

Chapter 40

A Tūfān

1836, *June* 28*th.*—A hurricane has blown ever since gun-fire; clouds of dust are borne along upon the rushing wind; not a drop of rain; nothing is to be seen but the whirling clouds of the tūfān. The old peepul-tree moans, and the wind roars in it as if the storm would tear it up by the roots. The pinnace at anchor on the Jumna below the bank rolls and rocks; the river rises in waves, like a little sea. Some of her iron bolts have been forced out by the pressure of the cables, and the sarang says, she can scarcely hold to her moorings. I am watching her unsteady masts, expecting the next gust will tear her from the bank, and send her off into the rushing and impetuous current. It is well it is not night, or she would be wrecked to a certainty. I have not much faith in her weathering such a tūfān at all, exposed as she is to the power of the stream and the force of the tempest. High and deep clouds of dust come rushing along the ground, which, soaring into the highest heaven, spread darkness with a dull sulphureous tinge, as the red brown clouds of the tūfān whirl swiftly on. It would almost be an inducement to go to India, were it only to see a hurricane in all its glory: the might and majesty of wind and dust: just now the fine sand from the banks of the river is passing in such volumes on the air, that the whole landscape has a white hue, and objects are indistinct; it drives through every crevice, and, although the windows are all shut, fills my eyes and covers the paper. It is a fearful gale. I have been out to see if the pinnace is likely to be driven from her moorings. The waves in the river are rolling high with crests of foam; a miniature sea. So powerful were the gusts, with difficulty I was able to stand against them. Like an Irish hurricane it blew up and down. At last the falling of heavy rain caused the abatement of the wind. The extreme heat passed away, the trees, the earth, all nature, animate and inanimate, exulted in the refreshing rain. Only those who have panted and longed for the fall of rain can appreciate the delight with which we hailed the setting in of the rains after the tūfān.

3*rd.*—This morning the Bāʾī sent down two of her ladies, one of whom is a celebrated equestrian, quite an Amazon: nevertheless, in stature small and slight, with a pleasant and feminine countenance. She was dressed in a long piece of white muslin, about eighteen yards in length; it was wound round the body and passed over the head, covering the bosom entirely: a part of it was brought up tight between the limbs, so that it had the appearance of full trousers falling to the heels. An embroidered red Benares shawl was bound round her waist; in it was placed a sword and a pistol, and a massive silver bangle was on one of her ancles. Her attendants were present with two saddle horses, decked in crimson and gold, and ornaments of silver, after the Mahratta fashion. She mounted a large bony grey, astride of course, and taking an extremely long spear in her hand, galloped the horse about in circles, performing the spear exercise in the most beautiful and graceful style at full gallop; her horse rearing and bounding, and showing off the excellence of her riding. Dropping her spear, she took her matchlock, performing a sort of mimic fight, turning on her saddle as she retreated at full gallop, and firing over her horse's tail. She rode beautifully and most gracefully. When the exhibition was over, we retired to my dressing-room: she told me she had just arrived from Juggernāth, and was now *en route* to Lahore to Runjeet Singh.[1] She was anxious I should try the lance exercise on her steed, which I would have done, had I possessed the four walls of a zenāna, within which to have made the attempt.

What does Sir Charles Metcalfe intend to do with the poor Bā'ī? what will be her fate? this wet weather she must be wretched in tents. The Lieutenant-Governor leaves Allahabad for Agra, in the course of a day or two.

In the evening I paid my respects to her Highness. I happened to have on a long rosary and cross of black beads; she was pleased with it, and asked me to procure some new rosaries for her, that they might adorn the idols, whom they dress up, like the images of the saints in France, with all sorts of finery.

[. . .]

[*July*] 5*th*.—The ladies of the station held a fancy fair at the theatre for the benefit of the Blind Asylum, which realized one hundred and eighty pounds.

8*th*.—Sir Charles quitted this station for Agra, leaving Allahabad to return to its usual routine of quietness. The thermantidotes have been stopped, rain has fallen plentifully, the trees have put on their freshest of greens, and the grass is springing up in every direction. How agreeable, how pleasant to the eye is all this luxuriant verdure!

[1] Ranjit Singh (1780–1839) was known as the Lion of the Sikhs. He founded a powerful Sikh empire which disintegrated after his death. Emily Eden describes the meeting between him and her brother the Governor-General in lively detail in her *Up the Country* (1866).

The report in the bazār is, that a native of much wealth and consideration went into his zenāna tents, in which he found two of his wives and a man; the latter escaped; he killed both the women. A zenāna is a delightful place for private murder, and the manner in which justice is distributed between the sexes is so impartial! A man may have as many wives as he please, and mistresses without number;—it only adds to his dignity! If a woman take a lover, she is murdered, and cast like a dog into a ditch. It is the same all the world over; the women, being the weaker, are the playthings, the drudges, or the victims of the men; a woman is a slave from her birth; and the more I see of life, the more I pity the condition of the women. As for the manner in which the natives strive to keep them virtuous, it is absurd; a girl is affianced at three or four years old, married, without having seen the man, at eleven, shut up and guarded and suspected of a wish to intrigue, which, perhaps, first puts it into her head; and she amuses herself with outwitting those who have no dependence upon her, although, if discovered, her death generally ends the story.

27*th.*—How weary and heavy is life in India, when stationary! Travelling about the country is very amusing; but during the heat of the rains, shut up in the house, one's mind and body feel equally enervated. I long for a bracing sea breeze, and a healthy walk through the green lanes of England; the lovely wild flowers,—their beauty haunts me. Here we have no wild flowers; from the gardens you procure the most superb nosegays; but the lovely wild flowers of the green lanes are wanting. Flowering trees are planted here on the sides of the roads, and I delight in bringing home a bouquet.

A steamer comes up every month from Calcutta; she tows a tug, that is, a large flat vessel, which carries the passengers. The steamers answer well; but what ugly-looking, mercantile things they are!

[. . .]

23*rd.*—During the night it began to blow most furiously, accompanied by heavy rain and utter darkness; so fierce a tūfān I never witnessed before. It blew without cessation, raining heavily at intervals; and the trees were torn up by their roots. At 4 A.M. the storm became so violent, it wrecked twenty large native salt boats just below our house; the river roared and foamed, rising in high waves from the opposition of the wind and stream. Our beautiful pinnace broke from her moorings, was carried down the stream a short distance, driven against the broken bastions of the old city of Prag, which have fallen into the river, and totally wrecked just off the Fort; she went down with all her furniture, china, books, wine, &c., on board, and has never been seen or heard of since; scarcely a vestige has been discovered. Alas! my beautiful Seagull; she has folded her wings for ever, and has sunk to rest! We can only rejoice no lives were lost, and that we were not on board; the sarang and khalāsīs (sailors) swam for their lives; they were carried some distance down the stream, below the Fort, and drifted on a sandbank. The headless image of the satī, that graced the cabin, had brought rather too much wind. When the sarang lamented her loss, I could only repeat, as on the day he carried off the lady, "Chorī ke mal nā'īch hazm hota,"—stolen food cannot be digested: *i.e.* ill deeds never thrive.

The cook-boat was swamped. On the going down of the river, although she was in the mud, with her back broken, she was sold, and brought the sum we originally gave for her when new;—such was the want of boats, occasioned by the numbers that were lost in the storm! The next morning, three of the Venetians and the companion-ladder of the pinnace were washed ashore below the Fort, and brought to us by a fisherman. We were sorry for the fate of the Seagull; she was a beautifully built vessel, but not to be trusted, the white ants had got into her. The mischief those white ants do is incalculable; they pierce the centre of the masts and beams, working on in the dark, seldom showing marks of their progress outside, unless during the rains. Sometimes a mast, to all appearance sound, will snap asunder; when it will be discovered the centre has been hollowed by the white ants, and the outside is a mere wooden shell. Almost all the trees in the garden were blown down by the gale.

[. . .]

Oct. 19th.—The Commander-in-Chief, Sir Henry Fane, arrived; his tents are pitched before the Fort, on the side of the Jumna; the elephants, the camels, and the horses in attendance form a picturesque assemblage, much to my taste.

21st.—The station gave a ball to Sir Henry and his party; he is a magnificent-looking man, with good soldier-like bearing, one of imposing presence, a most superb bow, and graceful speaking. I admire his appearance, and think he must have merited his appellation, in olden times, of the handsome aide-de-camp.

27th.—Sir Henry Fane reviewed the troops of the station, and a ball took place in the evening, at the house of Mr. Fane, the brother of the Commander-in-Chief. A few days afterwards, the ladies of his family requested me to accompany them to visit her Highness the Bāiza Bā'ī, which I did with much pleasure, and acted as interpreter.

Nov. 3rd.—We dined with Sir Henry in camp, and he promised to show me tiger-shooting in perfection, if I would accompany his party to Lucnow.

7th.—Some friends anchored under our garden, on their way to Calcutta; the sight of their little fleet revived all my roaming propensities, and, as I wished to consult a medical man at the Residency, in whom I had great faith, I agreed to join their party, and make a voyage down the river. The

Bāiza Bā'ī was anxious to see my friends; we paid her a farewell visit; she was charmed with Mr. C——, who speaks and understands the language like a native, and delighted with the children.

13*th.*—Our little fleet of six vessels quitted Allahabad, and three days afterwards we arrived at Mirzapore, famous for its beautiful ghāts and carpet manufactories.

17*th.*—Anchored under the Fort of Chunar, a beautiful object from the river; it was not my intention to have anchored there, but the place looked so attractive, I could not pass by without paying it a visit. The goats and sheep, glad to get a run after their confinement in the boat, are enjoying themselves on the bank; and a boy, with a basket full of snakes (cobra di capello), is trying to attract my attention. In the cool of the evening we went into the Fort, which is situated on the top of an abrupt rock, which rises from the river. The view, coming from Allahabad, is very striking; the ramparts running along the top of the rising ground, the broad open river below; the churchyard under the walls, on the banks of the Gunga, with its pretty tombs of Chunar stone rising in all sorts of pointed forms, gives one an idea of quiet, not generally the feeling that arises on the sight of a burial-place in India; the ground was open, and looked cheerful as the evening sun fell on the tombs; the hills, the village, the trees, all united in forming a scene of beauty. We entered the magazine, and visited the large black slab on which the deity of the Fort is said to be ever present, with the exception of from daybreak until the hour of 9 A.M., during which time he is at Benares. Tradition asserts that the Fort has never been taken by the English, but during the absence of their god Burtreenath. We walked round the ramparts, and enjoyed the view. The church, and the houses which stretch along the river-side for some distance, and the Fort itself, looked cheerful and healthy; which accounted for the number of old pensioners to be found at Chunar, who have their option as to their place of residence.

As you approach Benares, on the left bank of the river, stands the house of the Rājā of Benares, a good portly looking building. The appearance of the Holy City from the river is very curious, and particularly interesting. The steep cliff on which Benares is built is covered with Hindoo temples and ghāts of all sizes and descriptions; the first ghāt, built by Appa Sāhib, from Poona, I thought handsome; but every ghāt was eclipsed by the beauty of the one which is now being built by her Highness the Bāiza Bā'ī; the scale is so grand, so beautiful, so light, and it is on so regular a plan, it delighted me; it is the handsomest ghāt I have seen in India; unfinished as it is, it has cost her Highness fifteen lākh; to finish it will cost twenty lākh more; should she die ere the work be completed it will never be finished, it being deemed unlucky to finish the work of a deceased person. The money, to the amount of thirty-seven lākh, which the Bā'ī had stored in her house at Benares, to complete the ghāt, and to feed the Brahmāns, whose allowance was two hundred rupees, *i.e.* £20 a day, has been seized by the Government, and put into the Company's treasury, where it will remain until the point now in dispute is settled; that is, whether it belong to the Bā'ī or to her adopted son, the present Mahārāj of Gwalior, who forced her out of the kingdom. Several Hindoo temples are near this ghāt; a cluster of beauty. Two chiraghdanīs, which are lighted up on festivals, are curious and pretty objects; their effect, when glittering at night with thousands of little lamps, must be beautiful, reflected with the temples, and crowds of worshippers on the waters below; and great picturesque beauty is added to the scene by the grotesque and curious houses jutting out from the cliff, based on the flights of stone steps which form the ghāts. How I wished I could have seen Benares from the river during the Dewalī, or Festival of Lights! At sunset we went up the Minarets, built by Aurunzebe;[2] they are considered remarkably beautiful, towering over the Hindoo temples; a record of the Muhammadan conquest.

On my return to my budjerow, a number of native merchants were in waiting, hoping to dispose of their goods to the strangers; they had boxes full of Benares turbans, shawls, gold and silver dresses, kimkhwāb, and cloth of gold. This place is famous for its embroidery in gold, and for its tissues of gold and silver. I purchased some to make a native dress for myself, and also some very stiff ribbon, worked in silk and gold, on which are the names of all the Hindoo deities; the Hindoos wear them round their necks; they are holy, and called junéoo. The English mare and my little black horse met me here, *en route* to Calcutta.

The Bāiza Bā'ī told me by no means to pass Benares without visiting her ghāt and her house; some of her people having come down to the river, I returned with them to see the house; it is very curiously situated in the heart of the city. Only imagine how narrow the street is which leads up to it; as I sat in my palanquin, I could touch both the sides of the street by stretching my arms out, which I did to assure myself of its extreme narrowness. All the houses in this street are five or six stories high. We stopped at the house of the Bā'ī; it is six stories high, and was bought by her Highness as a place in which to secure her treasure. It is difficult to describe a regular Hindoo house such as this; which consists of four walls, within and around which the rooms are built story above story; but from the foundation to the top of the house there is a square in the centre left open, so that the

---

[2] Aurangzeb (1618–1707) was a Mughal emperor.

house encloses a small square court open to the sky above, around which the rooms are built with projecting platforms, on which the women may sit, and *eat the air*, as the natives call it, within the walls of their residence. I clambered up the narrow and deep stone stairs, story after story, until I arrived at the top of the house; the view from which was unique: several houses in the neighbourhood appeared much higher than the one on which I was standing, which was six stories high. The Mahratta, who did the honours on the part of her Highness, took me into one of the rooms, and showed me the two chests of cast iron, which formerly contained about eighteen thousand gold mohurs. The Government took that money from the Bā'ī by force, and put it into their treasury. Her Highness refused to give up the keys, and also refused her sanction to the removal of the money from her house; the locks of the iron chests were driven in, and the tops broken open; the rupees were in bags in the room; the total of the money removed amounted to thirty-seven lākh. Another room was full of copper coins; another of cowries; the latter will become mouldy and fall into dust in the course of time. One of the gentlemen of the party went over the house with me, and saw what I have described. Atr and pān were presented, after which we took our leave and proceeded to the market-place. The braziers' shops were open, but they refused to sell any thing, it being one of the holidays on which no worker in brass is allowed to sell goods.

The worship of Vishwŭ-kŭrma, the son of Brŭmha, the architect of the gods, was perhaps being performed. On that day blacksmiths worship their hammer and bellows; carpenters, the mallet, chisel, hatchet, saw, &c.; washermen, their irons; and potters, the turning-wheel, as the representative of this god. The festival closes with singing and gaiety, smoking and eating.

19*th.*—The hour was too early, and but few shops were open, which gave a dull look to this generally crowded and busy city.

The air is cool and pleasant; we float gently down the river; this quiet, composed sort of life, with a new scene every day, is one of great enjoyment.

I must not forget to mention that, after a considerably lapse of time, the treasure that was detained by the Government on behalf of the young Mahārāj of Gwalior, was restored to her Highness the Bāiza Bā'ī. [. . .]

1837, *Aug.*—The first few days in this month we were blessed with cooling and heavy rain. On the 6th, the annual festival of the Jenem, or birthday, and the sports of Krishnŭ, the Bāiza Bā'ī invited me to the camp:[3] on my

---

[3] Krishna is a Hindu god, one of the avatars of Vishnu the Preserver. He is often represented as a cow herd, sporting with female cow herds, the gopis. His beloved is Radha.

arrival I found her Highness seated under a large mango tree; from one of its boughs a swing was suspended, in which the Gaja Rājā and another lady were amusing themselves. This festival, in celebration of the sports of the most popular of the Hindoo deities, was held in all due form by the Mahrattas; it took place by torch-light, in the cool of the evening. In the forests on the banks of the Yamuna Krishnŭ passed his time, playing on the flute, swinging under the trees, dancing, and sporting with the gopīs. The young Princess was therefore amusing herself in the swing as a necessary ceremony; after which, some sixty or eighty Mahratta women came forward, and performed several dances sacred to the season, singing as they moved on the turf, in a circular dance called the rās, in imitation of the gopīs; and the "Songs of Govinda," as addressed by Kaniyā to Radha and her companions, were rehearsed at this festival, with a scenic representation of Kaniyā and the gopīs. "The listener could not depart after once hearing the sound of the flute, and the tinkling of the gopias' feet; nor could the birds stir a wing; while the pupils of the gopias' eyes all turned towards Creeshna."

[. . .]

The evening closed with the performances of some Mahratta nāch girls, after which I was allowed to depart, having first partaken of some sweetmeats, which they presented to me with a jar of dahī (curdled milk); the latter was excellent, and usually presented at this festival as the favourite food of the gopīs. I returned home late at night, accompanied as usual by the horsemen and torch-bearers of the Bāiza Bā'ī.

I have many idols, images of Krishnŭ, in divers forms . . . He has many names, Krishnŭ, Heri, Kaniyā, and is worshipped under many forms; the idols represent this popular god through many of the events of his life.

[. . .]

So devoted were the gopīs to Krishnŭ the beloved, that if he wished to ride an elephant, the lovely ladies, with most extraordinary dexterity, assumed the shape of the animal and bore him off in triumph. . . . "Kaniyā-jee and the Gōpia" is a fac-simile of an old Hindoo painting commemorative of this feat: the style in which the figures are grouped is very clever, and does much credit to the artist; the original is as highly finished as a miniature painting. The chatr, the emblem of royalty, is borne over his head; peacock's feathers form the ornament for his forehead; and in his hand is the ankus (the elephant goad) and a lotus flower. The gopīs carry with them their musical instruments; they are adorned with jewels, and the tail of the animal shows the beauty and length of their hair.

[. . .]

Chapter 41

The Famine

1837, *Aug.*—A gentleman who had been paying us a visit quitted us for Agra just before his baggage boat arrived, in which were two immense German dogs, one striped like a tiger,—most warlike animals; they eyed me fiercely, and pulled impatiently on their chains when brought into the verandah; they will be good guards at night, but their arrival at Agra will be a little too late;—like locking the door when the steed has been stolen. Mr. H——went out to dinner, and did not return home that night: some thieves took out a pane of glass, opened the door, carried off his two gun-cases and a writing-desk. A short distance from the house they broke open the cases, which they threw away, and made off with the guns, a gold watch, three seals, and a guard-chain. No traces have been discovered of the thieves, and our friend must resign himself to the loss, with the comfort of remembering that I told him several times he would lose his guns, unless he locked them up in some heavy, unwieldy chest, that could not readily be carried away.

Solitary confinement in the Fort of Allahabad, a punishment inflicted on rebellious sipahīs, is dreaded by them more than any other. The cells for prisoners in the Fort of Chunar are really solitary; you can neither see out of the window nor hear the sound of a human voice; both of which they contrive to do at Allahabad; therefore Chunar is held in all due horror.

Sept.—The fever, which, like the plague, carried off its thousands at Palee, has disappeared; the cordons are removed, the alarm is at an end, the letters are no longer fumigated, and the fear of the plague has vanished from before us.

On the 22nd of July, this year, the river had only risen eight feet above the usual mark; last year, at the same period, late as the rains were in setting in, the Jumna had risen twenty-four feet above the usual level; showing the great deficiency of rain this season.

24th—The Nawāb Hakīm Menhdī has been re-appointed minister in Oude; how happy the old man must be! He has been living at Fathīgar, pining for a restoration to the honours at Lucnow. The Nawāb quitted for Oude; on the first day of his march, the horse that carried his nakaras (state

The Famine

kettle-drums) fell down and died, and one of his cannon was upset;—both most unlucky omens. The Camp and the Minister were in dismay! To us it is laughable, to the natives a matter of distress. The right to beat kettle-drums, and to have them carried before you, is only allowed to great personages. Therefore the omen was fearful; it will be reported at Lucnow, will reach the ears of the King, and perhaps produce a bad effect on his mind;—the natives are so superstitious.

The Maharaj of Gwalior, the Bāiza Bā'ī's adopted son, who drove her out of the kingdom, announced a few days ago that a son and heir was born unto him. The Resident communicated the happy news to the Government; illuminations took place, guns were fired, every honour paid to the young heir of the throne of Gwalior. The Bā'ī sent her granddaughter on an elephant, in an amārī (a canopied seat), attended by her followers on horseback, to do pooja in the Ganges, and to give large presents to the Brahmāns. As the Gaja Rājā passed along the road, handfuls of rupees were scattered to the crowd below from the seat on the elephant. Six days after the announcement of the birth of a son, the King sent for the Resident, and, looking very sheepish, was obliged to confess the son was a daughter! The Resident was much annoyed that his beard had been laughed at; and, in all probability, the King had been deceived by the women in the zenāna: perhaps a son had really been born, and having died, a girl had been substituted;—the only child procurable, perhaps, at the moment, or approved of by the mother. A zenāna is the very birth-place of intrigue.

30th.—I am busy with preparations for a march; perhaps, in my rambles, I shall visit Lucnow, see the new King, and my old friend the Nawāb Hakīm Menhdī in all his glory. I should like very much to visit the zenāna, for, although the King be about seventy, there is no reason why he may not have a large zenāna, wives of all sorts and kinds,—"the black, the blue, the brown, the fair,"—for purposes of state and show.

Oct. 3rd.—At this moment a large fire is blazing away, and throwing up volumes of smoke at no great distance from our house. In this country they chop up straw very finely, as food for bullocks; an Hindū having collected a large quantity of bhūsā (this chopped straw), has of late been selling it at a very high price; in consequence, some one has set fire to the heap, and has destroyed some hundred mūns. My khansaman, looking at it, said very quietly, "He has of late sold his bhūsā at an unfairly high price, therefore they have secretly set it on fire; of course they would, it is the custom." The natives have curious ideas with respect to justice.

12th.—Called on the Bāiza Bā'ī;—really, the most agreeable visits I pay are to the Mahratta Camp.

17th.—The Padshah Begam and Moona-jah, the young Prince of Oude, whom she attempted to put on the throne, have arrived at Allahabad, state prisoners; they remained a day or two, their tents surrounded by double guards night and day. The Begam wished to remain here, but she was forced to march at last, and has proceeded to Chunar, where she is to remain a prisoner of state.

The preparations for a march up the country to visit my friends are nearly completed; my new tents have just arrived from Cawnpore, they are being pitched and examined, that I may have no trouble *en route*.

The Camp going to meet Lord Auckland at Benares passed through Allahabad yesterday; two hundred and fifty elephants, seven hundred camels, &c.,—a beautiful sight; they encamped very near our house, on the banks of the Jumna.

Nov. 23rd.—The Bāiza Bā'ī came down to go on board the steamer, which she was anxious to see. The vessel was drawn up to the ghāt, and enclosed with kanats (the canvas walls of tents). A large party of English ladies attended the Bā'ī, and several English gentlemen went on board with Appa Sāhib, after the return of her Highness, who appeared greatly pleased.

Dec. 1st.—The Governor-General Lord Auckland, the Hon. the Misses Eden, and Captain Osborne, arrived at Allahabad with all their immense encampment. The gentlemen of the Civil Service and the military paid their respects. Instead of receiving morning visits, the Misses Eden received visitors in the evening, transforming a formal morning call into a pleasant party,—a relief to the visitors and the visited.

7th.—I made my salām to Miss Eden at her tents; she told me she was going to visit her Highness the Bāiza Bā'ī with the Governor-General, asked me to accompany her, and to act as interpreter, to which I consented with pleasure.

8th.—The Gaja Rājā Sāhib went on an elephant in state, to bring the Misses Eden to call on the Bāiza Bā'ī. They arrived with Lord Auckland in all due form: his Lordship and Appa Sāhib sat in the outer room, and conversed with her Highness through the parda. I introduced the Misses Eden to the Bāiza Bā'i and her grand-daughter, with whom they appeared pleased and interested. Twenty-two trays, containing pairs of shawls, pieces of cloth of gold, fine Dacca muslin, and jewels, were presented to the Governor-General; and fifteen trays, filled in a similar manner, to each of the Misses Eden. They bowed to the presents when they were laid before them, after which the trays were carried off, and placed in the treasury for the benefit of the Government.

15th.—I quitted Allahabad on my road to the Hills, under the escort of our friend Mr. F——, near whose tents my own were to be pitched: the country was swarming with robbers; they follow the camp of the Governor-General, wherever it may be.

16th.—Arrived at my tents at Fathīpūr; the scene in the camp was very picturesque; the troops were drawn out before the tents of the Governor-General, and all was state and form, for the reception of the Chiefs of Bandelkhand; the guns were firing salutes; it was an animated and beautiful scene.

18th.—I mounted my black horse, and rode at daybreak with some friends. From the moment we left our tents, we were passing, during the whole march, by such numbers of elephants, so many strings of camels, so many horses and carts, and so many carriages of all sorts, attendant on the troops, and the artillery of the Governor-General and his suite, that the whole line of march, from the beginning to the end, was one mass of living beings. My tents were pitched near the guns of the artillery, outside the camp at Mulwah: a Rājā came to call on Lord Auckland, a salute was fired; my horses, being so near, became alarmed; the grey broke from his ropes, fell on the pegs to which he was picketed, and lamed himself; another broke loose; a camel lamed himself, and we had some difficulty in quieting the frightened animals.

19th.—I was unwell from over-fatigue, most uncomfortable. In the evening I roused myself to dine with Lord Auckland to meet Prince Henry of Orange. His Royal Highness entered the navy at eight years of age, and has been in the service ten years, in the "Bellona" frigate. Accompanied by his captain, he came up dāk to spend a few days with Lord Auckland. The Prince is a tall, slight young man, and, apparently, very diffident.

21st.—Arrived at Cawnpore, and paid a long promised visit to a relative. As the Misses Eden were at home in the evening, I accompanied Major P—— to pay my respects. We lost our way in the ravine from a dense fog: when we reached the tents the whole station was assembled there, quadrilles and waltzing going forward.

25th.—On Christmas-day the old Nawāb Hakīm Menhdī, the minister of Oude, of whom I have so often spoken, breathed his last at Lucnow. His death was announced to me in a very original note from his nephew and heir, the General Sāhib:—

"Dear Madam,—I have to inform you that my poor uncle Nawāb Moontuzim-ood-Dowlah Bahadur departed this life at the decree and will of Providence, at half-past three o'clock A.M., the day before yesterday, Monday, the 25th inst., after a short illness of six days only; consequently seeing him any more in this world is all buried in oblivion. The Begam Sāhiba tenders her kind remembrances to you. With best wishes, believe me to be, dear Madam, yours very faithfully, Ushruff-ood-Dowla Ahmed Ally Khan Bahadur."

I was sorry to hear of the death of the Nawāb. How soon it has followed on the bad omens of his march!

26th.—Received an invitation to breakfast with the son of the King of Oude (who had arrived from Lucnow), to meet the Governor-General's party: went there on an elephant: an immense party were assembled in a very fine tent. Shortly after, breakfast was announced: when it was over we returned to the former tent, when the presents were brought forth; they consisted of a fine elephant, with a howdah on his back, and the whole of the trappings of red cloth and velvet richly embroidered in gold. Two fine horses next appeared, their housings of velvet and gold; and the bridles were studded with rows of turquoise. A golden palanquin was next presented. On the ground, in front of the party, were twenty-three trays, the present to Lord Auckland; they were filled with Cashmere shawls in pairs, pieces of kimkhwāb, and necklaces of pearls, emeralds, and diamonds. Fifteen trays of shawls and cloth of gold, with fine pieces of Dacca muslin, were presented to each of the Misses Eden; two of the trays contained two combs set in superb diamonds, and two necklaces of diamonds and emeralds, such as are hardly ever seen even in India. All these fine things were presented and accepted; they were then carried off and placed in the Government treasury. The Government make presents of equal value in return.

26th.—The station gave a ball to the Governor-General and the Misses Eden; the next day Prince Henry of Orange, the Misses Eden, and Captain Osborne, went over to Lucnow for a few days, leaving Lord Auckland at Cawnpore; they returned on the 30th, when the Prince quitted the party, and went off with the Captain of "the Bellona" to visit Agra.

1838, *Jan. 1st.*—Sir Charles Metcalfe, who had arrived from Agra, resigned his power into Lord Auckland's hands, and departed for England.

I am very comfortable, every thing being *en regle*, having a double set of tents, two horses for the buggy, two Arabs for riding, ten camels to carry the baggage, and two bullock-carts for the women. The men servants march with the camels: every thing is required in duplicate. One tent, with the people, starts in the evening, and is pitched at the end of the march, and breakfast is there ready for me early the next morning.

3rd.—A cold day with a high wind: my tents are pitched on a dusty plain, without a blade of grass, the wind and dust careering up and down. My little tent is quite a pearl in the desert, so white and fresh: small as it is, it is too large to take to the hills, and I have this day written for two hill tents and a ghoont (a hill pony) to be bought for me, that they may be ready on my arrival.

4th.—Quitted Chobīpūr, and arrived early at the end of the march; found the tent only half pitched, no breakfast ready; in fact, the servants, leaving every thing about in every direction, had gone to sleep. The thieves, who are innumerable all over the country, taking advantage of their idleness, had carried off my dital harp with the French blankets and the pillows from my charpāī. These things were under the sentry, but he was asleep on his post. The box was found in a field, near the tent, but the dital harp was gone. I had always made a point of pitching my tents near the great camp, for the sake of the protection it afforded. "It is dark under the lamp,"[1] was exemplified;—a proverb used when crimes are committed near the seat of authority. Strict orders were of course issued to my people to be more on the alert in future. "When the wolf has run away with the child the door is made fast."[2] In the evening I dined with the Governor-General, and was much gratified with the sight of some of Miss Eden's most spirited and masterly sketches.

5th.—Arrived at Urowl. Here the famine began to show itself very severely;[1] I had heard it talked about, but had never given it much thought, had never brought the image of it before my mind's eye. No forage was to be procured for the camels or bullocks, therefore they went without it; it was not to be had for money, but gram was procurable, of which they had a meal. The horses got gram, but no grass; the country was so completely burnt up, scarcely a blade or rather a root of grass could be cut up, and every thing was exceedingly expensive.

6th.—At six A.M., when I quitted my tent to mount my horse, it was bitterly cold; the poor starving wretches had collected on the spot which my horses had quitted, and were picking up the grains of gram that had fallen from their nosebags; others were shivering over a half-burned log of wood my people had lighted during the night. On the road I saw many animals dead from over-exertion and famine; carts over-turned; at one place a palanquin garī had been run away with, the wheels had knocked down and passed over two camel drivers; one of the men was lying on the road-side senseless and dying.

On reaching the Stanhope, which had been laid half way for me, the horse gave some annoyance while being put into harness; when once in, away he went, pulling at a fearful rate, through roads half way up the leg in sand, full of great holes, and so crowded with elephants, camels, artillery,

[1] Oriental Proverbs.　　[2] Ibid.

[1] For further descriptions of the severe famine, see Emily Eden's *Up the Country* (1866). The famine was exacerbated by the enormous entourage of 1,200 that accompanied Lord Auckland and his sisters, with large numbers of elephants, camels and horses requiring forage.

cavalry, and infantry, and all the camp followers, it was scarcely possible to pass through such a dense crowd; and in many places it was impossible to see beyond your horse's head from the excessive dust. Imagine a camp of 11,000 men all marching on the road, and such a road!

Away rushed the horse in the Stanhope, and had not the harness been strong, and the reins English, it would have been all over with us. I saw a beautiful Persian kitten on an Arab's shoulder; he was marching with a long string of camels carrying grapes, apples, dates, and Tusar cloth for sale from Cabul. Perched on each camel were one or two Persian cats. The pretty tortoise-shell kitten, with its remarkably long hair and bushy tail, caught my eye;—its colours were so brilliant. The Arab ran up to the Stanhope holding forth the kitten; we checked the impetuous horse for an instant, and I seized the pretty little creature; the check rendered the horse still more violent, away he sprang, and off he set at full speed through the encampment which we had just reached. The Arab thinking I had purposely stolen his kitten, ran after the buggy at full speed, shouting as he passed Lord Auckland's tents, "Dohā'ī, dohā'ī, sāhib! dohā'ī, Lord sāhib!" "Mercy, mercy, sir! mercy, Governor-General!" The faster the horse rushed on, the faster followed the shouting Arab, until on arriving at my own tents, the former stopped of his own accord, and the breathless Arab came up. He asked ten rupees for his kitten, but at length, with well-feigned reluctance, accepted five, declaring it was worth twenty. "Who was ever before the happy possessor of a tortoise-shell Persian cat?" The man departed. Alas! for the wickedness of the world! Alas! for the Pilgrim! She has bought a cocky-olli-bird!

The cocky-olli-bird, although unknown to naturalists by that name, was formerly sold at Harrow by an old man to the boys, who were charmed with the brilliancy of its plumage,—purple, green, crimson, yellow, all the colours of the rainbow united in this beautiful bird; nor could the wily old fellow *import* them fast enough to supply the demand, until it was discovered they were *painted sparrows!*

The bright burnt sienna colour of the kitten is not tortoise-shell, she has been dyed with hinnā! her original colour was white, with black spots; however, she looks so pretty, she must be fresh dyed when her hair falls off; the hinnā is permanent for many months. The poor kitten has a violent cold, perhaps the effect of the operation of dyeing her: no doubt, after having applied the pounded menhdī, they wrapped her up in fresh castor-oil leaves, and bound her up in a handkerchief, after the fashion in which a native dyes his beard. Women often take cold from putting hinnā on their feet.

The Famine

Ancient Hindu Ruin

My tents were pitched near Meerunke Sarā's: in the evening, as I was riding into Kanauj, at the tomb of Bala Pīr, I met Captain C——on an elephant, and accompanied him to see the remains of a most ancient Hindū temple. Of all the ruins I have seen this appears to me the most remarkable and the most ancient: the pillars are composed of two long roughly-hewn stones, placed one upon the other, and joined by a tenon and mortise; no cement of any sort appears to have been used. The style of the building is most primitive, and there is a little carving—and but a little—on some of the stones; the structure is rapidly falling into decay. I regret exceedingly I cannot remember the marvellous stories that were related to me connected with this ruin and its inhabitants.

> "For they were dead and buried and embalm'd,
> Ere Romulus and Remus had been suckled:
> Antiquity appears to have begun
> Long after their primæval race was run."

On my return to the tents, my ayha complained bitterly of the annoyance she had experienced on the long march of thirteen miles and a half, over bad roads; she had been upset in her bailī, a native carriage, drawn by two bullocks, and her serenity was sadly discomposed.

7th.—This day, being Sunday, was a halt,—a great refreshment after toil; and Divine Service was performed in the tent of the Governor-General; after which, at 3 p.m., I went, on an elephant, to see two most ancient and curious specimens of Hindū sculpture, the figures of Rām and Lutchman,[2] which are about five feet in height, carved on separate stones, and surrounded by a whole heaven of gods and goddesses: the stones themselves, which are six or seven feet high, are completely covered with numerous images; and a devi (goddess), rather smaller, is on one side.

Passing through the bazār at Kanauj was a fearful thing. There lay the skeleton of a woman who had died of famine; the whole of her clothes had been stolen by the famished wretches around, the pewter rings were still in her ears, but not a rag was left on the bones that were starting through the black and shrivelled skin; the agony on the countenance of the corpse was terrible. Next to her a poor woman, unable to rise, lifted up her skinny arm,

---

[2] Rama is a Hindu deity, one of the avatars of Vishnu the Preserver. His brother was Laxman. One of the most famous epics of ancient India, the Ramayana, is based on their adventures to rescue Sita, the wife of Rama, who was kidnapped by the demon Ravana. They were helped by Hanuman, the Monkey-God.

and moaned for food. The unhappy women, with their babies in their arms, pressing them to their bony breasts, made me shudder. Miserable boys, absolutely living skeletons, pursued the elephant, imploring for bread: poor wretches, I had but little money with me, and could give them only that little and my tears: I cannot write about the scene without weeping, it was so horrible, and made me very sick. Six people died of starvation in the bazār to-day. Lord Auckland daily feeds all the poor who come for food, and gives them blankets; five or six hundred are fed daily;—but what avails it in a famine like this? it is merciful cruelty, and only adds a few more days to their sufferings; better to die at once, better to end such intolerable and hopeless misery: these people are not the beggars, but the tillers of the soil. When I was last at Kanauj the place was so beautiful, so luxuriant in vegetation,—the bright green trees, the river winding through low fields of the richest pasture: those fields are all bare, not a blade of grass. The wretched inhabitants tear off the bark of the wild fig tree (goolèr), and pound it into food; in the course of four or five days their bodies swell, and they die in agonies. The cultivators sit on the side of their fields, and, pointing to their naked bodies, cry, "I am dying of hunger." Some pick out the roots of the bunches of coarse grass, and chew them. The people have become desperate; sometimes, when they see a sipāhi eating they rush upon him to take his food; sometimes they fall one over the other as they rush for it, and having fallen, being too weak to rise, they die on the spot, blessed in finding the termination of their sufferings. The very locusts appear to have felt the famine; you see the wings here and there on the ground, and now and then a weak locust pitches on a camel. Every tree has been stripped of its leaves for food for animals. The inhabitants of Kanauj, about a lākh of people; have fled to Oogein and to Saugar. The place will be a desert; none will remain but the grain merchants, who fatten on the surrounding misery. There is no hope of rain for five months; by that time the torments of these poor wretches will have ended in death;—and this place is the one I so much admired from the river, with its rich fields, and its high land covered with fine trees and ruins!

I returned to the ancient Hindū building that had so much interested me, to sketch it at leisure, and was thus employed, when I was surrounded by numbers of the starved and wretched villagers. I performed my task as quickly as possible, and whatever errors there may be in the performance, must be attributed to the painful scene by which I was surrounded; some of the poor people flung themselves on the ground before me, attempting to perform pā-bos, that is, kissing the feet; wildly, frantically, and with tears imploring for food; their skeleton forms hideously bearing proof of starvation; the very remembrance makes me shudder. I quitted the ruin, and

Sketched in the Temple

BHAGWĀN.

and on Stone by

Figure 10   Bhagwān

returned to my tents. To-morrow we quit Kanauj, thank God! It is dreadful to witness and to be unable to relieve such suffering.

I picked up a curious piece of ancient sculpture, Mahadēo,[3] with Pārvatī in the centre, and a devi on each side, which I brought to my tent on the elephant. Considering it too heavy to carry about on the march, we buried it at night under a peepul tree, and shall take it away on our return home, if it will please to remain there.

At this place I learned the following legend. In the olden time, Kanauj was a great city. There were giants in those days, men of enormous stature, who dwelt at Kanauj, and with three steps could accomplish the distance hence to Fathīgarh. *En passant*, be it remarked, it took the feeble mortals in the camp of the Governor-General three long marches, during three long days, to pass over the same ground. The women were also very powerful; on brushing their houses of a morning, it was their custom to pitch the dirt a stone's throw from the door. Now, the women being as strong as the men, the dirt was thrown as far as Fathīgarh in a heap; and on the rising ground produced by these dirt-throwing damsels was afterwards erected the Fort of Fathīgarh.

[. . .]

Chapter 42

Pleasant Days in Camp

1838, *Jan. 8th.*—Arrived at Jellalabad without any adventures.
[. . .]
    10*th.*—Arrived at Fathīgarh.
[. . .]

[3] The Hindu triad consists of Brahma, the Creator, Vishnu, the Preserver, and Shiva, the Destroyer. Mahadeo is one of the forms of Shiva, the Destroyer. His consort is Parvati.

13th.—Crossed the river on a bridge of boats that had been erected for the accommodation of the Lord Sāhib, as the natives call the Governor-General.

They say there are about eleven thousand people with the camp, and elephants and camels innumerable, which, added to the Body guard, Artillery, and Infantry, form an immense multitude. It is said his Lordship's marching about the country costs the Government 70,000 rupees a month; the encampment encroaching on fields of grain often costs from 300 to 400 rupees a day to make up the loss sustained by the peasants. On the other side the bridge, the road was marked out by little flags,—and a most heartbreaking road it was; entirely through the dry bed of the river, nearly axle deep in fine sand: the day was bitterly cold, the wind very high, and the flying sand filled our eyes and mouths. I was too unwell to mount my horse, and the result was that the two greys had to drag me the whole way in the Stanhope. The first thing I discovered was my ayha in her cart fixed in the sand, and quite immovable. Some soldiers came forward and helped her out of her difficulty. All the Company's hackeries had come to an anchor. The soldiers, finding the bullocks had no power to extricate them from the sand, took out the animals, and harnessed themselves, some thirty or forty men to each cart, and dragged it until it reached better ground.

I came up to my tent at Imrutpūr, and found it was pitched close to the lines of the camp of the Governor-General; this could not be altered at the time, the other tent not having come up, and being ill I laid down to rest. The other tent did not come up until it was too late to pitch it; and in the evening I was annoyed at finding I was within the rules of the camp, within the sentries, which I had given strict orders to avoid, and which my people had disobeyed by mistake when pitching the tent during the night. Indeed, the long march over the sand of the river had harassed them, and when it is particularly cold, the natives are more stupid than usual.

14th.—I was quite ill, and much inclined to give up my journey altogether, but as my tent was pitched within the rules, I got up very early, had the other tent pitched without the rules, went into it, and struck the former. Captain C—— wrote to mention it had been observed that the tent had been pitched within the line of sentries, and to request I would give orders to my khalasīs to prevent the recurrence of the circumstance. I therefore determined to change my route; and a note having come from Mrs H——, saying their party having quitted the great camp were going to Alligarh, and requesting me to join them, I accepted the invitation with great pleasure.

19th.—Finished a march of fifteen miles before half-past eight A.M.;

halted at Nawabgunge; breakfasted with my friends; a most kind welcome, a bright fire, and an excellent breakfast, made me quite happy. The formality of the great camp I had just quitted formed a strong contrast to the gaiety and cheerfulness of marching under of the flag of the Resident of Gwalior.

23rd.—We arrived at Khāsgunge, and encamped in the Mango Tope just beyond the village. After breakfast, I drove four miles to see Mr. James Gardner, who had succeeded to his father's property, and was living at his house. I found the place quite deserted; Mr. Gardner was at one of his villages some miles off, but his wife, Mulka Begam, was at home. I sent word I would pay my respects to her if she could receive me. In the mean time I went into the garden, and visited all those spots where I had so often enjoyed the society of my dear friend Colonel Gardner. The pavilion in the centre of the garden, in which I had nursed him when he was so ill, recalled to mind the conversation we then had, which ended in his taking me to the tomb of his son just beyond the garden; we sat on that tomb, and the dear old man said, pointing to the spot, "I wish to be buried there, by the side of my son; another year will not pass ere I shall be placed there; you are very kind in trying to persuade me, my dear daughter, that I have still many years before me, but I feel I am going, my constitution is gone; it is well that with old age we feel all these pains and the ills that accompany it; were it not so, we should never be willing to quit this world." Our conversation lasted some time, afterwards he took my arm, and we returned slowly to the house. I visited his grave: his son had raised a tomb on the spot selected by his father; it was not quite finished. I knelt at the grave of my kind, kind friend, and wept and prayed in deep affliction. His Begam had only survived him a few days. She was buried in the same tomb, with her head to Mecca, towards which place the face of a true believer is always turned when laid in the grave. The corpse of a Muhammadan is laid on its back in the grave, with the head to the north and feet to the south, turning its face towards the kibla (or Mecca, *i.e.* west). The Shī'as make their tombs for men of the same shape as the Sunnīs make those for females; and for women like those of the Sunnīs for men, but with a hollow, or basin, in the centre of the upper part.

Mulka Begam received me very kindly; she showed me her little girl, the youngest, about two years old, whom she said was reckoned very like me. The child was shy, and clung to her ayha, frightened at a stranger; I could scarcely catch a glimpse of her face. The eldest boy was from home with his father; the second son, William Linnæus, so called after his grandfather, was at home; he is a very fine, intelligent boy. I requested leave to bring Mrs H—— to pay her a visit that evening, and then asking permission to depart, I returned to the tents. In the evening, our party set off for Khāsgunge: we walked in the garden, and visited the tomb. Major Sutherland spoke of Colonel Gardner as a most gallant officer, and recorded several most dashing actions in which he had distinguished himself in many parts of the country; gallantry that had not met the recompense due to it from Government;—the value of a spirit such as Colonel Gardner's had not been properly appreciated by the rulers of the land.

When the evening closed in, the gentlemen went into the outer house, and I took Mrs H—— into the zenāna: as dark beauties always look best by candle-light, I had selected a late hour to visit the Begam; she was sitting on her gaddī when we went in, surrounded by her three beautiful children, and was in herself a picture. The little girl, my likeness, had lost all her shyness, and was figuring about like a dancing girl; on remarking the extraordinary change from shyness to such violent spirits, Mulka said, "She has had some opium, that makes her so fearless." We sat an hour with the Begam, and then took our leave. We found the gentlemen in the outer house, sitting over a warm fire, and an excellent dinner of native dishes was ready; having dined, we returned by torch-light to the tents.

My friends were much gratified with their visit to Khāsgunge; I had spoken to warmly of the beauty of Mulka Begam, that I was pleased to find Mrs H—— admired equally both her person and manners.
[. . .]

Chapter 43

Ruins of Delhi

1838, *Feb*.—With the Neapolitan saying, "Vedi Napoli, e poi mori," I beg leave to differ entirely, and would rather offer *this* advice,—"See the Tājmahal, and then—see the Ruins of Delhi." How much there is to delight the eye in this bright, this beautiful world! Roaming about with a good tent and a good Arab, one might be happy for ever in India: a man might possibly enjoy this sort of life more than a woman; he has his dog, his gun, and his beaters, with an open country to shoot over, and is not annoyed with—"I'll thank you for your name, Sir." I have a pencil instead of a gun, and believe it affords me satisfaction equal, if not greater than the sportsman derives from his Manton.[1]

On my return from the theatre I sought my charpāī, and slept—Oh, how soundly!—was dressed, and on my horse by 6 A.M., having enjoyed four hours and a half of perfect rest. "Sleep is the repose of the soul."[1] I awoke from my slumber perfectly refreshed, and my little soul was soon cantering away on the back of an Arab, enjoying the pure, cool, morning breeze. Oh! the pleasure of vagabondizing over India!

16*th*.—We rode part of the distance, and drove the remainder of the march, sixteen miles; found the tents ready, and the khidmatgārs on the look out. Took a breakfast such as hungry people eat, and then retired to our respective tents. The fatigue was too much; the novel dropped from my hand, and my sleepy little soul sank to repose for some hours.

When the sun was nearly down, we roamed over the fields with the gentlemen and their guns, but found no game. Thus passed the day of the first march on the road to Delhi at Begamabad.

17*th*.—Arrived early at Furrudnagar, another long distance; a high wind, clouds of dust, and a disagreeable day. During the night the servants were robbed of all their brass lotas and cooking utensils. A thief crept up to my camels, that were picketed just in front of the tent, selected the finest, cut the rope and strings from his neck; then, having fastened a very long thin rope to the animal, away crept the thief. Having got to the end of the line, the thief gave the string a pull, and continued doing so until he rendered the camel uneasy; the animal got up,—another pull—he turned his head, another—and he quietly followed the twitching of the cord that the thief held; who succeeded in separating him from the other camels, and got him some twenty yards from the tent; just at this moment the sentry observed the camel quietly departing, he gave the alarm, the thief fled, and the animal was brought back to the camp;—a few yards more the thief would have been on his back, and we should have lost the camel.

18*th*.—Marched into Delhi: the first sight of the city from the sands of the Jumna is very imposing; the fort, the palace, the mosques and minarets,

---

[1] Oriental Proverbs.

[1] Joseph Manton (1766–1835) was a famous gunmaker in London.

all crowded together on the bank of the river, is a beautiful sight. "In the year of the Hijerah, 1041 (A. D. 1631–2), the Emperor Shāh-jahān founded the present city[2] and palace of Shāhjahānabad, which he made his capital during the remainder of his reign. The new city of Shāhjahānabad lies on the western bank of the Jumna, in latitude 28° 36′ North. The city is about seven miles in circumference, and is surrounded on three sides by a wall of brick and stone; a parapet runs along the whole, but there are no cannon planted on the ramparts. The city has seven gates: viz., *Lahore* gate, *Delhi* gate, *Ajimere* gate, *Turkoman* gate, *Moor* gate, *Cabul* gate, *Cashmere* gate; all of which are built of freestone, and have handsome arched entrances of stone, where the guards of the city kept watch."

We entered the town by the Delhi gate: during the rains, when the river flows up to and by the walls of the city, the view from a boat must be beautiful; at present the river is shallow, with great sand-banks in the centre. We crossed a bridge of boats, and encamped in front of the church.

The church was built by Colonel Skinner, planned by Colonel S——; I do not like the design: it was put into execution by Captain D——.[3] The dome appears too heavy for the body of the church, and in the inside it is obliged to be supported by iron bars,—a most unsightly affair. A man should visit the ruins of Gaur, and there learn how to build a dome, ere he attempt it. Colonel Skinner is a Christian; the ladies of his family are Musalmanīs, and for them he has built a mosque opposite the church. In the churchyard is the tomb of Mr. William Frazer,[4] who was murdered by the Nawab Shumsheodin: Colonel Skinner has erected a monument to the memory of his friend; it is of white marble, in compartments, which are inlaid with green stones, representing the weeping willow; the whole was executed at Jeypore, and cost, it is said, 10,000 rupees. On the top is a vase, and, in a compartment in front of the church is a Persian inscription. Below are these lines, and in front of the lines are two lions reposing: to none but an Irishman would it be clear that the *us* in the epitaph proceeds from the lions:—

[2] Shah Jahan (1592–1666) was a Moghul emperor who gained most fame for having the Taj Mahal built, dedicated to his wife Muntaz-i-Mahal. The walled city of Shahjahanabad, built by Shah Jahan in the seventeenth century, which is now called Old Delhi, was in those days called modern Delhi. In fact, the name continued to be used by authors till the present New Delhi was built. What Fanny Parkes calls Ancient Delhi is the ruins of the many former cities of Delhi.

[3] Colonel Skinner (known as Sikander Sahib) 1778–1841, fought for the Mahratta chief Scindia till 1803, when he had to resign, and then served under General Lake. He raised the force named Skinner's Horse and was later appointed a Lieutenant-Colonel in recognition of his services.

[4] William Fraser, Resident at Delhi.

"Deep beneath this marble stone
A kindred spirit to our own
Sleeps in death's profound repose,
Freed from human cares and woes;
Like *us* his heart, like *ours* his frame,
He bore on earth a gallant name.
Friendship gives to *us* the trust
To guard the hero's honour'd dust."

On the other side the monument is another inscription, also written by Colonel Skinner.

THE REMAINS
INTERRED BENEATH THIS MONUMENT
WERE ONCE ANIMATED
BY AS BRAVE AND SINCERE
A SOUL
AS WAS EVER VOUCHSAFED TO MAN
BY HIS
CREATOR!
A BROTHER IN FRIENDSHIP
HAS CAUSED IT TO BE ERECTED,
THAT, WHEN HIS OWN FRAME IS DUST,
IT MAY REMAIN
AS A
MEMORIAL
FOR THOSE WHO CAN PARTICIPATE IN LAMENTING
THE SUDDEN AND MELANCHOLY LOSS
OF ONE
DEAR TO HIM AS LIFE.
WILLIAM FRAZER
DIED MARCH 22ND, 1835.

In the evening the brother of the Bāiza Bā'ī, Hindū Rāo, sent me an elephant, and Colonel Skinner sent another; on these we mounted, and went through all the principal streets of the city. Dehlī or Dillī, the metropolis of Hindūstān, is generally called by Musalmāns Shāh-jahān-ābād, and, by Europeans, Delhi. The Chāndnī chauk, a very broad and handsome street, is celebrated; it has a canal that runs through and down the centre of it; but such is the demand for water, that not a drop now reaches Delhi, it being drawn off for the irrigation of the country, ere it arrive at the city. This fine stream is called *Nahr-i-Bihisht*, or "Canal of Paradise." "In the reign of Shāh-jahān, Ali Merdan Khan, a nobleman, dug, at his own expense, a canal, from the vicinity of the city of Panniput, near the head of the Doo-ab, to the suburbs of Delhi;—a tract of ninety miles in extent. This noble canal is called by the natives the 'Canal of Paradise,' and runs from north to south, in general about ten miles distant from the Jumna, until it joins that river nine miles below the city of New Delhi: it yielded formerly fourteen lákh of rupees per annum. At present it is out of repair, and in many places almost destroyed."

As we went round the Jáma Masjid, a fine mosque, I thought of the words of the Prophet,—"Masjids are the gardens of Paradise, and the praises of God the fruit thereof." On the high flight of steps leading to the mosque were hundreds of people in gay dresses, bargaining for cloth, sweetmeats, &c.

The inhabitants of Delhi appear to delight in dresses of the gayest colours, and picturesque effect is added to every scene by their graceful attire. Native gentlemen of rank, attended by large *sawárís* (retinues) on horseback, on elephants, or on camels, are met at every turn, rendering the scene very amusing and animated. Nevertheless, in spite of all this apparent splendour, a proverb is used to express the vanity and indigence prevalent in that city:—"Dillī ke dilwālī munh chiknā pet khālī;" "The inhabitants of Dihlī appear to be opulent, when, in fact, they are starving." A little beyond the Jáma Masjid is the wall of the palace,—a most magnificent wall; I was delighted with it and its gateways. Shortly afterwards we turned our elephants towards the tents, and returned, considerably fatigued, to dinner.

19th.—This morning we had decided on visiting the tomb of Humaioon, but, on mounting our horses, hearing firing at a distance, we rode off to see what amusement was going forward, leaving the visit to the tomb for another day. It was lucky we did so, I would not on any account have missed the scene. We galloped away, to save time, and found Lord Auckland and his party at a review; after looking at the review a short time, Captain S——, himself an engineer, took me to see a very interesting work: the sappers and miners had erected a mud-fort; trenches were regularly formed in front of the fort, to cover the attacking party, and mines were formed underground to a considerable distance. We walked through the long galleries, which were all lighted up, and Captain S——explained the whole to me. On our return, Lord Auckland came up, examined the fort, and walked through the miners' galleries. The attack commenced, the great guns blazed away at the bastion, which was blown up in good style by the miners; the soldiers mounted the breach and took the fort, whilst, on the right, it was scaled by another party. This mimic war was very animated; I like playing at soldiers, and it gave me an excellent idea of an attack, without the horror of the reality: another mine was sprung, and the warfare ended.

365

The sun was high and very hot,—we rode home as fast as our horses could carry us,—only stopping on the top of a rocky hill near the late Mr. Frazer's house, to admire the view of Delhi, which lay below a mass of minarets and domes, interspersed with fine trees. Near this spot Mr. Frazer was shot. The house was bought by Hindū Rāo for 20,000 rupees. Out of this rocky hill a sort of red gravel is dug, which forms the most beautiful roads.

After breakfast we struck our tents, and came to stay with a friend, who has a fine house in beautiful grounds, with a garden filled to profusion with the gayest flowers, situated just beyond the Cashmere gate of the city. Colonel Edward Smith, of the engineers, deserves great credit for the style and good taste he has displayed in the architecture of this gate of Delhi, and for several other buildings which were pointed out to me as of his design in other parts of the city. We found the tents very hot within the walls, with flies innumerable, like the plague of Egypt; at least, they must be quite as bad during the hot season. In the evening we went to a ball, given by Mr. Metcalfe to the Governor-General and his party.[5]

20*th*.—The ball gave me a head-ache, and I was suffering a good deal of pain, when a native lady came to see me, on the part of the Nawāb Shah Zamānee Begam, the Emperor's unmarried sister, from whom she brought a complimentary message, and a request that I would call upon her at the palace. The lady, finding me in pain, most kindly shampooed and mulled my forehead so delightfully, that my head-ache was charmed away;—shampooing is the great luxury of the East.
[. . .]

In the evening we drove through the ruins of old Delhi to the tomb of the Emperor Humaioon. The drive is most interesting; you cannot turn your eye in any direction but you are surrounded by ruins of the most picturesque beauty. The tomb of Humaioon is a fine massive building, well worth visiting: it is kept in good repair. There are several monuments within the chambers of the mausoleum that are of carved white marble. The tomb of the Emperor is very plain, and without any inscription. On the terrace is a very elegant white marble monument, richly carved, of peculiar construction, over the remains of a Begam. The different and extensive views from the terrace over the ruins of old Delhi are very beautiful.
[. . .]

---

[5] Thomas Theophilus Metcalfe, younger brother of Sir Charles, lived in Delhi for forty years, built Metcalfe House, and succeeded Fraser as Resident in 1835.

Chapter 44

The Zenāna at Delhi

1838, *Feb. 22nd.*—In the cool of the evening we mounted our horses, and rode to Ancient Delhi, or Indrapesta, now called Marowlie, the capital of the former Rajas. At this place, many houses were pointed out to us as having belonged to the mighty dead; but my attention was arrested by a bā'oli, an immense well. From the top of the well to the surface of the water the depth is sixty feet, and the depth of water below forty feet; just above the surface of the water the side of the well opens on a flight of stone steps, which lead to the upper regions. I peered over the well to see the water, and shuddered as I looked into the dark cold depth below; at that instant a man jumped from the top into the well, sank a great depth, rose again, and, swimming to the opening, came up the steps like a drenched rat; three more immediately followed his example, and then gaily claimed a "*bakshish,*" or reward, begging a rupee, which was given: we did not stay to see the sport repeated, at which the jumpers appeared disappointed.

Quitting the bā'oli, we visited the tombs of the three last emperors of Delhi,—Bahādur Shah, Shah'ālam, and Akbar Shah. The latter had been placed there within a few weeks; the tomb of Shah'ālam is of white marble, and about eighteen inches distant from that of the Emperor Bahādur Shah, over whose tomb flourishes a white jasmine. How are the mighty fallen! I had visited the tomb of Humaioon, and the still grander monument of Akbar at Secundra; had admired the magnificent building, its park and portal. The last Akbar reposes side by side with the two former emperors. Three marble tombs, prettily sculptured, in a small open court, the walls of which are of white marble, is all that adorns the burial-place of the descendants of Tamurlane![1]

The building that most interested me was the Royal Zenāna Ghār. At certain times of the year the Emperor of Delhi used to retire to this spot with all his ladies; the place is prettily situated amidst rocks and trees: there, seated at ease on his cushions of state, his amusement was to watch the

---

[1] The legendary Tartar conqueror Tamerlane invaded India in 1398 and is seen as the ancestor of the Moghuls.

sports of the ladies of the zenāna, as they jumped from the roof of a verandah into the water below, and then came up to jump in again. On the other side is another tank, with a sloping bank of masonry; on this slope the ladies used to sit, and slide down into the tank. In the water, amidst the trees, the graceful drapery of the Musulmanī and Hindū ladies clinging to their well-formed persons must have had a beautiful effect. During these sports guards were stationed around, to prevent the intrusion of any profane eye on the sacredness of the zenāna.

At 9 P.M. we revisited the minār: the night was remarkably fine, no moon, but a dark blue, clear star-light. The minār is fine by day, its magnitude surprising; but, by night, a feeling of awe is inspired by its unearthly appearance. If you ask a native, "Who built the Kutab?" his answer will generally be,—"God built it;—who else could have built it?"[2] And such is the feeling as you stand at the base, looking up to the top of the column of the polar star, which appears to tower into the skies: I could not withdraw my eyes from it; the ornaments, beautiful as they are by day, at night, shadowed as they were into the mass of building, only added to its grandeur. We roamed through the colonnades, in the court of the beautiful arches, and returned most unwillingly to our tents.

23rd.—Quitted the Kutab without revisiting Tuglukabad, our time not admitting of it; and I greatly regretted not having the power of visiting the tombs that surrounded us on every side the ruins of Ancient Delhi. The extent of these ruins is supposed not to be less than a circumference of twenty miles, reckoning from the gardens of Shalimar, on the north-west, to the Kutab Minār, on the south-east, and proceeding thence along the centre of the old city, by way of the mausoleum of Nizam-al-Deen, the tomb of Humaioon, which adjoins, and the old fort of Delhi, on the Jumna, to the Ajmeer gate of Shāhjahānabad. The environs to the north and west are crowded with the remains of the spacious gardens and country houses of the nobility, which in former times were abundantly supplied with water, by means of the noble canal dug by Ali Merdan Khan.

Franklin remarks,—"Ancient Delhi is said by historians to have been erected by Rajah Delu, who reigned in Hindūstan prior to the invasion of Alexander the Great: others affirm it to have been built by Rajah Pettou-var, who flourished at a much later period. It is called in Sanscrit *Indraput*, or the Abode of *Indra*, one of the Hindū deities, and is thus distinguished in the royal diplomas of the Chancery office."

[. . .]

---

[2] The Qutb Minar was built by the Muslim ruler Qutb-ud-Din Aybak in the early thirteenth century.

During my visit at Khāsgunge, Mr. James Gardner gave me an introduction to one of the princesses of Delhi, Hyat-ool-Nissa Begam, the aunt
of the present, and sister of the late king. Mr. James Gardner is her adopted
son. The princess sent one of her ladies to say she should be happy to receive
me, and requested me to appoint an hour. The weather was excessively hot,
but my time was so much employed I had not an hour to spare but one at
noon-day, which was accordingly fixed upon.

I was taken in a palanquin to the door of the court of the building set
apart for the women, where some old ladies met and welcomed me. Having
quitted the palanquin, they conducted me through such queer places, filled
with women of all ages; the narrow passages were dirty and wet,—an odd
sort of entrance to the apartment of a princess!

Under a verandah, I found the princess seated on a *gaddī*, of a green
colour. In this verandah she appeared to live and sleep, as her *charpāī*,
covered with a green *razā'ī*, stood at the further end. She is an aged woman;
her features, which are good, must have been handsome in youth; now they
only tell of good descent. Green is the mourning worn by the followers of
the prophet. The princess was in mourning for her late brother, the
Emperor Akbar Shah. Her attire consisted of trowsers of green satin, an
angiya, or boddice of green, and a cashmere shawl of the same colour: jewels
are laid aside during the days of *mātam* (mourning). I put off my shoes
before I stepped on the white cloth that covered the carpet, and advancing,
made my *bahut bahut adab salām*, and presented a *nazr* of one gold mohur.
The princess received me very kindly, gave me a seat by her side, and we
had a long conversation. It is usual to offer a gold mohur on visiting a
person of rank; it is the homage paid by the inferior to the superior: on the
occasion of a second visit it is still correct to offer a *nazr*, which may then
consist of a bouquet of freshly-gathered flowers. The compliment is graciously received, this homage being the custom of the country.

I had the greatest difficulty in understanding what the Begam said, the
loss of her teeth rendering her utterance imperfect. After some time, she
called for her women to play and sing for my amusement. I was obliged to
appear pleased, but my aching head would willingly have been spared the
noise. Her adopted son, the son of the present King Bahadur Shah, came
in;[3] he is a remarkably fine, intelligent boy, about ten years old, with a
handsome countenance. Several other young princes also appeared, and

[3] This must have been Mirza Jiwan Bukht, the youngest and favourite son of Bahadur Shah,
the last of the Moghul emperors—a mere puppet by this time. He was to accompany his
father into exile in Burma after the British defeat of the Indian Uprising of 1857. The real
heir-apparent at the time of Fanny Parkes' visit was Mirza Dara Bukht, eldest son of Bahadur
Shah, then aged thirty-six.

some of their betrothed wives, little girls of five and six years old: the girls
were plain. The princess requested me to spend the day with her; saying
that if I would do so, at 4 p.m. I should be introduced to the emperor (they
think it an indignity to call him the king), and if I would stay with her
until the evening, I should have nāches for my amusement all night. In the
mean time she desired some of her ladies to show me the part of the palace
occupied by the zenāna. Her young adopted son, the heir-apparent, took
my hand, and conducted me over the apartments of the women. The ladies
ran out to see the stranger: my guide pointed them all out by name, and I
had an opportunity of seeing and coversing with almost all the begams. A
plainer set I never beheld: the verandahs, in which they principally appeared
to live, and the passages between the apartments, were *mal propre*. The
young prince led me through different parts of the palace, and I was taken
into a superb hall: formerly fountains had played there; the ceiling was
painted and inlaid with gold. In this hall were three old women on charpāīs
(native beds), looking like hags; and over the marble floor, and in the place
where fountains once played, was collected a quantity of offensive black
water, as if from the drains of the cook rooms. From a verandah, the young
prince pointed out a bastion in which the king was then asleep, and I
quitted that part of the palace, fearing the talking of those who attended
me, and the laughing of the children, might arouse his majesty from his
noon-day slumbers.

On my return to the princess I found her sister with her, a good-
humoured, portly-looking person. They were both seated on chairs, and
gave me one. This was in compliment, lest the native fashion of sitting on
the ground might fatigue me. The heat of the sun had given me a violent
headache. I declined staying to see the king, and requested permission to
depart.

Four trays, filled with fruit and sweetmeats, were presented to me; two
necklaces of jasmine flowers, fresh gathered, and strung with tinsel, were
put round my neck; and the princess gave me a little embroidered bag filled
with spices. It is one of the amusements of the young girls in a zenāna to
embroider little bags, which they do very beautifully; these they fill with
spices and betel-nut, cut up into small bits; this mixture they take great
delight in chewing. An English lady is not more vain of a great cat and
kitten with staring eyes, worked by herself in Berlin wool, than the ladies
behind the parda of their skill in embroidery. On taking my departure the
princess requested me to pay her another visit; it gave her pleasure to speak
of her friends at Khāsgunge. She is herself a clever, intelligent woman, and
her manners are good. I had satisfied my curiosity, and had seen native life
in a palace; as for beauty, in a whole zenāna there may be two or three

handsome women, and all the rest remarkably ugly. I looked with wonder at the number of plain faces round me.

When any man wishes to ascend the minarets of the Jāma Masjid, he is obliged to send word to the captain of the gate of the palace, that the ladies may be apprised, and no veiled one may be beheld, even from that distance: the fame of the beauty of the *generality* of the women may be continued, provided they never show their faces. Those women who are beautiful are very rare, but then their beauty is very great; the rest are generally plain. In England beauty is more commonly diffused amongst all classes. Perhaps the most voluptuously beautiful woman I ever saw was an Asiatic.

I heard that I was much blamed for visiting the princess, it being supposed I went for the sake of presents. Natives do not offer presents unless they think there is something to be gained in return; and that I knew perfectly well. I went there from curiosity, not avarice, offered one gold mohur, and received in return the customary sweetmeats and necklaces of flowers. Look at the poverty, the wretched poverty of these descendants of the emperors! In former times strings of pearls and valuable jewels were placed on the necks of departing visiters. When the Princess Hyat-ool-Nissa Begam in her fallen fortunes put the necklace of freshly-gathered white jasmine flowers over my head, I bowed with as much respect as if she had been the queen of the universe. Others may look upon these people with contempt, I cannot; look at what they are, at what they have been!

The indecision and effeminacy of the character of the emperor is often a subject of surprise. Why should it be so? where is the difference in intellect between a man and a woman brought up in a zenāna? *There* they both receive the same education, and the result is similar. In Europe men have so greatly the advantage of women from receiving a superior education, and in being made to act for, and depend upon themselves from childhood, that of course the superiority is on the male side; the women are kept under and have not fair play.

One day a gentleman, speaking to me of the *extravagance* of one of the young princes, mentioned he was always in debt, he could never live upon his allowance. The allowance of the prince was twelve rupees a month!— not more than the wages of a head servant.

With respect to my visit, I felt it hard to be judged by people who were ignorant of my being the friend of the relatives of those whom I visited in the zenāna. People who themselves had, perhaps, no curiosity respecting native life and manners, and who, even if they had the curiosity, might have been utterly unable to gratify it, unless by an introduction which they were probably unable to obtain.

It is a curious fact, that a native lady in a large house always selects the smallest room for her own apartment. A number of ladies from the palace at Delhi were staying in a distant house, to which place a friend having gone to visit them, found them all in the bathing-room, they having selected that as the smallest apartment in which they could crowd together.

[*For health reasons Fanny Parks spent the next few months in Himalayan hill resorts, where she received a letter from the Ba'i (see below). After a pleasant, uneventful stay she received notice of the death of her father and resolved to return to England. In November 1838 she returned to Allahabad and proceeded by boat to Calcutta.*]

[. . .]

1838, *June 29th.*—Her Highness the Baïza Bā'ī did me the honour to send me a *kharītā*, that is, a letter enclosed in a long bag of *kimkhwāb*, crimson silk, brocaded with flowers in gold, contained in another of fine muslin: the mouth of the bag was tied with a gold and tasselled cord, to which was appended the great seal of her Highness,—a flat circular mass of sealing-wax, on which her seal was impressed. Two smaller bags were sent with it . . . each containing a present of bon-bons. The kharītā, as well as one of the small bags, is represented divested of its outer case of transparent muslin; the other little bag has on its white cover, and the direction is placed within the transparent muslin. The autograph of the Baïza Bā'ī is on the right hand side of the page; the letter was written in *Urdū* (the court language), in the Persian character, by one of her Highness's mūnshīs, and signed by the Bā'ī herself: the paper is adorned with gold devices. The letter commenced in the usual complimentary style; after which her Highness writes, that—"The light of my eyes—the Gaja Rājā—has been very ill; she has recovered, and her husband, Appa Sāhib Kanulka, having heard of her illness, has come from Gwalior to see her." Kharītās of this sort pass between the mighty men of the East, and between them and the public functionaries of Government.

[. . .]

Chapter 45

Departure from Allahabad

1838, *Nov.*—On my first arrival at Allahabad I thought I should never get through all the arrangements necessary before my departure for England; so many farewell visits were to be paid to my old friends, and so many preparations were to be made for the voyage. Her Highness the Bāiza Bā'ī was still at Allahabad, and she sent for me. One of the Italian greyhounds given me by Captain Osborne having died, I took the other two, and presented them to the Gaja Rājā Sāhib, the young princess having expressed a wish to have one: I gave her also a black terrier, and one of King Charles's spaniels.

One day a Mahratta lady came to my house, riding, *en cavalier,* on a camel, which she managed apparently with the greatest ease; she told me her Highness requested I would call immediately upon her. On my arrival in camp, after the ceremony of meeting had passed, the Bāiza Bā'ī said, "You are going to England,—will you procure for me three things? The first is, a perfectly high caste Arabian mare; secondly, a very, very little dog, just like a ball, covered with long hair, perfectly white, and having red eyes; and thirdly, a mechanical figure, that, standing on a slack rope, with a pole in its hand, balances itself, and moves in time to the music that plays below it."

I thought of the fairy tales, in which people are sent to roam the world in search of marvellous curiosities, and found myself as much perplexed as was ever knight of old by the commands of a fairy. The Bā'ī added, "You know a good Arab, I can trust your judgment in the selection; the little dogs, they say, come from Bombay: you can bring them all with you in the ship on your return."

I informed her Highness that very few Arabs were in England; that in her Majesty's stud there were some, presents from Eastern Princes, who were not likely to part with the apple of their eyes: that I did not think an Arab mare was to be had in the country. With respect to the little powder-puff dog with the red eyes, I would make enquiries: and the mechanical figure could be procured from Paris.

A few days after this visit one of her ladies called on me, and the following conversation ensued:—

Mahratta Lady—"You are going to England,—you will be absent eighteen months or two years,—have you arranged all your household affairs? You know how much interest I take in your welfare; I hope you have made proper arrangements."

I assured her I had.

"Yes, yes, with respect to the household, that is all very well; but with respect to your husband, what arrangement have you made? It is the custom with us Mahrattas, if a wife quit her husband, for her to select and depute another lady to remain with him during her absence;—have you selected such a one?"

"No," said I, with the utmost gravity; "such an arrangement never occurred to me;—will you do me the honour to supply my place?"

She laughed and shook her head. "I suppose you English ladies would only select one wife; a Mahratta would select two to remain with her husband during her absence."

I explained to her the opinions of the English on such subjects: our ideas appeared as strange to her as hers were to me; and she expressed herself grieved that I should omit what they considered a duty.

27th.—I called on the ex-Queen of Gwalior, and took leave in all due form; the dear old lady was very sorry to part with me,—the tears ran down her cheeks, and she embraced me over and over again. I was sincerely grieved to part with her Highness, with whom and in whose camp I had passed so many happy hours, amused with beholding native life and customs, and witnessing their religious ceremonies. The next day she sent me the complimentary farewell dinner, which it is the custom to present to a friend on departure: I partook of some of the Mahratta dishes, in which, to suit my taste, they had omitted musk or assafœtida; the cookery was good; pān, atr, and rose-water, as usual, ended the ceremony.

[. . .]

[Dec.] 20th.—When in the Hills, roaming in the interior, I met with an accident, a fall: coming down a rock, my long silk gown having caught on a projecting part of it, I was thrown headlong down; therefore I made a dress more suited for such expeditions, a black Paharī dress, somewhat resembling Turkish attire. My fair companion admired it exceedingly, and made one for herself after the same fashion; large round sailor-looking straw hats completed the costume: they were comfortable dresses on the river. My ayha, who accompanied me to the bazār last night, told me the natives said to her, "Ayha, ayha, is that a man or a woman?"—"A man." "Ayha, tell the truth, is it a man or a woman?"—"A man." "Then why are you with him?"—"Oh, the sāhib brought me to bargain for things in the bazar." I asked her why she had said I was a man? She replied, "They are great thieves,

and if they think you a man they are less likely to attempt to rob the boats." Her stratagem amused me. The purchases I made were certainly not feminine, consisting of sixty-five bamboos and some shot; and I superintended the fixing of some brass work on a musket that was out of repair.

We are at this moment surrounded by a great number of boats; the people belonging to them are singing and playing on all sorts of uncouth instruments; such a hum, and such a din!—it will be useless to attempt to rest until these perturbed spirits have sung themselves to sleep.

22nd.—Off Pointy, where the river is rapid and dangerous, we saw two vessels that had been just wrecked. The owner of the land (the jamīndar) was taking up the cargo from the wrecks; half becomes his share, and the owners of the vessels have only the remainder.

25th.—A stormy day; during a lull we attempted to cross the river; halfway over a heavy wind rendered my boat unmanageable, and we were driven by the wind upon a clump of bamboo stumps that were just above water in the middle of the stream: the crew were alarmed, and shouted "Rām! rām! āh'e Khudā! āh'e Khudā!" Fortunately, the boat being strong and new, she did not split open, and after a time we got her off again; the wind then drove us up a creek, and we lugāoed on a sandbank. The gale separated me from my fair friend, whose boat was driven to the opposite side of the river; her people were calling to know if I were safe; it was impossible to rejoin her; she heard the answering shouts of my men in the distance, and was satisfied. We were like the Brahmanī ducks, the chakwa chakwī, separated by the river, and calling through the live-long night "ā'o, ā'o," "come, come."

26th.—We anchored below the village of Downapūr, which had been washed away into the river during the last rains, by the force of the current having undermined its banks. My fair friend and I roamed in the beautiful moonlight by ourselves, attired in our Paharī dresses and straw hats, to a village at some distance. The women took us for cadets, and ran away in a great fright; nor was it for a length of time we could bring an ugly old hag to a parley; at last we succeeded, and bought a Bengalee goat and kid; the villagers were excessively afraid of us, and with great difficulty we persuaded them to bring the goats to the vessel. They asked my companion where her regiment was stationed; and imagined my wife was *parda nishīn* on board the boats. We did not undeceive them with respect to our manhood.

On my return I asked the sentry on my boat, "What hour is it?" The man answered, "When *Honey* is perpendicular over the mast it is midnight; it must now be eleven." His *Honey* are the three stars in Orion's belt.

27th.—Anchored below Sooty on the Bhagirathī. I was awakened from my sleep at 10 P.M. by the servants saying my cook had been missing since 7 in the evening; his age is twenty; and he had never quitted the boats before. We looked over all the boats, and searched the *jāngal* for miles around, and we began to fear a tiger might have taken him off, knowing that gentlemen are in the habit of coming to this part of the country tiger-shooting. My friend became uneasy, and was anxious to go to the opposite side of the river; to this I objected, offering to keep a bonfire blazing before the boats all night, but refusing to quit the spot until the boy's fate was ascertained. At last he was discovered on the top of my boat, hanging over the side as if he had fallen there; on moving him he groaned as if in severe agony, and appeared senseless; his jaw was locked, his eyes were fixed, and turned up under the lids. The poor fellow had been exposed in this state to the dews of a Bengal night for three hours. They brought him into my cabin, he fell into the most violent convulsions, and appeared dying. All the remedies for fits were applied; we placed him in a warm bath; after three hours and a half his jaw relaxed, his eyes moved as if the pressure was off them, and being better, the servants carried him, still apparently senseless, into the cook-boat. I had been up with him four hours in a damp foggy night, anxious for his recovery; his father was our cook, and this young native had been with us eleven years under his father. Mrs. B—— said, "I heard a native hint to another that the boy is not in a fit; and I have heard natives will sham illness, and deceive any body." I called a servant, and asked him if it were true. The man, standing on one leg, with the palms of both hands clasped together, said, "What can I say? will you forgive me? If you were my master I would tell you; but how can I utter such words of shame to my mistress? Say you will forgive me for uttering such words, and I will tell you, if you order me to do so." He then related what had passed, and said, the boy, hearing himself called, became alarmed, hid himself, and, on being discovered, shammed illness.

I desired the chaprasī to take a little riding whip in his hand, and accompany me into the cook-boat; the boy was better, but had not recovered from his fit,—the violent convulsions had gone off. I ordered the head man to cut off his hair, and apply leeches to his head; during the operation the itching of his head made him put up his hand and scratch it. I saw from his countenance he was angry, for the shaving of the head is, I believe, the sign of complete slavery with a native, and he found it difficult to sham illness. The operation over, the *khalāsī* gave him a sharp cut with the whip over his hand, desired him to leave off shamming, and come on deck. Finding his imposition was discovered, he got up, and in the most impudent manner said, "What fault have I committed?—what have I done that is wrong?" When I told a chaprasī to take charge of him, and take him to the nearest magistrate, the cook fell at my feet, confessed his crime, and begged I would not send him away; requesting a panchāyāt might be held on his conduct, or that I would punish him according to my pleasure. I told the people to hold a panchāyāt according to their own customs, to report the sentence to me, and it should be carried into execution. The whole of the people assembled in council under a sacred tree on the bank, and deliberated on the case: at the termination of the consultation the elders came to me saying they had decided as follows:—The cook was to receive twenty-two lashes, that he was to lose caste, and to have his *hukka panī bāndh*—that is, they would no longer allow him to associate with themselves, eat or smoke with them, or worship with the faithful. They requested I would turn him out of the boats, that they should be allowed to take him on shore, put him on an ass with his face to the tail of the animal, and followed by drums, and the hooting of the rabble, they should lead the donkey through the village, and then turn him off for ever. This was a severe sentence, and showed how angry the people of his own caste had become: they gave him the twenty-two lashes, he lost caste, and was not allowed to worship on deck as usual. I would not turn him out of service, knowing it would be his ruin, and I felt compassion for his pretty young wife, whom he had left at Allahabad; nor would I allow them to parade him on an ass. The panchāyāt took into consideration the conduct of the under-woman; the servants had told her if she had hidden the cook any where, if she would tell he should be released, and nothing should be said about it: that they would not awaken me; they only wanted to find him. She swore she had not seen him at all; she was present during the four hours he was pretending to be ill,—she saw how much alarmed I was,—also that during this time I was exposed to the night air; and she aided in the deception. They condemned her according to law, but as the sentence was very severe, I only allowed a part of it to be put into execution. She was obliged to blacken her own face with soot and oil as she sat on deck; all the servants came round her,—they laughed, hooted, and complimented her on her beauty; she cried bitterly,—the punishment was severe enough; she was afraid she should be paraded on the donkey, and was very glad to find I would not allow it. The next day she wanted the cook to marry her, and make her a Musalmanī, saying, her husband on her return would cut off her nose, and break into the zenāna of the cook. However, she was disappointed in her wish of becoming a follower of the Prophet, it being discovered she had another lover: this extra lover also lost caste, and had his *hukka panī bāndh*.

Knowing the natives are apt to administer poison in revenge, I mentioned the circumstance to my khansaman, and said, "It is immaterial to me, but, in case of my death, you will be answerable to the sāhib." The man made his salām, saying, "On my head be it: you have punished the man justly; there is nothing to fear: had he been punished unjustly he might have revenged himself by putting poison in your food." "Very well," said I, "it is your concern, not mine;"—and I finished my dinner.
[. . .]

31*st.*—Quitted Berhampūr. I have suffered so much during the last twelvemonth from the death of relatives and friends, that I now bid adieu to the past year without regret. May the new one prove happier than the last!
[. . .]

Chapter 46

Scenes on the Ganges

[*In January 1839 Fanny Parkes set sail for England. She only returned to Calcutta in April 1844, after rejoining her husband at the Cape of Good Hope, where her husband had been sent for convalescence. They proceeded to Allahabad by boat. Their voyage up the Ganges was largely uneventful, but she records a few interesting encounters.*]

1844, *Nov.* 20th.—To-day the scenery has been most uninteresting; nothing to be seen but sandbanks; the river is full of shallows, and there is no wind. Lugāoed on a fine open space in the middle of the river; it is really a good-sized island of fine and beautifully white sand. Four miles above Dinapūr is the junction of the Soane with the Ganges.

21st.—Sandbanks and shallows the whole day: we have advanced very little, and have moored as usual on a bank. Looking around me, I see nothing but a wilderness of sandbanks in the midst of the broad river, only terminating with the horizon—not a tree, not a house to be seen; here and there a distant sail. There is something very pleasing in this monotonous solitude; the only sound the roar of the sandbanks, as they give way and fall into the stream, with a noise like distant thunder. These high sandbanks are undermined by the strong current, and fall in in great masses—very dangerous to small vessels passing near them.

22nd.—"Twenty-two miles above Dinapūr," says the "Directory," "on the left bank, is the Civil station of Chuppra, the capital of the Sarun district. Steamers seldom touch here, even in the rains. Passengers for this place should arrange to land at Revelgunge, above it, where there is a steam agent. The latter place, which is twenty-seven miles by water above Dinapūr, on the left bank, is a very large grain and saltpetre mart, and noted for boat-building. An annual fair is held there. Steamers touch only to land passengers and a few packages to the steam agent's care. Thence up to Ghazipūr the villagers are said to be uncivil and dishonest."

We had a view of Chuppra from a distance, and then passed Revelgunge. The tents of a Rāja were pitched on the side of the Ganges, with the *khanats* extending on both sides into the river to screen the Rāja from the eyes of the curious, as he sat under a *shamiyana* (awning) in the centre. His camp contained several elephants, one most remarkably large, a number of fine horses and camels, and all the retinue of a wealthy native. Moored a little above Revelgunge.

23rd.—A fair wind. Lugāoed off a small *bastī* (village).

24th.—A fair wind. Anchored off Bulleah: a large fair was being held there on the banks of the river; we moored two miles away from it, but the din and uproar, even at that distance, was like the sound of waves breaking on a distant shore. I walked to the fair; it was late in the evening, and nothing was to be seen but thousands of people sitting in groups on the ground cooking their dinners, or lying there asleep. Some groups of people were watching the performance of nāch girls, *go'ālā log*, and dancing boys: every man had a long heavy bamboo in his hand, as a defence, and a walking staff.

The fakīrs had erected altars of mud, on the top of each of which was stuck a long bamboo, decorated with a flag. These holy personages, entirely naked, were sitting on the ground under some freshly-gathered boughs that were stuck up on one side. If one could but learn the real history of one of these men, it would give one a curious insight into human nature. A fakīr of this description is looked upon with respect by the natives; "No one inquires his caste or tribe; he has put on the sting, and is therefore a Brahman."[1]

These men sit up all night by a fire, smoking ganja, an intoxicating herb, eating sweetmeats and ghī, and drinking milk. They never put on any sort of clothing, and never sleep under shelter. They say they do not feel the cold, and they eat the offerings that are made to them. They must receive very large sums; the bearers give from one to four pāisa to these fellows, and a rich Hindū gives a rupee. Groups of people were sitting together singing and playing on tom-toms; the din was excessive, and the smoke very annoying from the innumerable fires around the pathway. To-morrow will be the last day of the fair.

25*th*.—From 7 A.M. until 11 o'clock we were striving to get the boats past the fair, which extended for miles along the bank of the river. It being the early morning, the people were bathing by thousands; the bank for miles was covered with moving figures ascending and descending the steep cliff in masses as thick as they could move. The river below was alive with the devout. Hindūs of all and every class were bathing and performing their devotions. The budgerow was stopped some time from the difficulty of passing her *gūn*, (tracking line,) over the tops of so many high masts; some persons cut the *gūn*, and they ran away with part of it, which theft detained us some time. The manner in which, by the aid of a bamboo, the tracking rope is carried to the top of a mast and thrown over it, is curious.

By the side of the river I saw several fakīrs bathing; they had thick heads of hair and enormous beards. One man had his hand and arm erect: it was only partly withered, his vow must therefore have been recently made, or the arm would have been withered to the bone and immovably fixed in its position. His body was covered with ashes, and his long elf locks, matted with cow-dung and yellow clay, hung down like so many rusty yellow tails. Hundreds of boats were bringing more people to the fair. The morning being cold, the people, wrapped up in great white sheets, were huddled together in the boats, as many as it was possible to cram together; and at a distance the vessels looked as if they were filled with bales of cotton.

Cows were numerous, and were undergoing the usual pūja. Sometimes a Brahman was seen seated on a charpāi with a chatr over his head, the charpāi supported on four bamboos that were erected in the river, and a fine triangular red flag flying from each end of the four bamboos. The effect was very picturesque: red and also white flags were in profusion, denoting the abiding place of a fakīr. Beauty was extremely scarce amongst the women. Some of the men had fine features—the skin of some of the latter

[1] Oriental Proverbs.

was almost of a transparent black, that of others of a dark brown hue, and some exhibited a bright *terra di sienna* tint. I saw no lepers, which is remarkable; it is usual to see one of the pink-coloured lepers amongst any great multitude bathing; and that leprosy not being catching, the people are not driven from the society of their fellows, as are those who are afflicted with the Arabian leprosy.

I think the number of people collected at this fair appears greater than the number I ever saw collected at Prāg; the cliff for miles was covered with a countless multitude. Perhaps the people were more conspicuous on the cliffs than on the flat sands at the Tribeni. A number of respectable-looking Hindoo women were in boats covered with an awning. This large native village of Bulleah is seventy-four miles above Dinapūr, on the left bank: it is a *dārogah* station, noted for the fair annually held there, as also for a grain mart.

[. . .]

Lugāoed close to a small and very pretty mandap or Hindū temple. I went up to see it; the Brahmān opened the door, and showed me his idols with much pleasure. They consisted of Seeta, Rām, and Lutchman, painted red, and decked with bits of gold and silver tinsel, and pieces of coloured cloth. Hūnoomān was displayed on the wall painted red, and decked also with red linen. The Brahmān gave me a ball of sweetmeat, which he said was the usual offering at the shrine. Two fine peepul-trees, which had been planted together, are on the high bank above the temple, and within their shade are three satīs, built of stone, of octagonal form, and surmounted by a dome: the point of the dome is ornamented with a kalsā formed like a crown with a hole in the centre, and on each of its points or horns, on certain days, a lighted lamp is placed. The cenotaph is hollow below; and there is a little arch, through which the relatives also on particular days place a small lamp, and offerings of flowers within the cavity of the little building, and in the same place the two *sīr* are deposited. The kalsās differ in form from those at Barrah; and the satīs are also of higher caste, being of stone and well built. If the moon rise in time, I will sketch the spot, but I am very much fatigued, and my head aches, not only from exposure to the sun, but from a blow I received upon it from the tracking rope this morning. The insects do not molest us now at night, with the exception of the musquitoes, which are very troublesome.

On the rising of the moon I went on shore to take the sketch, and was attracted by what appeared to be the figure of a man watching from under a tree on a high cliff. On going up to it I found a satī, which had fallen to ruin; the remains were whitewashed, and a large kalsā had been placed on the top, which being also whitewashed, at a distance produced the deception. . . . I brought the kalsā away with me; it will be replaced by the *kumhār*, or potter of the village, whose duty it is to restore all kalsās. On the other side of the old tree was another satī mound, and small *lotās*, earthen drinking vessels, were hung around the tree to receive the offerings of the devout. I had the curiosity to put my hand into one of them, and found one betel-nut which had been placed there as an offering. Peeping over a high bank, I saw an open space of ground, on which were some fine trees, and I could scarcely believe the number of mounds that met my eye were those of victimized women. By a little *détour* I found the entrance to this place of cenotaphs, and was shocked on counting eight-and-twenty satīs. I was alone; had a Hindū been with me, he would have made salām to each of them.

One was large and somewhat in the shape of a grave, after the form of the satī of the Brahmān at Barrah. The others were of various forms; the richer ones were of stone, of an octagonal shape, and surmounted by a dome; some were so small and low, they were not higher than one foot from the earth, like a little ant hill, but ornamented with a kalsā, which quite covered the little mound. Those of stone were from six to eight feet high, and of various forms. There is a hollow space within the satī, into which, through the little arch, the offerings are placed; and there also are deposited the two *sīr*, as they call them, which are made of stone, and are like a cannon ball split in halves. . . . One very old satī tomb, in ruins, stood on the edge of the high cliff above the river, shaded by a clump of bamboos. The spot interested me extremely. It is very horrible to see how the weaker are imposed upon; and it is the same all over the world, civilized or uncivilized—perhaps some of these young married women, from eleven to twenty years of age, were burnt alive, in all the freshness of youth; it may be with the corpse of some decrepit sickly old wretch to whom their parents had given them in marriage.

The laws of England relative to married women, and the state of slavery to which those laws degrade them, render the lives of some few in the higher, and of thousands in the lower ranks of life, one perpetual satī, or burning of the heart, from which they have no refuge but the grave, or the cap of liberty,—*i.e.* the widow's, and either is a sad consolation.

"It is this passive state of suffering which is most difficult to endure, and which it is generally the fate of women to experience. It is too commonly their lot to be deceived into a belief, that as they are the gentler sex, so they ought to be the weakest. Alas, it is far otherwise; the soldier covered with wounds of glory, the mariner warring with the elements, the sage consuming his strength with the midnight oil, or the bigot wearing life away with fanatical zeal in false devotion, require not the unshrinking firmness, the never-failing patience, the unbending fortitude which is expected from almost every woman."

The river has encroached so much upon the cliff, and so much ground has fallen in, that, probably, the place of the satīs was of much larger extent; next year, most likely, those that are now tottering on the edge of the cliff will fall into the depth below. From this place I returned to the mandap, and sketched the satīs I had first seen. Their kalsās had figures upon them, meant to represent the husband and wife; I brought three of these ornaments away,—they have received all the honours; their foreheads have been marked with red paint, lamps have been lighted and placed upon their points, and offerings have been laid before them. Pretty well fagged with my moonlight expedition, I returned to the boats and slept quietly,—a great blessing.

[. . .]

1844, *Dec. 5th.*—A friend accompanied me this morning to view Benares, or, as it is more correctly called, Bunarus: nothing pleases me more than driving about this city,—the streets, the houses, and the people are so well worth seeing. "A little to eat, and to live at Bunarus," is the wish of a pious Hindū; but a residence at this place is rather dangerous to any one inclined to violate the laws, as the following extract will testify:—"Kalū-Bhoirŭvŭ is a naked Shivŭ, smeared with ashes; having three eyes, riding on a dog, and holding in one hand a horn, and in another a drum. In several places in Bengal this image is worshipped daily. Shivŭ, under this name, is the regent of Kāshī (Bunarus). All persons dying at Benares are entitled to a place in Shivŭ's heaven; but if any one violate the laws of the shastrŭ during his residence there, Kalū-Bhoirŭvŭ at death grinds him betwixt two mill-stones."

[. . .]

6th.—Some of these people came down to the river-side, and displayed their snakes before the budgerow; they had two boa constrictors, one of which was of enormous size; the owner twined it about his neck after the fashion in which a lady wears her sable boa; the other, which was on the ground, glided onwards, and the man pulled it back, as it appeared to be inclined to escape into the water. They had a number of the cobra di capello, twenty or more, which, being placed on the ground, reared themselves up, and, spreading out their hoods, swayed themselves about in a fashion which the men called dancing, accompanied by the noise of a little hand-drum. The snake-charmers struck the reptiles with their hands, and the snakes bit them repeatedly on their hands, as well as on their arms, bringing the blood at each bite; although the venomous fangs have been carefully removed, the bite itself must be disagreeable; nevertheless, the natives appear not to mind it in the least. There was no trick in the case; I saw a cobra bite his keeper five or six times on his hand and arm, the man was irritating it on purpose, and only desisted when he found I was satisfied that there was no deception. At the conclusion of the exhibition they caught the cobras, and crammed them all into *ghar̄as* (earthen vessels); the boas were carried off in a basket.

In the evening I walked to a dhrumsāla or alms-house on the bank of the river, a little above Rāj ghāt; it is situated on the top of a high flight of steps, and is very picturesque. On the steps of the stone ghāt below is a gigantic image of Hunoomān, made of mud, and painted according to the most approved fashion. The natives were very civil, showing me the way to different places, and yet the Benares people have a *bud nām* (bad name) in that respect, being reckoned uncivil to strangers.

On the steps of the ghāt I met a very savage Brahmanī bull; the beast was snorting and attacking the people,—he ran at me, but some men drove him off; there were numbers of them in the bazār, but this was the only savage one I encountered; the rest were going quietly from gram-stall to gram-stall, apparently eating as much as they pleased. The merchants would be afraid to drive the holy bulls away with violence.

7th.—Quitted Rāj ghāt early, and tracked slowly past Benares, stopping every now and then to take a sketch of those beautiful ghāts. The minārs rear their slender forms over the city, and it is not until you attempt to sketch them that their height is so apparent, and then you gaze in astonishment at them, marvelling at the skill that has reared structures of such height and elegance, and at the honesty of the workmen, who have given such permanent cement to the stones.

A little farther on is a cluster of Hindū temples of extreme beauty and most elaborate workmanship, with a fine ghāt close to them; one of these temples has been undermined by the river, and has fallen—but not to the ground; it still hangs over the stream,—a most curious sight. How many temples the Ganges has engulphed I know not; some six or seven are now either deeply sunk in, or close to the water, and the next rains will probably swell the river, and undermine two or three more. A fine ghāt at the side of these has fallen in likewise.

Above this cluster of falling temples is a very beautiful ghāt, built of white stone,—I know not its name; but I sketched it from the boats. It is still uninjured by time, and is remarkable for the beauty of its turrets, over the lower part of which a palm-tree throws its graceful branches in the most picturesque manner. On the top of a small ghāt, just higher than the river, at the bottom of a long flight of steps, two natives were sitting, shaded from the sun by a large *chatr*; groups of people in the water were bathing and performing their devotions,—many were passing up and down the flight of stone steps,—whilst others, from the arched gallery above, were hanging garments of various and brilliant colours to dry in the sun. On the outside of some of the openings in the bastions straw mats were fixed to screen off the heat.

Just above this fine structure, on a small ghāt, a little beyond the minarets, is a gigantic figure in black stone of Bhīm Singh, a defied giant, of whom it is recorded that he built the fortress of Chunar in one day, and rendered it impregnable. The giant is represented lying at full length on his back, his head, adorned with a sort of crown, is supported on raised masonry; at his right side is erected a small altar of mud, of conical form, bearing on its top a tulsī plant; the natives water these plants, and take the greatest care of them. The tulsī had formerly the same estimation amongst the Hindūs, that the misletoe had amongst the ancient Britons, and was always worn in battle as a charm; on which account a warrior would bind a *mala* of tulsī beads on his person. The scene was particularly picturesque; below the ghāt, on which reposed the gigantic hero, were some native boats; and near them was a man dipping a piece of cloth embroidered in crimson and gold into the water; while, with a brilliant light and shade the whole was reflected in the Ganges.

A little distance beyond I observed a number of small ghāts rising from the river, on each of which a similar conical tulsī altar was erected, and generally, at the side of each, the flag of a fakīr was displayed from the end of a long thin bamboo. A man who appeared to be a mendicant fakīr, came down to the river-side, carrying in one hand a long pole, and in the other one joint of a thick bamboo, which formed a vessel for holding water, and from this he poured some of the holy stream of the Ganges on the little shrub goddess the tulsī.

In the midst of hundreds and hundreds of temples and ghāts, piled one above another on the high cliff, or rising out of the Ganges, the mind is perfectly bewildered; it turns from beauty to beauty, anxious to preserve the memory of each, and the amateur throws down the pencil in despair. Each ghāt is a study; the intricate architecture, the elaborate workmanship, the elegance and lightness of form,—an artist could not select a finer subject for a picture than one of these ghāts. How soon Benares, or rather the glory of Benares—its picturesque beauty—will be no more! Since I passed down the river in 1836 many temples and ghāts have sunk, undermined by the rapid stream.

The Baiza Bā'ī's beautiful ghāt has fallen into the river,—perhaps from its having been undermined, perhaps from bad cement having been used. Her Highness spared no expense; probably the masons were dishonest, and that fine structure, which cost her fifteen lākh to rear a little above the river, is now a complete ruin.

The ghāt of Appa Sāhib is still in beauty, and a very curious one at the further end of Benares, dedicated to Mahadēo, is still uninjured; a number of images of bulls carved in stone are on the parapet of the temple, and forms of Mahadēo are beneath, at the foot of the bastions.

We loitered in the budgerow for above six hours amongst the ghāts, which stretch, I should imagine, about three miles along the left bank of the Ganges.

At the side of one of the ghāts on the edge of the river sat a woman weeping and lamenting very loudly over the pile of wood within which the corpse of some relative had been laid; the friends were near, and the pile ready to be fired. I met a corpse yesterday in the city, borne on a flat board; the body and the face were covered closely with bright rose-coloured muslin, which was drawn so tightly over the face that its form and features were distinct; and on the face was sprinkled red powder and silver dust; perhaps the dust was the pounded talc, which looks like silver.

How soon the young Hindūs begin to comprehend idolatry! A group of children from four to seven years old were at play; they had formed with mud on the ground an image of Hunoomān, after the fashion of those they had seen on the river-side; and they had made imitations of the sweetmeat (*pera*) in balls of mud, to offer to their puny idol.

I was at Benares eight years ago (in November, 1836); the river since that time has undermined the ghāts, and has done so much damage, that, in another ten years, if the Ganges encroach at an equal rate, but little will remain of the glory of the most holy of the Hindū cities. The force of the stream now sets full upon the most beautiful cluster of the temples on its banks; some have been engulphed, some are falling, and all will fall ere long; and of the Bāiza Bā'ī's ghāt, which was so beautiful when last I visited the place, nothing now remains but the ruins! Her Highness objected greatly to the desire of the Government, to force her to live in this holy city: poor lady! her destiny exemplifies the following saying,—"He who was hurt by the *bel* (its large fruit falling on his head) went for refuge to the *bābūl*, (the prickles of which wounded his feet,) and he that was hurt by the *bābūl* fled to the *bel*."[1]

The Rajah of Sattara resides a state prisoner at Bunarus.

A buggy is to be hired at Secrole for four rupees eight ānās a day, which is preferable to a palanquin: in visiting the city the better way is to quit

[1] Oriental Proverbs.

your buggy, and proceed in a tānjān, if you wish to see the curious and ancient buildings to advantage.

I am so much fagged with the excitement of the day, gazing and gazing again, that I can write no more.

[. . .]

1844, *Dec.* 11*th*.—We lugāoed early in the evening four miles above Mirzapūr at the far-famed Bindachun.[1] The first remarkable object on approaching the place is the ghāt of the *Devī* (goddess) which stands out into the river; it is adorned with six bastions, which present a very fort-like appearance, and just above it we moored our boats. Taking an old bearer with me, whilst our people were preparing their evening meal, I hastened up to see the famous temple of Bhawānī, the place of resort of the Thugs, where they meet and take the vows. I ascended the steps of the ghāt of which there are about eighty, and very steep; from their summit you enter the bazār. This is a most curious place, and it is so narrow it can scarcely be called a street, being not more than six feet in the widest part, and in many places the breadth does not exceed three or four. It is lined on both sides with native shops, as thick as possible, and paved throughout with flag-stones. The people from the shops called out to me, "Will you not buy a garland for the goddess, or a *tāgah?*" "Will you not buy sweetmeats for the shrine?" Garlands of fresh flowers were in profusion for sale.

The Temple of Bhawānī

I encountered a man who happened to be *an hajjām*, a cupper and scari-fier. Now, in all Eastern stories a personage of this description appears to be a necessary appendage, and mine, who was also a barber and an Hindū, offered to show me the way to the temple of the Devī. The road, which is straight through the narrow paved alley of the bazār, must be half a mile or more in length: in time we arrived at the temple; three flags were flying from an old peepul-tree, and the noise of the bells which the Brahmāns were tinkling for worship told of the abode of the goddess. The temple, which is built of stone, is of rectangular form, surrounded by a verandah, the whole encompassed by a flight of five steps. The roof is flat, and the pillars that support it of plain and coarse workmanship. On the left is the entrance to the Hindū holy of holies. The Brahmāns begged me to take off my shoes, and said I might then enter and see the face of the goddess. I thought of the Thugs, and my curiosity induced me to leave my shoes at

[1] The temple is at Bindachal.

the door, and to advance about three yards into the little dark chamber. The place was in size so small, that when six people were in it, it appeared quite full; the walls were of large coarse stones. The worshippers were turned out of the apartment, and they gave me a full view of the Devī, the great goddess, the renowned Bhagwān!

The head of the figure is of black stone with large eyes, the whites of which are formed of plates of burnished silver: these glaring eyes attract the admiration of the Hindūs:—"Look at her eyes!" said one. Thrown over the top of her head, strings of white jasmine flowers (the double sweet-scented chumpa) took the place of hair, and hung down to the shoulders. If you were to cut a woman off just at the knees, spread a red sheet over her, as if she were going to be shaved, hiding her arms entirely with it, but allowing her feet to be seen at the bottom, making the figure nearly square—you would have the form of the goddess. The two little black feet rested on a black rat, at least they called it so, and a small emblem of Mahādēo stood at the side. Six or eight long chaplets of freshly-gathered flowers hung from her neck to her feet festooned in gradation,—they were formed of the blossoms of the marigold, the chumpa, or white jasmine, and the bright red pomegranate. The figure stood upon a square slab of black stone. It was about four feet in height, and looked more like a child's toy than a redoubtable goddess. The Brahmān or the Thug, whichever he might be, (for at this shrine all castes worship,) took a white flower, and gave it to me as a present for the goddess, at the same time requesting a rupee as an offering at the shrine. I had no money, but the old bearer had five paīsa (about one penny three farthings), which he gave to the Brahmān, who said, "This is not enough to buy a sweetmeat for the goddess!" I made answer,

> "I give thee all, I have no more,
> Though poor the offering be."

The man saw it was the truth, and was satisfied. The old bearer then requested me to hold my sketch-book for a few moments whilst he went in and put up a prayer: this I did, and the old man returned very quickly, much pleased at having seen the Devī.

I sketched the goddess when before the shrine, the Brahmān holding the lamp for me. Over her head was suspended from the ceiling an ornament of white flowers, and a lamp like that in the robber's cave in "Gil Blas" was also hanging from the roof. There was also a lamp on the black slab, which had the appearance of a Roman lamp. Ornaments worn on the wrists of Hindū women, called *kangan*, formed of a small hank of red, or rather flame-coloured cotton, intermixed with yellow, were offered to the Devī: the Brahmāns put them on her shoulders, as arms she had none. Why and wherefore the *kangan* is offered, I know not. Before a satī ascends the funeral-pile, some red cotton is tied on both wrists. This may, probably, account for the *kangan* offered to Bhagwān, the patroness of satīs.

I thought of the Thugs, but mentioned not the name in the temple; it is not wise "to dwell in the river and be at enmity with the crocodile."[1] In the verandah of the temple were two massive bells of a metal looking like bronze.

I can fancy terror acting on the Hindoos when worshipping the great black hideous idol, Kali Ma, at Kalī-ghāt, near Calcutta; but this poor stump of a woman, with quiet features, staring eyes of silver, and little black feet, inspires no terror:—and yet she is Bhagwān—the dreaded Bhagwān!

The temple was crowded by men and women coming and going, as fast as possible, in great numbers. The month of *Aghar* is the time of the annual meeting; it begins November 15th, and ends the 13th of December; therefore Bindachun must be full of rascals and Thugs at this present time, who have come here to arrange their religious murders, and to make vows and pūja.

This visit to Bindachun interested me extremely; the style of the temple surprised me; it is unlike any of the Hindoo places of worship I have seen, and must be of very ancient date. The pillars are of a single stone without ornament, rough and rude. Some of the shops in the bazār, like the one on the right where sweetmeats are sold, are of curious architecture; stone is used for all the buildings, quarries being abundant in this part of the country.

The people crowded around me whilst I was sketching the exterior of the temple, but were all extremely civil: the Brahmāns and beggars clamoured for *paisa* (copper coins), but were civil nevertheless. It is a disreputable neighbourhood: I hope they will not rob the boats to-night, as all the rascals and murderers in India flock to this temple at the time of the annual fair, which is now being held. Having made my salām to the great goddess, I was guided by the barber to another idol, which he said was worshipped by very few people. It was a female figure, very well executed in stone, with four or five figures around it, carved on the same block. I was much inclined to carry it off; it is one of the handsomest pieces of Hindū sculpture I have seen. A few flowers were lying withered before it in the hovel where it stood, placed there, it may be, by the piety of the barber. Even my husband was induced to climb the steps of the ghāt, and to walk through the bazār to the temple, but he did not enter it. A number of idols were under a peepul-tree in the bazār; they were a great temptation, but in this high place of superstition it might be dangerous to carry off a god.

[1] Oriental Proverbs.

This wandering life is very delightful; I shall never again be content "to sit in a parlour sewing a seam," which the old song gives forth as the height of feminine felicity! Much sooner would I grope through a dark alley idol hunting—*Àpropos*, by the idols under the peepul-tree was a satī mound, broken and deserted, not even a kālsa was there to claim the passing salām of the Hindū, nor a flower to mark the spot: perhaps the great goddess draws off the worshippers from the deified mortal, although all satīs are peculiarly under her protection.
[. . .]

[In March 1845 Charles Parkes gains permission to return to England on furlough. In August 1845 Fanny Parkes and her husband set sail from Calcutta, never to return.]

Chapter 47

The Farewell

And now the pilgrim resigns her staff and plucks the scallop-shell from her hat,—her wanderings are ended—she has quitted the East, perhaps for ever:—surrounded in the quiet home of her native land by the curiosities, the monsters, and the idols that accompanied her from India, she looks around and dreams of the days that are gone.

The resources she finds in her recollections, the pleasure she derives from her sketches, and the sad sea waves,[1] her constant companions, form for her a life independent of *her own* life.

"THE NARRATION OF PLEASURE IS BETTER THAN THE PLEASURE ITSELF."[2]

[1] Written at St. Leonard's-on-Sea.   [2] Oriental Proverbs.

And to those kind friends, at whose request she has published the history of her wanderings, she returns her warmest thanks for the pleasure the occupation has afforded her. She entreats them to read the pilgrimage with the eye of indulgence, while she remembers at the same time that,

"HAVING PUT HER HEAD INTO THE MORTAR, IT IS
USELESS TO DREAD THE SOUND OF THE PESTLE."[1]

To her dear and few surviving relatives,—and to her friends of many years,—the Pilgrim bids adieu:

"THE BLESSING OF HEAVEN BE UPON THEIR HEADS."[2]
"Ap ki topīyan par salāmat rahī."

"THE PEN ARRIVED THUS FAR AND BROKE ITS POINT."[3]
i.e. It is finished.

SALĀM! SALĀM!

---

[1] Oriental Proverbs.   [2] Ibid.   [3] Ibid.

Oriental proverbs and sayings

"*Masal i mdrūf pirāyah-e-zabānhā*"
"A proverb is an ornament to language"

"*Har chi bādābād-i-mā kishte dar āb āndākhtem.*"
No. 1. "Let the result be what it may, I have launched my boat."
i.e. The die is cast.   The bolt is shot.

"*Ghosh kh'ābānīh.*"
2. Lit.—"He put his ears to sleep."

"*Tu marā dil dih o dilīrī bīn.*
Rubah-e-kh'esh kh'ān o shere bīn."
3. "Encourage me, and then behold my bravery:—call me your own fox, and
then you will see me perform the exploits of a lion!"

"*Chi bāk az mauj-i-bahr ānrā ki bāshad Nauh kishtibān.*"
4. "What fear need he have of the waves of the sea, who has Noah for his
pilot?"
i.e. He is safe who has a powerful protector.

"*Kalandar har-chi goyad dīdah goyad.*"
5. "Whatever the wandering traveller says, he does so from having seen that
of which he speaks."

"*Unt dāgh hote the makrā abhī dāgh hone ko āyā.*"
6. "The camels were being branded (with hot irons for the public service),
and the spider came to be marked also."

"*Mekke gaye na Medine gaye bīch hī bīch hājjī the.*"
7. "He neither went to Mekka nor Medina, but was a pilgrim nevertheless."

"*Dharyāre men kahūn lauharyāre to kān de.*"

No. 8. "I speak to those who have daughters, and let those who have sons listen."

"*Bālā-e-tawīlah bar sar-i-maimūn.*"

9. "The misfortunes of the stable (fall) on the head of the monkey."
It is the custom in Hindostān to keep a monkey in or near a stable, to guard the horses from the influence of evil eyes. This proverb is applied whenever a poor man or a servant is punished for the crimes of his superior.

"*Sūndhī bawā chatāī kā lahangā.*"

10. "A handsome sister, with a mat for a petticoat."

"*Dekha shahr-i-Bangālā dant lāl munh kālā.*"

11. "I have seen Bengal, there the teeth are red, and the mouth is black."
i.e. From chewing betel.

"*Karz shauhar-i-mardān ast.*"

12. "Debt is a man's husband."
i.e. A man in debt is always at the mercy of his creditors, as a woman at her husband's.

"*Ek aur ek igārah.*"

13. "One and one make eleven."
From the way of writing (11) in figures.

"*Āmadan ba irādat raftan ba ijāzat.*"

14. "Coming is voluntary, but departing depends upon permission."

"*Fakīr kī surat hī sawāl hai.*"

15. "The appearance of a fakīr is his petition in itself."

"*Shāh-isparam az do barg paidā ast.*"

16. "The sweet basil is known by its two leaves."

"*Sonā jāne kase aur mānus jāne base.*"

17. "Gold is known by the touchstone, and a man by living with him."

"*Zahir-āsh az shaikh bātin az Shaitān.*"

18. "Externally he is a saint, but internally he is a devil."

"*Nīm na mithā ho sech gar ghī se.*"

19. "The nīm-tree (which is very bitter) will not become sweet, though watered with syrup and clarified butter."

"Tum ghī ke dīye jalāo."

No. 20. "Light thou the lamp of ghī."
(Clarified butter.)

"Hawā ke ghore par sawār hain."

21. "He rides a steed of air."
"Chateaux d'Espagne."—To build castles in the air.

"Jā ko piyā chāhen wuhī suhāgan."

22. "She who is beloved is the wife."

"Kyā dam kā bharosā hai?"

23. "What reliance is there on life?"

"Bakht-i-bad bā kase ki yār bavad
Sag gazad gar shutur-sawār bavad."

24. "He who has ill luck for his companion will be bitten by a dog, although mounted on a camel."

"Bhūkhe se kahā do aur do kyā? kahā chār rotīyān."

25. "If you ask a hungry man how much two and two make—he answers Four loaves."

"Shirīn zabānī o lutf o khūshī Tu agar pīle bā mūe kashī."

26. "By sweet words and gentleness you may lead an elephant by a hair."

"Ghawās gar andeshah kunad kām-i-nihang
Hargiz na kunad dar girān-māyah."

27. "If the diver were to think on the jaws of the crocodile, he would never gather precious pearls."

"Kāle ke āge chirāgh nahīn jaltā."

28. "The lamp burns not before the black snake."
(Which is supposed to carry a precious jewel in its head.)

"Khatt pona to adhā mulākāt."

29. "A letter is half an interview."

"Gharīb-parwar salāmat."

30. "Cherisher of the poor—peace be unto you."

31.   *"Allah, Muhammad, Ali, Fatima, Hussun, Hussein."*

"Chyūnte kī jo maut ānī hai to par nikalti hai."

32. "When ants are about to die they get wings."

"*Nayā naukar hiran māre.*"

No. 33. "A new servant will catch deer."

"*Rāst darogh ba gardan-i-rāwī.*"

34. "The truth or falsehood of the story rests on the head of the narrator."
i.e. I tell you the story as it was told to me, but I am not answerable for the truth of it.

"*Baghl men chhurī munh men Rām! Rām!*"

35. "The dagger in his bosom and salutation in his mouth."

"*Fāl-i-bad bar zabān bad bāshad.*"

36. "A bad omen ought not to be mentioned."

"*Ishk o mashk panhān na mī-mūnad.*"

37. "Love and musk do not remain concealed."

"*Har jā ki parī-rukhī ast dīve bā o ast.*"

38. "Wherever there is a fairy-faced damsel, she is attended by a demon."

"*Bhale bābā band pare Gobar chhor kashīde pare.*"

39. "Oh! Father! I have got into a strange difficulty, I have left off picking cow-dung, and am employed in embroidery."

"*Rīsh-i-khudrā ba dast-i-dīgare ma-dih.*"

40. "Do not put your beard into the hands of another."
i.e. Do not put yourself into the power of another person.

"*Admī sā pakherū koi nahīn.*"

41. "There is no bird like a man."
i.e. So volatile and unsteady.

"*Kal kase dekhā hai?*"

42. "Who has seen to-morrow?"
i.e. Enjoy to-day, no one knows what may happen to-morrow.

"*Us se achhā khudā kā nām.*"

43. "The name of God is better than this."
i.e. This is the best of all.

"*Āh dar jigar na mānad.*"

44. "There was not left even a sigh in his heart."
i.e. He was totally destitute.

"Dūdhon nahāo pūton phaliyo!"

No. 45. "May you bathe in milk and be fruitful in children!"

"Tū ki īn kadar az khwāb mahzūzī chirā na mi-mīrī?"

46. "You who are so fond of sleep, why don't you die at once?"

"Ber tale kā bhūt."

47. "A demon under a Ber-tree."

That attached to Bér-trees (Ficus Indica) is said to be exceedingly obstinate—hence applied to a very importunate person of whom you cannot get rid.

"Us ki jar hain to Pātāl ko pahunch gaye hain."

48. "Its roots have already reached to Pātāl."

i.e. The infernal regions. Said of a person who has established himself firmly in any situation.

"Apnī Rādhā ko yād kar."

49. "Attend to your own Rādhā."

i.e. Attend to your own business.

"Jhūth-bolne men to sarfah kyā?"

50. "What need of economy in telling lies?"

51.   *"Jhūth na bole, to pet na phut jāe?"*

"Khānah-i-khālī dīv mī-gīrānd."

52. "Demons take possession of an empty house."

"Zamīndārī dūb kī jar hai."

53. "Landed property is like the root of the Dūb-grass."

i.e. It is not easily destroyed.

"Shamlah ba mikdār-i-îlm."

54. "The pendant part of the turban should be in proportion to the learning."

It was formerly the custom of the learned to have the end of the turban hanging down the back.

"Gāchh men kathal honth men tīl."

55. "The jack fruit is upon the tree, and oil on your lips."

"Hāl men fāl dahī men mosal."

56. "Talking to a man who is in ecstasy (of a religious nature, feigned or practised by fakīrs) is like beating curds with a pestle."

"Merā māthā tabhī thonkā thā."

No. 57. "It was hammered upon my forehead."

"Takdīr chū sābik ast tadbīr chi saud?"

58. "What is the use of taking precautions, since what has been pre-ordained must happen?"

"Jaisā des waisā bhes."

59. "Every country hath its own fashions."

"Jādū hakk hai karne-wālā kāfir."

60. "Magic is truth, but the magician is an infidel."

"Gul se hamāre nishīn Siwā kānte ke nahīn."

61. "My only portion of the rose is the thorn."

"Nigāh-e-darwesh âīn-i-sawāl."

62. "The sight of a beggar is a request personified."

"Ek gharīb ko mārā thā to nau man charbī."

63. "I have killed such a poor man as you, and have got nine mūns of fat out of him."

"Jal men basī kamudinī chandā basī ākās.
Jo jan jā ke man basī so jan tā ke pās."

64. "The Nymphæa dwells in the water, and the moon in the sky, (but) he that resides in the heart of another is always present with him."
The Nymphæa expands its flowers in the night, and thence is feigned to be in love with the moon.

"Himmat-i-mardān hārhā dārad."

65. "Resolution overcomes great difficulties."

"Har-kirā sabr nīst hikmat nīst."

66. "He who has not patience, possesses not philosophy."

"Ki gumbad har chi goyī goyad-at bāz."

67. "Whatever you say to a dome, it says to you again."

"Kab mue kab kire pare."

68. "When he died and when the worms ate him (I know not)."

"Ab bhī merā murdah tere zinde par bhārē hai."

69. "My dead are better than your living."

397

"*Har ki dil pesh-i-dilbarē dārad,*
Rīsh dar dast-i-dīgare dārad."

No. 70. "Whoever hath given his heart to a beloved object, hath put his beard into the hands of another."

"*Bī-tāb-i-îshk har-chi kunad hakk ba dast-i-o ast.*"

71. "Whatever a man does who is afflicted with love, he must be excused for it."

"*Laili ko Majnūn ke ankhon se dekhnā.*"

72. "One must behold Laīlī with the eyes of Majnūn."

"*Dah darwesh dar kalīme bi-khuspand*
Do pādshāh dar iklīme na ganjand."

73. "Ten derveshes may sleep under the same blanket, but two kings cannot exist in one kingdom."

"*Hūr bhī saugan koden se burī.*"

74. "A contemporary wife, although a hūri, is worse than a she-devil."

"*Saut chun kī bhī burī.*"

75. "The very voice of a rival wife is intolerable."

"*Sautīyā dāh mashhūr hai.*"

76. "The malice of a rival wife is notorious."

"*Saut mūrat kī bhī burī.*"

77. "A contemporary wife is intolerable even in effigy."

"*Saut bhalī sautela burā.*"

78. "A contemporary wife may be good, but her child is bad."

"*Āsūdah kase ki buz na dārad.*"

79. "The man is happy who has no she-goat."

"*Būnd kā gharon dhal gayā.*"

80. "The house may be filled with the falling of drops."

"*Ham māl ba-dast āyad o ham mār na ranjad.*"

81. "To get possession of the wealth without disturbing the snake that guards it."

"*Saidrā chūn ājal āyad sū-e-sayyād rawad.*"

82. "When death approaches the game it goes towards the sportsman."

"Apnī guriyā sanwār-denā."

No. 83. "To dress one's own doll."

"Ghar kar ghar kar sattar balā sir dhar."

84. "He who builds a house and takes a wife, heaps seventy afflictions on his head."

"Jahān dekhe to ā barat.
Wahān gāwe sārī rāt."

85. "Where there is a marriage they may sing all night."

"Jis dūlhah tis banī barāt."

86. "The nuptial procession is proportioned to the rank of the bridegroom."

"Hamahrā yak mār gazīdah ast."

87. "One snake has bit them all."

"Rānī dīwānī hoyī oron ko patthar apnon ko laddū mār kī."

88. "The princess is grown foolish, she pelts her own relations with sweetmeats, others with stones."

"Tātorah bu hawā pāshīdah and."

89. "They have scattered datūra (thorn-apple) in the air."
i.e. The people are all gone mad.

"Man motion byāh Man chāwalon byāh.

90. "A marriage may be celebrated with a mŭn of rice, as well as with a mŭn of pearls."

"Nakāre bāj damāme bāj gaye."

100. "The sound of the nakaras and dumana has ceased."

"Misi kājil kisko Miyān chale bhasko."

101. "For whom should I stain my teeth and blacken my eyelashes? the master is turned to ashes."

"Zabān-i-khūsh mārrā az sorākh bar mī-ārad."

102. "A pleasant voice brings a snake out of a hole."

"Kharbūzāh chhurī par gire, yā chhurī kharbuze par to kharbūze
kā zarūr."

103. "Whether the melon falls on the knife, or the knife on the melon, the melon is the sufferer."
i.e. The weakest go to the wall.

"*Dhūl kī rassī batnā.*"

No. 104. "To twist a rope of sand."

"*Az bīwah kīr gadā'ī.*"

105. "To beg a husband from a widow."

"*Āthon gānth kumīt.*"

106. "Bay in all his eight joints."

"*Māmū jī juhār.*"

107. "God save you, uncle!"

"*Ek nahīn sattar balā taltī hai.*"

108. "Not one, but seventy misfortunes it keeps off."

"*Kāne kī ek rag siwā hotī hai.*"

109. "One-eyed men have a vein extra."

"*Thorā khānā aur Banāras rahnā.*"

110. "A little to eat and to live at Benares."
The wish of a pious Hindū.

"*Zabar-dast kā thengā sir par.*"

111. "The cudgel of the powerful must be obeyed."
Club law—the weakest always suffer.

"*Jiskī lāthī us kī bhains.*"

112. "He who has the stick, his is the buffalo."
To express that the most powerful is generally the most successful in all
disputes. Club law.

"*Jis ne na dekhā ho bāgh wuh dekke bilāī.*
Jis ne na dekhā ho thag wuh dekhe kasāī."

113. "He who has never seen a tiger let him look at a cat; and he who has
never seen a Thug, let him look at a butcher."

"*Zauk-i-chaman'z khātir-i-bulbul na mī-rawad.*"

114. "The desire of the garden never leaves the heart of the nightingale."

"*Ghar gūr to bāhir mamāke.*"

115. "A gooroo at home, but a beggar abroad."

"*Gharīb ko kaurī ashrafī hai.*"

116. "A kourī is a gold mohur to a pauper."

"Hazār niamat aur ek tand-rastī."
No. 117. "Health alone is equal to a thousand blessings."

"Chirāgh tale andherā."
118. "It is dark under the lamp."

"Larke ko jab bheriyā le-gayā tab tattī bāndhī."
119. "Fasten the door when the wolf was run away with the child."

"Khwāb āsāīsh-i-jān ast."
120. "Sleep is the repose of the soul."

"Agar firdause bar rū-e-zamīn ast
Hamen ast, hamen ast, hamen ast."
121. "If there be a Paradise upon earth, it is this, it is this."

"Dar-i-khānah-e khudā dāim bāz ast."
122. "The gate of the house of God is always open."

"Jitnā chhota itnā khota."
123. "Vicious as he is little."

"Tārīkī-i-shab surmah-e-chashm-i-mūsh-i-kūr ast."
124. "The darkness of the night is collyrium to the eyes of the mole."

"Sabz bar sang na-rawad chi gunah-e-bārānrā?"
125. "If grass does not grow upon stones, what fault is it in the rain?"

"Ek jorū sāre kumbe ko bas hai."
126. "One wife is enough for a whole family."

"Murdah ān ast ki nām ash ba nikūī na burand."
127. "He only is dead whose name is not mentioned with respect."

"Roz-i-tangī siyāh ast."
128. "The days of distress are black."
i.e. White and red amongst the Persians denote good.

"Shutur-ghamze karte hain."
129. "They cast camels' glances."

"Chhīnkte khāē, chhīnkte nahāe chhīnkte par ghar na jāe."
130. "After sneezing you may eat or bathe, but not go into any one's house."

> *"Astarrā guftand, pidar ast kīst? Guft asp khāl-i-man ast*
> *yā mādar-am mādiyān ast."*

No. 131. "The mule was asked 'Who is your father?' he answered, 'The horse is my maternal uncle, and the mare is my mother."

> *"Wahm kī dārū hī nahīn."*

132. "There is no physic for false ideas."

> *"Āb dar jaughan kobīdan."*

133. "To pound water in a mortar."
Labour in vain.

> *"Ām machhli bahtā ho hī rahtā hī."*

134. "Mangoes and fish meet of necessity."

> *"Murdan ba-izzat bih ki zindagānī ba-mazallat."*

135. "It is better to die with honour than live with infamy."

> *"Bhāgalpūr ke bhagliye aur Kahalgaon ke thag,*
> *Patne ke diwāliye tīnon nām-zad."*

136. "The hypocrite of Bhagulpūr, the thugs of Kuhulgaon, and the bank-rupts of Patna are famous."

> *"Zāt bhānt puchhe na koi, jatio pahan kar Bahman hoe."*

137. "No one enquires his caste or tribe, he has put on the string and is there-fore a Brahman."

> *"Rānd sānd sīrhī sanyāsī*
> *In chāron se bache Kāshī."*

138. "At Benares you should be upon your guard against the women, the sacred bulls, the stairs, and the devotees."

> *"Bel ke māre babūl tale. Babūl ke māre bel tale."*

139. "He who was hurt by the bel (its large fruit falling on his head) fled for refuge to the babūl (the prickles of which wounded his feet), and he who was hurt by the babūl, fled to the bel."

> *"Mānte to deo nahīn to bhīt kā leo."*

140. "If you believe, it is a god—if not, plaister detached from a wall."

> *"Daryā men rahnā aur magar machh se bair karnā."*

141. "To dwell in the river and be at enmity with the crocodile."

> *"Khudā shakar-khore ko shakar detā hai."*

142. "God gives sugar to him who eats sugar."
i.e. He provides for his creatures according to their wants.

"*Na burad kazz-i-narmrā tegh-i-tez.*"

No. 143. "A sharp sword will not cut raw silk."

"*Nakl-i-âish bih az âïsh.*"

144. "The narration of pleasure is better than the pleasure itself."

"*Ukhle men sir diyā to dhamkon se kyā dar.*"

145. "I have put my head into the mortar; it is useless to dread the sound of the pestle."

"*Āp kī topī par salāmat rahī.*"

146. "The blessing of heaven be upon your head."

"*Kalam īn jā rasīd o sar bi-shikast.*"

147. "The pen arrived thus far and broke its point."
i.e. It is finished.

RAM! RAM!

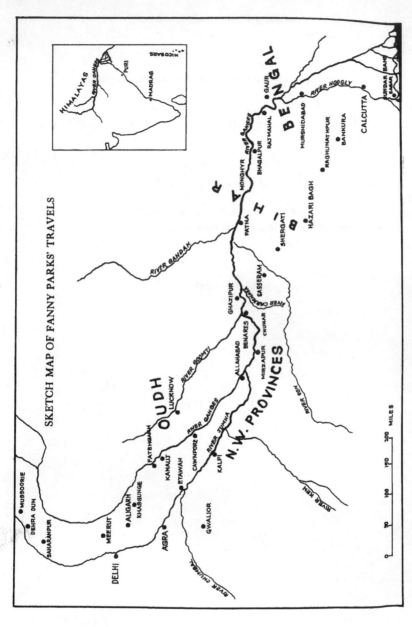

SKETCH MAP OF FANNY PARKS' TRAVELS

Source: E. Chawner (ed.) 1975, Fanny Parks, *Wanderings of a Pilgrim in Search of the Picturesque* (Oxford University Press, Karachi, Oxford in Asia Historical Reprints).

Appendix

No. I.—*Copy of the inscription in the church of Tanworth, Warwickshire*

"Heu Pietas! heu prisca Fides!"

"Sacred to the memory of Andrew Lord Archer, Baron of Umberslade, who died April 25th, 1778, ætatis forty-one, and lies interred in the family vault beneath. He was the last male descendant of an ancient and honourable family that came over with William the Conqueror, and settled in the county of Warwick in the reign of King Henry the Second, from whom his ancestors obtained grants of land in the said county. He married Sarah, the daughter of James West, Esquire, of Alscot, by whom he has left four daughters.

"To perpetuate his fair fame this monument is erected by her who knew and loved his virtues."

In the Peerage of England by Arthur Collins, Esq., vol. vii. p. 359, 4th edition, is the following account:—
"This family, one of the most ancient in Warwickshire, came out of Normandy, where some of the name, bearing the same arms, are yet existing. In Stow's Annals, printed in 1615, is a list taken from a table anciently in Battle Abbey, of those who came into England with William Duke of Normandy, in which the name of Archer is inserted; also in an ancient roll, cited by Stow, of the names of the chief noblemen, &c. who, in 1066, accompanied William the Conqueror into England, collected by Thomas Scriven, Esq., the name of Archer occurs."
Edward Gwynn, Esq., a learned antiquary in the reign of King James the First, demonstrates very clearly, that Fulbert l'Archer, with his son Robert, came into England with William the Conqueror; and that the said Fulbert was in England, and of eminent degree, is apparent, by his being witness to several concessions of Geffery de Clinton, a Norman, who was treasurer and lord chamberlain to King Henry the First, and founder of the monastery of Kenilworth in Warwickshire.
Mr. Gwynn in his dissertation further recites, that Robert l'Archer also accompanied his father Fulbert into England with William the Conqueror; and was in such estimation for his learning, that the said king appointed him to instruct

405

his son, King Henry the First (then prince), who, to his tutor's credit, was (as Gemmeticencis saith) "Justitiæ ac pacis sectator, religionis amator, iniquorum, et furum ferventissimus punitor, inimicorum suorum, non solum excellentium Principum, et Comitum, verum et nominatissimonum Regum fælicissimus Triumphator." How well he deserved the respect and esteem of the said prince, and how well he was rewarded by him, when he came to be king, the following grant fully manifests: "*Henricus, Dei Gratia, &c. Sciatis Nos dedisse et concessisse, Roberto l'Archer, magistro meo, et hæred. suis, &c. Manor de Aldermanson, Fynchampsted, Coletrope, Speresholt, Chewlewe, &c. in com. Berks.*" Which manors and lands thereunto belonging King Henry II. confirmed to William l'Archer, his son. King Henry I.'s estimation of the said Robert l'Archer, and the account he made of his service, may be conceived in vouchsafing to call him his master, also by his liberal donations to him."

No. II.—*To freeze ice cream in an English freezing pail, enough for a large party*

The freezing pail should always be of pewter,—those from England are the best. The natives make them of a composition that answers well, but it is necessary to be careful in this respect, lest, having a portion of lead in them, the ice should be rendered poisonous from the effect of the lime-juice. The lid of the freezing pail ought to be made with a catch to prevent its coming off when the pail is turned round by the hand in the bucket of ice. The freezing pail should be of pewter, because it prevents the contents of the vessel from congealing too quickly, and there is time to mix them thoroughly; for on this, in a great measure, depends the excellence of the ice: if it be made of tin, the congelation is too rapid, and the materials have not time enough to allow of their being well mixed.

When an article is iced, it does not lose its sweetness; no additional sugar or syrup is requisite; the loss of sweetness arises from the materials not being properly mixed or worked with a bamboo or spaddle when in the freezing pail. The natives do not open the freezing pail and stir the mixture with a spaddle; on the contrary, they fasten the lid down securely by putting paste all round the edges: consequently, their cream ice is as hard as real ice itself. Properly stirred it resembles hard snow, after the fashion of the Parisian ice cream.

No. III.—*Strawberry or raspberry ice cream*

Cream three-fourths, fresh milk one-fourth, five large table-spoonfuls of jam; two ditto of fresh lime-juice, one ditto of colouring mixture. If you find it not sweet enough, add a little syrup or melted sugar, not pounded sugar. Beat the cream, milk, and jam through a hair sieve, and mix them well; add the lime-juice and the colouring mixture; stir it well, and put it into the freezing pail. The pail holds about two quarts. Take a deep ice basket, lay a bazār blanket inside, place within it a clean dry bucket, put the freezing pot into the bucket.

No. IV.—*Freezing mixture*

Half *ser* *nowshādar* (sal ammoniac), one *ser* common salt, one *ser* saltpetre, with eight or ten *ser* of ice. The saltpetre and salt should be previously roughly pounded. Mix the whole of this together quickly in a blanket; put the mixture into the bucket until it is nearly up to the top and all round the freezing pail; turn the freezing pail round and round in the mixture, holding it by the handle for ten minutes, then leave it for a quarter of an hour, cover the top with ice; cover up all inside with the blanket, and put on the cover of the ice basket; do not let it stand near a *tattī*. In the course of ten minutes or a quarter of an hour, open the freezing pail, stir the cream round with a long wooden spoon, or a bit of bamboo, cut flat, or a spaddle. You will find it has congealed on the sides, but not in the centre; remove the spoon, put on the lid, turn the pail round for a short time, and cover it up again; this must be repeated until the cream is properly frozen, when it is fit for use. Should the cream not have frozen properly, the freezing mixture, if any remain over, or more ice, may be put into the bucket. In about an hour, or a little more, the cream ice will be ready. It should not be made until just before it is required for use.

Cream ices may be made with strawberry, raspberry, or any other jam in the above manner. The jam imported from France is finer and more reasonable than that sent from England.

No. V.—*To freeze two quarts of strawberry cream in a native kulfī*

The khānsāmāns make ice in a pewter vessel, called a *kulfī*; it contains a quart, and ought to have a removable lid. The bottom of the *kulfī* should be a fixture. For two *kulfīs* of this size take eight *chhattaks* of saltpetre, eight ditto salt, four ditto *nowshādar* (sal ammoniac); mix them together, having first pounded them separately. Mix these ingredients with ice sufficient to fill an earthenware pan, that with a broad mouth will hold two *kulfīs* standing erect in it. Having put your *kulfīs* in the jar, surround them with ice nearly to the rim; put the remainder of the ice into a napkin, and lay it over the top of the *kulfīs*; then cover over the whole with an earthenware cover. Open the *kulfīs* in a quarter of an hour, and stir the cream with a flat bamboo, which is a better thing than a spoon for the purpose; cover them up; open again in another quarter of an hour, stir, and leave them for four hours; no fresh ice need be added.

For one *kulfī* half the quantity of the mixture, and a smaller earthenware pan.

To keep the whole from the effect of the air and the *tattī*, it is better to place a bazār blanket in an ice-basket, then put in the earthenware pan, and having done all as above directed, cover the whole up with the blanket, and put on the cover of the ice-basket.

[. . .]

No. XI.—*To lacquer boxes*

Make your coloured wax of the best, clearest, and picked Chuppra *lakh*, only adding the colour necessary; whilst the box is on the lathe, having put a bit or two of lighted charcoal under it, turn the lathe, press the wax upon the box, the wax will come off and lacquer it; polish and smooth it with the dried leaf of the *ālū*.

No. XII.—*Karand patthar, corundum stone, or adamantine spar*

The cheapness and abundance of emery in Europe, and its being nearly equal to corundum in hardness, have, perhaps, prevented the Indian corundum from being brought home; but there appears every probability that the substance which has been lately sold at a high price in small quantities, under the name of *diamond powder*, said to be from the *diamond* mines of India, and applied to the purpose of sharpening razors and other cutlery, is nothing else than corundum reduced to a fine powder. The common *karand patthar* of India, the corundum or adamantine spar, so named from its hardness, will cut and polish all stones except the diamond. By the natives it is used with oil for removing rust from steel, after which the steel is re-polished with buffalo horn and a semicircular steel instrument.

No. XIII.—*Indian method of washing the hair*

A quarter of a *ser* of *basun*, the yolks of two large eggs (no whites), the juice of two or three limes; mix the whole in a basin with cold water, add some hot water, strain it through a towel. Rub it well into the roots of the hair, and wash it out by pouring warm water over the head, until the hair is perfectly clean. The operation is most agreeably performed in a *hummām*. In a bathing-room it is necessary to have ready prepared six *kedgerī* pots of boiling water, which can be mixed afterwards with cold. Having thoroughly dried the hair, put a small quantity of oil upon it. Use no soap. *Basun* is the pounded and sifted meal of *gram*, i.e. *chanā*.

No. XIV.—

Take seven *gelās* (seed of mimosa scandens), break and put the kernels into a *chhattak* of water for a night; pound them, and strain through muslin; add the juice of four or five limes, and the yolks of two or three eggs; wash the hair with the mixture.

No. XV.—*Ink for taking impressions off Hindūstanī seals*

Lampblack, one *paisā*, *gond*, (*i.e.* gum of the babūl, or gum Arabic,) two *chhattaks*. Having ground both, dry the whole on a plantain leaf. Mix two *paisā* of water with one of the mixture; boil, and strain it for use. If not good add one grain of salt. Lampblack made in unglazed pans is better than any other. The ink should be put on the seal with the point of the finger. It should be very black, and thick; but put on very thinly. The paper to be wetted with water on a bit of muslin, and just patted down before the seal is pressed on the spot. If the paper come off on the seal the former is not damp enough. Use thick Chinese paper, or common writing paper.

No. XVI.—*To recover the ink of faded writing*

Fill up one quarter of a pint bottle with pounded gall nuts, add spirits of wine or gin to fill the bottle. Put the letter in a plate, and cover it with the mixture; after a short time the writing will become visible.

No. XVIII.—*Treatment of cholera*

Our medical adviser said, he considered the best treatment was, "to give forty *measured* drops of laudanum in a glassful of brandy and water every time the bowels are moved, which is preferable to giving a greater quantity, as that would produce drowsiness. You give opium to abate pain and stop the sickness, not to dull the senses, which are too dull already. After the first few evacuations, all that follow are like pipeclay and water,—one of the signs of cholera."

Spirits of hartshorn in water we found very beneficial to the natives. Colonel Gardner said, "Half a wine glass of the juice of onions, rubbed up with ginger, red and black pepper, and garlic, I have seen administered in desperate cases of cholera with great success."

No. XIX.—*To prepare skeleton peepul leaves*

Put a quantity of the fresh and finest leaves of the peepul into a pan, containing two or three quarts of water. Leave the pan in some distant part of the garden until the water wastes away, and the green of the leaves is corrupt. In ten days' time take up a leaf, and if the green comes off, leaving the fibres perfect, it is time to remove the leaves; but if any of the green still adhere, replace the leaf, and let the whole remain in the dirty water for another ten days; after which take them out, wash them with pure water, and with a *soft* toothbrush gently brush off any part of the green that may still adhere to the fibres. Leave them in clean water for some days, and brush them daily, very gently, separately, and carefully, until the skeleton is quite perfect. If not of a good colour bleach them by exposure to the sun, and pour water over them now and then during the exposure.

No. XX.—*To copy drawings with talk*—i.e. talc

First make your lampblack in this manner: Put a cotton wick into an earthen saucer, such as are put under flower-pots, put common oil into the saucer, light the wick, and place over it another earthen saucer, so that the flame may blacken it; in a few hours a quantity of lampblack will collect on the upper saucer, which is of the very best sort. Mix a little of this lampblack with fine linseed oil, dip your pen into it, and trace on the *talk* with it, having first put your *talk* over the drawing you wish to copy. When you take off the *talk*, if you put white paper beneath it, you will see if any part require to be darkened: touch the distances lightly, and the foregrounds strongly. Be careful not to put too much oil with the lampblack, or it will run, and spoil the drawing. Having finished your tracing, damp a piece of China paper with a sponge, put it on the *talk* while it is *very damp*, take care not to stir it, put another piece of paper over it, and pass your hand steadily over all, when the impression will come off good and clear. Patterns for work may be copied in this manner: of course every thing is reversed. Ivory black will not answer.

No. XXI.—*To take off the impression from leaves and flowers*

Make your lampblack as above directed. Make two balls, about the size of your fist, with wool and wash-leather; put a bit of stick into the centre of each, to serve as a handle, and tie the leather tight upon it; flatten it to the shape of a printer's ball; the top of a white leather long glove will do, or chamois leather. With a spatula mix some lampblack with a little linseed oil, put it on the balls, rub both balls together until it is all smooth and even, put a freshly-gathered leaf between the balls, pat the leaf on both sides, put it between two sheets of paper, rub your finger carefully over the leaf; take up the paper, and you will have two beautiful impressions. Stalks and flowers may be done in the same way, and corrected with a pen and some of the oil and lampblack. The Chinese books sold in the *burā bazār*, Calcutta, are excellent for this purpose.

No. XXII.—*To arrange a turban*

The turban should be of fine India muslin, twenty-one yards in length, by fourteen inches and a half in breadth. Take one end, put it over your head, allowing a quarter of a yard to hang down your back; twist the muslin in front of your forehead, so that it may form a sort of skull cap on the top of your head; after which, begin to bind the turban round your head, and go on, until, in fanciful bands, you have used up the whole. Take the little end hanging down your back, turn it up, and stick it under one of the folds. This turban, when properly put on, is not at all large. Should it not set out enough, you must first bind a smaller and coarser turban around your head, and put the fine one over it. A Benares gold turban, or a Bengal muslin, spotted in gold, should be worn over a turban of this sort; they are too flimsy to set properly of their own accord. A long fine Cashmere shawl forms into a beautiful turban.

Another method.—Turbans are more generally put on in this manner than in the preceding: Take the middle of the cloth, put it over the front of the head, and pass the two ends behind. Take one end, and pass it round and round your head until it is all used up; after which take the other end, and pass it round in some different fashion; when you have used it all up it ought to set properly.

Almost all turbans are thus put on, with the exception of stiff turbans, which are made over a bamboo frame; they are formal, and want the graceful and fanciful ease of a turban formed of a strip of muslin hastily thrown around the head.

Some are formed on a light wicker frame; others, made up by regular turban makers in the bazār, are formed on blocks, and the muslin is plaited and put on in a very exact and regular style. Some turbans appear as if formed of coloured rope, so tightly do they twist the muslin into a cord ere it is wound round the head.

No. XXIII.—*The Coles, the Bheels, the Gonds, the Khonds, &c*

AN EXTRACT FROM "THE TIMES," NOV. 23, 1847

"Our readers are aware that the Hindoos are not the aboriginal inhabitants of India. Arriving from the north-west, they first occupied that moiety of the peninsula to the north of the Nerbudda called emphatically Hindostan, and subsequently crossed that river into the Deccan, or 'south' portion of the country, where they dispossessed the natives as before. There are reasons for concluding that this expulsion of the early inhabitants by the Brahminical Hindoos was characterized by great ferocity on the part of the invaders. The inferior tribes, however, were by no means exterminated. Under the various denominations of Bheels, Coles, Gonds, Khonds, &c., they still exist in the peninsula, to the number, it is computed, of at the least two or three millions. Whether they are branches of the same family or not appears hardly ascertained, but they all possess features in common, and are altogether distinct, not only from the Hindoo, but also from the Thibetan varieties of native tribes near the Himalayan range. They are small, dark, and active, with a peculiarly quick and restless eye, highly barbarous, and owning only a few importations of Hindoo superstitions or civilization. They have little clothing, few arms but bows and arrows, and no ordinary food beyond berries or game. They have no repugnance to killing or eating oxen, and bury their dead instead of burning them. Their religious rites involve much greater barbarism than the Brahminical precepts; indeed, it is alleged by the advocates of Hindoo excellence that the most objectionable practices attributed to the disciples of Brahma have either been imported from these tribes at a late period, or erroneously related by writers who confused the identity of the nations. This is said to have been particularly the case with human sacrifices, which had no place in the original code of the Vedas, while they were so inveterately established among these older tribes, that the disturbances of the present day have actually originated in the defence of the rite. The main retreat of these people from the persecution of the invaders was in the hills, which, under the names of the Vindhya and Santpoora ranges, rise on each bank of the Nerbudda, and form the barrier between the Deccan and Hindostan. At the eastern extremity these hills expand into a lofty mountain rampart on the confines of Orissa and Berar, forming, with the contiguous districts, the most barbarous and unreclaimed portion of the whole peninsula. Much of it, in fact, is unexplored to this day, as may be seen by a glance, in any map, along the western frontier of Orissa. Such are the actors, and such the scene of the present disturbances. A few words more will explain their origin and character.

"The eastern coast of India between the Delta of the Ganges and the mouths of the Kistna came into our possession by successive instalments. In 1765 the sagacity of Lord Clive demanded, and his power obtained, the cession of that maritime province known by the name of the Northern Circars, previously attached to the

Government of the Deccan, but readily and cheaply yielded by the emperor to the request of the victorious general. This carried the Madras presidency along the coast nearly up to the confines of Bengal; the sole interruptions to a continuity of English territory being the Southern Sircar of Guntoor at the lower end, still depending on the Deccan, and the province of Cuttack at the upper, claimed by the Mahratta Prince of Berar. The former, after considerable turmoil on both sides, was surrendered by Nizam Ali in 1788, and the latter by Bhonslay at the end of the first great Mahratta war of 1803. The contiguous districts, forming part of the ceded territories, were restored by the policy of Sir G. Barlow, and did not finally return to us till the conclusion of the war of 1818, when the inveterate hostility of Apa Saheb was punished by the demand of these peculiar territories on the Nerbudda, solely valuable as opening a communication between Bengal and Bombay. We found the eastern country in the hands of petty Rajahs of ancient standing, and some consideration amongst their subjects, though they were not of the aboriginal race, but individual families (apparently Rajpoots) of the invading nation who had contrived to establish themselves in hereditary power amongst the savages. As long as we were content to allow these people their ancient licence, to accept a small uncertain subsidy by way of rent, and leave them to their own privileges and habits, things went well enough; but as soon as the more scrupulous civilization of later times introduced or attempted reforms, disturbances at once ensued. A settlement of a fixed, though not extortionate, rent was imposed upon the Rajahs, and when this fell seriously in arrear they were dispossessed. Police were introduced in some of the villages, and civil courts established. The consequences were speedily visible. In 1816 the Goomsoor people rose in arms to demand an ejected Rajah; and though a force of 3000 men in the country repressed these outbreaks, yet they could not be prevented from aiding a similar insurrection in Cuttack immediately afterwards, nor was peace entirely restored for three long years, and then only after some conciliatory abolitions of the obnoxious institutions.

"In the present case the rebellion (in Goomsoor) is based on our interference with their Meriah sacrifices, in observance of which rite they store, fatten, butcher, and dissect some hundreds of children annually, distributing the fragments, as a propitiatory offer to the local Ceres, over the surface of their fields, and the old cry for their indulgent Rajahs is again raised. The Khonds—the precise tribe who gave us so much trouble in 1816—are again the chief insurgents, though common cause is eagerly made by all their neighbours. Their method of fighting is to lurk in their tangled thickets and shoot their arrows from the ambuscade. Recently, too, they exchanged a herd of bullocks which they captured, for some firearms, and they are said now to possess some 700 or 800 matchlocks. This, of course, does not make them less noxious, but their offensive warfare forms but a small part of the dangers of the campaign. The tracts about which they roam are, beyond all comparison, the most pestilential in India. The air of Shikarpoor is bracing and salubrious compared with the atmosphere of these territories. The malaria of their jungles is almost certain death, and a bivouac in the bush will cause far more havoc in an invading force than a battery of cannon. In addition to this, beasts of prey swarm in every cave and forest, numerous and ravenous enough to give a clean account of all stragglers. The ordinary briefness of an Indian campaign is here so far circumscribed, that there are very few weeks in the year when an inroad would even be attempted, and at this moment not 200 men of the regiment employed there are fit for duty.

"The Khonds are in nowise disaffected to us, nationally. On the contrary, when Sir G. Barlow surrendered their country again to Berao, against our compact and their entreaties, he was forced in decency to offer a home in Cuttack to those who chose still to live under English rule, and the struggle between the latter wish and the reluctance to quit their birthplaces produced some very tragical scenes. Towards the west, too, the Bheels are enrolled in local corps in the Company's service, and conduct themselves with very great credit. The only rebellion is that of a hardy, barbarous, and inaccessible race, against masters whose supremacy they gladly own, but whose civilization they are averse to borrowing."

No. XXIV.—*Bengal coins*

$$
\begin{aligned}
4 \text{ kauris} &= 1 \text{ gunda.} \\
20 \text{ gundas} &= 1 \text{ pun.} \\
4 \text{ puns} &= 1 \text{ ānā.} \\
4 \text{ ānās} &= 1 \text{ kāhan, 1280 kauris, or about one} \\
&\quad\text{quarter of a rupī.}
\end{aligned}
$$

Kauris, small white glossy shells, are made use of for small payments in the bazār. They rise and fall according to the demand there is for them, and the quantity in the market.

Accounts are kept in rupīs, with their subdivisions.

$$
\begin{aligned}
3 \text{ pie} &= 1 \text{ pāisa.} \\
4 \text{ pāisa} &= 1 \text{ ānā.} \\
16 \text{ ānās} &= 1 \text{ rupī.} \\
16 \text{ rupīs} &= 1 \text{ gold muhr.} \\
100,000 \quad '' &= 1 \text{ lākh.} \\
100 \text{ lākh} &= 1 \text{ karor, or } 100,000,000 \text{ rupīs.}
\end{aligned}
$$

No. XXV.—*Easy method of preserving small birds*

Birds to the size of a pigeon may be preserved from putrefaction by an easy process, and by a method which will effectually guard them against the attacks of insects. Carefully remove the abdominal viscera at the vent, by means of a wire bent to a hook at one end; then introduce a small piece of the antiseptic paste, and afterwards as much clipped cotton or tow as may be thought sufficient, with some of the paste mixed with it; remove the eyes and fill the orbits with cotton imbued with the paste; draw out the tongue, which remove, and pass a wire from the mouth into the cavity of the cranium, merely to give the antiseptic access to the brain; bind a piece of thread round the rostrum, another piece round the body and wings; then hand it up by the legs, and pour in at the vent from half an ounce to two ounces, according to the size of the bird, of alcohol; let it be hung in an airy situation, and it will soon dry without any unpleasant smell.

No. XXVI.—*Antiseptic paste*

Antiseptic paste is made by mixing eight parts of finely-powdered white arsenic, four parts of Spanish soap, three parts of camphor pulverized in a mortar, with a few drops of alcohol, and one part of soft soap. If it become too dry add a little spirits of wine.

No. XXVII.—*Arsenical soap*

Powdered arsenic one pound, white Marseilles soap one pound, powdered camphor three ounces; fine lime, in powder, three ounces; salt of tartar, six ounces; keep it corked in a jar. Melt the soap, and gradually mix the other ingredients. When required to be used, take a little out, mix it with water until it is of the consistence of thick cream; spread on the skin thinly with a brush. By using too much you render the skin brittle—put a little cotton wool on the part when done. Useful for the skins of quadrupeds, large birds, and also for insects, moths, and butterflies.

No. XXVIII.—*Dye for the moustache*

Mix one *ser* of large *hurs* (*hura*, ink-nut, myrobalan chebulic) with half a *pāisa* weight of *ghī*, fry them until they are quite black and split, take them out and cover them over with red-hot charcoal ashes at night. Wipe them clean, and separate the pulp, which reduce to a subtile powder in an iron mortar; add to every *tolā* of the above powder three-fourths of a *masha of tūtiyā tā'ūsi*, and half a *masha* of salt.

When you wish to dye your hair, take some of the powder, mix it with water so as to form an unctuous paste, and grind it very fine in an *iron* mortar; apply it to the hair, and tie it up with fresh-gathered castor oil leaves. Should the hair not be dyed as required, wet the hair with water, as also the leaves, and tie it up again, as the dye will not have the desired effect if the hair be not kept moist with it. The mortar must be of iron, or the mixture will be spoiled.

Eight *rattīs* (seed of abrus precatorius) make one *māsha*, twelve and a half *māshas* one *tolā* or *sicca rupī* weight.

No. XXIX.—*To dye the beard and moustache*

Boil four or five *anolas* (myrobalan emblic, Lin.) for a short time in water, till they impart their colour to it. Grind up indigo leaves (*busmuh*) on a *sil* (a rough slab of stone, with a stone roller), with the above decoction, and use the preparation as a dye, after having exposed it to the sun for a short time. This receipt was given me by Seyd Husain, an old *peshkār* at Prāg.

No. XXX.—*Perfumed tobacco cakes*

Tobacco, one *mŭn*; *gurh* (thick sugar), one *mŭn*; *gulkand* (*gūlabī*) conserve of roses, ten *sers*; *gulkand* (*séo*), five *sers*; *paurī*, three *tolās*; musk, one *tolā*; amber, one ditto; *ugur, pāo bur*, i.e. a quarter of a *tolā*; *tugger*, one quarter of a *tolā*.

The tobacco and *gour* to be mixed, and left in a *gharā* for five days, the other ingredients to be then added, and the whole buried for ten days before use. One of the cakes is sufficient for a quart bottle of rosewater, into which it is to be broken; and in this state of solution it is sufficient to impregnate with its flavour a *mŭn* of tobacco. This receipt was procured from one of the attendants on her Highness the Bāiza Bā'ī.

[. . .]

Glossary

Additional definitions are drawn from the glossary provided by Fanny Parkes or from Henry Yule and A. C. Burnell, *Hobson-Jobson: The Anglo-Indian Dictionary* (1886; Ware: Wordsworth Editions, 1996).

A.

Āb, water. *Ābdār*, water-cooler.
Abīr, red powder used in the Holī.
Ābnūs, ebony.
Achchhā, good.
Ādāb, salutation, respects, politeness.
Adālut, court of justice.
Ādam-khor, a cannibal.
Afgan, overthrowing.
Afghān, the name of a race of people who inhabit the country to the northwest of Lahore; called also *Pathans*. They are supposed to be of Jewish extraction.
Afīm, or *aphīm*, opium.
Agārī pichhārī, the ropes with which horses are tied.
Agast, æschinomene grandiflora.
Āghā, lord master.
Aghan, the eighth Hindū solar month.
Aghorī, professing *ughorpanth*, an order of religious mendicants, who eat every thing, however filthy, even human carcases; hence, a gross or filthy feeder.
Ā'ina, a mirror.
Akās, the sky, the firmament.
Ākās-bel, the air-creeper; it has no root nor leaves, but grows on the tops of trees.
Ākās-diya, a lamp which the Hindūs hang aloft on a bamboo in the month *Kārtik*.
Akbar, very good, greatest.
Akbarābādī, of Akbar.

'Alam, a spear, a standard.
'Alam-dār, standard-bearer (*Abbās*).
'Alam-gīr, conqueror of the universe.
Allāh, God. *Allāhuakbar*, God is great!
Ām, mango (mangifera Indica).
Amarī, a seat with a canopy to ride in on an elephant.
Ānā, a copper coin, the sixteenth part of a rupī.
Anannās, pine-apple.
Āndhī, storm tempest.
Angethī, chafing-dish, brazier.
Angiya, a native boddice.
Ankus, the elephant goad.
Arghā, a vessel shaped like a boat, used by the Hindūs for making libations in their devotions.
Ārsī, a mirror, particularly a mirror in a thumb-ring.
Āsan, a seat or small carpet.
Asārh, the third Hindū solar month (June and July).
Aswina, the first month of the Hindū lunar year.
Ātashbāzī, fireworks.
Ātāsh-khwar, fire-eater; name of a bird, the *chakor*.
Atr, perfume. *Atr-dam*, perfume-box.
Avatār, a descent.
Ayb, or *aib*, spot, mark, defect.
Ayha, a lady's maid.
Azan, the summons to prayers, generally proclaimed from the minars or towers of a mosque.

B.

Baba, child.
Baboo, a Hindū gentleman, a Calcutta merchant.
Babūl, mimosa Arabica.
Badrī-nāth, a celebrated place of pilgrimage.
Badshah, or *pādshāh*, a king.
Bāgh, a tiger.
Bāgh, a garden.
Bāgh-sira, gryllus monstrosus.
Bāghīchar, a small garden.
'Baghnā, an ornament made of tigers' claws.
Bahādur, champion, boaster.
Bahangī, a stick with ropes hanging to each end, for slinging baggage to, which is carried on the shoulder.
Bahut, much, most.
Bahut bahut adab salam, most respectful obeisance.
Bā'ī, mistress, lady amongst the Mahrattas.
Bailī, bullock carriage.
Bairāgī, a fakīr.
Bājrā, panicum spicatum.
Bakāyan, melia sempervirens.
Bakhshish, a gift; *bakhshnā*, to give.
Bakrā, he-goat.
Bandar, a monkey.
Bandh, an embankment.
Banglā, a thatched house.
Baniya, shop-keeper.
Bāns, the bamboo.
Bā'olī, a large well.
Barā, great.
Bara-dīn, a holiday.
Bāra-singha, twelve-horned stag (cervus elaphus).
Barāt, marriage procession.
Bardār, a bearer.
Barha'ī, a carpenter.
Bārī, a garden house.
Barkandāz, a native policeman.
Basantī, yellow, the favourite colour of Krishna.
Bastī, a village.
Bater, quail.
Batū'ā, a small bag.
Baunā, a dwarf.
Bāwarchī, cook.
Bayā, loxia Indica.
Bāzār, market.
Bāzūbands, armlets.
Begam, a Muslim lady.
Bel, ægle marmelos (cratæva religiosa).

Belā, jasminum zambac.
Bengālī, a native of Bengal.
Bér, or *bar*, ficus Indica.
Besan, flour or meal of pulse, particularly of *chanā* (cicer arietinum).
Betī, daughter.
Bhabhūt, ashes which the fakīrs use.
Bhagat, a devotee of a religious order, peculiar to the low tribes, whose initiation consists in putting a necklace of beads around the neck, and marking a circle on the forehead; after which the initiated person is bound to refrain from spirituous liquors, flesh, &c.
Bhāgulpūr, the town of.
Bhagwān, the Deity, the Supreme Being, fortunate.
Bhains, buffalo.
Bhaiyā, brother.
Bhang, or *bhengh*, cannabis Indica.
Bhātā, an extra allowance to troops on service.
Bhū'a, a father's sister.
Bhūsā, chopped straw.
Bichchhū, the scorpion.
Bidrī, a kind of *tutanag*, inlaid with silver, used to make *hukka* bottoms, cups, &c.
Bīghā, a quantity of land, containing 20 *katthās*, or 120 feet square, or 1600 square yards, which is nearly one-third of an English acre; in the Upper Provinces it is nearly five-eighths of an acre.
Bihisht, paradise.
Bihisht-ī, a water-carrier.
Bilva, or *bilwa*, cratæva marmelos (Linn.).
Binaulā, seed of the cotton tree.
Biskhopra, lacerta iguana.
Bismillāh, in the name of God.
Boxwālā, an itinerant merchant with a box of goods.
Brahm, or *Brŭmhŭ*, the one eternal God.
Brahma, the first person of the Hindū trinity.
Brahman, an Hindū priest.
Brahmand, the mundane egg of the Hindūs.
Brindāban, the forest of *Brindā*, in the vicinity of *Mathurā*, celebrated as the scene of Krishna's sports with the Gopīs.
Budgerow, a barge, often used while travelling on the Ganges.
Burāk, Muhammad's steed.
Burhiyā, old woman.
Burj, a bastion, tower; *burūj*, pl.

Burjī, a turret, a small tower.
Burka, a dress, a disguise.

C.

Chabenī, parched grain.
Chābuk, a whip.
Chabūtāra, a terrace to sit and converse on.
Chādir, Chādar, mantle, garment.
Chakkī, a mill-stone.
Chakor, partridge (perdix chukar).
Chakwā, Brāhmanical duck.
Chakwī, the female of the *chakwā*.
Chamār, currier, shoemaker.
Champā kalī, a necklace.
Chanā, gram (cicer arietinum).
Chānd, the moon.
Chandnī-chauk, a wide and public street or market.
Chandnī kā mār-janā, a disease in horses, supposed to proceed from a stroke of the moon. "The moonlight has fallen on him," is said especially of a horse that is weak in the loins.
Chāotree, or *chauthī*, a marriage ceremony, the fourth day.
Chapātī, a thin cake of unleavened bread.
Chaprāsī, a messenger or servant wearing a *chaprās*, badge.
Chār, four.
Charkhī, a spinning-wheel, &c.
Chārpāī, bed, four-legged.
Chatā'ī, mat.
Chatr, umbrella.
Chauk, market.
Chaukīdār, watchman.
Chaunrī, fly-flapper.
Chhach hūndar, musk-rat.
Chhallā, thumb or great toe ring.
Chhappar, a thatched roof.
Chhat, roof.
Chhattak, about an ounce.
Chilamchī, washhand basin.
Chirāgh, lamp.
Chirāgh-dān, stand for lamps.
Chiri-mār, bird-catcher.
Chītā, hunting leopard.
Chītthī, note.
Chob-dār, mace-bearer.
Chor, or *cho'ār*, thief.
Chūlee, a fire-place.
Chūnā, lime.
Chūrī, bracelets.
Chŭrŭk-pūja, a festival.

Chyūnta, black ant.
Compound, ground around a house.
Conch, a shell.
Corook. See *Kurk*.

D.

Dabāo, pressure.
Daftarī, the paper-ruler, penmaker, &c.
Dāk, post, post-office; transport by means of relays of porters.
Dakait, or *dākū*, a robber.
Daldal, bog, quagmire.
Dālī, basket of fruit.
Damrī, a coin, four to a *paisā*.
Dānd, oar.
Dāndī, boatman.
Darbār, hall of audience.
Dārogha, head man of an office, inspector.
Darwāza, a door; *darwān*, doordeeper.
Daryā-i, or *daryā*, the sea, river.
Darzī, a tailor.
Dastkhatt, signature.
Dastur, custom.
Dastūrī, perquisites paid to servants by one who sells to their master.
Daulut-khana, house of fortune.
Derā, a dwelling, a tent.
Devī, a goddess.
Dewālai, dewāl, or *dewālaya*, temple of idols.
Dewālī, an Hindū festival, celebrated on the day of the new moon of *Kārtik*; when the Hindūs, after bathing in the Ganges, perform a *shraddhā*, and at night worship Lakshmī; the houses and streets are illuminated all night; and in Hindostan the night is universally spent in gaming.
Dhān, rice before it is separated from the husks.
Dhanuk, a bow, a bowman.
Dhobī, washerman.
Dhotī, a cloth, passed round the waist, passing between the limbs, and fastening behind.
Dighi, a large tank or reservoir, in the form of an oblong square.
Dil, heart; *dil-kushā*, heart-expanding.
Dillī, or *Dihlī*, the metropolis of Hindūstan; generally called by Musalmāns Shah-jehan-abad, and by Europeans Delhi.
Dinghee, a small boat.
Dïwak, white ant.

Dīwan-i-am, public hall of audience.
Dīwān-i-khās, privy-council chamber.
Dogh, buttermilk.
Dohā'ī, or *duhā'ī*, mercy.
Dolī, a kind of sedan for women.
Domra, the name of a caste of Musalmāns, the males of which are musicians, and the females sing and dance in the company of females only.
Donī, a native vessel or boat.
Do-patta, or *du-patta*, a sheet of two breadths.
Do-shala, or *du-shāla*, two and shawl, two shawls being always worn together by the natives.
Dosūtā, two-threaded cloth.
Dūb, name of a grass (agrostis linearis).
Dūdhiyā, milky.
Duldul, a hedgehog; the name of the horse of 'Ali, the prophet's son-in-law.
Dūlhā, or *dūlha*, bridegroom.
Dulhān, bride.
Dumba, a kind of sheep with a thick tail.
Durbar, a court or levee.
Durga, one of the names of Bhawānī, the goddess Durgā.
Durga-pūja, the festival in honour of Durgā.
Durgah, a tomb, a shrine.

E.

Eed, a festival, a solemnity.

F.

Fajr, morning; *barī-fajr*, early dawn.
Fakhr, glory, nobility.
Fakīr, a religious mendicant.
Falīta, fusee; *falīta-dār*, a matchlock.
Fānūs, a shade to keep the wind from a candle.
Fath, victory.
Fātịma, the daughter of the prophet, and the wife of the caliph 'Ali.
Fidwī, devoted (your devoted servant).
Fīl, elephant.
Fīl-khāna, elephant shed.
Fīl-pāī, elephantiasis.

G.

Gaddī, sovereign's throne.
Gāgrī, a water-vessel of brass.

Gainā, a species of small bullock.
Gaini, a carriage for a *gainā*.
Galahi, forecastle.
Gal'haiya, boatswain, forecastle-man.
Gālī, abuse.
Gāndar, a kind of grass, of which *khaskhas* is the root (andropogon muricatum).
Ganjha, or *gānja*, the young buds on the leaves of the hemp-plant.
Garh, a fort, as *fatīh-garh*.
Gari, a cart, a carriage.
Garī-wan, carter, driver.
Gaur, an ancient city, formerly the capital of Bengal.
Ghantā, a clock.
Ghar, a house.
Gharā, an earthen waterpot.
Gharāmī, a thatcher.
Gharī, an instrument for measuring time, a water-clock.
Gharis, division of time.
Ghariyāl, a crocodile, a plate of brass for beating time.
Ghariyali, the person who attends the *gharī*, and strikes the hours.
Gharnā'ī, a raft supported by empty pots (*gharā*, an earthen waterpot).
Ghāt, landing place on a river, with steps leading down to the water.
Ghī, clarified butter.
Ghirgut, or *girgut*, lizard, chameleon.
Ghulām, slave.
Ghunghrū, a small bell, or little bells on a string for the ankles.
Ghur, or *ghorā*, a horse.
Ghur-daur, race-course.
Ghuwā, a coarse kind of cotton cloth.
Go-mukhī, a cloth bag, containing a rosary, the hand being thrust in counts the beads; the chasm in the Himalaya mountains, through which the Ganges issues.
Gobar, cow-dung.
Gola, a granary.
Gop, a cow, a caste.
Gopī, feminine of *gwālā*, a cowherd.
Gor-istān, burying-ground.
Gosā'īn, a holy man.
Gram, grain or pulse.
Gul-āb, rose-water.
Gul-badan, a kind of silk cloth.
Gulistān, rose garden.
Gun, track rope.
Gunga, the Ganges.

Gūnth, a pony.
Gurū, spiritual director.

H.

Hājī, pilgrim.
Hajjām, a barber.
Hakīm, a physician, a learned man.
Hakrī, a cart.
Hammām, a hot bath.
Hān, yes.
Hāndī, a pot, a small cauldron.
Hār, a necklace of pearls, a wreath, a chaplet of flowers.
Hargilla, the adjutant, or gigantic crane.
Harkāra, running footman.
Harphārewrī, or *harpharaurī*, the name of a sour fruit (averrhoa acida, Linn.).
Hāth, the hand, a cubit, or eighteen inches.
Hāthī, an elephant.
Hathī-wān, elephant-driver.
Hawāldār, a native military officer of inferior rank.
Hāzim, digestive.
Hāzir, present.
Hāzirī, breakfast.
Hazrat, a title addressed to the great; majesty; highness.
Hazrat'īsā, Jesus Christ.
Hinnā, the tree lawsonia inermis; a reddish dye used as a cosmetic.
Hirdāwal, the name of a defect in horses.
Hisāb, accounts, computation.
Howā, air.
Howdah, a seat to ride in on an elephant, without a canopy.
Hubāb, a bubble.
Hubāb-i, bubbling.
Hukāk, stone-cutter, lapidary.
Hukka, or *hooqŭ*, a pipe.
Hukka-bardar, pipe-bearer.
Hukm, order.
Huzūr, the presence.

I. J.

Jādū, enchantment.
Jadū-garī, magic.
Jafari, lattice-work.
Jāgīr, land given as a reward for service.
Jahānārā, world adorning.
Jahān-gīr, world-taking.
Jahān-pannāh, world protection, his majesty, your majesty.

Jahannam, the infernal regions.
Jahaz, a ship.
Jahāzi, a sailor.
Jai, or *jaya*, triumph, victory, bravo! huzza! all hail!
Ja'ī, oats.
Jamadār, head of the *harkāras*.
Jān, life, soul, spirit.
Janao, Brāhmanical thread.
Jangal, forest.
Janglī-kawwa, a raven.
Janwār, an animal.
Jawāb, an answer.
-Jee, suffix denoting respect.
Jhaīhar, cymbals or bells for the ankles.
Jhāmā, pumice-stone, bricks burnt to a cinder.
Jhāmp, a matted shutter.
Jhārū, a broom.
Jhārū-bardar, a sweeper.
Jinn-ī, genii.
Ikbal, good fortune.
Imām, a leader in religious affairs.
Indra, the Hindū heaven.
Joār, or *jwār*, millet (andropogon sorghum).
Ishk-peshā, ipomea quamoclit.
Islām, the religion of Muhammad.
Istrī, a smoothing iron, a wife.
Jum'a, Friday.
Jum'a-rāt, Thursday, eve of Friday.
Izār-bund, the string with which trowsers are tied.

K.

Ka'ba, the temple of Mecca.
Kabr, a grave, a tomb.
Kabūl or *ḳubūl*, consent, assent.
Kābul, the capital of Afghanistān.
Kacharī, or *kacherī*, court of justice, an office.
Kachchhī, a horse with a hollow back, from the province of Kachchh, on the banks of the Sind.
Kachnār, bauhinia variegata.
Kadam, a footstep.
Kadam-bos, one who kisses the feet of a superior.
Kadam-chūmnā, to kiss the feet, to bid adieu.
Kāfir, infidel.
Kāfūr, camphor.
Kāghaz, paper.
Kāghazī, paper-case.
Kāhan, an aggregate number, consisting of

17 *pans*, or 1280 *kaurīs*.
Kahār, a palkī bearer.
Kahwa, coffee.
Kālā, black.
Kālā chor, an unknown person, a domestic thief.
Kālā namak, a kind of rock salt, impregnated with bitumen and sulphur.
Kālā pānī, the ocean, the black water.
Kālā zīra, the seeds of the nigella Indica.
Kalam, a pen, a reed.
Kalam-dan, inkstand.
Kalghī, an ornament on a turban, an aigrette, a plume.
Kālī, the goddess; or, *Kali Ma*, the black mother.
Kalsā, the spire or ornament on the top of a dome, a pinnacle.
Kam-bakht, unfortunate.
Kam de'o, the god of love.
Kamān, a bow.
Kamān-dār, an archer.
Kamar-band, a girdle.
Kammal, a blanket.
Kanāt, canvas enclosure, walls of a tent.
Kanauj, the ancient city.
Kangan, an ornament worn on the wrists of Hindū women, a bracelet.
Kangni, millet (panicum Italicum).
Kanhaiyā, a name of *Krishna*.
Kans, or *Kansa*, the tyrant whom *Krishna* was born to destroy.
Kapās, cotton undressed, the cotton plant (gossypium herbaceum).
Kaprā, cloth.
Karbalā, the name of a place in Irāk, where Husain, the son of 'Ali, was murdered.
Karbī, the stalk or straw of *jo'ār* or *bājrā* (holcus sorgum and spicatus).
Kār-khāna, workshop.
Kark-nath, a fool with black bones.
Karn-phūl, a kind of ear-ring.
Karor, ten millions.
Kārtik, a Hindū month, our October and November.
Karwā-tel, oil made from mustard-seed. bitter oil.
Kās, a kind of grass of which rope is made (saccharum spontaneum).
Kasā'ī, a butcher, cruel, hard-hearted.
Kāshī, the city of Benares.
Kāsid, courier, a runner.
Kath, an astringent vegetable extract.
Katmiram, (vulgo: *catamaran*,) a very small

raft, used as a fishing boat on the coast of Madras.
Kaurī, a cowrie, a small shell used as a coin (cypræa moneta).
Kāwar, the baskets in which the holy water is carried.
Kawwā, a crow.
Kāzi, a judge.
Khāla, mother's sister.
Khalāsī, a sailor, a native artilleryman, a tent pitcher.
Khān, a lord, a title of respect.
Khāna, a house.
Khānā, food.
Khānā-pīnā, meat and drink.
Khānsāmān, head table-servant.
Kharītā, bag, a letter.
Khas-khas, root of *gāndar*.—See *Gāndar*.
Khatrī, the second of the four grand Hindū castes, being that of the military.
Kazānchī, treasurer.
Khet, a field.
Khidmatgar, table-servant.
Khil'at, dress of honour.
Khīsā, a rubber used in baths.
Khraunchī, a native carriage.
Khudā, God.
Khudā-wand, master.
Khudā-yā, O God!
Khūnd, a well, a spring.
Khush-bo, perfume, odour.
Khusrū, the king; *Khusrau*, the sultan.
Kibla-gāh, the place turned to when at prayer; a father, or the one beloved.
Kibla, Mecca, an altar.
Kimkhwab, silk brocade worked in gold and silver flowers.
Kishan, the Hindū god *Krishna*.
Kishtī, (prop. *kashtī*), a ship, boat, barque.
Kismat, fate, destiny.
Kitāb, a book.
Kohī, mountain.
Kohī-nūr, the mountain of light, the great diamond.
Kohirawān, the moving mountain, *i.e.* the elephant.
Kot, a fort.
Kotwal, police officer.
Krānī, a clerk.
Krishna, a descent of *Vishnū*.
Kū'ā, a well.
Kudalī, a small pickaxe.
Kulfī, a cup with a cover, in which ice is moulded.

Kulsa, ornament on the top of a dome, particularly a sati mound.
Kumbhīr, an alligator.
Kumhār, potter.
Kum'hir, a crocodile.
Kur'ān, (vulgo: *koran*,) the precepts of Muhammad.
Kurand, corundum stone (adamantine spar).
Kurk, an order made public, that no one may be seen on the road on pain of death.
Kurtā, a kind of shirt, a tunic.
Kurtī, a short garment for women, jacket for soldiers, coat.
Kusūr, fault.
Kutb, the polar star, the north pole.
Kuttā, a dog.
Kutwāl, native magistrate, head of the police.

L.

Lachhman, the half-brother of Rāmachandra.
Lachhmī, the goddess of beauty.
Lailī, also *Lailā*, the beloved of Majnūn.
Lākh, one hundred thousand; *gum lac*, a kind of wax formed by the coccus lacca.
Lāt, or *lāth*, obelisk, pillar, club, staff.
Lāthī, staff, stick.
Lāw, a rope, cable.
Līchī, a fruit (dimocarpus litchi).
Līl, indigo.
Log, people.
Lon, salt.
Lota, a drinking vessel.
Lubāda, or *labāda*, a wrapper, great coat.
Lugao, to lay a boat alongside the shore or wharf.
Lūnī, the salt that effloresces from walls.
Lunj, or *langrā*, lame.

M.

Mā, mother.
Ma-bāp, mother and father, parents.
Machh, or *Machchh*, the name of the first avatār.
Machchhar, a gnat.
Machhlī, or *Machhī*, a fish.
Madrasa, a Muhammadan college.
Magar, an alligator.
Magrela, a seed (nigella Indica).

Mahā-bhārat, the great war.
Mahādēo, or *Mahā-deva*, a descent of Shiva.
Mahā-kalī, or *Kalī-mā*, a terrific form of Durgā, the consort of Shiva.
Māhā-nimba, melia sempervirens.
Mahā-rāj, great king, excellency.
Mahā-rājā, an Hindū emperor.
Mahal, house.
Mahāwat, elephant driver.
Mahū'ā, or *mahu'ā*, bassia longifolia, bearing flowers which are sweet, and from which a spirituous liquor is distilled; the nuts afford an oil used instead of butter.
Maidān, a plain.
Makka, vulgo: *Mecca*.
Makrī, a spider.
Mālā, Hindū rosary, a garland.
Mālī, gardener, florist.
Mālik, lord, master.
Mandap, or *mandul*, a house, a temple.
Mangūs, or *newalā* (viverra mungo), ichneumon.
Mānjhī, master of a vessel, steersman.
Masālah, spices, drugs, materials.
Mash'al, a torch.
Mash'al-chi, torch-bearer.
Mashk, water bag.
Masīh, or *Masīhā*, the Messiah, Christ our Lord.
Masjid, mosque.
Masjid-i-jāmī, a great mosque.
Masnad, a throne, a large cushion.
Māyā, idealism, illusion; a deception depending on the power of the Deity, whereby mankind believe in the existence of external objects, which are in fact nothing but idea.
Melā, a fair.
Mem sāhiba, madam, the lady of the house.
Menhdī, lawsonia inermis; *menhdi*, the plant whose leaves afford the henna used for dyeing.
Mihtaranī, sweeper's wife.
Mik'hal, the instrument with which collyrium is applied to the eyes.
Minar, turret.
Mirg, a deer.
Mirg nābbī, musk, a bag of musk.
Mirzā, a prince.
Misī, or *missī*, a powder to tinge the teeth black.
Misrāb, a steel frame for the fore-finger when playing on the sitar.

Motī, a pearl.
Muazzin, the call to prayers.
Mufassal, the country.
Mugdar, a club.
Muhammad, the Arabian prophet.
Muharram, the first Muhammadan month.
Mulākāt, interview.
Mulk, kingdom, realm.
Mumtāz, distinguished, exalted.
Mūn, a weight, forty ser.
Mund-māl, a necklace of human heads.
Munh, mouth.
Muniyā, amadavat.
Munkir, Nakīr, the names of the two angels who examine the dead in the tomb.
Murabbā, a preserve, confection.
Musāfir, a traveller.
Musāhib, aide-de-camp, companion.
Musallā, a carpet to pray upon.
Musalmān, a Muhammadan.
Musalmanī, fem. of *Musalmān*.
Mushk, musk.
Mut'h, Hindū temple.

N.

Nāch, an Indian dance.
Nadī, or *naddī*, a river.
Nadir-shāh, the king.
Nā'echa, a small reed *hukka* snake.
Nāgā, the holy serpent.
Nahīn, or *nā'īch*, not, no.
Nālā, a rivulet.
Nālkī, a sort of litter used by people of rank.
Nānd, a large earthen pan.
Nārangī, an orange.
Nārjīl, cocoa-nut, or cocoa-nut tree.
Nasīb, fortune; *balā-nasīb*, unfortunate.
Nawab, vulg. Nabob; a Muslim prince or landowner.
Nazr, a gift especially offered to a superior.
Newala, mungoose (viverra mungo).
Newār, tape.
N'hut, a nose-ring.
Nīl-gāw, lil-gā'ī, or *rojh*, the white-footed antelope of Pennant, antilope picta of Pallos.
Nīm, or *neemb*, margosa tree (melia azadirachta).
Nīmbu, or *līmu*, a fruit, the lime.
Nūn, *non*, or *lon*, salt.
Nūr, light.
Nut-log, tumblers.

P.

Pābos, kissing the feet.
Pachāsī, a game, so named form the highest throw, which is twenty-five.
Padshāh, a king.
Pāgal, fool; *pāgal-i-nāch*, a fancy-ball.
Pahār, a mountain.
Pahar, a watch of three hours.
Pahare-wālā, a sentry.
Pahār-i, a hill, a mountain.
Pā'ī, the fourth part of an *ānā*.
Paisā, copper coin.
Pājāma, trowsers, long drawers.
Pakkā, real, exact, expert, built of brick.
Palang, couch, cot.
Palīta, match (of a gun).
Pālkī, or *palkee*, a palanquin.
Palwār, a boat.
Pān, leaves of piper betel.
Panchāyāt, a court of inquiry.
Pānī, water.
Pankhā, a fan.
Pā-posh, slipper.
Pāras-patthar, the philosopher's stone.
Parbatī, pārvatī, mountaineer.
Parbut, mountain.
Parda, seclusion of women.
Parda-nishīn, remaining behind the curtain.
Parī, fairy.
Pāt, a leaf, ornament worn in the upper part of the ear.
Pātā, a plank on which washermen beat clothes.
Pātāl, the infernal regions.
Patelā, or *patailā*, a flat-bottomed boat.
Patelī, a small flat-bottomed boat.
Pāthur, or *patthar*, a stone.
Pattar, puttī, or *pattī*, a leaf.
Pattū, a kind of woollen cloth.
Pera, a sweetmeat.
Peshkār, minister, deputy.
Peshwā, Mahratta minister.
Peshwāz, a gown.
Phāns, a bamboo.
Phānsī-gār, a strangler, a *Thag*.
Phānsnā, to noose.
Phurr, the noise of a bird, as a partridge or quail, suddenly taking wing.
Phuslānā, to decoy.
Phuslā'ū, wheedling.
Pīlī-bhīt, the name of a town in Rohilkhand, famous for the smallness and fineness of its rice.

Glossary

Pinnace, a yacht.
Pīpal, ficus religiosa.
Pīr, a saint.
Pitārā, a basket.
Piyāla, a glass, a cup.
Pooja, religious worship.
Prāg, the ancient name of Ilāhābād, commonly Allahabad.
Pūjā, worship, adoration.
Pul, a bridge.
Pulā'o, a dish of flesh and rice.
Pur, a town, a city.
Purā, a large village, a town.
Purāṇ or *purāṇa*, the Hindū mythological books.
Putla, a puppet, an image.
Pūtlū, a small puppet or image.
Puwāl, straw.

R.

Rahīm, merciful, compassionate.
Rahmān, forgiving.
Ra'īyat, tenants, subjects.
Rāj, kingdom.
Rājā, a prince, a king.
Rāj-rānī, a queen, royal consort.
Rāj-put, a descendant of a *rājā*, the name of a celebrated military caste.
Rākkī, a bracelet or amulet, which the Hindūs tie on their arms on a certain festival, held in the full moon of *Sāwan*, in honour of *Krishṇa*.
Rām, the seventh Hindū incarnation.
Rām-rām, a Hindū form of salutation.
Rāmtur'aī, hibiscus longifolius.
Rānī, a Hindū queen or princess.
Rā'ō, a prince.
Rās, the circular dance performed at the festival of Krishna.
Rās-dhārī, a dancing boy.
Rasūl, a messenger.
Rāt-alū, the yam (dioscorea sativa).
Rat-aundhā, blindness at night (nyctalopia).
Rath, a four-wheeled carriage.
Rauza, mausoleum.
Rāwtī, a kind of tent.
Rezai, or *razā'ī*, a native counterpane.
Rikhi or *rishi*, a sage, a saint.
Rohū, a fish (cyprinus denticulatus).
Rotī, wheaten cakes baked on an iron plate, called *tawā*.
Rūpiya, a rupee.
Rustam, a hero.

S.

Sach, truth.
Sāchak, hinnā presented to the bride on the day of marriage.
Sadr'adālut, supreme court of justice.
Sāgar, the sea, the ocean.
Sāgūn, teak, a forest tree.
Sahajnā, horseradish tree.
Sāhib, master, gentleman of the house.
Sāhiba, lady.
Sā'īs, a groom.
Sajjāda, a carpet or mat on which the Muhammadans kneel at prayers.
Sālagrām, a stone containing the impression of one or more ammonites.
Salām, salutation, peace, safety.
Salāmut, salvation, safety.
Sallam, cloth.
Sālotarī, horse doctor.
Samāt, signs.
Samudr, the sea.
Sānchā, a mould.
Sang-i-miknātīs, the loadstone.
Sang-i-sulaimānī, agate, onyx.
Sang-tarāsh, a stonecutter, lapidary.
Sang-i-yashm, a kind of jasper or agate.
Sangtara, an orange (cintra).
Sankh, a conch which the Hindūs blow, a shell.
Sānkho, shorea robusta.
Sarā'e, a native inn.
Sarā'ī, a small cover.
Sārangī, a musical instrument like a fiddle.
Sāras, a species of heron (ardea antigone), saras phenicopteros.
Sardar, headman.
Sarhang, (corrupt: *serang*,) or *galaiya*, master of a vessel, commander.
Sarī, a dress, consisting of one long piece of cloth or silk, worn by Hindū women.
Sarkār, a superintendent.
Sarp, a serpent.
Sarpat, a kind of reed or grass (saccharum procerum).
Sarpesh, an ornament worn in the turban.
Sarposh, cover, lid.
Satï, a woman who burns herself on her husband's funeral pile, chaste, virtuous, constant.
Sawār, a horseman.
Sawari camel, riding camel.
Ser, two pounds.
Shab-bo, polianthes tuberosa.

Shaddā, the banners that are carried with the Taziya in the Muharram.
Shādī, a wedding, marriage.
Shāh, king.
Shāh-bāsh! bravo!
Shāh-zāda, a prince.
Shahī, kinglike.
Shaikh, (vulgo: *Shekh*) a chief, a venerable old man.
Sharāb, wine.
Sharm, shame.
Shāstr, Hindū scriptures.
Shatrang-i or *sutraengī*, a kind of carpet.
Sher, a tiger, a lion.
Shī'a, a follower of the sect of 'Alī.
Shikār, chase.
Shīsha, glass.
Shīsha-mahul, a house adorned with glass.
Shīsham, dalbergia sissoo (Roxb.).
Shiva, the third person of the Hindū triad.
Sholā, (commonly pronounced *sola*,) æschynomene paludosa (Roxb.).
Sirdar-bearer, head of a set of palanquin-bearers or head valet.
Sihnī, a chaplet worn on the head by the bridegroom and bride at the marriage ceremony.
Sila, the stone on which cooks grind, with the looreea or rolling pin of stone.
Singhārā, trapa natans.
Sipāh'ī, (whence seapoy,) a soldier.
Sir, head.
Sircar. See *Sarkār*.
Sirjāh-tālū, black mouthed.
Sītalpatī, a fine and cool mat.
Siwālā, or *shīwālā*, a temple dedicated to Mahadēo.
Sonā, gold; *sonahla*, golden.
Sontā, a club.
Sonte-bardār, a mace-bearer; a person in the retinue of the great, armed with a short curved club, generally covered with silver.
Sraddha, funeral obsequies in honour of ancestors.
Srī or *Shrī*, a name of *Lakshmī*, the wife of *Vishnu*. It is written as a mark of respect at the beginning of Hindū proper names of persons.
Sū'ar, a hog.
Sūbadār, governor of a province.
Sulaimān, Solomon.
Sultān, king, emperor.
Sunn, hemp.

Sunnī, an orthodox Muhammadan, who reveres equally the four successors of Muhammad. The Turks are *Sunnīs*, the Persians are *Shi'as*.
Sūp, a kind of basket for winnowing corn.
Supyārī, betel nut.
Surāh-ī, a long-necked goblet.
Surma, collyrium, eye salve.

T.

Taat, paper made of hemp, i.e. *sunn*.
Tāj, a crown.
Takā, a copper coin, equal to two *paisā*.
Takht, a throne; *padshah-i-takht*, the king's throne.
Taksāl, the mint.
Tamāshā, fun, sport.
Tana, a spider's web.
Tanjan, a chair carried by natives.
Tarāi, marsh meadows.
Tasar, a cloth.
Tattī, a screen or matted shutter.
Tattoo, a pony.
Tawā, the iron plate on which (*rotī*) bread is baked.
Taziya, the representation of the tomb of Hasun and Husain, used during the Muharram.
Thaili, purse, bag.
Thermantidote, a kind of mechanical fan.
Thiliyā, water pot.
Tīkā, a mark or marks made with coloured earths, or unguents, upon the forehead and between the brows, either as ornament or sectorial distinction; an ornament worn on the forehead.
Tilak, a mark the Hindūs make on the forehead.
Tiriyā, wife.
Tiriyā-raj, Amazon country, petticoat government.
Top, cannon.
Tope, plantation.
Tri-benī, or *tri-venī*, the junction of the three sacred rivers.
Tūfān, a hurricane, a storm of wind whirling round.
Tulsī, a plant, basil (ocymum sanctum).

U. V.

Uchchat tilak, a religious ceremony
Vishnu, the second person of the Hindū triad.

Ulāk, a small boat.
Ummed-wār, an expectant.
Voirājī, or *bairāgī*, a religious mendicant.
Uplā, cakes of dried cowdung.

W.

Walī-uhd, heir apparent.

Y.

Yāk, the small cow of Thibet.
Yug, or *yuga*, an age of the world. The Hindūs reckon four *yugas*, or ages, since the creation of the present world.

Yugānt, the end of the four *yugas*, or ages, when, according to the Hindūs, a total destruction of the universe takes place.

Z.

Zaban-i-urdū, the court language.
Zāmin, guarantee.
Zamīndar, landlord.
Zanāna, or *zenāna*, female apartments, feminine, effeminate.
Zūl-jana, the horse of Husain, *i.e.* the winged wolf.
Zunnār, the Brahmanical thread.

Bibliography

Ahmed, L. (1982) "Western ethnocentricism and perceptions of the harem", *Feminist Studies*, 8/3, pp. 521–34

Ballhatchet, K. (1980) *Race, Class and Sex Under the Raj: Imperial Attitudes and Policies and their Critics 1793–1905*, Weidenfeld and Nicolson, London

Bayly, C. (1989) *Imperial Meridian: The British Empire and the World 1780–1830*, Longman, Harlow

Bermingham, A (1986) *Landscape and Ideology: The English Rustic Tradition, 1740–1860*, University of California Press, Berkeley

Bermingham, A. (1994) "The picturesque and ready-to-wear femininity", in Copley, S. and Garside, P. (eds) *The Politics of the Picturesque*, Cambridge University Press, Cambridge, pp. 81–119

Bhabha, H. (1994) *The Location of Culture*, Routledge, London

Blake, S. (1992) "A woman's trek: what difference does gender make?", in Chaudhuri, N. and Strobel, M. (eds) *Western Women and Imperialism: Complicity and Resistance*, Indiana University Press, Bloomington, pp. 19–34

Bohls, E. (1995) *Women Travel Writers and the Language of Aesthetics*, Cambridge University Press, Cambridge

Burton, A. (1994) *Burden of History: British Feminists, Indian Women, and Imperial Culture, 1865–1915*, University of North Carolina Press, Chapel Hill, NC

Callan, H. and Ardener, S. (eds) (1984) *The Incorporated Wife*, Croom Helm, London

Copley, S. and Garside, P. (eds) (1994) *The Politics of the Picturesque: Literature, Landscape and Aesthetics Since 1770*, Cambridge University Press, Cambridge

Edney, M. (1997) *Mapping an Empire: The Geographical Construction of British India 1765–1843*, University of Chicago Press, Chicago and London

Foucault, M. (1972) *The Archaeology of Knowledge*, Tavistock, London

Fox, J. (1982) *White Mischief*, Penguin, Harmondsworth

Gartrell, B. (1984) "Colonial wives: villains or victims?", in Callan, H. and Ardener, S. (eds) *The Incorporated Wife*, Croom Helm, London, pp. 16–85

Ghose, I. (1998a) *Women Travellers in Colonial India: The Power of the Female Gaze*, Oxford University Press, Delhi

Ghose, I. (ed.) (1998b) *Memsahibs Abroad: Writings by Women Travellers in 19th Century India,* Oxford University Press, Delhi

Grewal, I. (1996) *Home and Harem: Nation, Gender, Empire and the Cultures of Travel,* Leicester University Press, Leicester

Guha, R. (1983) *Elementary Aspects of Peasant Insurgency in Colonial India,* Oxford University Press, Oxford

Hutchins, F. G. (1967) *The Illusion of Permanence: British Imperialism in India,* Princeton University Press, Princeton

Hyam, R. (1990) *Empire and Sexuality: The British Experience,* Manchester University Press, Manchester

James, L. (1994) *The Rise and Fall of the British Empire,* Abacus, London

Jayawardena, K. (1995) *The White Woman's Other Burden: Western Women and South Asia During British Rule,* Routledge, London

Jeffery, P. (1979) *Frogs in a Well: Indian Women in Purdah,* Zed Press, London

Kabbani, R. (1986) *Europe's Myths of Orient: Devise and Rule,* Macmillan, London

King, A. (1976) *Colonial Urban Development: Culture, Social Power and Environment,* Routledge and Kegan Paul, London

King, A. (1984) *The Bungalow: The Production of a Global Culture,* Routledge and Kegan Paul, London

Lewis, R. (1996) *Gendering Orientalism: Race, Femininity, and Representation,* Routledge, London

Melman, B. (1992) *Women's Orients: English Women and the Middle East, 1718–1918; Sexuality, Religion and Work,* Macmillan, Basingstoke

Mills, S. (1991) *Discourses of Difference: Women's Travel Writing and Colonialism,* Routledge, London

Mills, S. (1994) "Knowledge, gender and empire", in Blunt, A. and Rose, G. (eds) *Writing Women and Space: Colonial and Postcolonial Geographies,* Guildford, New York

Mills, S. (1997) *Discourse,* Routledge, London

Mohanty, C. (1988) "Under Western eyes: feminist scholarship and colonial discourses", *Feminist Review,* 30, pp. 68–88

Mulvey, L. (1975) "Visual pleasure and narrative cinema", *Screen,* 16.3, pp. 6–18

Mulvey, L. (1981) "Afterthoughts on 'Visual Pleasure and Narrative Cinema' inspired by Duel in the Sun", *Framework,* 15/16/17, pp. 12–15

Pratt, M. L. (1992) *Imperial Eyes: Travel Writing and Transculturation,* Routledge, London

Richards, T. (1993) *The Imperial Archive: Knowledge and the Fantasy of Empire,* Verso, London

Robinson, J. (1990) *Wayward Women: A Guide to Women Travellers,* Oxford University Press, Oxford

Said, E. (1978) *Orientalism,* Routledge and Kegan Paul, London

Sharpe, J. (1993) *Allegories of Empire: The Figure of Woman in the Colonial Text,* University of Minnesota Press, Minneapolis

Stacey, J. (1994) *Star Gazing: Hollywood Cinema and Female Spectatorship*, Routledge, London

Stanford, J. (ed.) (1962) *Ladies in the Sun: The Memsahibs' India 1790–1860*, Galley Press, London

Stoler, A. (1989) "Making Empire respectable: the politics of race and sexual morality in 20th-century colonial cultures", *American Ethnologist*, 16, pp. 634–40

Suleri, S. (1992) *The Rhetoric of English India*, University of Chicago Press, Chicago

Whitehead, N. (1997) "Introduction" to *Walter Ralegh's The Discoverie of the Large and Bewtiful Empyre of Guiana*, Manchester University Press, Manchester

Young, R. (1993) *Colonial Desire: Hybridity, Theory, Culture and Race*, Routledge, London

Youngs, T. (1994) *Travellers in Africa: British Travelogues 1850–1900*, Manchester University Press, Manchester

Youngs, T. (1997) "Buttons and souls: some thoughts on commodities and identity in women's travel writing", *Studies in Travel Writing*, 1, pp. 117–40

Yule, H. and Burnell, C. (eds) (1886) *Hobson-Jobson: The Anglo-Indian Dictionary*, Wordsworth Editions, Ware

Index

430

Index